AI for Smart, Secure, and Sustainable Systems

Mashael M. Asiri
King Khalid University, Saudi Arabia

IGI Global
Scientific Publishing
Publishing Tomorrow's Research Today

Vice President of Editorial	Melissa Wagner
Director of Acquisitions	Mikaela Felty
Director of Book Development	Jocelynn Hessler
Production Manager	Mike Brehm
Cover Design	Jose Rosado

Published in the United States of America by
IGI Global Scientific Publishing
701 East Chocolate Avenue
Hershey, PA, 17033, USA
Tel: 717-533-8845 | Fax: 717-533-7115
Website: https://www.igi-global.com E-mail: cust@igi-global.com

Library of Congress Cataloging-in-Publication Data

LCCN: 2026033417 (CIP Data Pending)
ISBN13: 979-8-2600-3280-0
Isbn13Softcover: 979-8-2600-3281-7
EISBN13: 979-8-2600-3282-4
British Cataloguing in Publication Data
A Cataloguing in Publication record for this book is available from the British Library.

Table of Contents

Detailed Table of Contents

ML is an important branch of AI, which allows a computer to get patterns based on the data & make decisions/predictions without any explicit programming. ML methods are used in many fields due to fast development of digital technologies & access to massive data. In this chapter, we give a review of two important ML paradigms - supervised & unsupervised learning. Labelled datasets are utilized to supervised learning to train predictive models based on classification, regression tasks with algorithms like decision trees, random forests, naive bayes, support vector machines, & neural networks. Unsupervised learning analyses unlabelled data to extract concealed trends & associations in the data. Pattern discovery & exploratory data analysis techniques like dimensionality reduction & clustering, are frequently employed to analyse data patterns. The chapter also addresses the performance evaluation metrics, ML issues, & their use in practice, with a focus on the ways in which these methods contribute to process of making decisions & informing about the capability to analyse complex data.

The digital age has brought amazing levels of connectivity, but also new levels of exposure and risk to ever more sophisticated cyber threats. Old security is frequently

This chapter discusses the application of artificial intelligence (AI) in aerospace engineering, focusing on aerodynamic analysis, structural design, aerospace materials, and autonomous systems. Machine learning, deep learning and physics-informed models help to rapidly generate an approximation (surrogate model) and minimize reliance on computational expensive simulations like the computational fluid dynamics (CFD). These methods include increasing the prediction accuracy, aiding in real-time optimization, and uncertainty analysis. The chapter also discusses generative design and topology optimization of lightweight aircraft structures. The use of AI in Aerospace Materials facilitates faster property prediction and material discovery, digital twins enable predictive maintenance and intelligent monitoring. Data quality, model validation, interpretability and certification requirements are key challenges.

With the quick development of smart home technology, new ways to improve daily living via automation and intelligent systems have emerged. Finding and analysing common household behaviours is a crucial part of this progress, since it may significantly increase safety, comfort, and energy efficiency. The goal of this chapter is to develop a machine learning-based model that can identify typical behaviours in smart homes using feature selection, neural networks, and the load signatures of household appliances. To assess the effectiveness of the suggested approach, a thorough experimental setup is constructed in a simulated smart home environment. A wide range of everyday chores and appliance usage patterns are included in the dataset used to evaluate the model. By assessing the model's ability to adjust to novel and unforeseen difficulties, it also demonstrates its potential for ongoing learning and development. The study's findings show that feature selection and neural networks may significantly improve the accuracy and robustness of smart home daily activity detection.

The study uses a multi-source data fusion approach to assess online course effectiveness. The research combines student engagement metrics, learning performance, and course content quality using the 3P (Presage-Process-Product) model. The structured questionnaire was taken from undergraduate students from five regional colleges, and a total of 685 responses were collected, 583 of which were valid samples. The data were analyzed using SPSS 25.0 and AMOS 24.0 for reliability and validity testing. A backpropagation neural network (BPNN) was used to forecast learning performance related to course interaction, selection rates, and engagement metrics. Hypothesis testing was performed to check the links between course quality, engagement, and learning performance. Structural equation modeling was applied to find direct and indirect effects, leading to an unbiased approach for course effectiveness evaluation. The findings direct specific approaches to increase online course delivery, student engagement, and attainment of educational outcomes.

In the context of decision-making in public health settings amidst uncertainties, the effective fusion of human intelligence and artificial intelligence (AI) plays an important role. In this research paper, we introduce the CI framework as a solution to effectively incorporate the two forms of intelligence via a layered structure comprised of predictive modeling, explainability, and decision validation by experts. Our proposal includes a confidence-weighted fusion technique that leverages the confidence values assigned by both humans and machines to facilitate effective collaboration between the two. Based on our experiments performed based on empirical data from epidemiology cases pertaining to COVID-19, our proposed CI technique has the advantage of offering improved accuracy, robustness, and consistency of decisions compared to the human-only and AI-only baseline approaches. Finally, our work also bridges the gap between theoretical formulation and implementation. Although we observe promising performance gains, there are some limitations in terms of expert simulation.

In recent years, there has been a shift in the way people think about finance due to an increasing awareness and concern for issues such as environmental damage, social injustice, and poor governance. Financial decisions that were once made based only on short-term profits and how much wealth a company creates for its shareholders are now being analyzed using a longer-term perspective of the risks and/or opportunities that long-term sustainability issues present. Therefore, Environmental, Social, and Governance (ESG) principles will be essential in order to integrate measurable criteria of sustainability into financial decision-making and business strategies, investment decisions, and risk management practices. An ESG approach provides stakeholders with an all-encompassing understanding of how well a business performs; it takes into account not only the financial returns produced by a business but also how committed that business is to being environmentally responsible, socially responsible to the communities where it operates, and ethical in its corporate governance.

Preface

INTRODUCTION

Artificial intelligence has rapidly evolved from a specialized field of computer science into one of the most transformative technologies of the twenty-first century. Today, AI influences nearly every aspect of society, from healthcare and education to cybersecurity, aerospace engineering, environmental sustainability, agriculture, finance, and intelligent infrastructure. As organizations continue to embrace digital transformation, the demand for intelligent systems capable of making informed decisions, improving operational efficiency, and addressing complex global challenges has grown significantly. At the same time, ensuring that these systems remain secure, trustworthy, and sustainable has become equally important.

AI for Smart, Secure, and Sustainable Systems brings together a diverse collection of research that reflects the multidisciplinary nature of artificial intelligence and its growing impact across industries. The contributions within this volume demonstrate how machine learning, deep learning, intelligent data analytics, collaborative intelligence, and predictive modeling are being leveraged to solve real-world problems while supporting innovation and responsible technological development. Rather than focusing on AI as a theoretical concept alone, this book highlights practical applications that address pressing societal and industrial needs.

One of the defining characteristics of this volume is its emphasis on balancing technological advancement with responsibility. As AI systems become increasingly autonomous and interconnected, concerns surrounding cybersecurity, transparency, ethical implementation, sustainability, and human collaboration have become central to ongoing research. The chapters in this book recognize these challenges while presenting innovative solutions that strengthen the reliability and effectiveness of intelligent systems. Readers will discover how AI can not only improve performance but also contribute to safer digital environments, more sustainable practices, and better-informed decision-making.

This edited collection is intended to serve as a valuable resource for researchers, academics, graduate students, engineers, technology professionals, and policymakers interested in the rapidly evolving landscape of artificial intelligence. By bringing together perspectives from experts representing multiple disciplines and institutions around the world, this volume offers both foundational knowledge and forward-looking insights into the future of smart, secure, and sustainable AI-driven systems.

OVERVIEW OF THE CHAPTERS

The book begins with **Chapter 1**, *Supervised and Unsupervised Learning – A Brief Overview*, which establishes the theoretical foundation of machine learning by introducing supervised and unsupervised learning paradigms. The chapter discusses widely used algorithms, performance evaluation metrics, and practical applications while highlighting the strengths and limitations of each learning approach.

Building upon these fundamentals, **Chapter 2**, *Neural Shields: AI's Proactive Cyber Defense Revolution*, explores the growing role of artificial intelligence in cybersecurity. The authors examine how machine learning and behavioral analytics enable proactive threat detection, intrusion prevention, malware classification, and automated incident response while also addressing challenges such as adversarial AI and ethical considerations. Continuing the cybersecurity theme, **Chapter 3**, *Phishing E-mail Detection Using Ensembled ML Models*, presents a sophisticated ensemble learning framework that combines multiple machine learning techniques to improve the identification of phishing emails through advanced feature engineering and text analysis.

Expanding into engineering applications, **Chapter 4**, *Aerodynamic Design Optimization AI Creation Systems Applications in Aerospace Engineering*, demonstrates how artificial intelligence accelerates aircraft design, structural optimization, materials discovery, digital twins, and predictive maintenance. The chapter illustrates AI's ability to reduce computational costs while improving engineering precision and performance.

The focus then shifts toward intelligent living environments in **Chapter 5**, *Smart Home System Based on Feature Selection and Load Signature of Appliances*. This chapter investigates machine learning techniques for recognizing household activities using appliance load signatures, neural networks, and feature selection methods to improve energy efficiency, automation, and resident safety. **Chapter 6**, *A Hybrid Data Fusion Model for Online Education Evaluation in Intelligent Classroom Environments*, examines how multi-source data fusion and neural network models can enhance educational assessment by integrating student engagement, learning performance, and instructional quality into comprehensive evaluation frameworks.

Healthcare and collaborative decision-making are addressed in **Chapter 7**, *Intelligent Teaming in Public Health Management: A Collaborative Intelligence Framework*. The authors introduce an innovative framework that combines human expertise with artificial intelligence to improve decision-making during public health crises. Using confidence-weighted collaboration and explainable AI, the chapter demonstrates how hybrid intelligence can outperform either human-only or AI-only approaches.

Financial sustainability becomes the focus of **Chapter 8**, *AI-Driven ESG Analytics on Cloud Platforms for Sustainable Financial Decision*, which explores how artificial intelligence supports Environmental, Social, and Governance (ESG) analysis. The chapter illustrates how cloud-based AI technologies enable organizations and investors to incorporate sustainability metrics into strategic planning, investment evaluation, and corporate governance.

The volume concludes with **Chapter 9**, *An Effective Algorithm for Potato Disease Classification Utilizing Deep Learning*, highlighting the role of artificial intelligence in precision agriculture. Through image processing, transfer learning, and deep neural networks, the authors present an efficient approach for detecting potato diseases, demonstrating how AI can contribute to increased agricultural productivity, food security, and sustainable farming practices.

Collectively, these chapters illustrate the remarkable breadth of artificial intelligence applications while reinforcing the importance of designing intelligent systems that are secure, ethical, efficient, and capable of addressing both present and future societal challenges.

CONCLUSION

Artificial intelligence continues to redefine the boundaries of innovation, enabling new possibilities across science, engineering, business, healthcare, education, finance, agriculture, and public services. As these technologies become increasingly embedded within our daily lives, the need for systems that are not only intelligent but also secure, transparent, and sustainable has never been greater. The research presented throughout this volume demonstrates that meaningful technological advancement requires balancing computational power with responsible design, ethical implementation, and human-centered decision-making.

The chapters in this collection showcase the remarkable diversity of contemporary AI research while emphasizing practical solutions to real-world challenges. From strengthening cybersecurity defenses and optimizing aerospace engineering to advancing smart homes, intelligent education, collaborative healthcare, sustainable finance, and precision agriculture, each contribution reflects the expanding role of AI as a catalyst for innovation. Together, these studies reveal how interdisciplinary collaboration continues to drive the development of intelligent systems capable of creating measurable social and economic impact.

Although tremendous progress has been achieved, the field of artificial intelligence remains dynamic and rapidly evolving. Emerging challenges—including explainability, fairness, cybersecurity risks, regulatory frameworks, environmental impact, and responsible governance—will require continued collaboration among researchers, practitioners, industry leaders, and policymakers. The knowledge presented within this volume not only documents current advances but also identifies opportunities for future investigation and technological development that will shape the next generation of AI-enabled solutions.

As editor, I extend my sincere appreciation to all contributing authors for sharing their expertise, dedication, and innovative research. Their scholarly efforts have made this volume possible and have enriched its multidisciplinary perspective. I also express my gratitude to the reviewers and publishing team whose thoughtful guidance and support ensured the quality of this collection. It is my hope that *AI for Smart, Secure, and Sustainable Systems* will serve as a valuable reference for researchers, educators, students, and professionals while inspiring continued exploration and collaboration in the pursuit of intelligent technologies that benefit society and contribute to a more secure and sustainable future.

Mashael M. Asiri
King Khalid University, Saudi Arabia

Chapter 1
Supervised and Unsupervised Learning: A Brief Overview

Krutika Patre
http://orcid.org/0009-0001-7969-4409
Ajeenkya D.Y. Patil University, India

Kritikka Kunte
http://orcid.org/0009-0002-4820-8831
Ajeenkya D.Y. Patil University, India

Sunil Sankathala
Ajeenkya D.Y. Patil University, India

Susanta Das
http://orcid.org/0000-0002-9314-3988
Ajeenkya D.Y. Patil University, India

ABSTRACT

ML is an important branch of AI, which allows a computer to get patterns based on the data & make decisions/predictions without any explicit programming. ML methods are used in many fields due to fast development of digital technologies & access to massive data. In this chapter, we give a review of two important ML paradigms - supervised & unsupervised learning. Labelled datasets are utilized to supervised learning to train predictive models based on classification, regression tasks with algorithms like decision trees, random forests, naive bayes, support vector machines, & neural networks. Unsupervised learning analyses unlabelled data to extract concealed trends & associations in the data. Pattern discovery & exploratory data analysis techniques like dimensionality reduction & clustering, are frequently

DOI: 10.4018/979-8-2600-3280-0.ch001

employed to analyse data patterns. The chapter also addresses the performance evaluation metrics, ML issues, & their use in practice, with a focus on the ways in which these methods contribute to process of making decisions & informing about the capability to analyse complex data.

1. INTRODUCTION

Machine Learning (ML) has also become a big field of artificial intelligence that allows computers to learn behaviours on data and make predictions or choices without explicit coding. Due to the rapid development of digital technologies and the rise of large datasets, machine learning methods are widely used in medicine, finance, telecommunications, psychology, and social sciences. Such methods can help the researcher and organization to study, analyse, and extract meaningful insights using complex data in order to make data-driven decision-making (Nettleton et al., 2010; Usama et al., 2017; Naeem et al., 2023). Analyses of data and study of relationship between variables have traditionally been performed by use of statistical methods. The methods are based on mathematical models which can usually make given assumptions about data distributions, linear relationships and preset model forms. The relationships between the predictor and the outcome are normally defined by the researchers in advance to conduct an analysis. Although these methods have been effective with small and structured datasets, they may prove difficult with current datasets which are large, complex, and high-dimensional. These data sets can have a nonlinear relationship and interaction between several variables thus, it is difficult to control the latent patterns using the predictable statistical methods (FY et al., 2017; Verma et al., 2019; Burkart & Huber, 2021). Machine learning provides solutions to these limitations by providing adjustable methods of computation that can learn patterns in large amounts of data automatically. Algorithms are self-improving and develop their work based on historical data with time, which allows them to identify involved relations that are not always easy to identify using traditional statistical methods (Jordan et al., n.d.; Jiang et al., 2020). There are broadly four categories of machine learning; these are supervised, unsupervised, semi-supervised, and reinforcement learning. The most common ones are supervised and unsupervised learning. Supervised learning involves labelled datasets to carry out classification and regression with any of the decision trees, logistic regression, support vector machines, random forest, naive Bayes, and neural networks (Nasteski, 2017; Jiang et al., 2020). These methods are typically used in prediction of diseases and fraud detection (Stonier et al., 2023; Hilas & Mastorocostas, 2008). Equally, unsupervised learning processes the data without labels and finds the latent patterns by use of clustering and dimensionality reduction algorithms like K-means, hierarchical clustering, and Principal Component Analysis (Aissaoui et al., 2019; Tyagi et al., 2021).

2. SUPERVISED LEARNING

2.1. Concept and Working of Supervised learning

One of the most popular machine learning methods of prediction and classification is supervised learning. In this technique, labelled data are used to train the models in which the input features as well as the output values are known. The key task is to determine the connection between the inputs and outputs in order to have the model capable of correctly prediction the outcomes of new and unknown data (Nasteski, 2017; Jiang et al., 2020). The learning process is usually supervised by first gathering and preparing known pairs of inputs and outputs in the form of training data. The algorithm processes this data during training and comes up with patterns and relationship between features and target values. The model is also tested on new data after it has been trained to determine its predictive accuracy and the parameters can be modified to enhance its performance. Classification and regression problems are solved by supervised learning algorithms. Algorithms that are popular are Support Vector Machine (SVM), Naive Bayes, Decision Trees, and Neural Networks. Their high predictive accuracy is why these techniques are used in the real world to diagnose diseases, detect fraud, predict finances, identify images, and detect patterns (Nettleton et al., 2010; Pandey et al., 2019).

2.2. Role of Labelled Data

Labelled data is an important part of supervised learning as it gives the information needed by the algorithm in order to learn the right relations between input and output. In a labelled dataset, there is an input of features and the correct output / category in each observation. Such labels act as reference points that regulate the learning of the model of machine learning (Usama et al., 2017). To prove, the variables to be considered as input in a healthcare dataset in disease prediction might be age, blood pressure, cholesterol, and lifestyle, whereas the label of the output variable denotes whether a patient has a specific disease. This labelled information is used by the machine learning algorithm to know how various features are affected by the outcome. This is highly useful since the labelled data can greatly improve the performance of the supervised learning models since the algorithm can obtain clear feedback during the training process. The model is able to measure the errors of prediction by obtaining the differences between the predicted outputs and the actual labels to make corrections on its internal parameters and achieve an increased accuracy. However, labelled data can be hard, costly, or time-intensive to get in certain cases due to their possible need to be explained manually or require expert experience. In spite of such difficulties, labelled datasets are still necessary to create the high-quality supervised learning models (Usama et al., 2017).

2.3. Types of Supervised Learning

There are usually two broad categories of supervised learning problems, namely, classification and regression. The differences between these categories are the kind of output that the model is likely to predict.

2.3.1. Regression

The other type of supervised learning that is of relevance is regression in which the output variable is continuous and not categorical. Regression is in attempt to determine the prediction of the numeric value of a target variable using the relationship of the input ones. Unlike classification where the data points are put into a category, regression approximates the quantities or readings (Nasteski, 2017). Regression models find application in the forecasting and prediction operations. This could be the prices of houses based on location and property features, prediction of temperature variations, prediction of sales revenue, or determination of the riskiness of certain disease based on patient health records. The regression analysis can be done using various algorithms which include the linear regression algorithm, the support vectors regression algorithm, the decision trees and the neural networks. These algorithms rely on historical data and come up with mathematical models that can explain the relationship between predictors and the continuous outcome variable. With the assistance of these models, new data can be approximated when being trained in order to calculate the numerical results (Jiang et al., 2020).

2.3.2. Classification

A supervised learning task is known as classification in which the output variable is discrete. The objective of classification is to categorize the input data into a known pattern of existing training data into a preset class or category. In other words, the algorithm can forecast the group to which a particular piece of data is related (Nasteski, 2017). The popular classification models have a number of applications in the real world. As a sample, machine learning models may be implemented in the healthcare system to indicate the presence or absence of a certain disease. The email filtering systems are categorized using the categorization algorithms to determine whether an email is spam or legitimate email. On a different note, fraudulent behaviour patterns can be discovered by use of user behaviour patterns on the same telecommunications networks through a fraudulent behaviour classification model (Hilas & Mastorocostas, 2008). Many algorithms are extensively used in classification and they include decision trees, logistic regression, support vectors machines, random forest, naive bayes classifiers and artificial neural networks. They analyse the training input, learn relationships between attributes and create models, which are able to classify new observations with high accuracy (Jiang et al., 2020).

2.4. Supervised Learning Algorithms

2.4.1. Decision Tree

The Decision trees are popular learning algorithms that are used in classification and prediction. They work according to the principle of division of the dataset into smaller groups by the conditions of input features. The model is in the form of a tree where the internal nodes are the decisions made based on the attributes, the branches are the outcomes of the decisions and the terminal node is the final label of class or prediction. During training, the algorithm selects those features that most characterize the data, most suitably, into the different classes and will divide the data into smaller groups repeatedly, until no further division of the data can improve the accuracy of the predictions. The Decision Trees can handle both categorical and numerical data and are easy to interpret as compared to most of the machine learning models. Their simplicity and the ability to inform us of the significance of features make them very popular in predictive modelling, data analysis, and decision systems (Nasteski, 2017; Jiang et al., 2020; Nettleton et al., 2010).

(a) Advantages

I. Automatically identifies complex interaction among predictors and risk factors in datasets (Jiang et al., 2020)
II. Helps classify individuals into different risk categories such as suicide risk (Jiang et al., 2020)
III. Detects non-linear relationship (FY et al., 2017)
IV. Supports pattern discovery in complex healthcare datasets (Verma et al., 2019)

(b) Weakness

I. Individual decision trees may suffer from instability in predictions (Nettleton et al., 2010)
II. Likely to to overfitting when trained on specific datasets (Jiang et al., 2020)

(c) Limitations

I. Limited overview to new datasets without validation (Jiang et al., 2020)
II. Requires external validation (Jiang et al., 2020)
III. It does not perform efficiently on high dimensional datasets (Verma et al., 2019)

2.4.2. Random Forest

Random Forest is a supervised ensemble-based learning algorithm, a better prediction accuracy is worked out by a combination of multiple decision trees. Unlike the only decision tree model, the algorithm of the Random Forest generates many decision trees on different subsets of the training material, and on different subsets of inputs. Each of the trees comes up with a prediction and the final prediction will be the result of the consolidation of the outcomes of the trees. The advantage of the ensemble method is that it helps reduce the chances of overfitting i.e. a model can be highly effective in training data but it fails in new data. Random Forest calculates a more solid and trustworthy model with averaging the results of a large number of decision trees. The method also helps in establishing the relative importance of different elements that occur in the data set and therefore the researcher can ascertain which variables have the most favourable role in the prediction of the findings. Random Forests were prevalent in predictive modelling because they could be used with big and complex data with lots of variables. (Jiang et al., 2020; Burkart & Huber, 2021).

(a) Advantages

i. Prediction accuracy increases by combining multiple decision trees (Jiang et al., 2020)
ii. Reduce overfitting (FY et al., 2017)

(b) Weaknesses

i. Complex to understand than simple models (Nasteski, 2017)

ii. Requires more computational resources (Nettleton et al., 2010)

(c) Limitations

i. Noise and inaccurate data affect performance (Jiang et al., 2020)
ii. Not best for all datasets (Nasteski, 2017)

2.4.3. Naïve Bayes

Naive Bayes is a probabilistic based supervised learning algorithm, and typically used in classification tasks. It is an algorithm based on the probability theory and it is used to estimate the probability of a single instance of data to fall under a certain class based on the values of the input features. A significant feature of the Naive Bayes algorithm is that it presupposes that the variables considered as the input do not depend on the rest of the variables. Although the assumption is not practically applicable to real-world data, this algorithm is effective in most tasks of classification because of its simplicity and low computational cost. It is a statistical model which is founded on the statistical probabilities founded on the training data in order to draw on the likelihood of each label of the class. Naive bayes classifier is also typically used in pattern detection, document classification and spam detection among other applications because they are also used in processing large amounts of information. (Nettleton et al., 2010; Jiang et al., 2020).

(a) Advantages

i. Simple methods model (Nettleton et al., 2010)
ii. It works well with text classification and pattern detection (Nettleton et al., 2010)
iii. Fast classification performance (Nasteski, 2017)

(b) Weakness

i. Less flexible compared to other models (Nasteski, 2017)
ii. Accuracy gets reduced when predictors are correlated (Stonier et al., 2023)

(c) Limitations

i. Depends on probability assumptions (Nettleton et al., 2010)
ii. Performance varies across datasets (Nasteski, 2017)

2.4.4. Support Vectors Machines (SVM)

Support Vector Machines (SVM) are state-of the art supervised learning algorithms used in the classification and regression applications. The major goal of SVM is to obtain an optimum decision boundary which will divide the data points of the different classes. The algorithm can extract patterns in the data that are used to classify the classes in a superior manner because of transforming the original data into a high dimensional space. It is this that helps SVM to be a useful tool when dealing with high dimensional datasets. The applications Support Vector Machines are favoured by predictive modelling because of their good generalization behaviour and their capability of making accurate predictions even in the circumstances where the dataset on which it is being applied is large. They are applicable to the majority of data analysis and classification due to their possibility to identify important trends in complex data sets (Nasteski, 2017; Jiang et al., 2020).

(a) Advantages

i. Good for classification tasks such as PTSD prediction (Jiang et al., 2020)
ii. Works well with large and complex datasets
iii. Capture non-linear relationships in datasets (Verma et al., 2019)

(b) Weakness

i. Performance depends on pre-processing and parameter selection (Nettleton et al., 2010)
ii. Complexity increases with large datasets (Nasteski, 2017)

(c) Limitations

i. Labelled data for training (FY et al., 2017)
ii. Sensitive with noise and measurement errors
iii. Need validation for generalization (Jiang et al., 2020)

2.4.5. Neural Networks

The supervised learning networks are the Artificial Neural Networks that are grounded on the architecture of human brain and its functionality. These models consist of members comprising of networked layers of the modelled neurons which process data and learn patterns based on data. All the neurons are provided with certain input values, work with the input with the help of mathematical functions and transmit the result to other neurons in the network. The weights of the connections between the neurons are adjusted by the neural networks in the training stage to reduce the errors in the prediction. This is achieved progressively so that the model acquires association between intricate input features and output variables. The more the training examples that are inputted into the network, the more the predictive accuracy. The neural networks are particularly used in the analysis of large and complex data sets where the ordinary statistical models may not be in a position to establish nonlinear relationships. (Nettleton et al., 2010; Jiang et al., 2020).

2.5. Challenges in Supervised Learning

a) Noise in Training Data

Noise in training data is the greatest challenge of the supervised learning. There would be noise in case of errors, irregularities, or mislabelled data in the data that will be used to train the model. The studies of machine learning have been associated with labelled datasets to train on the models to facilitate the algorithms to learn the associations between the input variables and their expected results. However, when the data being used in training contains measurements errors or misplaced labels then the learning algorithm can simply accommodate these mistakes as opposed to major trends. According to researchers, the most significant issues that may affect the accuracy of machine learning predictions are called noise and measurement errors. Models that have been trained on noisy data are thus able to make imperfect predictions and they do not extrapolate well with new noisy data in this issue are medical and psychological research fields where data is typically complex, sensitive, and can be collected at more than one site (Jiang et al., 2020).

b) Sensitivity of Algorithm

The other major issue as regards to supervised learning is that machine learning algorithms are also conditional with the data type. Different algorithms respond different to changes in data scale, feature distribution, and complexity of data. Since of this sensitivity, a certain algorithm may perform well on a certain dataset, but not on another dataset. Comparative analysis of learning algorithms has shown that there does not exist a single best algorithm that is applicable and efficient in every dataset and problem situation. The efficiency of a machine learning model is greatly determined by the characteristics of datasets such as the number of variables and relations between predictors (Nasteski, 2017). It is also discovered that the rate of learning, the cost of computation calculated, and prediction error will depend on the dataset (Nettleton et al., 2010). The other challenge is overfitting whereby a model is trained to capture the trends of the training data and fails to predict novel data (Jiang et al., 2020).

c) Strength of Naive Bayes as Compared to Another Model

The notion of robustness is used to explain how machine learning algorithm can be steady and robust even when the circumstances of the data shift or contain uncertainties. The other common supervised learning algorithm is Naive Bayes due to the simplicity and the probabilistic nature of the algorithm. This is because it is popular since it is able to handle data in large quantities and it is quick at classifying data. The assumption the algorithm presumes is that the characteristics of inputs are independent of each other with respect to the task of making prediction in relation to the labelling of classes and this renders it easy to compute and makes the process of making classification to be faster. However, in the majority of real-life data, it is possible that most predictor variables are highly correlated and this may reduce the precision of Naive Bayes predictions (Stonier et al., 2023). Document classification and text mining studies show that the algorithms such as Naive Bayes, Support Vector Machines and k-Nearest Neighbour are commonly used algorithms in the process of classification. These studies indicated that preprocessing and feature selection is important in increasing the model accuracy and strength (Nettleton et al., 2010). Comparative analysis also shows that ensemble techniques, such as Random Forest, are more predictive and robust because they are made up of multiple models to remove the variance and overfitting (Nasteski, 2017).

2.6. Case Studies

Several applications of supervised learning have been applied in diverse areas such as healthcare, business analytics, telecommunications and education. These are methods that use labelled data to train models that are able to predict outcomes and also classify data in the correct style. Various sources suggest that complicated data may be processed with the help of supervised learning algorithms and may be useful in making effective decisions. The fact of predicting the likelihood of suicide among the military personnel following the psychiatric hospitalization is also a significant case study. The employees fitted the Elastic Net algorithm to a data set that comprised of demographic, behavioural and clinical variables such as age, gender, medical history of psychiatric diagnoses, treatment history and attempt to commit suicide. The model considered hundreds of predictors and was able to classify persons as high risk with regard to suicide. Major predictors included the previous suicidal behaviour, mental illnesses and certain demographic factors. This predictive action assisted medical care providers in identifying persons who could be at high risk at earlier stage and placing preventative actions (Lowry & Milford, 2016; Naeem et al., 2023).

The other application of supervised learning is in the retailing marketing whereby organizations engage in trying to predict the customer buying behaviour. The customer information considered in a retail company in this case included the age, level of income, history of browsing, history of purchase and time spent on the site. A predictive model was developed based on labelled results indicating a purchased or non-purchased customer as well as the use of a decision tree algorithm. The model could establish the trend of the customer behaviour and could predict the likelihood of repeat purchase later hence enabling businesses to make personalised marketing strategies and improve customer relationships (Nettleton et al., 2010).

Supervised learning is also greatly used in the detection of telecommunications fraud. The researchers analysed call detail records of a private branch exchange system that included such information as the caller identification, the length of the call, the number to which the call was placed and the time of the call. All the records were categorized as being legitimate or fraudulent. The neural network with multilayer perceptron was used to classify the call activities based on the patterns of user behaviour. The authors unveiled that the model could effectively identify the frauds based on the unusual calling patterns and help the telecommunication providers to reduce the financial losses (Hilas & Mastorocostas, 2008; Dike et al., 2018).

3. UNSUPERVISED LEARNING

3.1. Concept and Characteristics

Another important machine learning technique is unsupervised learning, which analyses the sets of data with no predefined labels or values of the output. In this method algorithms establish the existence of concealed patterns, forms or relationships in data without prior knowledge of the correct answers. It is based on the fact that underlying structure of real-life datasets can be learnt with the assistance of the computational analysis (Tyagi et al., 2021). As contrasted to the supervised learning, in the unsupervised learning, the labelled data is not applied to train the system: the input data are applied to produce similarities and differences between data points. This allows algorithms to automatically group information, identify patterns as well as extract valuable information out of complex data. According to the researchers, unsupervised learning could be utilized specifically during the exploratory data analysis to reveal some pattern without the direct observation with the assistance of the traditional method (Aissaoui et al., 2019). One of the advantages of unsupervised learning is that it may work with large volumes of unstructured or unlabelled data. The most effective way of the analysis of raw data without supervision is by the unsupervised methods since labelled datasets can be quite expensive and time-consuming to produce (Dike et al., 2018). These are clustering and dimensionality reduction techniques which typically enable simplification of complex data and identifying meaningful correlations between variables (Tyagi et al., 2021).

3.2. Pattern Discovery and Data Exploration

One of the goals of unsupervised learning is pattern discovery, in which algorithms are used to discover natural structures and relationships among data without any prior labels. Such patterns can consist of groups of comparable observations, variable-to-variable relationships, or anomalies that show abnormal behaviour (Tyagi et al., 2021). Clustering methods like K-means and hierarchical clustering are algorithms that allow grouping data points into similar clusters to assist the researcher to identify meaningful categories in large datasets (Aissaoui et al., 2019). The unsupervised learning also contributes to the exploration of data with the help of such techniques as Principal Component Analysis (PCA) that reduces data dimensions and preserves significant information. The approaches assist in visualizing complex information and uncovering the latent patterns in disciplines such as healthcare and marketing (Tyagi et al., 2021; Aissaoui et al., 2019; Usama et al., 2017).

3.3. Unsupervised Learning Techniques

In the analysis of unlabelled data and in learning the underlying structures in data, the unsupervised methods of learning are extremely significant. Clustering algorithms (K-Means and Hierarchy Clustering) can be used to find natural clusters in a dataset and dimensionality reduction algorithms (PCA) help to simplify complex data structures and enhance computational efficiency. These techniques are widely applicable in many applications in the fields of networking, predictive maintenance, detecting fraud and theft, healthcare analytics and behavioural analysis, and other areas (Tyagi et al., 2021; Aissaoui et al., 2019; Usama et al., 2017; Amruthnath et al., 2018; Hilas & Mastorocostas, 2008; Dike et al., 2018). Generally, unsupervised learning provides exploitative data analysis and pattern discovery tools of significant strength. Such techniques enable the researchers and organizations to discover valuable information and support in their decision-making process with the help of data to locate the latent relationships and structures in datasets and are applied to complex real-world settings (Amruthnath et al., 2018).

3.3.1. Clustering Methods

Clustering is one of the most widespread techniques of unsupervised learning. The key objective of the clustering is to divide a set of data into clusters referred as clusters whereby items in a cluster share similarity but those in different clusters are radically different. The clustering techniques allow the researcher to reveal the underlying structure and pattern of the data without knowing that a dataset has a structure (Tyagi et al., 2021; Aissaoui et al., 2019). The clustering algorithms have been used in different applications such as customer segmentation and image processing, document classification, fraud detection and behavioural analysis. One such example of application has been in the separation of abnormal calling patterns in telecommunication fraud by sorting similar user behaviours and detecting abnormalities that may indicate telecommunication fraud (Hilas & Mastorocostas, 2008). In predictive maintenance systems in the industrial sector, clustering algorithm is made to work on sensor data acquired by the machines with an aim of classifying the operational statuses in both normal and abnormal modes. These algorithms make it possible to detect possible mistakes and improve the decision-making process related to maintenance based on the similarity of data points (Amruthnath et al., 2018).

(a) Advantages

i. Works without labelled data
ii. Discovers hidden patterns (Tyagi et al., 2020)
iii. Useful for exploratory data analysis (Casolla et al., 2019)

(b) Weakness

i. Difficult to understand results (Nasteski, 2017)
ii. Depends on parameter selection (Tyagi et al., 2021)

(c) Limitations

i. Sensitive to data quality (Nasteski, 2017)
ii. Restricted by dataset size and techniques used (Casolla et al., 2019)

K-Means Clustering and Hierarchical Clustering are two of the most popular clustering methods that appear on the literature.

3.3.1.1. K- Means Clustering

K-means clustering is one of the most popular yet simplest clustering algorithms of machine learning. The algorithm divides a dataset into a specified number of clusters that are referred to as centres. The main aim of the algorithm is to minimize the gap between the data points and the cluster centres (Tyagi et al., 2021; Aissaoui et al., 2019). The fact that K-Means algorithm is widely used is because it is simple, scalable in addition to being useful in executing calculations. It has been used in many fields, including pattern recognition, image segmentation, customer behaviours analysis, and document clustering (Tyagi et al., 2021 Aissaoui et al., 2019 Usama et al., 2017). In networking studies, K-Means clustering has been used in network traffic pattern analysis and detection of abnormal network behaviour (like cyber-attack or traffic bursts) in the networks. The algorithm can spread the patterns which are abnormal to the normal network behaviours by fusing the similar traffic flows together (Usama et al., 2017). Similarly, K-Means is also applied as a clustering algorithm in predictive maintenance to cluster the machine operation conditions by the sensor data. Such clusters are the reflections of the different states of machines and can be employed in detecting the early signs of equipment malfunction (Amruthnath et al., 2018).

3.3.1.2. Hierarchical Clustering

The other prominent unsupervised learning algorithm that is used to cluster data points is the hierarchical clustering, which can be used to cluster similar data points. Unlike in the K-Means clustering, hierarchical clustering does not require prior knowledge of the number of clusters that is going to be used. Instead, it creates a pyramid of clusters that surround the connections among data points (Tyagi et al., 2021; Aissaoui et al., 2019).

Normally there are two different hierarchical clustering methods:

(a) Agglomerative Clustering

Agglomerative clustering follows the bottom-up approach where the first stage is to create a cluster of each of the data points individually. The algorithm then sequentially merges clusters in terms of measure of similarity until a cluster is created with all the data points.

(b) Divisive Clustering

Divisive clustering is a top-down algorithm in which one cluster is created initially having the complete dataset. The algorithmic algorithm is to divide the cluster into smaller groups according to the distinctions between the data points.

In visualizing the results of hierarchical clustering, a dendrogram (tree-like structure of relationships between clusters) is a widely used type of visualization. The dendrogram enables the researcher to determine how many clusters best fit the data and to get to know about the hierarchical connections among subsets of data (Tyagi et al., 2021; Aissaoui et al., 2019). Some of the fields that have implemented hierarchical clustering include in fraud detection, networking as well as health care data analysis. An example of this is that hierarchical clustering might be employed in the detection of traditional telecommunication fraud since the clusters of patterns of calls and the deviation of the normal pattern of calls are utilized in the detection process (Hilas & Mastorocostas, 2008).

3.3.2. Association Rule Mining

The other important data mining technique that can be utilized to identify relation between the variables in huge datasets is referred to as association rule mining. It establishes patterns that exhibit the presence of some items or events with respect to each other. This technique is usually used in market basket analysis, recommendation systems and analysis of customer behaviours. The common patterns algorithms such as ECLAT (Equivalence Class Clustering and Bottom-Up Lattice Traversal) and Frequent Pattern development (FP-Growth) are usually used in the mining of association rule. However, in the provided paper, they are only said to be a mere example of the association rule mining methods and the details of how they work are not explained in detail. The literature reviewed mainly focuses on the clustering algorithms and dimensionality reduction techniques in the context of unsupervised learning (Tyagi et al., 2021; Dike et al., 2018).

3.3.3. Dimensionality Reduction

High dimensional data has redundant or irrelevant features, which has a high degree of complex calculation and analysis. The aim of the dimensionality reduction techniques is to reduce the variables, and yet retain the most useful data in the data set. They can be helpful to improve the visualization, reduce the computational cost, and performance of a machine learning model (Tyagi et al., 2021; Aissaoui et al., 2019).

One of the most popular ways of dimensionality reduction is Principal Component Analysis (PCA).

3.3.3.1. Principal Component Analysis (PCA)

Principal Component Analysis (PCA) is a statistical procedure applied to reduce the large dimensional data to a few non-correlated variables referred to as the principal components. These attributes grasp as numerous as can be data variation in the dataset and reduce the quantity of variables (Tyagi et al., 2021). In PCA, the original data is transformed into a new set of coordinates where the first largest principal component represents the highest variance of the data followed by the second largest principal component, etc. By doing so, datasets can be simplified and the most important information is not lost (Tyagi et al., 2021; Aissaoui et al., 2019). PCA can be proactively applied to any kind of work and investigation such as image recognition, anomaly detection, data visualization, and predictive maintenance. PCA is applied in sensor data analysis in industrial monitoring to detect abnormal behaviour of the machine by detecting a variation in the operational parameters (Amruthnath et al., 2018). PCA has been applied to networking to reduce the complex traffic data of the network traffic and to detect abnormal trends of cyber-attack or network failures. The PCA helps to decrease the dimensions of data to make the calculations more efficient and to improve the performance of the system of anomaly detection (Usama et al., 2017).

3.4. Applications

A. Computer Vision

Unsupervised learning has become an important part of computer vision where the computers are trained to understand and process visual data such as pictures and videos. The unsupervised forms of learning are typical when the data of interest is images and there is no labelling to detect patterns and structures of the visual representations. PCA finds vast applications in images analysis to reduce the image data dimensions without visual data that is significant. PCA simplifies the artificially complicated large datasets and improves the effectiveness of the calculations by transforming the image data into the limited number of major elements (Tyagi et al., 2021). Along with PCA, autoencoders and other unsupervised representation models based on deep learning are popular in learning image representations, as well. Autoencoders decrease the dimensionality of pictures to lower-dimensional representations and recover the original images back to images where neural networks can learn pertinent visual representations without the use of labels (Dike et al., 2018). They are utilized in the process of object recognition, image compression, pattern recognition, and face recognition, analysis of medical images (Tyagi et al., 2021; Aissaoui et al., 2019).

B. Speech Recognition

In speech recognition machines can be in a position to recognize and read the spoken words whereby the sounds are processed and transformed into the text. The unsupervised methods of learning will be utilized in speech recognition as there is generally a considerable amount of audio data that do not have transcripts labelled. The unsupervised neural network-based models can be trained to obtain audio speech representations to improve recognition by investigating the patterns in audio properties, e.g. frequency, pitch, and time variation, through their examination (Dike et al., 2018). The dimensionality reduction techniques like the Principal Component Analysis (PCA) are also used to reduce the complexity of the thus high-dimensional acoustic data, without loss of important data. This improves the processing system of speech (Tyagi et al., 2021). In addition to this, the clustering is also the process that finds speech patterns that are similar and this allows the identification of phonetic patterns and improves language modelling. The voice assistants, automatic transcription, and speech to text technologies are the common applications (Dike et al., 2018; Tyagi et al., 2021).

C. Nature Language Processing (NLP)

The objective of Natural Language Processing (NLP) is to help machines to understand human language. Learning without supervision is also applicable in NLP because much of textual information is not marked. Clustering algorithms can be typically applied to group together similar semantically similar documents or sentences. This may be utilized to ascertain what is present in vast document collections and it can automatically arrange the written content. Such clustering methods are popular in document classification, topic modelling and information retrieval systems (Tyagi et al., 2021; Aissaoui et al., 2019). The NLP uses are also significant in the dimensionality reduction techniques. High dimensional text data contain thousands of distinct features or words that are normally unique to them thus making computations more complicated. The analysis of the text is made easier, since using such techniques as PCA can reduce the number of features and preserve the most important semantic information (Tyagi et al., 2021). Deep learning-based models (unsupervised models) such as autoencoders and generative models can also be trained to learn meaningful representations of textual data. The models are applied to uncorrelated all the latent relations between words and sentences, and the subsequent application might be language translation, sentiment analysis, and chatbots (Dike et al., 2018).

4. SUPERVISED AND UNSUPERVISED LEARNING COMPARATIVE ANALYSIS

Predictive modelling Supervised learning has a high potential in predictive modelling because it is based on labelled training datasets to guide the learning process. Supervised models may be highly precise with the processing of tasks involving classification and regression through the analysis of known relation between input and output. The decision trees, support vector machine, neural networks, and the logistic regression are some of the popular algorithms that have been widely applied in healthcare classification, financial forecasting, and risk evaluation (Sathya & Abraham, 2013; Nettleton et al., 2010). Supervised learning however has its limitations as well. One of the key problems is the large labelled datasets required because they are occasionally difficult and expensive to obtain. Data labelling could be time-consuming, and experts working in the domain could need to label the data (Usama et al., 2017; Burkart & Huber, 2021). Unsupervised learning on the other hand is the one that analyses with unlabelled data sets and is more common in the real world. Some of the algorithms include K-means clustering, hierarchical clustering and association rule mining algorithms such as Frequent Pattern Growth (FP-Growth) and Equivalence Class Clustering and Bottom-Up Lattice Traversal (ECLAT) (Tyagi et al., 2021; Amruthnath et al., 2018). Despite the advantages, unsupervised models are difficult to evaluate since they have no labelled results that can be compared to them, and trends identified do not always have an easy interpretation in the real world (Nasteski, 2017; Verma et al., 2019).

4.1. Advantages and Limitation

Predictive modelling Supervised learning has a high potential in predictive modelling since it relies on labelled training datasets to direct the learning process. Supervised models can be very accurate when processing tasks that include classification and regression by analysing known input output relationships. Some of the common algorithms are decision trees, support vector machine, neural networks, and logistic regression that are extensively used in classification of healthcare, financial forecasting, and risk assessment (Sathya & Abraham, 2013; Nettleton et al., 2010). There are however limitations to supervised learning too. The large labelled datasets needed are one of the main issues as they are sometimes hard and costly to get. Labelling data can be laborious, and it might be necessary to annotate the data by domain experts (Usama et al., 2017; Burkart & Huber, 2021). Unsupervised learning, on the other hand, analyses using unlabelled data sets, and this is more prevalent in the real world. K-means clustering, hierarchical clustering, and association rule mining algorithms like Frequent Pattern Growth (FP-Growth) and Equivalence Class

Clustering and Bottom-Up Lattice Traversal (ECLAT) are some of the algorithms that are used to detect concealed relationships and group similar data points (Tyagi et al., 2021; Amruthnath et al., 2018). In spite of the benefits, it is challenging to assess unsupervised models as they lack labelled results to compare them to, and patterns found do not necessarily have a simple interpretation into the real-world (Nasteski, 2017; Verma et al., 2019).

4.2. Algorithm Performance

One of the essential factors in the selection of machine learning algorithms is the performance. In the case of sufficient labelled training data, the predictive accuracy of the supervised learning models is much greater. According to the established performance indicators, such as accuracy, precision, and recall and F1-score, which allow assessing the performance of these models in solving classification and regression tasks, these models can be evaluated (Burkart & Huber, 2021; Jiang et al., 2020). The problem of overfitting, noisy data, and imbalanced dataset however can hurt the supervised learning algorithms. The features and data preparation have to be carefully chosen so that the successful model performance could be ensured (Nettleton et al., 2010; Sathya & Abraham, 2013). Algorithms that do not require supervision are more interested in discovering patterns and not the ability to predict specific outputs. The similarity measures, the clustering initializing, and feature representation determine their work. As an example, different results would be produced by clustering algorithms depending on the distance measures applied and the number of clusters to form during model training (Amruthnath et al., 2018; Nasteski, 2017). Such dimensionality reduction algorithms as PCA may assist in minimizing the performance of an algorithm by reducing the dimensionality of data and still reflecting on essential data. Optimization of computational efficiency and the ability to process massive data through machine learning models can also be achieved with the help of the given process (Tyagi et al., 2021; Verma et al., 2019).

4.3. Real-Life System Practical Limitations

There exist a few restrictions in the selection of machine learning techniques in the real world. One of the most important ones is data availability and quality. Supervised learning requires labelled datasets which are not accessible in all applications, such as in healthcare, cybersecurity and behavioural science research (Burkart & Huber, 2021). Another important weakness is the computational complexity. Machine learning algorithms may also be very intensive in terms of processing power when handling large datasets. The methods that may make the complex data simple are clustering and dimensionality reduction that may improve the efficiency of the calculations in large-scale systems (Amruthnath et al., 2018; Tyagi et al., 2021). Moreover, the problems of interpretability and dependability are other factors of consideration when implementing the machine learning models in the real world. The supervised learning models are clearly defined in terms of value metrics and as such, it is not hard to justify their performance. In contrast, the unsupervised learning models are more likely to require the knowledge of the domain in order to interpret the patterns found by the algorithms (Nasteski, 2017; Verma et al., 2019).

5. TYPES OF LEARNING APPROACHES

5.1. Deep Learning

Deep learning is a subset of machine learning and is advanced of machine learning that uses artificial neural networks with multiple layers of nodes in the middle to learn and recognize complex patterns from large information. In contrast to machine learning methods such as Logistic Regression and Support Vector Machine need to extract features manually, deep learning automatically discovers and learns useful features from raw data. It is this ability to process highly abstract information and obtain high accuracy for solving a real-world problem, that makes deep learning systems so powerful. As high-performance computers continue to evolve, there is an incredible amount of data and the development of GPU technology, deep learning has gradually become a hot topic in the last few years, such as image recognition, speech processing, natural language processing, high-level autonomous systems and high-level intelligent decision making (Hao, 2019). Many kinds of data, including images, text, audio, video, sequential, and tabular data, can be used in deep learning models. Typically, a deep learning model is designed and trained, validated and interpreted following the pre-processing of a data set. Deep learning systems are usually trained using the support of robust hardware and massive amounts of data since deep neural networks consist of a number of calculations and parameters. Training deep learning models can be time consuming, but once trained, can give you results faster. In different application areas, there are different important deep learning architectures. They are the Multi-Layer Perceptron (MLP), Convolutional Neural Networks (CNN), Recurrent Neural Network (RNN), Long Short-Term Memory (LSTM), Deep Belief Network (DBN), Restricted Boltzmann Machine (RBM), Autoencoder (AE), and Generative Adversarial Network (GAN). CNNs are mainly used in image processing and computer vision, while the RNNs and LSTMs can be used for sequential and time series data such as language processing and speech recognition tasks. GANs and Autoencoders are commonly used to perform Generative and Unsupervised learning tasks. The potential of deep learning has been successfully shown in healthcare, cybersecurity, robotics, smart cities, recommendations systems, intelligent assistants, and transportation systems. The advantages of these deep learning models include flexibility, automated feature extraction, high performance, but there are also disadvantages, including the need for large amounts of labelled data, the opacity or "black box" nature of many models, and the fact that they require significant computational resources. The researchers continue to improve the efficiency and real-world applicability of deep learning by incorporating transfer learning, hybrid models, and lightweight architectures. Researchers are still working on improving the efficiency and real-world applicability of deep learning, which is done by incorporating transfer learning, hybrid models and lightweight architectures (Hao, 2019; Sarker, 2021).

5.2. Self-Supervised Learning (SSL)

Self-Supervised Learning (SSL) is one of the most important machine learning approaches that require little or no manual explanations to learn meaningful representations of features from a large amount of unlabelled data. Instead of being labelled by humans, SSL learns goals automatically, known as pretext tasks, allowing the model to learn patterns, structures, textures, edges, shapes and relationships that are implicit in their information. This approach is useful when the data is labelled, but this is expensive and time-consuming in some applications such as medical image analysis. There are generally two stages to self-supervised learning: During the first step, the model is pretrained with only unlabelled data to capture feature representations in a general way. The second step is to perfect the pre-trained network using a small labelled dataset for the final classification/prediction task. The process enables the model to start supervised learning with a well-established knowledge of features from the unlabelled data (Huang et al., 2021). Popular self-supervised learning methods, such as SimCLR, MoCo, BYOL and Rotation Prediction and Context Restoration, these methods can help the model with providing helpful visual and structural information from images without when needed.

5.3. Semi-Supervised Learning

Semi-Supervised Learning (Semi-SL) is a machine learning approach which combines a few labelled data samples and a large number of unlabelled data samples to improve learning and model performance. It can be very useful when labelled information is not readily available, and is more expensive to label, but unlabelled information is available. For example, in medical image classification, it is hard to get labelled images, as medical specialists are needed to label them, and the labelling process is expensive. To overcome this a method of semi-supervised learning that utilizes the labelled and unlabelled data for training the model and drastically reduces the need for extensive annotated data while ensuring high classification accuracy. The concept of semi-supervised learning in terms of patterns and relationships in the few labelled data, and then generalising that to the many unlabelled data. The model will attempt to discover structures in the data, and will be able to learn from the data even on samples that are not labelled (Wen et al., 2024). Typically, semi-supervised learning techniques have two major objectives for training. The first goal is to classify the labelled data correctly and the second goal is to make stable and consistent predictions on unlabelled data. An important assumption of this method is that if there are no labels, similar data samples result in similar predictions (Huang et al., 2021). In SRL, several widely-used approaches exist for effectively using unlabelled data. They include pseudo-labelling, consistency regularization, graph-based methods and Virtual Adversarial Training (VAT). There are lots of methods which produce pseudo-labels for unlabelled data and employ these pseudo labels to boost the learning process. Several important semi-supervised learning techniques like Mix Match, Fix Match, Mean Teacher, Pseudo-Labelling and VAT. Of these, Mix Match outstood in terms of performance uniformity with respect to various medical data sets. Experimental results indicate that semi-supervised learning has better classification accuracy than fully supervised learning in the scenario of limited amount of labelled data. The model is trained simultaneously on both labelled and unlabelled data, and learns to make predictions more reliably about the target classification task with more flexibility to learn from the labelled data. However, the hyperparameter optimization (HPO) of semi-supervised learning (SSL) techniques is also highly sensitive and requires careful tuning of the hyperparameters to achieve the best results (Huang et al., 2021; Wen et al., 2024).

6. CRITICAL ANALYSIS

6.1. Comparison

Comparisons of supervised learning algorithms, including Support Vector Machines (SVM), neural networks, decision trees, random forests, and Naive Bayes have established that ensemble techniques tend to be more predictive and robust and no single algorithm is always best as it depends on data properties (Nettleton et al., 2010; Nasteski, 2017). Machine learning models have been applied in applied fields, especially in mental health research, to predict disorders and diagnoses like PTSD and suicide risk based on demographic, clinical, and behavioural data, and decision tree-based and random forest models have discovered important risk factors and enhanced early intervention plans (FY et al., 2017; Verma et al., 2019). Moreover, regularization methods (including Ridge Regression, LASSO, Elastic Net) can be used to handle high-dimensional data, and, moreover, ensemble methods (like the Super Learner) can be applied to improve the performance of the model by adding additional algorithms to it (Jiang et al., 2020; Lowry & Milford, 2016; Naeem et al., 2023 A technique of feature selection (such as Information Gain and Chi-square) is another instrumental tool to enhance the model efficiency by selecting pertinent variables, particularly in high-dimensional data (Chin & Mirzal, 2015) . Under the name of unsupervised learning, developments around Gaussian Mixture Models and deep learning-based autoencoders have expanded conventional clustering methods, and dimensionality reduction methods like Principal Component Analysis (PCA) continue to be vital in simplifying complicated data sets (Tyagi et al., 2021). Moreover, the integration of machine learning in the IoT-based systems has allowed analysis of behavioural data through sensor technologies, but most of the studies are based on small datasets, which suggests that more sophisticated data analysis methods are required (Casolla et al., 2019). Although they have been made, the current literature also identifies such critical issues as overfitting, noisy data, and absence of external validation, which requires more detailed, comparative, and strengthening research methods to enhance the reliability and generalizability of machine learning models (Jiang et al., 2020; FY et al., 2017).

6.2. Model Interpretability

The concept of model interpretability is the capacity to comprehend the decision-making and predictions of a machine learning model. It is also a requirement in most applications, particularly in systems with considerable amounts of critical decision-making, that models be not only accurate, but also transparent and explainable. The literature emphasizes that a complex model, especially the one applied in supervised learning, is usually viewed as a black-box system, as it is not easy to comprehend the internal decision-making process. In an effort to deal with this problem, scholars have come up with methods as part of Explainable Artificial Intelligence (XAI). These methods consist of interpretable models, surrogate models and explanation methods that assist users in comprehending the impact of input features on predictions. Features importance analysis, local explanations, and rule extraction among others are popular approaches to enhance transparency (Burkart & Huber, 2021). The interpretability is especially necessary in the field of healthcare, where machine learning models are applied to diagnose and plan treatment. Here, it is possible to construct trust by knowing the rationale behind predictions, accountability, and allows the professionals to justify the model outputs. It also aids in determining faults or discrepancies in model behaviour (Doshi-Velez & Kim, 2017).

6.3. Bias and Fairness

Bias and fairness are critical concerns in machine learning, especially when models are applied to sensitive domains such as healthcare and public health. Bias occurs when a model produces systematically unfair or inaccurate predictions due to imbalanced or unrepresentative training data. The literature indicates that machine learning models rely heavily on the quality and structure of input data, and any bias present in the data can directly affect model outcomes. In applications involving personal or behavioural data, such as mental health prediction or public health monitoring, biased models may lead to unequal treatment of individuals or groups. This raises concerns about fairness, accountability, and transparency in automated decision-making systems. Researchers emphasize that ensuring fairness requires careful data selection, preprocessing, and evaluation to avoid discriminatory outcomes. The literature also highlights the importance of ethical considerations in data usage, particularly when dealing with sensitive information. Responsible data governance and adherence to ethical guidelines are necessary to ensure that machine learning systems do not reinforce existing inequalities (Jordan et al., n.d.).

6.4. Scalability and Deployment Challenges

Some of the key challenges in the real-world implementation of machine learning systems are scalability and deployment. Although models can be effective in the controlled laboratory environment, to apply them to the real-world environments, it is necessary to manipulate large volumes of high-dimensional data. The literature emphasises that machine learning algorithms should be able to handle large volumes of data, being accurate and computationally efficient. Generalization where the model trained on a particular dataset should be able to work on new and unseen data is one of the most important challenges. The most widespread problem is overfitting that can restrict scalability because models might not fit various environments. As a result, effective validation methods like cross-validation and external validation are needed to achieve the robustness. Moreover, deployment in the real world needs to be integrated with other existing systems, including healthcare systems, IoT platforms, or industry. The literature suggests that the handling of high-dimensional data, effective calculation, and sustenance of the model performance over time are vital issues. The models also need to be constantly monitored and updated to fit the changing patterns of data (Jiang et al., 2020).

7. CONCLUSION

Machine learning has become among the key technologies to process big and sophisticated data and give smart decision-making in different areas. The chapter has provided a detailed description of two critical models used in machine learning supervised and unsupervised learning. The supervised learning methods utilise labelled data in order to learn predictive models which can be applied to do classification and regression tasks. Other significant algorithms that are widely applied in several applications such as disease prediction, fraud detection and customer behaviour analysis can be decision trees, random forests, naive Bayes, support vectors machine and neural networks. Unsupervised learning, in its turn, is geared towards the exploration of unlabelled data to discover the hidden structures and patterns. The dimensionality reduction and clustering methods including the K-means clustering, hierarchical clustering, and PCA will enable the researcher to explore and find insights in high-level data. These methods are particularly applied in anomaly detection, customer segmentation, computer vision, natural language processing and autonomous systems. As the relative analysis in this chapter indicates, the choice between supervised learning and unsupervised learning largely is determined by the existence of the labelled data, nature of the problem and factors of computation. Even though the unsupervised learning has very high ability to analyse data, the supervised learning is more predictive in the cases where labelled data is not readily available. Overall, the machine learning techniques are still dynamic to the current data analysis and artificial intelligence. These algorithms provide an advantageous addition to the research, decision-making, and technological innovation in a broad scope of applications in the real world as they enable systems to learn through information and find complex patterns.

REFERENCES

Aissaoui, O. E., Madani, Y. E. E., Oughdir, L., & Allioui, Y. E. (2019). Combining supervised and unsupervised machine learning algorithms to predict the learners' learning styles. *Procedia Computer Science, 148*, 87–96. DOI: 10.1016/j.procs.2019.01.012

Amruthnath, N., & Gupta, T. (2018). A research study on unsupervised machine learning algorithms for early fault detection in predictive maintenance. In *5th International Conference on Industrial Engineering and Applications* (p. 355). IEEE. DOI: 10.1109/IEA.2018.8387124

Burkart, N., & Huber, M. F. (2021). A survey on the explainability of supervised machine learning. *Journal of Artificial Intelligence Research, 70*, 245–317. DOI: 10.1613/jair.1.12228

Casolla, G., Cuomo, S., Di Cola, V. S., & Piccialli, F. (2019). Exploring unsupervised learning techniques for the internet of things. *IEEE Transactions on Industrial Informatics, 16*(4), 2621–2628. DOI: 10.1109/TII.2019.2941142

Chin, J. A., & Mirzal, A. (2015). Supervised, unsupervised and semi-supervised feature selection: A review on gene selection. In *IEEE/ACM Transactions on Computational Biology and Bioinformatics*. DOI: 10.1109/TCBB.2015.2478454

Dike, H. U., Zhou, Y., Deveerasetty, K. K., & Wu, Q. (2018). Unsupervised Learning based on Artificial Neural Network: a review. *2018 IEEE International Conference on Cyborg and Bionic Systems (CBS)*, 322–327. DOI: 10.1109/CBS.2018.8612259

Osisanwo, F.Y., Akinsola, J.E.T., Awodele, O.,, Hinmikaiye, J. O., Olakanmi, O., & Akinjobi, J. (2017). Supervised Machine Learning Algorithms: Classification and comparison. *International Journal of Computer Trends and Technology, 48*(3), 128–138. DOI: 10.14445/22312803/IJCTT-V48P126

Hao, Z. (2019). Deep learning review and discussion of its future development. MATEC Web of Conferences, 277, 02035. DOI: 10.1051/matecconf/201927702035

Hilas, C. S., & Mastorocostas, P. A. (2008). An application of supervised and unsupervised learning approaches to telecommunications fraud detection. *Knowledge-Based Systems, 21*(7), 721–726. DOI: 10.1016/j.knosys.2008.03.026

Huang, Z., Jiang, R., Aeron, S., Hughes, & M. C. (2021). Systematic comparison of semi-supervised and self-supervised learning for medical image classification. In *Tufts University, School of Engineering*.

Jiang, T., Gradus, J. L., & Rosellini, A. J. (2020). Supervised machine learning: A brief primer. *Behavior Therapy, 51*(5), 675–687. DOI: 10.1016/j.beth.2020.05.002

Jordan, M. I., Mitchell, T. M., De Choudhury, M., Counts, S., Horvitz, E., Hoff, A., Brownstein, J. S., Freifeld, C. C., Madoff, L. C., Eysenbach, G., Broniatowski, D. A., Paul, M. J., Dredze, M., Sadilek, A., Kautz, H., Silenzio, V., White, R. W., Harpaz, R., Shah, N. H., ... M. Schrems. (n.d.). *Machine learning: Trends, perspectives, and prospects*. https://www.cs.cmu.edu/~tom/pubs/Science-ML-2015.pdf

Lowry, S., & Milford, M. J. (2016). Supervised and unsupervised linear learning techniques for visual place recognition in changing environments. *IEEE Transactions on Robotics, 32*(3), 600–613. DOI: 10.1109/TRO.2016.2545711

Naeem, S., Ali, A., Anam, S., & Ahmed, M. M. (2023). An Unsupervised Machine Learning Algorithms: Comprehensive Review. *International Journal of Computing and Digital Systems, 13*(1), 911–921. DOI: 10.12785/ijcds/130172

Nasteski, V. (2017). An overview of the supervised machine learning methods. *HORIZONS B, 4*, 51–62. DOI: 10.20544/HORIZONS.B.04.1.17.P05

Nettleton, D. F., Orriols-Puig, A., & Fornells, A. (2010). A study of the effect of different types of noise on the precision of supervised learning techniques. *Artificial Intelligence Review, 33*(4), 275–306. DOI: 10.1007/s10462-010-9156-z

Pandey, D., Niwaria, K., Chourasia, B., (2019). Machine Learning Algorithms: A Review. *International Research Journal of Engineering and Technology (IRJET), 06*, 916. https://www.irjet.net

Sarker, I. H. (2021). Deep Learning: A comprehensive overview on techniques, taxonomy, applications and research directions. *SN Computer Science, 2*(6), 420–420. DOI: 10.1007/s42979-021-00815-1

Sathya, R., & Abraham, A. (2013). Comparison of supervised and unsupervised learning algorithms for pattern classification. *International Journal of Advanced Research in Artificial Intelligence* 2(2), pp. 34–38. https://thesai.org/Downloads/IJARAI/Volume2No2/Paper_6-Comparison_of_Supervised_and_Unsupervised_Learning_Algorithms_for_Pattern_Classification.pdf

Stonier, A. A., Gorantla, R. K., & Manoj, K. (2023). Cardiac disease risk prediction using machine learning algorithms. *Healthcare Technology Letters, 11*(4), 213–217. DOI: 10.1049/htl2.12053

Tyagi, K., Rane, C., Sriram, R., & Manry, M. (2022). Unsupervised learning. In R. Pandey, S. K. Khatri, N. k. Singh, & P. Verma (Ed.) *Artificial Intelligence and Machine Learning for EDGE Computing*, pp. 33-52. Academic Press. DOI: 10.1016/B978-0-12-824054-0.00012-5

Usama, M., Qadir, J., Raza, A., Arif, H., & Yau, K.-L. A. (2017). Unsupervised machine learning for networking: techniques, applications and research challenges. *ArXiv*. https://arxiv.org/abs/1709.06599v1

Verma, K. K., Singh, B. M., & Dixit, A. (2019). A review of supervised and unsupervised machine learning techniques for suspicious behavior recognition in intelligent surveillance system. *International Journal of Information Technology*, *14*(1), 397–410. DOI: 10.1007/s41870-019-00364-0

Wen, Z., Pizarro, O., & Williams, S. (2024). Active self-semi-supervised learning for few labeled samples. *Neurocomputing, 614,* 128772. DOI: 10.1016/j.neucom.2024.128772

KEY TERMS AND DEFINITIONS

Artificial Intelligence: A branch of computer science that enables machine learning to simulate human intelligence, allowing them to learn from data, reason, sole problems, and make decisions.

Clustering: Unsupervised machine learning technique that automatically groups similar data points into clusters, ensuring high similarity within groups and low similarity between them.

Decision Tree: A widely used supervised machine leaning algorithm that uses a hierarchical, flowchart-like structure of questions and rules to make predictions or classify data.

Labelled Data: Raw data paired with meaningful tags or annotations that provide context from supervised machine learning models to learn pattern and make predictions.

Machine Learning: ML is a subset if artificial intelligence that trains software to learn patterns from the data and make predictions or decisions without being explicitly programmed.

Supervised Learning: A type of machine learning where models are trained using labelled datasets, meaning each input data point is paired with the correct output.

Unsupervised Learning: A machine learning technique where algorithms analyse and cluster unlabelled datasets, discovering hidden patterns.

Chapter 2
Neural Shields:
AI's Proactive Cyber Defense Revolution - A Systematic Study

Willson Joseph C.
http://orcid.org/0009-0004-6882-5241
Rajagiri School of Engineering and Technology, India

Venkateswaran Radhakrishnan
http://orcid.org/0000-0003-1096-0278
College of Computing and Information Sciences, Oman

K. Tharageswari
Karpagam Academy of Higher Education, India

S. Aruna
http://orcid.org/0000-0002-1052-3572
Dayananda Sagar College of Engineering, India

Anirudh N. M.
Dayananda Sagar College of Arts, Science, and Commerce, India

Keerthana N. V.
http://orcid.org/0000-0001-8878-2083
Velalar College of Engineering and Technology, India

ABSTRACT

The digital age has brought amazing levels of connectivity, but also new levels of exposure and risk to ever more sophisticated cyber threats. Old security is frequently no match for new attacks and AI is game-changing in cybersecurity. AI supports instant detection, identification of anomalies, and anticipated threat-intelligence using advanced machine learning applications, such as deep machine learning and behavioral algorithmics. They improve detection of intrusion, categorization of malware and automation of response, cutting reaction time and damage. AI can predictIdentify and Respond, beyond the detection of vulnerabilities, AI will enable organization to see something bad is happening before it does and allocate resources to respond. Yet, challenges including adversarial AI, ethical considerations, algorithmic bias and high implementation costs need to be formalized.

DOI: 10.4018/979-8-2600-3280-0.ch002

1. INTRODUCTION

Human error is one of the important elements of cybersecurity weaknesses. Such developments have grave cybersecurity threats, which highly affect critical infrastructure. As an example, when there are many IT teams in the process of setting up, one may not get an effective configuration of the system. Due to constant innovation, computer security has been advanced than ever. The challenging situation in cybersecurity is changing as 6G networks are promoted, and devices associated with the Internet of Things (IoT) are spread (Kulandaivel & Kulandaivel, 2025). The implementation of AI and quantum computing in cybersecurity has opportunities and challenges. Cybersecurity is currently a priority to the leadership of both the public and commercial organizations. Cybersecurity has become one of the most important issues in cyberspace nowadays. Neural networks and other AI models can be primarily trained on cybersecurity systems to identify anomalies, which can result in a cyberattack.

"Time is of the essence" is a saying that shows extraordinary importance in the field of cybersecurity. Cybersecurity is the art of protecting information confidentiality, integrity, and availability, as well as the practice of safeguarding networks, devices, and data from unauthorised use or access (Sandhia et al., 2025). Cyber defensive mechanisms, on the other hand, appear at the application, network, host, and data levels. Grand View Research approximated the global Artificial Intelligence (AI) market size at USD 93.5 billion in 2021 and anticipates a Compound Annual Growth Rate (CAGR) of 38.1% between 2022 and 2030 to measure this phenomenon statistically. AI has been applied widely recently across various sectors, including cybersecurity. Many cybersecurity-related products and technologies are aimed at fighting attacks against network systems and applications that exist within an organization's internal or external periphery.

AI is increasingly being used in life. The cybersecurity strategy is based on the capability of AI as a developing technology that has demonstrated massive growth potential. The ability of AI to respond to the evolving security concerns is very much possible due to its versatility, speed, and precision, and not only are there tactical consequences of weapon handling, but also implications of decision-making. One of the primary technologies of the Fourth Industrial Revolution, or Industry 4.0, is AI, which can protect Internet-connected devices from web-based threats, attacks, damage, and unlawful access (De Azambuja et al., 2023). "AI-driven cybersecurity" can potentially be a powerful part of smart cybersecurity management and services (Riza et al., 2025).Cybersecurity computing can become more automated and intelligent through security intelligence modeling based on AI techniques. AI makes cyberspace security controllable in a reasonable amount of time and presents potential remedies. Similarly, the worldwide cybersecurity industry was estimated by

Mordor Intelligence to be worth $156.24 billion in 2020 and is projected to increase at an annual pace of 14.5% to reach $352.25 billion by 2026. All organizations' information system analysts are in charge of educating staff members about cyber threats so they may make informed judgments that will maximize the company's security (Behera, Vedashree, Kumar, & Upreti, 2025).

Cybersecurity also places a stress on non-repudiation to prevent Grand Viewd-enial of communications or activities and authentication for identity verification purposes of users. Its scope encompasses such as network security to secure channels of communication, incident response to effectively deal with intrusions, application security to secure software, and data security to secure sensitive information. Cyber-security is mandatory for individuals and organizations to protect themselves from cyberattacks. It secures data, networks, and systems by following the three basic principles of the CIA triad: Confidentiality, Integrity, and Availability. Confidentiality states that confidential data is secure from unauthorized access using practices like encryption and access controls. In everyday life, cybersecurity finds application in all areas—network security, protecting communication media; application security, securing software; and data security, securing information while stored as well as in transit. It also covers endpoint security for computers, cloud security to defend against data storage in cloud infrastructure, and operational security for protecting workflows (Keerthana & Suresh, 2016). In addition, cybersecurity includes incident response to manage breaches and disaster recovery to recover from attacks. Cyber security is now imperative for reducing risks and helping companies stay regulatory compliant because of our growing dependency on technology (Kanimozhi, Keerthana, Pavithra, Ranjitha, & Yuvarani, 2021).

To develop modifications of known Failure Mode, Effects, and Criticality Analysis (FMECA) techniques (table-based templates, algorithms for analyzing failures/intrusion modes and effects criticality, criticality matrices, and sets of countermeasures applied by various actors), their integrated option, and the corresponding ontology model. The development of a methodological framework and protocols for assessing cybersecurity is the main contribution of the research.

2. FUTURE SECURITY: ROLE OF AI IN CYBERSECURITY

2.1 Traditional Vs AI-Driven

Traditional cybersecurity methods primarily employ signature-based detection methods. These methods involve matching system logs and network traffic against predetermined patterns of known malicious behavior. It is challenging to function effectively due to large sets of data and high false alarm rates, particularly when businesses move to cloud-based architecture and acquire more data. Inspection of advanced threat standards and high-level data analysis in cyber-threat intelligence and cybersecurity. The goal of AI is to create cheaper and high-quality products that are more personalized. The technology of wireless and AI allows creating a fundamental shift in production. The introduction of AI to cybersecurity raises serious concerns over the issues of privacy, autonomy, and responsibility. The advent of AI has transformed cybersecurity into a new form through the introduction of new solutions to improve its threat prevention, detection, and response capabilities. The signature-based techniques were disadvantaged as far as identifying polymorphic malware and the zero-day attacks were concerned (Ramezanpour & Jagannath, 2022).

For many years, digital security tactics have been built on top of traditional cybersecurity techniques. To identify risks, these techniques mostly use pre-established rules and signatures. For improved security, it is then evident to use more robust security measures and algorithms that support stronger cryptographic keys. Because diverse nodes in an Internet of Things network handle different data formats and communication technical standards, they are susceptible to a range of assaults and exploit risks. It can be challenging to identify some of the new security risks of today with conventional security and privacy methods and procedures. As a result, creative approaches are desperately needed to provide security and privacy in intelligent Cyber-Physical Systems (CPS) (Alowaidi, Sharma, AlEnizi, & Bhardwaj, 2023). A sophisticated grasp of the security frameworks used by different cloud providers is required due to the heterogeneity of cloud platforms and services. A fragmented security landscape is the outcome of the different capabilities, configurations, and security mechanisms offered by each cloud environment.

To maintain a consistent security posture across many environments, organizations must manage these variations. IoT adoption appears to be very promising, but if a failure arises, it could cause a power chain catastrophe. These problems are simpler to fix because majority of conventional network failures are brought about by either equipment failures or changes in parameters.

- Explainability and Trust
- Computational Cost
- Adversarial Attacks
- Evolving Threat Landscape
- Data Requirements

Conventional cybersecurity techniques emphasise rule-based systems and signature-based detection, which are reactive rather than proactive. These techniques can only identify assaults that match predetermined criteria because they are based on predefined rules and recognised threat signature patterns. These systems are unable to keep up with the increasing sophistication and evolution of cyber threats. Therefore, ML-based AI has also been employed to enable security for those CPS in addition to standard security measures. According to an analysis by ABI Research, 44% of energy, healthcare, public safety, transportation, water, waste treatment, and other infrastructure management initiatives will receive cybersecurity funding in smart city projects. The study explores the conventional cybersecurity techniques used in Master Data Management (MDM) systems (Inan, Namin, Pogrund, & Jones, 2016). This covers network security, authentication procedures, encryption, and access controls. The literature assesses these metrics' efficacy critically and emphasises their function in setting a baseline for protecting private data inside MDM. The following subsections offer a concise overview of several AI models, datasets, assessment metrics, and research projects related to zero-day attack detection.

The performance of generative AI models can also be affected by the data poisoning attack. For instance, a rain-removal deep generative model trained by a poisoned training dataset can turn the traffic light from red to green while removing the rain of an input image, posing a severe risk to road safety. Adversarial instances include minor adjustments to the input attributes that are invisible to human observers or disturbances of the raw input data. However, these disruptions are deliberately designed to trick the AI model into generating incorrect results. A cybersecurity methodology based on AI, in particular the K-Nearest Neighbour (KNN) algorithm and the Enhanced Encryption Standard (EES) encryption and decryption algorithm, has been used to accomplish the research's goals.

Experts are exploring new solutions as traditional security measures failed to ward off cyberattacks, data breaches, financial loss, and brand damage (Mishra, 2023). Classic rule-based solutions usually cannot deal with the complexity of advanced persistent threats (APTs), zero-day attacks, or other sophisticated cyberattacks. AI solutions can provide preemptive, responsive, and self-adaptive solutions to threat detection, prevention, and response, including machine learning (ML) and deep learning (DL). The key to interference discovery is AI methods that allow even unknown threats to be dealt with prior to their spreading. Because people cannot scale anymore to defend the dynamic enterprise attack surface, AI gives detailed insights and notifications so threat detection can be simpler for cybersecurity experts to minimize the number of breach risks and enhance overall security (Jawaid, 2023). In contrast to standard methods, SDN programmability allows for the development of AI-enabled defense capabilities without the necessity for specific hardware devices, making it yet another reasonable and adaptable solution. Sinha, Singla, & Victor (2023) demonstrate that it is already being used to detect anomalies and mitigate threats.

2.2 Modern Cyber Defense with AI

In our digitally connected world, the fight against cyber threats is being fought on many fronts, mostly due to the continual evolution of tactics employed by attackers to bypass defenses. In this continuous arms race, AI is a powerful partner in improving cybersecurity defenses. AI was basically just digital human intelligence. Advanced ML would need to automatically detect assaults and intelligently recommend ways to prevent attackers from launching new ones to properly respond to cyberattacks, which have increased at previously unheard-of rates. The authors describe the development and deployment of a smart cyber assistant that helps security analysts by quickly and effectively thwarting both emerging and existing attacks to successfully address these issues.

The creation of targeted cyber intelligence for use in defense or offense—that is, to improve or jeopardise the security of networks, data, and users—is one prospective use of AI. These technologies can be used to integrate several aspects of the cyber intelligence process, specifically the "collection," "processing," and "analysis" of information, as the literature has noted (Bonfanti, 2022).The following abilities make AI a valuable technology in cyber defense and information security because of

- Pattern forecasting and prediction (e.g., impending server downtime)
- Effective analysis of massive amounts of data (e.g., log files)
- Pattern analysis and recognition
- Grouping and classifying (such as spam, phishing, or malware).
- Anomaly detection (e.g., 10,000 login attempts per second, i.e., possible cyber-attack detected)

While ML and AI have been used to combat cyber attacks and their spread, cyber defense provides an enormous benefit to cybersecurity. By integrating blockchain technology and AI, this approach provides a multi-layered security that strengthens the proactive and reactive elements of cybersecurity. It is possible to consider ways to spot adversarial samples that could potentially harm the model, and then strengthen the pre-trained classifier against poisoning attacks to resolve the cybersecurity issue. There are many methods designed to contribute to more robust models like poisoning training including defensive distillation, gradient obfuscation, feature squeezing, etc.

Speed and Accuracy: The best advantage that AI can offer to the cybersecurity industry is the real-time detection and remediation of threats. The AI programs through network traffic monitoring are capable of automatically detecting any unusual activities or actions that can pose a threat to your security.

Continual Learning and Response: AI does not only assist security systems to respond to emerging forms of threats and attack vectors at a fast pace, it also assists in keeping security systems ahead of the hackers.

Efficiency and scalability: AI can be used in comparison to human analysts to efficiently and effectively quantify and catalog large amounts of data in a short period of time. AI takes some of the operational load off the shoulders of security practitioners to enable them concentrate on more challenging and complicated problems.

AI response would loosely suit phishing email attacks in particular, where it has the potential to process and structure the vast volume of data, discover fine-tuning relationships between features, and learn dynamically regarding the cyber defense environment. Most of the strategic benefits of AI lead to cybersecurity, which includes:

- Enhanced Accuracy
- Threat Prioritization
- Quicker Data Analysis
- Increased Automation
- Improved Threat Detection

2.3 Key Technologies for AI Enablement in Cyber Security

Threat Detection Enhancement: Real-time analysis of massive data sets by ML algorithms enables the identification of subtle irregularities and attack patterns that have not been observed before (A. R. P. Reddy, 2021). By having such a proactive approach, businesses can detect threats before they attain a critical level of influence.

Automated Incident Response: The first thing that comes after a security incident has happened is time. Artificial intelligence may work in real-time to isolate all the affected systems, end communications with a malicious entity, and initiate the remediation process. The faster the reaction, the fewer the destruction and recovery time the attack caused (Ochieng, Cogburn, and Wong, 2025).

Advanced Malware Detection: The modern anti-virus detectors rely on the use of signatures to detect malware. The analysis of the malware behavior by artificial intelligence can be used to detect the new and emerging threats. Machine Learning algorithms can even be used to help differentiate between benign and malicious activity that is present within the behavior of a malware family, even in the case of malware that has never been observed before (Sinha et al., 2023).

Data-Driven Risk Assessment: The AI evaluates vulnerabilities within the system, as well as past data on the system's past and uses it to create a risk score in general. Data-based security assessments enable security teams to identify the most essential vulnerabilities and focus their efforts on eliminating them first.

Constant Learning and Adaptation: The AI models are always learning and adapting to new data and new cyber threats. This enhances security controls since the AI and ML security systems keep on learning; therefore, security models are always being updated to adapt new cyber threats.

Behavioural Analytics: AI is able to detect abnormal user behavior through behavioral analysis. Behavioral analytics would be a good solution to internal threat detection or account compromise. The AI systems adapt and learn to identify abnormal behavior and other suspicious activity.

Fraud Detection: AI is detecting financial and e-commerce fraud. Artificial intelligence systems scan transaction history and behavior of users. Fraudulent transactions are being detected by AI systems and they also reduce the chances of losses.

AI & ML: AI has the potential to reshape cybersecurity and the detection of various cyberthreats. Machine Learning (ML) is a computer system's ability to learn from data and use algorithms to perform tasks without programming, which is defined as learning (Wazid, Das, Chamola, & Park, 2022). Defensive systems utilizing deep learning (DL) methods, specifically artificial intelligence in cybersecurity, are being utilized to automate the detection of cyberattacks and gradually develop and improve their systems. AI-based cybersecurity techniques for IoT, IoE, IoH, and IoV.

- AI-enabled digital investigation.
- Advanced AI techniques to secure future Internet architectures/protocol.
- Full-proof security of ML models.
- Enhanced effectiveness of cyber security met.
- Limited requirements of human intervention.
- Quick scanning and mitigation.

Zero Trust Architecture (ZTA): Zero Trust Architecture (ZTA): An approach to meeting security needs in a network with untrusted infrastructure is zero trust architecture or ZTA (Ramezanpour & Jagannath, 2022). We also make the case for utilizing 5G networks' Multi-access Edge Computing (MEC) capabilities to give resource-constrained devices the computational power they need to achieve the intended i-ZTA. Zero Trust Principles are,

- Zero Trust.
- Trust/Risk Evaluation.
- Least Privilege.
- Dynamic Policy.
- Integrity Check.

Blockchain: Blockchain is a decentralized safe storage paradigm that saves data following appropriate verification and authentication (Mohamed, Taherdoost, & Madanchian, 2025). Smart contracts, keys, files, transaction information, etc. It is a decentralized consensus system that uses safe algorithms to store and retrieve data. With proper mutual authentication or key agreement, peer-to-peer data transmission is possible. Higher-level applications of blockchain utilize smart contracts.

- Decentralization.
- Transparency.
- Immutability.
- Pseudonymity.
- Traceability.
- Programmable.
- Autonomy.

Proactive Threat Detection: Real-time analysis of network traffic is accomplished using AI algorithms leveraging questionable behaviors and indicators of imminent attack, prior to manifesting as serious attacks.

Adaptive Defense: AI systems are good learners and adapt to new threats, behavior, etc.

Automated Security Processes: AI is capable of automating various security tasks, including incident management, applying patches, and vulnerability detection, in addition to learning and adapting over time.

Enhanced Accuracy: AI systems are capable of identifying and categorizing network intrusions with high accuracy. Neural networks are used in DL, a subset of machine learning, to analyze and learn from data.

Reinforcement Learning (RL): RL is a type of ML in which agents, or software, learn how to make decisions through trial and error. In the context of cyber security, RL provides several benefits shown in Figure 1. By utilizing ML and DL, AI-based systems provide proactive, automated, and adaptive mechanisms for threat assessment, prevention, and response. Intrusion Detection Systems (IDS) powered by Deep Learning (DL) have received much interest because they use complex processes of decision making, which produce substantial filtering between normal and suspicious states. Large Language Models (LLMs) such as Bidirectional Encoder Representations from Transformers (BERT) and Bidirectional and Auto-Regressive Transformers (BART) are among the recent tools that enable the emergence of proactive threat detection methods by identifying network behaviors and aberrations (Diaf, Korba, Karabadji, & Ghamri-Doudane, 2024).

Figure 1. Advantages of RL usage in Cyber Defense

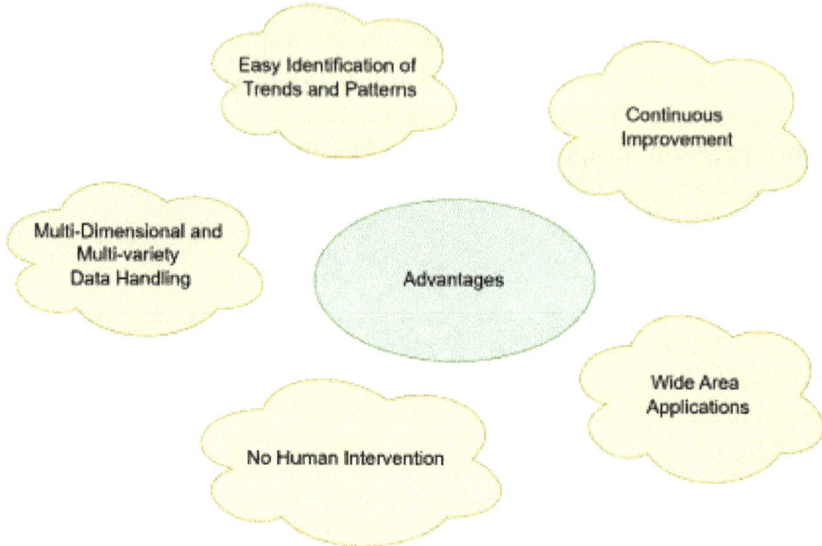

3. CYBER ATTACK DETECTION WITH AI

By facilitating the proactive detection of abnormalities and hitherto undiscovered attack patterns, ML promises a paradigm leap in threat detection. The area of ML has been growing at a pace unprecedented in history (Ferrag, Maglaras, Moschoyiannis, & Janicke, 2020). As the agency cannot depend on the old, conventional process anymore, it has found an alternative process to avert attacks prior to their occurrence. the necessity of understanding cyber safety techniques and how applying ML algorithms and artificial neural networks might result in enhanced abilities.A comprehensive analysis of papers on cybersecurity ML from 2013 to 2018, foundations and respective defenses against cyberattacks, the basics of the most popular ML algorithms, and proposed ML and cybersecurity data mining plans for features, dimension reduction, classification, and detection were incorporated.

AI-powered threat detection systems employ advanced ML methods, DL models based on neural networks to identify abnormal activities and detect potential threats in multi-cloud environments. Several studies employ ML algorithms to detect, monitor, contain, and eliminate security threats. Examples such as Dynamic malware analysis, spam and phishing detection, intrusion detection and classification, security analysis that includes event correlation and network user profiling, network user authentication, safeguarding vital infrastructure, and cybersecurity risk management.

Figure 2. Role of ML and AI in Cyber Security

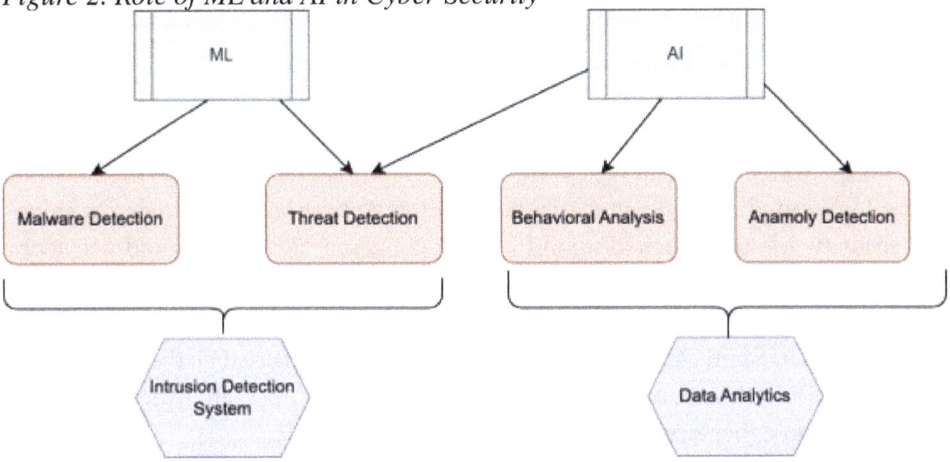

Incident Report Analysis: Natural Language Processing (NLP) can be used to automate incident report summarization and classification to enable cybersecurity teams to react faster to the incident, patterns, enhance the quality of threat identification, and eliminate false positives.

Image and Video Analysis: DL methods can scan image and video information for security, e.g., surveillance mechanisms that identify illegitimate entry or track abnormal activities in restricted areas.

Malware Detection: Whether malware is embedded or completely new, DL models can efficiently search binary code and executables to detect malicious signatures and patterns.

Active Scanning and Probing: Through adapting and improving themselves over time in the identification of threats, ML models improve the inspection of network traffic, system logs, and behavior, providing accurate threat detection and improved security overall.

Understanding Cybersecurity Data: In order to construct an IDS dataset, Defence Advanced Research Project Agency (DARPA) attempted the earliest in 1998.In recent years, a well-organized market involving large amounts of money has become the malware industry.

3.1 Role of Neural Networks in Cyber Security

The ANN architecture boasts a high score of accuracy at 99.97 percent, a Receiver Operator Characteristic (ROC) area of an average size of 0.999, and a false positive mean of only 0.001 (Sarker, 2021). Such architectures comprise multiple layers of artificial neurons capable of identifying complex data patterns were modelled after the structure and functions of the human brain. Convolutional Neural Networks (CNN) are particularly well-suited to analyze image and network traffic data. They can be taught to recognize patterns characteristic of malware or other vectors of attack by looking for patterns characteristic of malware or other vectors of attack. A Recurrent Neural Network (RNN) is especially capable of recognizing patterns in time in the data. They are thus perfectly suited for analyzing network traffic logs and identifying attack paths that emerge with time.The topics of safety and security are also touched upon by these concerns. Several DL and ML techniques, along with CNN and Long Short-Term Memory (LSTM) networks, have been documented. Unsupervised ML (UML) can be utilized to find anomalies in CPS, claims (Al Siam, Alazab, Awajan, & Faruqui, 2025). Based on the Deep Belief Network (DBN), the neural networks listed below in Figure 3, are examples of DL applications in cybersecurity.

Figure 3. Example DL Models

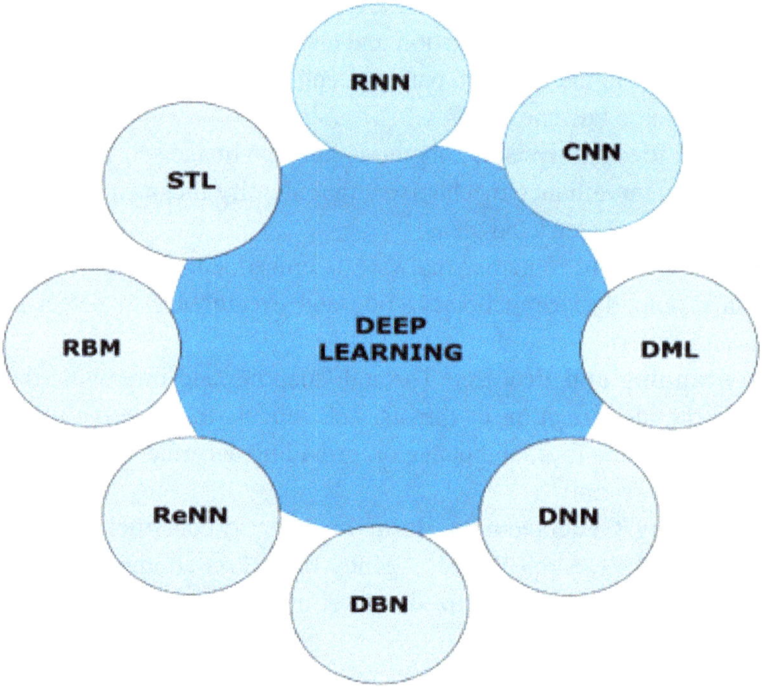

Deep Neural Network (DNN): Tang et al. utilized a DL method to explain an intrusion detection system in a software-defined network paper. An IDS was utilized in a networked software paper that was fully dependent on the DL methodology.

By integrating the suggested IDS network into the SDN controller, any OpenFlow Ethernet switch can be effortlessly monitored.

RNN: A cyber-physical IDS to identify cyberattacks on automobiles. Compared to conventional ML methods, the system's deep multilayer perceptron and recurrent neural network design provide higher accuracy and more consistency.

CNN: To detect anomalies in packet data in a state estimator based on phasor measurement units. They extract event signatures from phasor measurement units using a data filter based on a convolutional neural network.

Restricted Boltzmann Machine (RBM): A comparative study of restricted Boltzmann machines for cyber-intrusion detection. Specifically, the research demonstrates how limited Boltzmann machines are able to distinguish normal and abnormal NetFlow traffic to achieve outstanding detection speed and accuracy.

Deep Belief Network (DBN): DBN can be used in a broad category of high-dimensional data applications within the cybersecurity domain. It can efficiently extract features and classify features in a broad category of high-dimensional data applications.

Deep Migration Learning (DML): For intrusion detection in cybersecurity. Specifically, the research combines an IDS with a DL model. It results in a high accuracy and false alarm rate.

Self-Taught Learning (STL): For the detection of intruders in cybersecurity. The proposed technique segments the process of classification into steps, including learning feature representation and using the learned representation for the classification task.

Replicator Neural Network (ReNN): For the intrusion of identifications in cybersecurity. For identifying abnormalities, the study utilizes the dropout method.

3.2 Phishing and Social Engineering Attack Detection using NLP

NLP analyses textual information to perform intelligent recognition and performs semantic analysis of text to detect harmful intent. It provides a comprehensive answer to this problem (Ochieng et al., 2025). The method also uses NN and DL frameworks. NLP analyses textual information to perform intelligent recognition and performs semantic analysis of text to detect harmful intent. It provides a comprehensive answer to this problem (Ochieng et al., 2025). The method also uses NN and DL frameworks. Phishing email detection is now bounded by the employment of NLP technology instead of DL methodologies, which entirely disregard the disparities between anti-phishing emails and other objectives and partly disregard contextual details.

Data protection is in jeopardy as phishing attacks persist to trap both individuals and organisations because of the adoption of more advanced tactics by assailants, e.g., customised and highly compelling messages (Ferrag et al., 2020). NLP techniques have become vital tools for extracting beneficial information from unstructured text data. This approach proved the utility of NLP in enhancing threat intelligence by providing early warning signals for emerging ransomware threats (Nithya, Chandrasekaran, Mahendrakumar, Keerthana, & Keerthana, 2026).

Applying NLP, ML algorithms, and optimization techniques, text features of phishing emails, dataset or resources used within phishing emails, and assessment metrics, the primary study topics in phishing email detection (Roshanaei, Khan, & Sylvester, 2024). To date, there is zero research conducted on several systematic literature reviews on phishing email detection using NLP methods (Benavides-Astudillo, Fuertes, Sanchez-Gordon, Nuñez-Agurto & Rodríguez-Galán, 2023). The most common phishing types are technological deception (like malware installation) and social engineering (like fake emails).But other traditional methods (such as pharming) are also utilized to scrape users' personal information from the Internet. This study makes use of clustering, NLP, and ML methods based on NN to detect phishing attempts by examining the email content before recipients view it.

Types of Phishing:

- Malware Phishing.
- Smishing.
- Standard Phishing.
- Search Engine Phishing.
- Clone Phishing.
- Malvertising.
- Business Email Compromise.
- Pharming.
- Vishing.

The best performance of 99.57% accuracy rate for phishing URL identification was achieved by utilizing the random forest method with only NLP in Internet of Things (IoT) environments, according to the testing data. More than 87 research studies employing DL algorithms for phishing URL identification from 2018 to 2022 can be found by conducting a Google Scholar search.

This qualitative awareness of cybersecurity gains a potent, universal capability with the application of NLP. Moreover, pre-trained representation-based AI models can generalize predictions of cyber jobs without being trained on task-related data, which represents the path that NLP is taking in cyber workforce capacities (Ganesh Kumar & Sengan, 2020). The literature has only recently recognized some of the issues related to automatic processing of NLP text through establishing and defining custom ML approaches based on commonly applied NLP approaches.

Threat and Vulnerability Analysis using ML Models:

- Prediction Models based on Software Metrics using supervised ML approaches.
- Anomaly detection techniques that use UML techniques to automatically mine rules or extract a model of normalcy from software source code, identifying vulnerabilities as deviations from the norm;
- Susceptible Code Pattern Recognition, which uses supervised ML techniques to identify patterns in numerous vulnerability code samples that contain susceptible code segments. d
- Miscellaneous Approaches, which belong to the other AI and ML-based approaches that cannot be categorized in the previous categories.

Social engineering detection: One of the most straightforward methods of learning more about a target is through social engineering, which takes advantage of human flaws seen in all organizations (Diaf et al., 2024). Social engineering has emerged as one of the most pernicious and hazardous techniques in the field of cybersecurity because it plays on feelings and trust. Some of the methods employed in social engineering attacks are listed below in Figure 4.

Figure 4. Social Engineering Model

3.3 Anomaly Detection and Behavioural Analytics

The concept of "behavioural analytics" refers to processes that rely on data to study behaviours user. It suggests considering user behaviours and actions, which finely tunes on the data related to how users are interacting with IT systems (Silvestri, Islam, Papastergiou, Tzagkarakis, & Ciampi, 2023). Since departures from accepted baselines are potential indicators of an insider threat, each user action is tracked in real-time with unique behaviours identified as a security risk prior to inflicting any damage. Behavioural analytics systems take advantage of many data sources to generate a baseline of acceptable behaviours of users within an organisation. One significant contributor to the success of behavioural analytics is its ability to combine ML algorithms and adapt over time (Bergadano & Giacinto, 2023).

The first step to allow AI to identify anomalies is establishing proper baselines that includes operations commonly present in the cloud ecosystem. It is through continuous sensing and learning that AI can identify normal interactions and examples across frameworks, applications, and individuals. A wide-ranging perspective is complemented by efficiently identified aberrations that may indicate security risks.

Additionally, AI systems can modify and improve their understanding of normalcy since behaviours of users, network activity, and systems uniquely evolve through a continual studying process which will help ensure that baselines will still be relevant in the face of changing user behaviours or system settings (Arora, Arora, & McIntyre, 2023). Once the baselines are established, AI becomes skilled at identifying system anomalies (deviations from baselines, or unexpected behaviours) very quickly. It is important to note that anomalies can appear in many forms, including odd data transfers or fluctuating access behaviours.

The models are usually divided into two classes (i) Legitimate and (ii) Abnormal Intrusion is considered to occur whenever there is a deviation to abnormal marks from a legitimate design. The project aims to enhance cybersecurity defences of the ever-evolving network environments with more sophisticated cyber-attacks, based on the potential of ML, statistical modelling, and adaptable parameters. Anomaly detection is a form of study that has been carried out over several years in academic literature. Many advanced techniques are used to detect data anomalies. Many applications of anomaly detection models, including cybersecurity, network intrusion detection, fault detection, streaming, hyper-spectral imaging, and anomalous activity in videos, use anomaly detection models such as the one illustrated in Figure 5.

Figure 5. Anomaly Detection Model

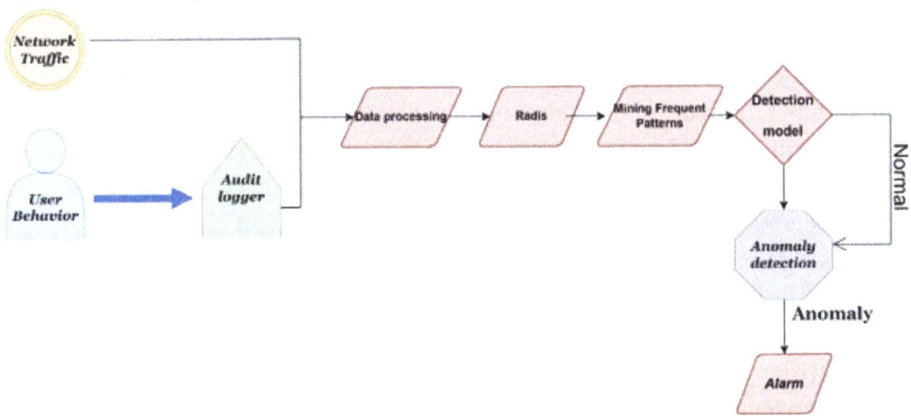

Anomaly detection can be defined as the process of detecting outliers or unusual data occurrences that are not in accordance with the expected behaviour. Anomaly detection is one of the basic techniques for immediately identifying cyberattacks. It can detect new unknown threats with no indicators. Anomaly detection is essential in cybersecurity in order to detect possible fraud or system weaknesses, or other security violations. Adaptive learning, data collecting, pattern recognition, and real-time analysis are some of the core areas of anomaly detection. Anomaly-based techniques analyse typical system and network behaviour, and identify outliers as deviations from that behaviour. This is appealing because of its ability to identify zero-day attacks. Anomaly detection models utilize graph-based analysis, autoencoders, or clustering algorithms to identify network activity that is different from what is expected. This is applicable in fraud detection to capture abnormal or unexpected behaviour, such as a spike in account activity or an unusually large transaction from an unknown source. One promising method of fraud detection is behavioural analysis. (ML) algorithms can analyse historical transaction and spending information, as well as online activity to establish a baseline of behavior. For the ongoing assessment of a behaviour pattern system, ML systems can determine anomalies (i.e., a user behaving out of their established norm) and put potentially suspicious accounts on hold for evaluation. Organizations can take a proactive stance and stop the fraudulent activity before it happens.

3.4 Intrusion Detection and Prevention System (IDPS)

The observation of network or system activity, ML improves IDS's capacity to detect intrusions. Intrusion Prevention Systems (IPS) take it further by possessing the ability to block attacks immediately, something not always necessary for IDS (Illy & Kaddoum, 2023). AI techniques such as neural networks and fuzzy logic are also vital alongside ML. Nine defence against flood attack IDPS models were constructed by one research using traditional, DL, and AI. An intrusion prevention system is required to guard endpoints against malware and malicious access. Machine learning and deep learning can be used to enhance IDPS so as to combat cyberattacks more efficiently. Moral and legal issues are present in the use of AI in company operations (Mtukushe, Onaolapo, Aluko, & Dorrell, 2023). IDPS is one of the cyber defence mechanisms guarding digital valuables. Intrusion detection is the cornerstone of CPS security. Some of the IDS methodologies are anomaly detection, which identifies deviations from normal behaviour, and misuse detection, which identifies well-known attack patterns. IDPS, which offers a hybrid model, risk and performance analysis, classification, and prevention, has been explored in ML and DL.

Figure 6. Intrusion detection and prevention system

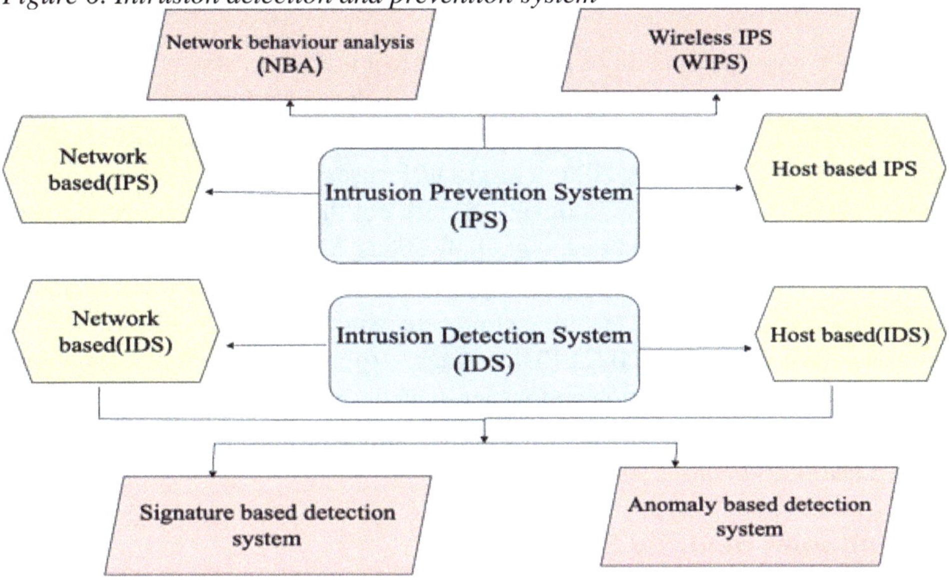

New IDPS detect attacks, logs them, and notifies Incident Response (IR) teams. An IDPS pipeline examines IDPS logs at multiple levels, locates applicable incidents, correlates them to vulnerable applications, and blocks attacks. It makes use of two models: a sophisticated Deep Neural Network (DNN) on cloud servers to classify attacks (to determine appropriate countermeasures) and a lightweight DNN for local server anomaly identification (for immediate response) (Odufisan, Abhulimen, & Ogunti, 2025). It uses a priority concept, where the abnormal traffic is categorized by the second model. It presents four main contributions:

- Analyses DNN time complexity.
- Suggests a collaborative DL-based IDS and its architecture for ICS.
- Proposes detection features, DNN algorithms, and IRS methods.
- Showcases the effectiveness of the strategy through experiments.

Intrusion detection is essential to system security. Through anomaly detection, adaptive learning, and real-time analysis of massive amounts of data, AI-powered IDS improves threat identification. Through the use of machine learning (ML) for quick threat detection, monitoring, and response, AI-driven IDPS provides autonomous real-time defence (Purnamadewi & Zahra, 2025). Because it categorises threats and starts automated responses, it is better than antivirus software, SIEM, and EDR.

3.5 Malware Analysis and Classification

Malware with AI capabilities is a danger since it is always changing to avoid detection and improve on ransomware attacks. This malware circumvents conventional protections by adapting through machine learning. While XDR monitors the entirety of the kill chain across many IT systems, EDR focuses on the endpoints to provide wider visibility and response to threats. Security at the endpoint protects devices that connect to networks via endpoint applications from a cyberattack. Endpoint metadata is used to identify endpoint applications through network connections. Endpoint security uses a full feature set to secure remote-connected devices (Heino, Jalio, Hakkala, & Virtanen, 2022). EDR utilizes AI to analyse behaviour at endpoints in real time for threat detection and response while EPP uses signatures (Tauseef, 2022). EDR systems collect and analyse data at the endpoint in a central database to alert teams of threats.

3.6 Endpoint Security Solutions

While XDR monitors the entirety of the kill chain across many IT systems, EDR focuses on the endpoints to provide wider visibility and response to threats. Security at the endpoint protects devices that connect to networks via endpoint applications from a cyberattack. Endpoint metadata is used to identify endpoint applications through network connections. Endpoint security uses a full feature set to secure remote-connected devices (Heino, Jalio, Hakkala, & Virtanen, 2022). EDR utilizes AI to analyse behaviour at endpoints in real time for threat detection and response while EPP uses signatures (Tauseef, 2022). EDR systems collect and analyse data at the endpoint in a central database to alert teams of threats. AI drives EDR with ML and deep neural networks. The models involved in endpoint security are represented in Figure 7.

Figure 7. Endpoint Security

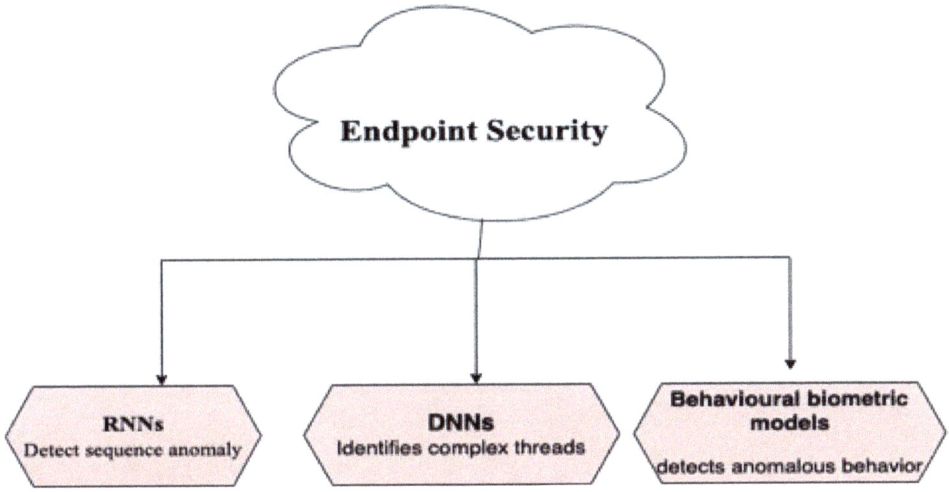

3.7 Phishing Detection and Mitigation

In general, phishing is derived from "phone phreaks," a cyberattack where the attacker is trying to steal sensitive information deceptively. Detection includes DL, machine learning, scenario-based learning, and hybrid learning (Mughaid et al., 2022). With AI, risk management ends up being automated as it can respond rapidly to threats and learn new security policies based on those responses. Steps can also be taken to mitigate the risk, with 38% using awareness training and 17% using AI/ ML. ML & NLP analyse email content to categorize phishing (Keerthana, Suresh, Kulandaivel, & Kulandaivel, 2025). It is caused by security vulnerabilities, weak passwords, and insufficient endpoint detection. AI amplifies phishing campaigns by producing highly personalized, realistic fakes represented in Figure 8.

Figure 8. Phishing Detection

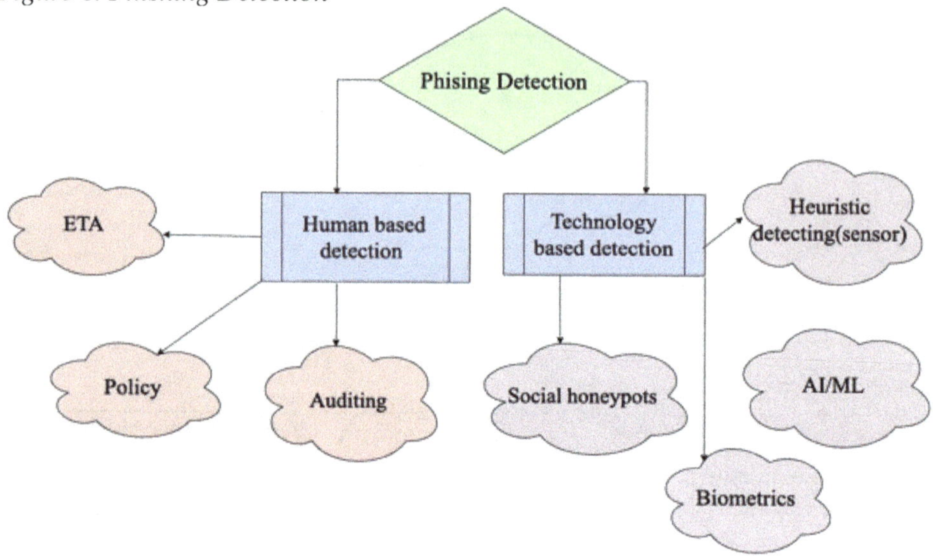

4. AI IN THREAT INTELLIGENCE AND VULNERABILITY MANAGEMENT

AI sorts through large data sets seeking potential risk, and pattern-recognition weaknesses are addressed by ML algorithms. AI integration presents with many challenges, such as complexity, trust requirements, adversarial attacks, domain-expert knowledge, as well as high-quality data (Alanezi, 2022). AI helps enhance human resource management for a firm by better allocating resources to address pressing needs, solve current issues, and protect against constantly changing cyber attacks. Threat intelligence and vulnerability management increase with AI support, enhancing overall cybersecurity. These tasks are accomplished due to proactive risk elimination, predictive inspection, and effective risk identification and prioritization.

4.1 AI-Powered Cybersecurity Solutions in Industry

AI is critical to industrial cybersecurity today and has moved from abstraction levels of theory to applicability in practices occurring in the banking or maritime industries now.' AI is applied through anomaly detection and pre-emptive protective measures, as well as optimizing security algorithms and threat analysis (Rahman, Yi, & Khalil, 2022). The ML and DL approaches will require several methodologies to interconnect various types of complex threats and risks, such as CNNs, DAEs, and GANs. The structured knowledge of cyberthreats can also be more accessible through the implementation of cybersecurity ontologies, which facilitate the process of risk assessment and the overall security posture in all industrial settings.

4.2 Successful Use Cases of AI in Preventing Major Cyber Attacks

Artificial intelligence has prevented significant cyberattacks on vital industries. AI endpoint protection and behavioural analytics became an important ransomware and insider threat defence in healthcare. The AI anomaly detection helped a financial organization to automatically detect and prevent phishing and credential stuffing attacks, reduce the risk and safeguard confidential information and transactions. These are some of the ways AI can make predictions to offer proactive solutions to augment cyber defence.

5. LESSONS LEARNED AND BEST PRACTICES

Cybersecurity is now an important aspect of a sustainable digital future that calls for actions across policies and economic opportunity. Developing cyber talent and raising awareness in communities are also important. A further consideration is to incorporate cybersecurity into alliances such as NATO (Erola, Agrafiotis, Goldsmith, & Creese, 2022). There are lessons learned from our use of AI in terms of AI challenges in incident response that will inform the employment of AI in security in the future. There are likely many businesses that can learn from one another about the security associated with digital transformation and automation. Current trends reflect a movement towards stronger authentication, such as MFA, as well as security assessments, particularly for IoT security.

5.1 Enhanced Detection Accuracy

AI greatly improves accuracy in threat detection (about insider threats and zero-day exploits) and often performs better than other methodologies. Coupling AI with automation focuses the alarm and saves time for security personnel (Abdullahi et al., 2022). In many cases, advancements to defences improve the bad guy's sophistication of attack; nevertheless, the effectiveness of AI in detection applications is based on the same principles as any tool - it must be able to recognize new malware and anomalies in intrusion detection. By applying techniques like AdaBoost, Gradient Boost, and XGBoost, detection accuracy can be further enhanced through samples from large datasets, and AI can recognize a pattern that appears to be affably malicious (Dash, Ansari, Sharma, & Ali, 2022).

5.2 Faster Response Times

AI streamlines the cybersecurity incident response process by escalating the speed at which threats are detected, systems are isolated, and recovery is automated. The more swiftly you respond less the amount of damage and recovery time. Supplier AI-enabled SIEM and SOAR operations incorporated to employ real-time monitoring, automated response workflows, and actionable evidence-based decision-making enable them to respond faster and more effectively than conventional methods of response when identifying the subject matter (A. Reddy, 2022). AI offers the capability of learning and analysing, and can initiate a 'hot' and timely containment as soon as an incident occurs, greatly impacting the traditional response time.

5.3 Scalability and Adaptability

In AI cybersecurity, scalability refers to controlling the performance and expenses of resources and the systems that utilize them as they expand. The ability of AI to use ML and iterative or continuous learning in response to shifting regulations and threats is known as adaptability (Babu, 2024). The scaling up of AI applications also requires good software engineering practices, good data/ML practices, and attention to ethical and legal considerations. Common roadblocks to scaling include technology barriers, generalizing lab environment performance, and ethical issues like bias. AI-oriented automation provides scalability and allows for a quicker response to threats, the commitment of faster and more resources, and the release of security professionals for additional work.

5.4 Proactive Threat Mitigation

Cybersecurity is substantially improved when proactive threat detection strategies based on risk mitigation evaluation are implemented, allowing AI to predict attacks, identify deviations much earlier, and reduce response time, especially with ML models such as a NARX ANN. In addition, some organizations have reported 92.5% accuracy when identifying threats while having a false positive rate of 3.2%. Dynamic load balancing, real-time monitoring, and predictive analytics should allow intrusions to be 20% less impactful. Proactive mitigation types like threat intelligence, patch management, and end-user training will augment defences against attackers' changing tactics and result in a more capable overall system (Keerthanaa, Rojab, Santhiyac, & Sowndharyad).

6. CHALLENGES AND LIMITATIONS OF AI IN CYBERSECURITY

Adversarial attacks against AI are disruptive to the cybersecurity landscape, taking advantage of vulnerabilities in AI models to create deceptive inputs, usually as adversarial examples that misguide the decision path of the AI model. Adversarial attacks adversely impact critical infrastructure and/or industry domains, such as smart autonomous medical systems, autonomous vehicles, smart grids, etc (Peri, Asokan, Goel, Anjali, & Keerthana, 2025). Adversarial attacks typically go undetected by conventional detection mechanisms. RL environments are more susceptible since attacks by adversaries introduce perturbations that may not trigger significant modification of the AI model's decision process but result in misclassification to take advantage of vulnerabilities (Subramanian, Subramaniam, Natarajan, & Thangavel, 2024). Adversarial training, input sanitizing, and ensemble modelling have been suggested as defence to help AI models with adversarial attack robustness, although there is no silver bullet to completely eliminate vulnerability to such attacks. As noted above, data availability and data quality are still primary issues since noisy, incomplete, and/or biased data will undermine the performance of the AI model. Operational interfacing of AI with legacy systems involves drastic infrastructural changes and process re-engineering. Ethical and privacy issues augment the situation to call for ethical application of AI responsibly that may entail abiding by the principles of legal instruments on data protection (e.g., GDPR, CCPA, etc.) and providing sufficient informed consent, so as not to inadvertently reveal sensitive information and/or be exploited (Ragab et al., 2025). Privacy-oriented technologies, such as federated learning, train AI models without ever sending applicable raw data. There was some thought behind AI and cybersecurity, which has a lot of potential. The intrusion detection solution, LSTM-based solutions have some advanced defences, VLAN segmentation, TLS encryption and multilayered access that may be implemented as a layered security solution. Regarding innovation and technological advancement, IBM has introduced the Adversarial Robustness Toolbox in addition to the hybrid DL framework of NGCAD-EDLM that promotes the emergence of proactive and adaptive defence systems. Overall, the amount of relevant AI innovation in cybersecurity is vast, and the construction of practical AI systems will require not only the active search for innovation and technology but also compliance with ethical theory, legal practices, and intersectoral and industry collaboration. Since AI is superimposing and replacing current and developing infrastructure, which has been developed at a fast pace over the last few years, a carefully thought-out collection of proactive and cooperative methods will add confidence and safety to sensitive settings against the approaching complexity of cyber threats.

7. FUTURE TRENDS IN AI AND CYBERSECURITY

The development of the AI algorithms and systems has seen a significant enhancement in the component of cyber defense resulting in the capabilities to detect, respond, and prevent a threat among others. Malware analysis, phishing detection, endpoint security, and autonomous incident responses are the improvements in AI technologies (supervised and unsupervised learning, DL, RL, and NLP), which are dynamic processors and analyzers of massive data sets in real time (Behera et al., 2025). As much as AI systems have numerous advantages, they have their shortcomings. Some of the inherent weaknesses of AI technologies include adversarial attack vulnerabilities, computational constraints, and black box decision-making. The problems mentioned above raise the issue of explainability and trust in AI systems (Ghanem, Chen, Ferrag, and Kettouche, 2023). The creation of Explainable AI (XAI) is essential in the formation of trust in AI and an ethical duty to utilize such tools to make decisions in a transparent way in an ethical manner in cybersecurity. Moreover, since AI-led threats are also on the rise (e.g., AI-based phishing and deepfake social engineering attacks), AI will also be in demand to assist the adaptive countermeasures in fighting the threats. The collaboration of human and AI is relevant in the harmonization of automated accuracy, as well as human contextual knowledge. The human-in-the-loop models and expert systems will be more equipped to offer options in decision making and responsibility as well as endorse the core nature and purpose of AI and will facilitate the further development of ethical and legal consequences (Kanimozhi et al., 2021). Cybersecurity in CPS, IoT, and MANETs does not only require intentional AI techniques, but it is also necessary to ensure that it is secured with an effective encryption to safeguard their intricate multilayered ecosystems (Wazan & Cuppens, 2023).Finally, AI-supported cybersecurity must continually be developed through interdisciplinary measures, continuous education, and the establishment of an adequate balance between automation and supervised human intervention where it is necessary. Resilience to the current, complex hacker cyber threat activity will imply the creation and implementation of AI solutions in responsible, transparent, adaptive, and secure ways.

8. CONCLUSION

The two situations of AI-driven technology concerning cybersecurity are twofold since it can be used to enhance cybersecurity in thrilling ways and simultaneously, new threats have been brought by advanced technology. Artificial intelligence will add most of the capabilities to our cybersecurity systems, such as detecting threats in real-time, automatically reacting to them when a threat is detected, and providing more effective protection of the possibility of an anomalous behavior. Besides this, AI gives enemies the capability to create advanced architectures of cyberattacks and is a more easy target to scale, such as AI-generated phishing and deepfakes. Continuous innovation, reasonable application of AI, and continuous development of methods of protection of our digital assets are required. It suggests an increased willingness to find a common solution that involves the use of computational capabilities of AI and the rationality of humans, and the level of experience and reliability to have possession of the final decision reached. To foster an illusion of trust in the consideration of the problem of socio-ethical challenges embedded in AI decision-making, without having knowledge about AI hardware and technical foundations, explainable AI (XAI) should be provided.

We discussed the balance in terms of DL, concerning resilience and interpretability, and maintained the effectiveness of DL. The second frontier of intelligent, scalable and secure solutions is the developing cybersecurity environment, particularly the automotive networks and technologies that fall under the CPS category. With the threats constantly moving as fast as light, the old techniques of using a fixed response will no longer be viable. Consequently, further debates on AI development are to concentrate on such aspects of AI development as the creation of monitoring as opposed to a fixed premise, the adaptability of risk management, cross-disciplinarity, among others. This is because the opportunity to study AI decision-making, ethically coupled with human judgment, should result in a more responsive and resilient capacity to react to cyber incidents that pose a threat to a globalized and diverse world. With our innovations running at a faster rate than the need to reflect on ethical practice to contextualize response, there will still be more tensions as we attempt to shape the direction of our technology.

REFERENCES

Abdullahi, M., Baashar, Y., Alhussian, H., Alwadain, A., Aziz, N., Capretz, L. F., & Abdulkadir, S. J. (2022). Detecting cybersecurity attacks in internet of things using artificial intelligence methods: A systematic literature review. *Electronics (Basel), 11*(2), 198. DOI: 10.3390/electronics11020198

Al Siam, A., Alazab, M., Awajan, A., & Faruqui, N. (2025). A Comprehensive Review of AI's Current Impact and Future Prospects in Cybersecurity. *IEEE Access : Practical Innovations, Open Solutions, 13*, 14029–14050. DOI: 10.1109/ACCESS.2025.3528114

Alanezi, M. A. (2022). Vulnerabilities, threats and challenges on cyber security and the artificial intelligence based internet of things: A comprehensive study. *International Journal of Computer Science & Network Security, 22*(2), 153–158.

Alowaidi, M., Sharma, S. K., AlEnizi, A., & Bhardwaj, S. (2023). Integrating artificial intelligence in cyber security for cyber-physical systems. *Electronic Research Archive, 31*(4), 1876–1896. DOI: 10.3934/era.2023097

Arora, A., Arora, A., & McIntyre, J. (2023). Developing chatbots for cyber security: Assessing threats through sentiment analysis on social media. *Sustainability (Basel), 15*(17), 13178. DOI: 10.3390/su151713178

Babu, C. S. (2024). Adaptive AI for Dynamic Cybersecurity Systems: Enhancing Protection in a Rapidly Evolving Digital Landscap. In *Principles and applications of adaptive artificial intelligence* (pp. 52-72): IGI Global Scientific Publishing.

Behera, A., Vedashree, A., Kumar, M. R., & Upreti, K. (2025). Artificial Intelligence and Cybersecurity Prospects and Confronts. In *Navigating Cyber-Physical Systems With Cutting-Edge Technologies* (pp. 155–184). IGI Global Scientific Publishing.

Benavides-Astudillo, E., Fuertes, W., Sanchez-Gordon, S., Nuñez-Agurto, D., & Rodríguez-Galán, G. (2023). A phishing-attack-detection model using natural language processing and deep learning. *Applied Sciences (Basel, Switzerland), 13*(9), 5275. DOI: 10.3390/app13095275

Bergadano, F., & Giacinto, G. (2023). *Special Issue "AI for Cybersecurity: Robust Models for Authentication, Threat and Anomaly Detection"* (Vol. 16). MDPI. DOI: 10.3390/books978-3-0365-8265-8

Bonfanti, M. E. (2022). *Artificial intelligence and the offence-defence balance in cyber security. Cyber Security: Socio-Technological Uncertainty and Political Fragmentation.* Routledge.

Dash, B., Ansari, M. F., Sharma, P., & Ali, A. (2022). Threats and opportunities with AI-based cyber security intrusion detection: A review. [IJSEA]. *International Journal of Software Engineering and Its Applications, 13*(5).

De Azambuja, A. J. G., Plesker, C., Schützer, K., Anderl, R., Schleich, B., & Almeida, V. R. (2023). Artificial intelligence-based cyber security in the context of industry 4.0—A survey. *Electronics (Basel), 12*(8), 1920. DOI: 10.3390/electronics12081920

Diaf, A., Korba, A. A., Karabadji, N. E., & Ghamri-Doudane, Y. (2024). *Bartpredict: Empowering iot security with llm-driven cyber threat prediction.* Paper presented at the GLOBECOM 2024-2024 IEEE Global Communications Conference. DOI: 10.1109/GLOBECOM52923.2024.10901770

Erola, A., Agrafiotis, I., Goldsmith, M., & Creese, S. (2022). Insider-threat detection: Lessons from deploying the CITD tool in three multinational organisations. *Journal of Information Security and Applications, 67*, 103167. DOI: 10.1016/j.jisa.2022.103167

Ferrag, M. A., Maglaras, L., Moschoyiannis, S., & Janicke, H. (2020). Deep learning for cyber security intrusion detection: Approaches, datasets, and comparative study. *Journal of Information Security and Applications, 50*, 102419. DOI: 10.1016/j.jisa.2019.102419

Ganesh Kumar, K., & Sengan, S. (2020). Improved network traffic by attacking denial of service to protect resource using Z-test based 4-tier geomark traceback (Z4TGT). *Wireless Personal Communications, 114*(4), 3541–3575. DOI: 10.1007/s11277-020-07546-1

Ghanem, M. C., Chen, T. M., Ferrag, M. A., & Kettouche, M. E. (2023). ESASCF: Expertise extraction, generalization and reply framework for optimized automation of network security compliance. *IEEE Access : Practical Innovations, Open Solutions, 11*, 129840–129853. DOI: 10.1109/ACCESS.2023.3332834

Heino, J., Jalio, C., Hakkala, A., & Virtanen, S. (2022). A method for endpoint aware inspection in a network security solution. *IEEE Access : Practical Innovations, Open Solutions, 10*, 44517–44530. DOI: 10.1109/ACCESS.2022.3170456

Illy, P., & Kaddoum, G. (2023). A collaborative DNN-based low-latency IDPS for mission-critical smart factory networks. *IEEE Access : Practical Innovations, Open Solutions, 11*, 96317–96329. DOI: 10.1109/ACCESS.2023.3311822

Inan, F. A., Namin, A. S., Pogrund, R. L., & Jones, K. S. (2016). Internet use and cybersecurity concerns of individuals with visual impairments. *Journal of Educational Technology & Society, 19*(1), 28–40.

Jawaid, S. A. (2023). Artificial intelligence with respect to cyber security.

Kanimozhi, N., Keerthana, N., Pavithra, G., Ranjitha, G., & Yuvarani, S. (2021). *CRIME type and occurrence prediction using machine learning algorithm.* Paper presented at the 2021 International conference on artificial intelligence and smart systems (ICAIS). DOI: 10.1109/ICAIS50930.2021.9395953

Keerthana, N., & Suresh, P. (2016). Security driven multi-constrained scheduling for computational grid. *International Journal of Scientific and Engineering Research, 7*(2), 43–49.

Keerthana, N., Suresh, P., Kulandaivel, M., & Kulandaivel, S. (2025). Critical Strategies for Phishing Defense and Digital Asset Protection: A Case Study Approach. In *Critical Phishing Defense Strategies and Digital Asset Protection* (pp. 221-244): IGI Global Scientific Publishing. Keerthanaa, N., Rojab, S., Santhiyac, S., & Sowndharyad, L. Data Security Using Certificateless Signature Cryptosystem. DOI: 10.4018/979-8-3693-8784-9.ch011

Kulandaivel, S., & Kulandaivel, M. (2025). Intelligent and Optical Security Monitoring for 6G Communications. In *RFID, Microwave Circuit, and Wireless Power Transfer Enabling 5/6G Communication* (pp. 417-444): IGI Global Scientific Publishing.

Mishra, S. (2023). Exploring the impact of AI-based cyber security financial sector management. *Applied Sciences (Basel, Switzerland), 13*(10), 5875. DOI: 10.3390/app13105875

Mohamed, N., Taherdoost, H., & Madanchian, M. (2025). Comprehensive Review of Advanced Machine Learning Techniques for Detecting and Mitigating Zero-Day Exploits. *EAI Endorsed Transactions on Scalable Information Systems, 12*(1).

Mtukushe, N., Onaolapo, A. K., Aluko, A., & Dorrell, D. G. (2023). Review of cyberattack implementation, detection, and mitigation methods in cyber-physical systems. *Energies, 16*(13), 5206. DOI: 10.3390/en16135206

Mughaid, A., AlZu'bi, S., Hnaif, A., Taamneh, S., Alnajjar, A., & Elsoud, E. A. (2022). An intelligent cyber security phishing detection system using deep learning techniques. *Cluster Computing, 25*(6), 3819–3828. DOI: 10.1007/s10586-022-03604-4 PMID: 35602317

Nithya, T., Chandrasekaran, V., Mahendrakumar, S., Keerthana, N., & Keerthana, A. P. (2026). Digital Innovation as the Backbone of Developing Economies: A Study. In *Digital Technologies and Transformations in Public Administration, Engineering, and Sustainable Business* (pp. 263-294): IGI Global Scientific Publishing.

Ochieng, T., Cogburn, D., & Wong, H. (2025). Introduction to the Minitrack on AI Safety, Cybersecurity, and Inclusion through Advanced Text Analytics.

Odufisan, O. I., Abhulimen, O. V., & Ogunti, E. O. (2025). Harnessing Artificial Intelligence and Machine Learning for Fraud Detection and Prevention in Nigeria. *Journal of Economic Criminology*, 100127.

Peri, S. S. S. R. G., Asokan, D., Goel, D., Anjali, A., & Keerthana, N. (2025). *Strategic Leadership and Digital Disruption: A Roadmap for Organizational Expansion using Adaptive Boosting (AdaBoost).* Paper presented at the 2025 3rd International Conference on Self Sustainable Artificial Intelligence Systems (ICSSAS).

Purnamadewi, Y. R., & Zahra, A. (2025). Enhancing detection of zero-day phishing email attacks in the Indonesian language using deep learning algorithms. *Bulletin of Electrical Engineering and Informatics*, *14*(1), 505–512. DOI: 10.11591/eei.v14i1.8759

Ragab, M., Basheri, M., Albogami, N. N., Subahi, A., Abdulkader, O. A., Alaidaros, H., Mousa, H., & AL-Ghamdi, A. A. L.-M. (2025). Artificial intelligence driven cyberattack detection system using integration of deep belief network with convolution neural network on industrial IoT. *Alexandria Engineering Journal*, *110*, 438–450. DOI: 10.1016/j.aej.2024.10.009

Rahman, Z., Yi, X., & Khalil, I. (2022). Blockchain-based AI-enabled industry 4.0 CPS protection against advanced persistent threat. *IEEE Internet of Things Journal*, *10*(8), 6769–6778. DOI: 10.1109/JIOT.2022.3147186

Ramezanpour, K., & Jagannath, J. (2022). Intelligent zero trust architecture for 5G/6G networks: Principles, challenges, and the role of machine learning in the context of O-RAN. *Computer Networks*, *217*, 109358. DOI: 10.1016/j.comnet.2022.109358

Reddy, A. (2022). The Future of Cloud Security: Ai-Powered Threat Intelligence and Response. *International Neurology journal.*

Reddy, A. R. P. (2021). The role of artificial intelligence in proactive cyber threat detection in cloud environments. *NeuroQuantology : An Interdisciplinary Journal of Neuroscience and Quantum Physics*, *19*(12), 764–773.

Riza, A. Z. B. M., Jennsen, L., Anggani, P., Rafeen, A. I., Ruth, P. N. J., Sookun, D., . . . Luximon, L. (2025). Leveraging Machine Learning and AI to Combat Modern Cyber Threats.

Roshanaei, M., Khan, M. R., & Sylvester, N. N. (2024). Enhancing cybersecurity through AI and ML: Strategies, challenges, and future directions. *Journal of Information Security*, *15*(3), 320–339. DOI: 10.4236/jis.2024.153019

Sandhia, G., Ranjani, M., Nithiyanandam, N., Prakash, U., Srinivasan, R., Girirajan, S., . . . Ramaprabha, J. (2025). Cybersecurity: The Part Played by Artificial Intelligence. In *Analyzing Privacy and Security Difficulties in Social Media: New Challenges and Solutions* (pp. 213-246): IGI Global Scientific Publishing.

Sarker, I. H. (2021). Deep cybersecurity: A comprehensive overview from neural network and deep learning perspective. *SN Computer Science*, *2*(3), 154. DOI: 10.1007/s42979-021-00535-6 PMID: 33778771

Silvestri, S., Islam, S., Papastergiou, S., Tzagkarakis, C., & Ciampi, M. (2023). A machine learning approach for the NLP-based analysis of cyber threats and vulnerabilities of the healthcare ecosystem. *Sensors (Basel)*, *23*(2), 651. DOI: 10.3390/s23020651 PMID: 36679446

Sinha, A. R., Singla, K., & Victor, T. M. M. (2023). Artificial intelligence and machine learning for cybersecurity applications and challenges. *Risk Detection and Cyber Security for the Success of Contemporary Computing*, 109-146.

Subramanian, D., Subramaniam, S., Natarajan, K., & Thangavel, K. (2024). Flamingo Jelly Fish search optimization-based routing with deep-learning enabled energy prediction in WSN data communication. *Network (Bristol, England)*, *35*(1), 73–100. DOI: 10.1080/0954898X.2023.2279971 PMID: 38044853

Tauseef, A. (2022). Technology Under Siege: Reinforcing Device and Cloud Security Against Cyber Threats.

Wazan, A. S., & Cuppens, F. (2023). Cybersecurity in networking: Adaptations, investigation, attacks, and countermeasures. *Annales des Télécommunications*, *78*(3), 133–134. DOI: 10.1007/s12243-023-00956-9 PMID: 36950453

Wazid, M., Das, A. K., Chamola, V., & Park, Y. (2022). Uniting cyber security and machine learning: Advantages, challenges and future research. *ICT Express*, *8*(3), 313–321. DOI: 10.1016/j.icte.2022.04.007

KEY TERMS AND DEFINITIONS

Adversarial Attacks: An activity of trying to deceive or corrupt machine learning models with inputs designed very carefully so that they result in wrong output.

Behavioral Analytics: Applying data analysis techniques to help understand patterns of human or system behavior, usually for identifying anomalies or threats.

Cyber-Physical System (CPS): A combination of computation, networking, and physical processes where embedded systems monitor and control the process through actuators interfaced to physical systems.

Cybersecurity: Measures that are taken in securing a computer network from malicious attacks or unauthorized access; the state of being protected against the criminal or unauthorized use of electronic data, or the measures taken to achieve this.

Master Data Management (MDM): The ability to create and maintain a single, accurate, and consistent view of the critical business data spread throughout an organization.

Secrecy: Ensuring that secrets are seen only by those who have the right to view them and not viewed by those who should not see/learn.

Zero Trust Architecture (ZTA): A security model in which no user or device is considered trusted by default, and verification of access to resources happens constantly.

Chapter 3
Phishing E-Mail Detection Using Ensembled ML Models

V. N. Krishna Addepalli
http://orcid.org/0009-0004-1160-0148
School of Engineering and Technology, Christ University, India

Aayush Paudel
Christ University, India

Arnav Makhija
Christ University, India

Chhandak Mukherjee
Christ University, India

ABSTRACT

Phishing attacks continue to represent a major cybersecurity threat in modern digital communication. Attackers frequently use deceptive emails that imitate legitimate mes- sages to trick users into revealing confidential information such as passwords, financial details, or personal credentials. Traditional detection approaches based on rule-based filtering systems often struggle to identify new and evolving phishing patterns. based on a stacking ensemble learning framework. The proposed ap- proach combines two widely used machine learning algorithms, Ran- dom Forest and XGBoost, within a stacking architecture to improve classification ac- curacy and robustness. Email data is first preprocessed and transformed into numerical features using TF-IDF vectorization, along with additional indicators such as suspicious URLs, inconsistencies in sender information, and structural character-

DOI: 10.4018/979-8-2600-3280-0.ch003

istics of the email content. By combining predictions from multiple classifiers, the ensemble model aims to capture complex patterns in phishing emails and reduce misclassification errors.

1. INTRODUCTION

Electronic mail has become one of the most widely used digital communication mecha- nisms in modern society. It is extensively utilized in personal, academic, governmental, and corporate environments for exchanging information, coordinating activities, and conducting business transactions. Due to its convenience, speed, and low operational cost, email has evolved into a critical component of global digital communication in- frastructure. However, the increasing reliance on email systems has also made them a frequent target for cyberattacks and malicious activities. Among various forms of cyber threats, phishing attacks represent one of the most prevalent and damaging forms of email-based cybercrime (Altwaijry et al., 2024).

Phishing emails are fraudulent communications designed to pose as reputable compa- nies, banks, or service providers in an effort to trick recipients into divulging private information. Attackers frequently try to obtain private information, including security verification codes, bank account information, login passwords, and personal identifying details. These attacks frequently take advantage of psychological ma- nipulation strate- gies, such as authority, fear, and urgency, to raise the possibility that users would inter- act with malicious attachments or links. Traditional security measures frequently fail to recognize newly developing attack patterns as phishing attempts continue to get more sophisticated.

Typically, rule-based systems, blacklist verification, domain reputation checks, and signature-based detection techniques are used in traditional email filtering systems. These methods work by comparing incoming communications to known malicious sources or established patterns. Although these methods work well against threats that have already been detected, they often miss newly generated phishing emails that have slightly altered language patterns, disguised URLs, or dynamically generated content. As a result, attackers can send misleading messages straight to users' inboxes by getting over static filtering restrictions.

To overcome these limitations, machine learning techniques have emerged as an ef- fective alternative for automated email threat detection. Machine learning algorithms enable systems to learn patterns directly from large volumes of email data and iden- tify statistical characteristics associated with phishing attempts. By analyzing textual content, structural attributes, and embedded metadata within email messages, machine learning models can detect suspicious behavior without relying solely on predefined rules. Several studies have demonstrated that machine learning methods significantly improve phishing detection performance when compared to traditional rule-based sys- tems (Bountakas et al., 2021).

Even with these developments, applying independent machine learning models to in- tricate cybersecurity datasets may provide challenges. Nonlinear correlations between several variables found in phishing emails are frequently difficult for individual classifiers to capture. Additionally, real emails greatly outnumber phishing samples in phishing databases, which often suffer from class imbalance. Such an imbalance may result in less accurate detection of minority phishing cases and biased model predictions.

To address Class imbalances, the dataset is studied for better class ratios and weights to address the issue of classification of minority phishing values. This helps in the optimisation of precision and recall which further increases the accuracy of the model. For the stacking design, a regression is used to combine base model predictions. This addresses the overfitting issue associated with testing and training data sets which improves the probability for acceptable risk scoring.

By pooling predictions from several machine learning models, ensemble learning approaches offer an efficient way to deal with these issues. Ensemble approaches in- corporate multiple learners rather than a single classifier to enhance overall predictive performance and lower variation. Ensemble models can achieve higher classification accuracy and better generalization across unseen data samples by utilizing the complementing characteristics of various methods.

Stacking-based frameworks have shown excellent performance in email categorization tasks among other ensemble learning techniques. Stacking creates the final forecast by combining outputs from several base models and applying a meta-learning method. By combining information from many classification techniques, this method allows the machine to discover the best decision limits. Recent research indicates that stacking ensembles significantly enhances phishing email detection performance compared to individual classifiers (Adnan et al., 2024).

Inspired by these findings, this project suggests PhishGuard, an intelligent phishing email detection solution. The Random Forest and XGBoost models are integrated into the system's stacking-based ensemble learning framework. While XGBoost has excel- lent gradient boosting capabilities that may learn intricate feature interactions, Random Forest gives robust decision tree aggregation and significant variance reduction.

Email preprocessing, feature engineering, machine learning categorization, and real- time inference are just a few of the processing steps carried out by the suggested sys- tem. Together with tailored phishing indications, feature extraction techniques like TF- IDF representation are used to clean and modify email content. The ensemble learning model is then used to assess these characteristics in order to ascertain if the email is a genuine communication or a phishing attempt.

The trained model is implemented utilizing a FastAPI-based backend architecture to show the created system's practical usability. Through a web-based interface, the de- ployed service facilitates real-time phishing email analysis. Users can submit email con- tent and receive instantaneous classification results along with comprehensible phishing risk indicators. Such deployment-oriented approaches contribute toward the develop- ment of scalable and production-ready cybersecurity solutions capable of protecting modern communication platforms (Fang et al., 2019).

1.1 Problem Statement

Phishing attacks continue to evolve rapidly as cybercriminals adopt more sophisticated techniques for deceiving users and bypassing existing security defenses. Modern phishing emails frequently employ advanced strategies such as domain spoofing, misleading hyperlinks, deceptive branding elements, and carefully crafted language designed to mimic legitimate communications. These techniques make phishing messages increasingly difficult to distinguish from genuine emails.

Traditional detection mechanisms often rely on static filtering rules or known attack sig- natures. While these approaches can detect previously identified phishing campaigns, they frequently fail to adapt to newly emerging threats that exhibit subtle variations in content or structure. As a result, many phishing emails remain undetected until they reach end users, exposing individuals and organizations to significant security risks such as identity theft, financial fraud, and unauthorized system access (Champa et al., 2024).

1.1.1 Need for Intelligent Detection Systems

The rapidly evolving nature of phishing attacks necessitates the development of intelligent detection systems capable of learning adaptive patterns from email datasets. Conventional filtering methods are insufficient for addressing dynamically changing attack strategies because they depend heavily on manually defined rules.

Machine learning–based detection systems offer the capability to analyze complex relationships among multiple features present within email content. By learning statistical patterns and behavioral characteristics associated with phishing attempts, such systems can identify suspicious messages even when they differ from previously known attack signatures. Consequently, intelligent detection frameworks have become an important research direction in modern cybersecurity applications (Altwaijry et al., 2024).

1.2 Problem Formulation

The problem addressed in this project can be formulated as the development of an automated classification framework capable of accurately distinguishing phishing emails from legitimate email communications. The system must be capable of analyzing di- verse email characteristics, including textual content, structural features, and suspicious indicators embedded within the message body.

Additionally, the proposed framework must maintain reliable prediction performance despite the presence of imbalanced datasets, where legitimate emails significantly out- number phishing samples. Achieving high detection accuracy while minimizing false positives is essential for ensuring user trust and system usability.

To address these challenges, the proposed solution adopts a stacking-based ensemble learning architecture combining Random Forest and XGBoost classifiers. Ensemble learning techniques improve model robustness by integrating predictions from multiple algorithms, thereby reducing the limitations associated with individual classifiers. The formulation therefore focuses on developing a scalable and accurate phishing detection framework capable of supporting real-time email security applications (Adnan et al., 2024).

1.3 Problem Statement & Objectives

The primary objectives of the proposed project are listed below:

- Enhance model learning capability by capturing complex feature interactions present in phishing email datasets.
- Integrate Random Forest and XGBoost classifiers using a stacking ensemble frame- work to improve phishing email classification accuracy.
- Strengthen prediction reliability by combining multiple machine learning learners into a unified classification model.
- Address class imbalance challenges to ensure accurate detection of minority phish- ing samples.
- Achieve improved performance across evaluation metrics such as accuracy, pre- cision, recall, and F1-score.
- Develop a deployable phishing detection system capable of performing real-time email analysis through a web-based interface.

1.4 Limitations

Although the proposed system demonstrates promising performance for phishing email detection, certain limitations remain within the scope of this academic project.

The quantity, variety, and quality of the training datasets that are available have a significant impact on how well machine learning models work. The vast range of attack tactics used in real-world settings might not be adequately represented by publicly accessible phishing statistics.

Large-scale experimentation and ongoing model retraining are also limited by project duration and computer resource limitations. Large-scale company email datasets might be used for more thorough training, which might enhance detection performance even more.

The analysis of linguistic and structural elements taken from email content is the main emphasis of the current system. Sophisticated spear-phishing campaigns, dynamically produced web pages, and malicious file attachments are examples of advanced attack components that might demand for more detection methods outside the purview of the current implementation.

Additionally, testing has mostly taken place in confined experimental settings, despite the created system's successful deployment via a web-based interface. Additional fac- tors including system scalability, security hardening, and continuous monitoring tech- niques would need to be taken into account for large-scale integration into enterprise email infrastructure.

2. LITERATURE SURVEY AND REVIEW

A comprehensive literature survey plays a vital role in understanding existing research contributions related to phishing email detection and identifying suitable machine learn- ing techniques for improving classification performance. A literature review is the start- ing point for new study ideas in academic research. It enables researchers to look at previously suggested solutions, assess their advantages and disadvantages, and pinpoint areas that need more development.

Email systems are now an essential component of daily communication due to the quick growth of digital communication platforms and internet services. But the ubiquitous use of email has also drawn hackers who use email infrastructure to launch phishing scams. Phishing attacks entail the use of misleading emails intended to fool recipients into divulging private information or carrying out nefarious tasks like clicking on phony links or downloading dangerous attachments.

Conventional security measures like rule-based filtering and blacklist verification fre- quently fail to identify freshly created phishing emails as phishing assaults become more sophisticated. This has spurred researchers to investigate sophisticated machine learn- ing methods that can extract patterns from massive email data sets. To identify question- able activity, machine learning models might examine URL architecture, sender details, email content, and other features.

Recent studies highlight that ensemble learning techniques, which combine predictions from multiple machine learning models, can significantly improve classification accu- racy and robustness in phishing detection tasks. Ensemble frameworks are particularly useful in cybersecurity applications because they reduce prediction variance and im- prove the ability of models to generalize across unseen datasets (Altwaijry et al., 2024) (Dietterich, 2000).

The literature survey presented in this chapter examines several research contributions related to phishing email detection, machine learning classification techniques, and ensemble learning methodologies. By analyzing the existing research landscape, important insights can be obtained regarding effective detection strategies, dataset preparation methods, and algorithm selection.

The chapter is divided into two major sections:

- Literature collection and segregation
- Critical review of selected literature

2.1 Literature Collection and Segregation

Initial research efforts in automated email filtering focused on probabilistic and rulebased learning techniques. One of the earliest influential works was conducted by Sahami et al., who introduced Bayesian learning approaches for automated email classification. Their research demonstrated that statistical analysis of word frequencies within email messages could be used to differentiate spam emails from legitimate messages. The Bayesian filtering technique operates by calculating the probability that a message belongs to a particular class based on the occurrence of specific words within the email text.

This study provided important evidence that machine learning algorithms could be successfully applied to email filtering problems. Although the primary focus of the work was spam classification, the fundamental concepts introduced by this research later influenced the development of phishing detection systems (Sahami et al., 1998).

Subsequent studies investigated a wide range of supervised machine learning algorithms for detecting phishing emails. Abu-Nimeh et al. conducted one of the earliest comparative studies evaluating several machine learning techniques, including Support Vector

Machines, Decision Trees, Na¨ıve Bayes classifiers, and rule-based learners. The re- searchers performed extensive experiments using phishing datasets and analyzed performance of each algorithm under different feature configurations.

The results of their experiments revealed that different classification algorithms exhibit varying levels of effectiveness depending on dataset characteristics and feature selection methods. Their work demonstrated that machine learning models can significantly outperform traditional rule-based filtering approaches when trained using properly engineered features. The study also highlighted that the selection of appropriate classification algorithms plays an important role in achieving high phishing detection accuracy (Abu-Nimeh et al., 2007).

With the increasing complexity of phishing attacks, researchers began exploring more robust classification techniques capable of handling high-dimensional email datasets. Basnet et al. proposed machine learning models utilizing decision tree–based classifiers for detecting phishing emails. Decision tree algorithms are particularly useful in classification problems because they construct hierarchical decision rules based on feature values.

Their research demonstrated that decision tree–based models are capable of capturing complex feature interactions while maintaining interpretable decision structures. Experimental results showed that tree-based models achieved strong detection performance and were able to effectively classify phishing emails using structural and textual features extracted from email messages. The study also emphasized the importance of feature engineering in improving the effectiveness of phishing detection systems (Basnet et al., 2014).

A major advancement in machine learning research occurred with the introduction of ensemble learning techniques. Ensemble learning involves combining predictions from multiple models in order to produce more reliable classification results. Instead of re- lying on a single classifier, ensemble models aggregate the predictions of several base learners to reduce prediction errors and improve robustness.

Dietterich provided a comprehensive theoretical analysis of ensemble learning methods and demonstrated that combining multiple classifiers can significantly reduce model variance and improve prediction stability. Ensemble methods have therefore become widely adopted in classification problems where high accuracy and reliability are re- quired (Dietterich, 2000).

Among ensemble learning algorithms, the Random Forest model proposed by Breiman has received significant attention in classification research. Random Forest operates by constructing multiple decision trees using random subsets of training data and features. Each decision tree produces a prediction, and the final classification is obtained by aggregating the predictions through majority voting.

This approach improves model robustness and reduces the risk of overfitting, particularly when applied to large and noisy datasets. Random Forest models have therefore been widely adopted in various cybersecurity applications, including phishing email detection and spam filtering systems (Breiman, 2001).

Boosting-based ensemble methods further improved machine learning performance by iteratively correcting classification errors during the training process. The XGBoost algorithm introduced by Chen and Guestrin represents a highly optimized implementation of gradient boosting capable of handling large datasets efficiently. XGBoost incorporates several optimization techniques, including parallel processing, regularization mechanisms, and efficient tree pruning strategies.

These characteristics enable XGBoost to achieve high predictive performance while maintaining computational efficiency. Consequently, XGBoost has become one of the most widely used algorithms in machine learning competitions and real-world classification applications (Chen & Guestrin, 2016).

A particularly relevant contribution to phishing email detection is the stacking ensemble framework proposed by Adnan et al. In their research, multiple base classifiers such as Logistic Regression, Decision Trees, Naive Bayes, and K-Nearest Neighbour were combined using a meta-learning model that generated the final prediction. The stacking approach allows the system to learn how to combine predictions from different models in order to produce a more accurate classification result.

The study utilized TF-IDF feature representation and benchmark email datasets includ- ing SpamAssassin and Enron email corpora. Experimental results demonstrated that the stacking ensemble achieved higher accuracy, precision, recall, and F1-score compared to individual classifiers. This work clearly demonstrated the effectiveness of stacking- based ensemble frameworks for email classification tasks (Adnan et al., 2024).

TF-IDF Vectorization: This model maps the text form to an alpha Numerical form by considering its relative value in a document to a set of documents. It ignores the generic terms like "is", "the" and so on and works on keywords in identifying their relative value in a set of pages.

Stacking Ensemble Learning: A stacked ensemble model is an ensemble technique that combines different learning models, like base models, level-0, into a single predictive model. It considers a level-1 to learn how to optimise the models to get the best predicted results.

Recent research has also emphasized the importance of dataset quality and feature en- gineering in phishing detection systems. Champa et al. highlighted that carefully cu- rated datasets containing diverse phishing samples significantly improve the training

effectiveness of machine learning models. The study suggested that incorporating both textual and structural email features can enhance detection accuracy by providing richer information to classification algorithms (Champa et al., 2024).

Furthermore, Kyaw et al. conducted a comprehensive survey of phishing detection techniques and reported that machine learning–based detection systems consistently outperform traditional rule-based filtering mechanisms. Their survey also highlighted the increasing importance of ensemble learning and hybrid detection frameworks for handling sophisticated phishing attacks (Kyaw et al., 2024).

In addition to machine learning methods, recent studies have explored deep learning ar- chitectures for phishing detection. However, these models often require significant com- putational resources and large volumes of labeled training data. Murti et al. reported that lightweight machine learning models combined with ensemble learning techniques can provide a more practical solution for real-world deployment environments where computational efficiency is essential (Murti & Naveen, 2023).

Table 1. Summary of Key Literature in Phishing Email Detection

Author	Method Used	Dataset	Key Findings
Sahami et al.	Bayesian Learning	Spam Dataset	Early machine learning based email filtering
Abu-Nimeh et al.	SVM, Decision Trees	Phishing Dataset	Comparative evaluation of classifiers
Basnet et al.	Decision Tree Models	Email Dataset	Improved detection us- ing tree-based models
Breiman	Random Forest	Various datasets	Robust ensemble learn- ing model
Chen & Guestrin	XGBoost	Structured datasets	Efficient gradient boosting algorithm
Adnan et al.	Stacking Ensemble	Enron + SpamAs- sassin	Improved phishing classification accuracy

2.2 Critical Review of Literature

Although significant progress has been achieved in phishing detection research, several limitations remain evident in existing approaches. Many early studies relied on individual machine learning classifiers, which may struggle to capture complex relationships among multiple email features. Such models may also exhibit reduced performance when applied to imbalanced datasets where legitimate emails significantly outnumber phishing samples.

Comparative analyses indicate that relying on a single classifier may lead to inconsistent detection performance in real-world applications. Bountakas et al. reported that classification accuracy can vary depending on dataset characteristics, feature selection methods, and algorithm configuration (Bountakas et al., 2021).

By merging predictions from diverse classifiers, stacking-based ensemble learning meth- ods overcome these constraints. Stacking ensembles can capture complementary deci- sion patterns and enhance classification performance by combining outputs from sev- eral models. Nevertheless, previous stacking frameworks frequently depended on tradi- tional machine learning algorithms and did not thoroughly investigate the incorporation of powerful tree-based ensemble learners that could manage intricate feature spaces. Therefore, incorporating Random Forest and XGBoost models into a stacking architecture presents a viable method for raising the accuracy of phishing detection. The growing need for phishing detection systems that can function in real-time settings is another significant finding from recent research. Many deep learning models have significant processing overhead and might not be appropriate for use in settings with limited resources.

Therefore, optimized ensemble learning frameworks offer a good trade-off between computing efficiency and classification accuracy. These models can deliver high detection performance while maintaining fast inference speed suitable for practical deployment scenarios (Altwaijry et al., 2024) (Fang et al., 2019).

Overall, the reviewed literature highlights the growing importance of ensemble learn- ing techniques in phishing email detection. The collective findings strongly motivate the proposed work, which develops a stacking-based ensemble framework integrating Random Forest and XGBoost classifiers to improve classification accuracy while sup- porting efficient real-time deployment.

3. RESEARCH METHODOLOGY

Research methodology defines the systematic procedures adopted to analyze the re- search problem, design the proposed solution, and validate experimental outcomes.A clear methodology guarantees a logical, repeatable, and scientifically structured ap- proach in academic research. The research process for machine learning-based cy- bersecurity applications must encompass the entire workflow, from data collection and problem analysis to model building, assessment, and practical implementation.

Phishing email detection is a complicated classification problem that calls for careful treatment of textual input, method selection, feature extraction, and performance val- idation. In contrast to conventional software systems, machine learning systems are highly dependent on the caliber of the training data and the feature representation de- sign that is utilized to identify pertinent patterns. As a result, the methodology used for this project places a strong emphasis on dependable evaluation techniques, robust model construction, and methodical data processing.

The goal of the suggested research approach is to provide a workable and deployable system for phishing email detection that can accurately identify malicious messages while preserving computing efficiency. To provide a scalable cybersecurity solution, the methodological design integrates concepts from software deployment, experimental assessment, and machine learning engineering.

Figure 1. Overall research methodology adopted for the proposed phishing email detection system.

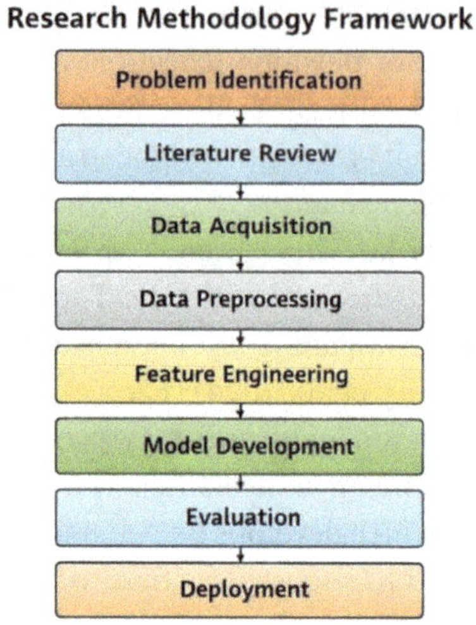

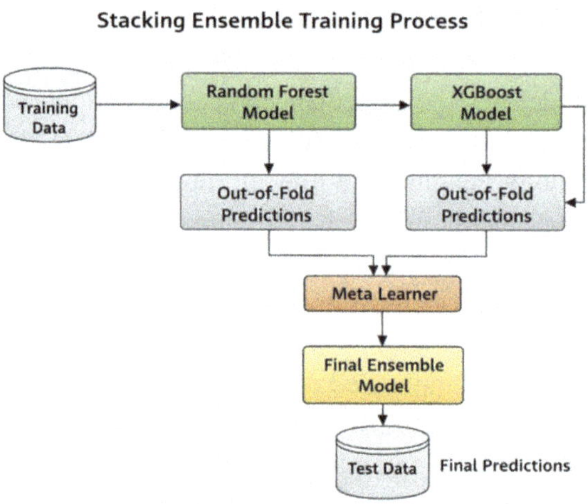

The overall research methodology illustrated in Figure 1 represents the structured workflow followed during the development of the proposed system. The methodology integrates several phases including data collection, data preprocessing, feature engineer- ing, model development, experimental evaluation, and deployment integration.

3.1 Overview and Approach

The research follows an empirical and engineering-driven methodology consisting of multiple interconnected phases. Each phase contributes to the overall objective of de- veloping an intelligent phishing email detection system capable of identifying malicious messages with high reliability.

The major stages involved in the research process are described below:

1. **Problem Analysis and Background Study:** An extensive study of existing phishing detection mechanisms was conducted to understand limitations associated with rule-based filtering systems and traditional classification approaches.
2. **Data Acquisition and Preparation:** We gathered representative datasets from publicly accessible repositories that included both legitimate and fraudulent emails.
3. **Feature Engineering:** Both textual and structural indications were used to con- vert email information into machine learning feature representations.
4. **Model Design:** To enhance predictive performance, a stacking-based ensemble framework combining Random Forest and XGBoost classifiers was created.
5. **Model Training and Evaluation:** Multiple assessment metrics and stratified cross-validation approaches were used to train and evaluate the classification models.
6. **Deployment and Integration:** Using a FastAPI-based backend architecture, the trained model was implemented in a real-time inference system.

Ensemble learning methodologies have been widely adopted for classification problems because they combine predictions from multiple models to produce more stable and reliable results. Such approaches reduce prediction variance and improve generalization capability across unseen datasets (Dietterich, 2000).

3.2 Problem Identification and Preliminary Study

A preliminary investigation was conducted to analyze the limitations of existing phish- ing detection mechanisms. Traditional rule-based filtering systems rely on predefined rules, keyword patterns, and blacklist verification techniques. While these approaches can detect known phishing messages, they often fail to recognize newly generated at- tacks that employ modified language patterns or obfuscated URLs.

Furthermore, standalone machine learning classifiers frequently exhibit inconsistent performance when applied to diverse phishing datasets. Earlier comparative studies have demonstrated that individual classification algorithms may perform well on spe- cific datasets but fail to generalize effectively across different phishing campaigns (Bountakas et al., 2021) (Abu-Nimeh et al., 2007).

These observations highlight the need for more robust classification frameworks capa- ble of integrating multiple predictive models. Ensemble learning approaches offer an effective solution by combining the strengths of different algorithms while minimizing their individual limitations.

The preliminary study therefore motivated the adoption of a stacking-based ensemble architecture capable of improving classification stability and detection reliability.

3.3 Data Acquisition

Data acquisition represents a critical step in machine learning projects because model performance depends heavily on the quality and diversity of training datasets. In this re- search, publicly available phishing and legitimate email datasets were utilized to ensure a wide variety of email content, sender behavior patterns, and URL characteristics.

Using publicly available datasets provides several advantages, including accessibility, reproducibility of experiments, and comparability with results reported in previous re- search studies. Dataset selection followed recommendations from recent phishing detection research emphasizing the importance of curated and representative data collections (Champa et al., 2024).

The collected datasets were carefully inspected to remove redundant records, eliminate corrupted samples, and ensure consistent label definitions. Data inspection procedures were also applied to verify that sensitive personal information was not retained during the experimental process.

Maintaining dataset diversity is particularly important in phishing detection because at- tackers frequently modify email structures, domain names, and textual content in order to evade detection.

3.4 Data Preprocessing

Raw email messages typically contain unstructured textual content, metadata fields, embedded hyperlinks, and formatting elements. Before machine learning models can be applied, the raw email data must be transformed into structured representations suitable for algorithmic processing.

Preprocessing operations included header extraction, normalization of textual content, removal of duplicate messages, and label harmonization across different datasets. Text normalization involved converting characters to lowercase, removing unnecessary symbols, and standardizing whitespace patterns.

These preprocessing steps help reduce noise within the dataset and improve the ability of machine learning algorithms to learn meaningful patterns from the email content.

Such preprocessing strategies are widely adopted in machine learning–based email filtering systems and have been shown to improve classification performance by ensuring consistent feature representation (Murti & Naveen, 2023).

Maintaining identical preprocessing procedures during both training and deployment stages is also essential to ensure prediction consistency within real-time applications.

3.5 Feature Engineering

Feature engineering is one of the most important stages in machine learning pipeline design. In phishing detection systems, effective feature extraction enables models to capture meaningful patterns that differentiate malicious emails from legitimate communications.

In this research, feature engineering combines textual features derived from email con- tent with metadata-based indicators related to sender behavior and URL characteristics.

TF–IDF vectorization was used to represent lexical patterns within email content. This technique converts textual data into numerical vectors based on the importance of words within the document corpus. TF–IDF has been widely adopted in email classification research because it effectively captures distinguishing textual patterns within messages (Sahami et al., 1998).

In addition to textual features, several engineered attributes were included to capture structural characteristics of phishing emails. These attributes include URL indicators, domain verification signals, stylistic writing patterns, and statistical measures of email content.

Hybrid feature representations combining textual and structural signals have been shown to significantly improve phishing detection accuracy by providing richer contextual in- formation to machine learning algorithms (Kyaw et al., 2024).

3.6 Model Design and Training

The proposed system employs a stacking ensemble learning framework designed to integrate complementary machine learning algorithms. Ensemble learning approaches combine predictions from multiple base learners in order to improve classification ac- curacy and reduce prediction variance.

- **Random Forest:** Introduced by Breiman, Random Forest utilizes bagging principles to construct multiple decision trees using randomly selected subsets of training data and features. The aggregation of multiple decision trees improves model stability and reduces overfitting (Breiman, 2001).
- **XGBoost:** Gradient boosting algorithms such as XGBoost improve predictive accuracy by iteratively correcting misclassified samples during sequential training iterations. XGBoost incorporates optimization techniques that enable efficient training and high predictive performance (Chen & Guestrin, 2016).
- **Stacking Strategy:** In the stacking ensemble architecture, predictions generated by the base learners are used as inputs to a meta-classifier that produces the final prediction. This approach enables the model to learn optimal combinations of base learner predictions, resulting in improved classification performance (Adnan et al., 2024).

Class imbalance, which is common in phishing datasets, was addressed using stratified sampling and class-weight adjustments. These techniques ensure that minority phishing samples receive adequate representation during model training.

3.7 Hyperparameter Tuning and Validation

Hyperparameter optimization is an important component of machine learning model development. Proper selection of hyperparameters can significantly influence model accuracy, training efficiency, and generalization capability.

In this study, model parameters were optimized using grid-search and randomized search strategies combined with stratified cross-validation. These techniques allow systematic exploration of parameter combinations while preventing overfitting during training.

Multiple evaluation metrics including precision, recall, F1-score, and ROC-AUC were monitored during the validation process. Balanced evaluation practices are particularly important for cybersecurity classification problems involving skewed datasets (Basnet et al., 2014).

3.8 Evaluation Metrics and Experimental Setup

Model performance was evaluated using several standard classification metrics com- monly used in machine learning research.

- Accuracy, Precision, Recall, and F1-score.
- Confusion matrix analysis for minority-class evaluation.

- Inference latency measurements to assess real-time capability: Inference latency in phishing email detection, while considering for ML & DLM Models, maps for time taken to show the email as a legitimate one or a phishing one. Thus, lightweight models like Random Forest and XGBoost can consider inference time below 100ms, which makes it acceptable under security mechanisms

Using multiple evaluation metrics provides a comprehensive assessment of model per- formance and prevents biased interpretation of classification results.

Such multi-metric evaluation frameworks are widely adopted in modern phishing de- tection research to ensure reliable experimental analysis (Altwaijry et al., 2024).

3.9 Deployment and Integration

To demonstrate practical applicability, the trained ensemble model was deployed using a FastAPI-based REST architecture. Deployment pipelines replicate preprocessing and feature extraction stages used during training to maintain consistency between offline experiments and production inference environments.

Deployment-oriented machine learning systems are increasingly recommended for real- world cybersecurity applications because they bridge the gap between research proto- types and operational security solutions (Fang et al., 2019).

3.10 Ethical Considerations and Privacy

Email datasets may contain sensitive information including personal identifiers, financial data, and confidential communications. Therefore, privacy-preserving practices were followed throughout the research process.

These practices include anonymization of personal data, restricted storage of sensitive information, and minimal logging of user inputs during system deployment.

Ethical data handling practices are essential for responsible machine learning development in cybersecurity domains.

3.11 Reproducibility and Code Management

Reproducibility is an important requirement in academic research. To ensure reproducibility of experimental results, preprocessing pipelines, feature engineering procedures, and trained models were packaged into serialized pipeline artifacts.

Version control mechanisms and environment documentation were also maintained to enable replication of experiments and future extension of the proposed system.

3.12 Limitations of Methodology

Although the adopted methodology balances accuracy, interpretability, and deployment feasibility, certain limitations remain. Dependence on available labeled datasets may restrict exposure to novel phishing strategies that emerge in real-world email environments.

Additionally, TF–IDF feature representations primarily capture lexical patterns and may not fully represent deeper semantic relationships present in sophisticated phishing messages.

Future work may therefore explore advanced natural language processing techniques capable of capturing contextual meaning within email content.

3.13 Summary

The presented methodology establishes a systematic pathway from problem analysis to deployment of a stacking-based ensemble model integrating Random Forest and XGBoost classifiers. The approach emphasizes robust validation, reproducibility, and real-time applicability, forming the foundation for the implementation and experimental analysis described in subsequent chapters.

4. ACTUAL WORK

After identifying and formulating the research problem and completing a comprehensive literature survey, the practical implementation of the proposed phishing email detection system, namely **PhishGuard**, was undertaken. The move from conceptual re- search and methodological preparation to the creation of a fully working system that can identify phishing emails under actual operating conditions is represented by the actual work phase.

In order to determine whether the suggested theoretical framework can be converted into a workable solution that can handle actual cybersecurity issues, the implementation stage is crucial. In order to create a cohesive phishing detection framework, the system architecture, machine learning pipeline, data processing modules, and deployment infrastructure were meticulously planned and integrated throughout this phase.

The real work done for this project focuses on practical usability and deployment practicality in addition to algorithmic performance. Machine learning models must be ac- curate, efficient, scalable, and able to make predictions in real time for use in contemporary cybersecurity applications. In order for the created system to function well in actual email filtering environments, particular attention was paid to assuring repeatability, scalability, and operational efficiency.

The experimental design, system architecture, machine learning model integration, deployment strategy, and prototype validation carried out throughout the project are all covered in detail in this chapter.

4.1 Methodology for the Study

The implementation of the proposed system followed a structured and incremental workflow beginning with dataset preparation and ending with real-time deployment of the trained model. In machine learning applications, maintaining consistency between the training pipeline and prediction environment is a critical requirement for ensuring reliable performance during real-world usage.

For this reason, identical preprocessing and feature engineering procedures were main- tained across both development and deployment stages. This design ensures that the model receives the same type of input features during prediction as it was exposed to during training, thereby preventing inconsistencies that could negatively impact classification accuracy (Altwaijry et al., 2024).

Figure 2. Workflow of the Proposed Phishing Email Detection Process

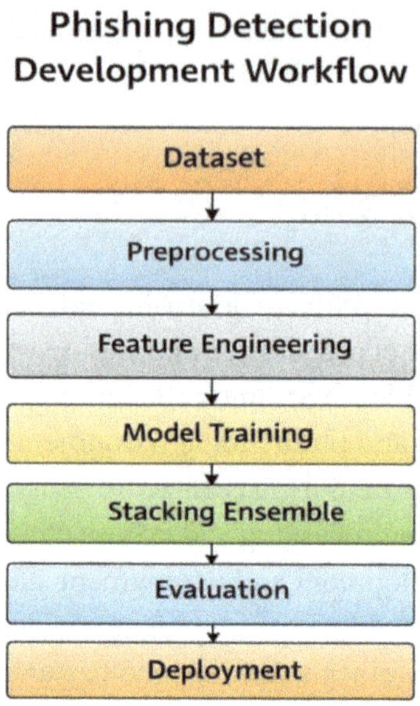

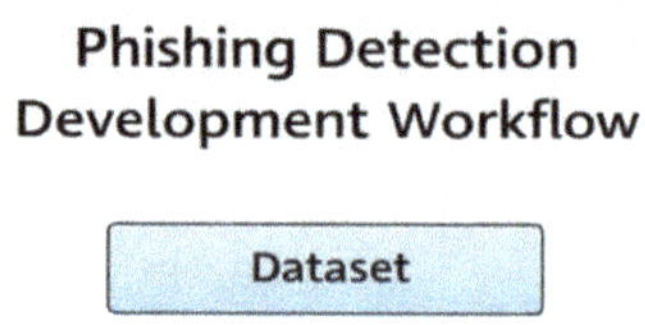

Figure 2 illustrates the overall workflow adopted during system development. The workflow is designed to ensure that each stage of the machine learning pipeline is executed systematically and efficiently. By following a structured workflow, potential errors during model training and deployment can be minimized. This work shows a phishing detection system where the input data is cleaned and then mapped to identifying characteristics. These characteristics are studied by multiple machine learning models working in parallel to identify suspicious patterns, to check whether the email is safe or not.

The major stages involved in the study are listed below:

1. Collection of phishing and legitimate email datasets from publicly available repositories, ensuring diversity in email patterns and phishing techniques.
2. Prior to model training, email content is preprocessed and normalized to eliminate irrelevant noise, standardize textual representation, and enhance data quality.
3. Random Forest and XGBoost classification models are trained to determine base- line learning capacity and assess the effectiveness of different algorithms.
4. Using stacking ensemble learning, base learners are integrated to increase classification stability and predictive performance.
5. Deployment of the trained model via an online application that facilitates risk assessment and real-time phishing detection.

This structured methodology enables a smooth transition from data-driven model development to production-level deployment, ensuring that the developed system remains both reliable and scalable.

4.2 Experimental and/or Analytical Work Completed in the Project

Experimental analysis was conducted to evaluate the effectiveness of individual ma- chine learning classifiers as well as the proposed ensemble learning framework. The primary objective of the experimentation phase was to determine whether integrating multiple machine learning algorithms improves phishing detection capability compared to standalone models.

Initially, Random Forest and XGBoost models were trained independently in order to establish baseline performance levels. Evaluating individual model performance pro- vides valuable insights into the strengths and weaknesses of each algorithm before they are combined into an ensemble architecture.

Tree-based learning algorithms are widely adopted for structured cybersecurity datasets due to their robustness, interpretability, and ability to capture nonlinear feature relation- ships (Breiman, 2001)(Chen & Guestrin, 2016). These models also demonstrate strong resistance to noisy data, which is commonly observed in real-world email datasets containing diverse message formats and content structures.

The preprocessing pipeline converts raw email data into structured numerical representations suitable for machine learning models. Raw email messages often contain unstructured textual content, embedded hyperlinks, metadata fields, and formatting elements. These components must be carefully processed before they can be used for machine learning classification.

Text normalization, token filtering, and feature extraction ensure that meaningful lin- guistic and structural information is retained while irrelevant noise such as punctuation and redundant tokens is removed. The resulting feature vectors provide numerical rep- resentations that allow machine learning algorithms to identify patterns associated with phishing emails.

The prediction outputs of both models were subsequently combined using a stacking ensemble strategy, enabling the meta-classifier to learn optimal decision boundaries from complementary learners. Stacking-based integration has been shown to improve classification reliability compared to standalone models in email filtering tasks (Adnan et al., 2024).

Performance evaluation was carried out using accuracy, precision, recall, and F1-score metrics to ensure balanced detection of phishing emails under class-imbalanced condi- tions. Particular attention was given to recall performance since failure to detect phish- ing emails may lead to serious security consequences.

Table 2. Comparative Performance of Implemented Models

Model	**Accuracy**	**Precision**	**Recall**	**F1-score**
Random Forest	87	86	85	85.5
XGBoost	88	87	86	86.5
Stacking Ensemble	93.3	92	91	91.5

The experimental results demonstrate that the stacking ensemble model achieved improved performance compared to individual classifiers. The improvement indicates that ensemble learning effectively combines strengths of different algorithms to enhance prediction accuracy. A statistical significance test such as McNemar's test may be considered to clarify whether ensemble models give better results than individual models. For example by considering the accuracy results of XGBoost and Ensembled model, we can see that the accuracy increased from 88% to 93.3%. If the p-value is below 0.05, it may be considered that the ensemble model specifies a considerable statistical betterment which says that the results are genuine.

4.3 Modeling, Analysis, and Design

Figure 3. Architecture of the Proposed Phish-Guard Phishing Email Detection System

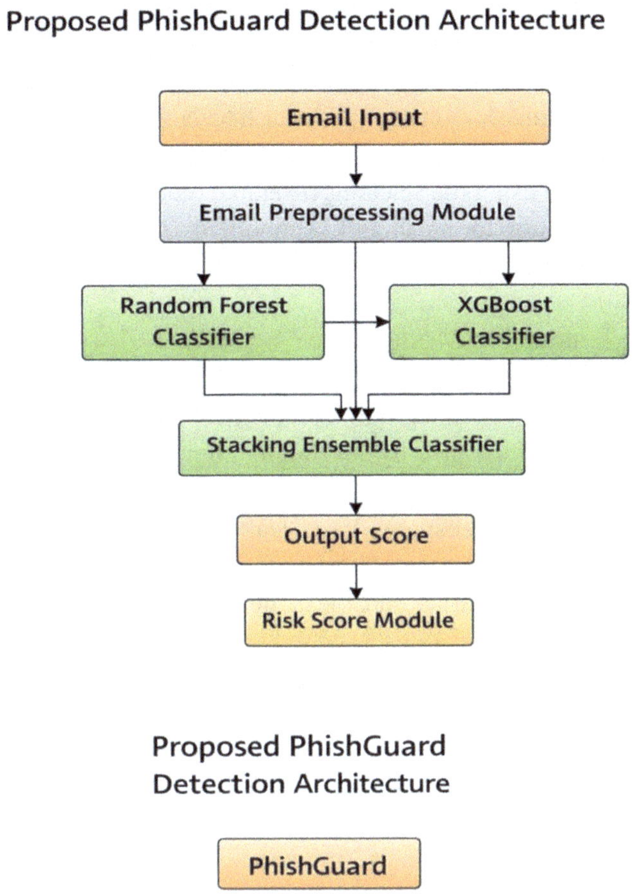

The architecture identifies phishing emails by preprocessing raw email data into identifiable features. These features are studied in parallel by models like Random Forest and XGBoost, which independently predict high target risks. The outputs is merged by combining a stacking ensemble to achieve better accuracy and precision in generating a final prediction score. This score is mapped to risk, enabling users to check whether the mail is safe or not.

The proposed phishing detection system follows a modular and layered architecture in- tegrating preprocessing modules, machine learning inference components, and deploy- ment infrastructure. Modular architectures improve scalability and simplify integration of intelligent detection systems into real-world platforms (Fang et al., 2019).

The overall system architecture illustrated in Figure 3 demonstrates how incoming email data flows through different stages of the detection pipeline before a final prediction is generated.

The operational workflow consists of:

- Email content submission through the user interface.
- Automated preprocessing and feature extraction.
- Feature evaluation using the stacking ensemble model.
- Probability estimation for phishing likelihood.
- Generation of classification output and risk-level feedback.

4.3.1 Stacking Ensemble Model

The ensemble framework integrates complementary learning paradigms to improve pre- diction performance by leveraging strengths of both bagging and boosting strategies.

Random Forest operates as a bagging-based learner that reduces variance through ag- gregation of multiple decision trees (Breiman, 2001). In contrast, XGBoost functions as a gradient boosting learner capable of iteratively improving classification accuracy by correcting previously misclassified samples (Chen & Guestrin, 2016).

A meta-classifier combines probability outputs from both models to produce a final pre- diction, improving generalization capability through ensemble decision fusion (Dietterich, 2000). This hybrid learning strategy enables improved phishing detection accuracy while maintain- ing computational efficiency suitable for real-time deployment.

4.4 Implementation Details

The phishing email detection system was implemented using Python- based machine learning libraries and deployed through a FastAPI backend service to enable real-time inference. Python was selected due to its extensive ecosystem of machine learning libraries, including Scikit-learn, XGBoost, and data processing frameworks.

Table 3. Implementation Components of the Proposed System

Component	Description
Dataset Processing	Email parsing and preprocessing
Feature Engineering	TF-IDF and phishing feature extraction
Machine Learning Models	Random Forest and XGBoost
Ensemble Method	Stacking-based learning
Backend Framework	FastAPI REST API
Model Storage	Joblib serialized pipeline
Deployment Platform	PhishGuard Web Application (Vercel)
Prediction Output	Risk score and classification result

Deployment-oriented machine learning systems are increasingly recommended to bridge the gap between experimental models and real-world cybersecurity applications (Murti & Naveen, 2023). The backend API loads trained models during initialization to minimize response la- tency and ensure efficient processing of incoming requests.

Users interact with the deployed PhishGuard web application, which communicates with the backend service to obtain predictions and phishing risk explanations in real time.

4.5 Prototype and Testing

A functional prototype of the phishing detection system was developed and evaluated under practical operating conditions to validate system reliability and responsiveness.

Testing procedures included:

- Validation using labelled phishing and legitimate email samples.
- Real-time testing through the deployed web interface.
- Measurement of prediction latency.
- Verification of classification stability across diverse inputs.

Experimental testing confirmed that predictions are generated within milliseconds, demon- strating suitability for real-time deployment. Efficient inference capability is an essential requirement for modern email security systems operating under continuous data streams (Altwaijry et al., 2024).

The successful implementation and deployment of the PhishGuard application demon- strate the feasibility of integrating stacking-based ensemble learning models into scal- able and practical cybersecurity solutions capable of supporting future enterprise-level deployment.

4.6 Ethical and Security Implications

Any user's sensitive data to be protected using techniques like Encryption to maintain ethical and security implications. The standard data protection procedures to be followed while handling email datasets. To maintain ethical and security standards, transparency by avoiding biased training data and maintain transparency in model decisions. The proposed model must be free from adversarial attacks like unclear text or false URLs, by using proper training, continuous learning, and defective pattern detection. The system can also continuously support standard model updates, considering feedback, and real-time threat models to detect any new phishing

4.7 Scalability and Deployment Geography

Cloud-based services support scalability in Business environments. It also supports for parallel processing mechanisms to support the scalability of applications. The scalability in Horizontal mode helps in enhancing performance at organizations of varying size. The data must be aligned with Data protection regulations, which maintain strict control by Law enforcement agencies. The data security is to be maintained against cross-border regions based on mutually acceptable laws and international standards.

5. RESULTS, DISCUSSIONS AND CONCLUSIONS

This chapter presents a comprehensive evaluation of the proposed PhishGuard (phishing email detection system) developed during the course of this project. The efficacy of the stacking-based ensemble learning framework is evaluated by a thorough analysis of the experimental results from the model training, validation, and deployment phases.

In order to assess system dependability, generalization potential, and deployment viability in actual cybersecurity settings, the acquired results are assessed from both analytical and practical viewpoints. In addition to focusing on numerical performance measures, the investigation assesses the system's response to actual phishing scenarios.

To determine the relative contributions of each learning algorithm in the suggested architecture, a comparative evaluation of the ensemble framework and individual machine learning models is carried out. The installation cost, system performance observations, and wider implications of the suggested solution in relation to contemporary email security systems are also covered in this chapter. Lastly, conclusions drawn from the experimental data are provided, along with possible avenues for further study and system improvements.

5.1 Results and Analysis

The performance evaluation of the developed phishing email detection system was con- ducted using widely accepted machine learning classification metrics including accuracy, precision, recall, and F1-score. Together, these measures offer a fair evaluation of classifier efficacy, especially when working with datasets that show a class imbalance between phishing and legitimate emails.

By calculating the proportion of phishing emails that are genuinely harmful, Precision assesses the system's capacity to reduce false positive warnings. To avoid excessive false alarms that could erode user confidence in automated detection systems, high precision is crucial. Recall shows how well the model can recognize phishing emails in the dataset. Recall is especially crucial in cybersecurity situations because unnoticed phishing emails can result in financial fraud, credential theft, or illegal system access. The F1-score offers a balanced measure of classification performance by combining precision and recall into a single metric.

To establish baseline learning performance, the Random Forest and XGBoost models were first trained individually during the experiment. The results showed that nonlinear correlations seen in textual and manufactured phishing indicators can be efficiently captured by tree-based ensemble methods. These algorithms are particularly well suited for cybersecurity datasets because they can handle high-dimensional feature spaces and noisy input data. Subsequently, the stacking ensemble framework combined probability outputs generated by both base learners. The meta-classifier learned optimal decision boundaries by leveraging complementary strengths of bagging and boosting mechanisms. This integration significantly improved prediction robustness and reduced model variance.

Hybrid feature engineering using TF-IDF representation alongside domain-specific phishing attributes enabled the learning models to identify subtle linguistic and structural characteristics commonly observed in phishing emails. Experimental observations con- firmed that combining textual semantics with engineered indicators enhances classification capability beyond traditional single-feature approaches.

The confusion matrix provides deeper insight into classification behaviour by showing the distribution of correct and incorrect predictions. The matrix demonstrates that the ensemble model successfully distinguishes between legitimate and phishing emails with a relatively low rate of false positives and false negatives.

The results indicate that the stacking-based ensemble model achieves a balanced trade-off between detection sensitivity and prediction stability, making it suitable for deployment in real-world email filtering environments.

5.2 Comparative Study

To further validate system effectiveness, a comparative analysis was performed between standalone machine learning classifiers and the proposed stacking ensemble framework.

This comparison helps determine whether combining multiple algorithms produces significant performance improvements over individual classifiers. The Performance Comparison of Implemented Models is as follows.

Table 4. Performance Comparison of Implemented Models

Model	Accuracy	Precision	Recall	F1-score
Random Forest	87	86	85	85.5
XGBoost	88	87	86	86.5
Stacking Ensemble Model	93.3	92	91	91.5

The comparative results summarized indicate that although individual models achieve competitive performance levels, the stacking ensemble model consistently provides superior generalization capability.

Figure 4. Performance comparison of Random Forest, XGBoost, and stacking ensemble models across evaluation metrics.

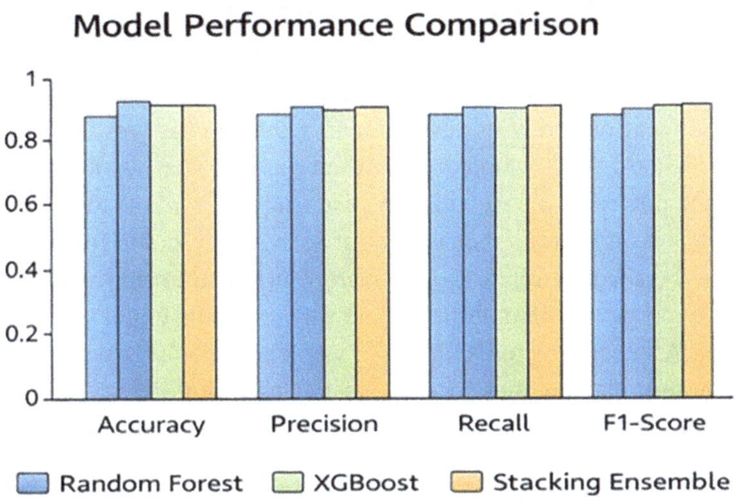

As illustrated in Figure 4, the ensemble model achieves balanced improvements across all evaluation metrics. Random Forest contributes stability through variance reduction, while XGBoost enhances learning efficiency by iteratively correcting classification errors.

The stacking mechanism effectively combines these strengths, allowing the meta-classifier to adaptively learn from prediction patterns generated by base learners. This collaborative learning approach improves classification consistency and enhances resilience against overfitting when exposed to unseen email data.

5.3 Discussions

The experimental findings reveal several important insights regarding machine learning–based phishing detection systems.

First, preprocessing and feature engineering significantly influence model performance. Words weighed right help machines make sense of text, when scaled properly they adjust for frequency. Instead of raw counts, importance shifts by how rare terms are across documents. This way common words matter less while distinctive ones stand out more. Through rescaling, patterns emerge clearer for analysis to follow

Count the email's words by number yet keep how people naturally speak showing clear differences phishing messages from legitimate communications. One reason they handle noise better is how multiple models work together instead of alone

A single model on its own? The Random Forest approach sharpens accuracy by spreading out errors across many trees. Instead of relying on one path, it leans on a crowd of decisions made separately Yet XGBoost-like methods shift attention during training toward tougher classification cases One after another, these examples show how blending methods opens doors to using two kinds of learning at once. One key point stands out when thinking about how well it can be set up. It differs from approaches that only rely on testing apart from standard testing setups, the suggested PhishGuard setup worked well when put into real-world trials with a FastAPI backend powering the web display, live trials showed the forecast held up

Even with delays under a few thousandths of a second, tasks still run as needed in real situations cybersecurity applications. Apart from that, the setup's separate parts make it easier to connect with enterprise One way to handle email safety involves using gateways. Another uses tools built into web browsers. This setup forms part of a broader system made earlier so it connects classroom ideas with real world smart tools security solutions.

5.4 Cost Estimation Model

The economic feasibility of deploying intelligent cybersecurity solutions is an important consideration for both academic and industrial environments. The estimated Cost Analysis of the Proposed System is as follows.

Table 5. Estimated Cost Analysis of the Proposed System

Component	**Estimated Cost**
Dataset Acquisition	Free (Public datasets)
Development Tools (Python Libraries)	Free/Open Source
Model Training Resources	Existing Hardware
Backend Development (FastAPI)	Free
Cloud Deployment (Vercel)	Free Tier
Maintenance Cost	Minimal

Since the proposed system relies entirely on open-source software libraries and pub- licly accessible datasets, implementation costs are significantly reduced. Training and experimentation were conducted using standard computing hardware without the need for specialized GPU infrastructure.

The lightweight deployment architecture further ensures scalability without introducing substantial operational expenses. As a result, the proposed phishing detection frame- work represents a cost-effective solution suitable for small organizations, academic in- stitutions, and prototype enterprise deployments.

The cost model must maintain a balance between detection accuracy and computational complexity, and the overhead of resources. When an ensemble model is used, it increases performance and accuracy but at the same time increases space and time complexity. But in real-time environments with the available high-speed and high computing resource systems, this can be achieved at a minimal cost model. The added cost is a bit low, considering that the available high-end resources for high security is considered to be an acceptable model.

5.5 Conclusions

This project successfully designed and implemented an intelligent phishing email detection system based on stacking ensemble learning. The primary objective of the research was to improve detection accuracy while maintaining deployment feasibility within real-world email security environments.

Random Forest meets XGBoost in learning system Other choices shape the outcome, leading to steadier results when sorting things out several ways to measure success. Tests showed steady outcomes across When it comes to how correct the results are, along with their consistency, completeness, and overall balance between them. With PhishGuard rolled out, its real-world usefulness became clear through actual use integrating machine learning–based cybersecurity solutions into real-time operational Not just one model, but a team of them working together shows how machine learning adapts across different settings. This setup proves that combining methods improves results when handling complex data landscapes Turning lab-made ideas into real tools people can actually use often works out fine Users might spot possible phishing risks with its help. A solid setup takes shape when speed meets consistency without breaking down. One part grows easily, another holds steady under pressure, while the third keeps things moving smoothly. Efficiency shows up not through force but by design. Stability arrives quietly, built into each layer. What stands out is how little it demands over time One way to spot fake emails helps make online protection stronger against email-based attacks.

A hyper parameter search may provide for better exploration and accuracy and addresses theOverfitting problem but it needs to be balanced between learning rate and controlled complexity, which suits more for ensemble models Ensemble stacking methods provide better performance while considering different features of data set, while models like BERT measure better semantics at high data set size and computational overhead. Hybrid approaches may balance both the advantages and limitations of the proposed models, which may provide more generalisations in a real-time environment while capturing phishing emails.

To improve the strength and security of the model during deployment, it must be supported with minimal feature distribution and delayed performance. It should be supported with Proper privacy mechanisms like encryption techniques and non-linear access control mechanisms while minimising log-based data to resist exposure risks. The illegal or proxy intrusions and deceptive payloads are to be measured to reduce web vulnerability with unauthorized requests. The model must be tuned to predict and identify suspicious tokens and URL's in betterment of predictions and decision-making.

5.6 Scope for Future Work

Although the proposed system achieves strong phishing detection performance, several enhancements may further improve its capabilities.

In order to maintain adaptation against new attack techniques, future work may incor- porate ongoing model retraining utilizing evolving phishing datasets. Contex-tual com- prehension of complex phishing content may be improved by integrating deep learning architectures like transformer-based language models.

A multi-layered detection architecture that can handle intricate attack patterns can be created by integrating additional security modules like URL reputation analysis, attach- ment inspection, and behavioral email profiling.

Additionally, explainable AI systems could be used to provide comprehensible justi- fication for classification choices. Transparency and confidence in automated security systems can be increased by giving consumers explanations for forecasts.

The system can also be expanded into a business email gateway or browser-based solu- tion that can analyze messages directly within webmail platforms and provide real-time phishing alerts.

Figure 5. Proposed future enhancement integrating PhishGuard with a browser-based phishing detection extension.

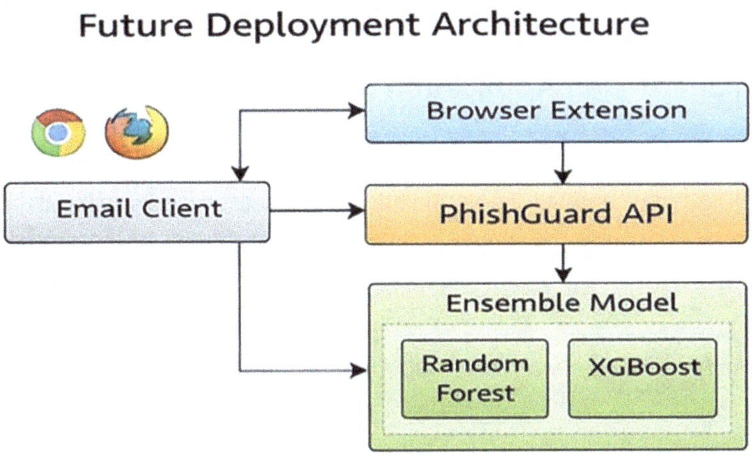

Future optimization initiatives might also concentrate on automated security response systems, distributed inference, and large-scale deployment. These advancements may result in the creation of completely autonomous intelligent email security systems that can defend consumers against quickly changing phishing threats.

For real-world applications, anti-phishing systems can be implemented at enterprise mail servers to scan the reaching mails for possible threats before they reach users. In most of the applications, the model is combined with proper filtering mechanisms to study content, generate a risk score and differentiate them to spam or non-spam models. The model can also check URL's page information to check for possible phishing attacks. But the challenges like low latency, mischievous content may affect the risk score, which may affect the privacy concerns and belief in Business structures.

The comparison between Term Frequency–Inverve Document Frequency: In TF only text features and in IDV hybrid features (text + URL + metadata) are considered which provides a phase shift from content-based analysis to a total analytical approach that improves accuracy in ML tasks, especially in phishing detection

By providing a confusion matrix, false negatives will identify attacks in phishing mode and mimic trusted brands with emails. False positives may also arise due to possible suspicious models and patterns. In some cases, newer techniques of feature extraction and better model tuning may improve accuracy in predicted results.

B. SYSTEM INTERFACE AND PREDICTION OUTPUTS

This appendix presents the graphical user interface and sample prediction results generated by the developed **PhishGuard** phishing email detection system.

B.1 PhishGuard Web Application Interface

The PhishGuard system provides an interactive web-based platform that allows users to analyze email content for potential phishing threats. Users can input the email subject and body text into the interface, after which the backend system performs preprocessing, feature extraction, and ensemble model prediction automatically.

Figure 6. PhishGuard web interface used for real-time phishing email analysis.

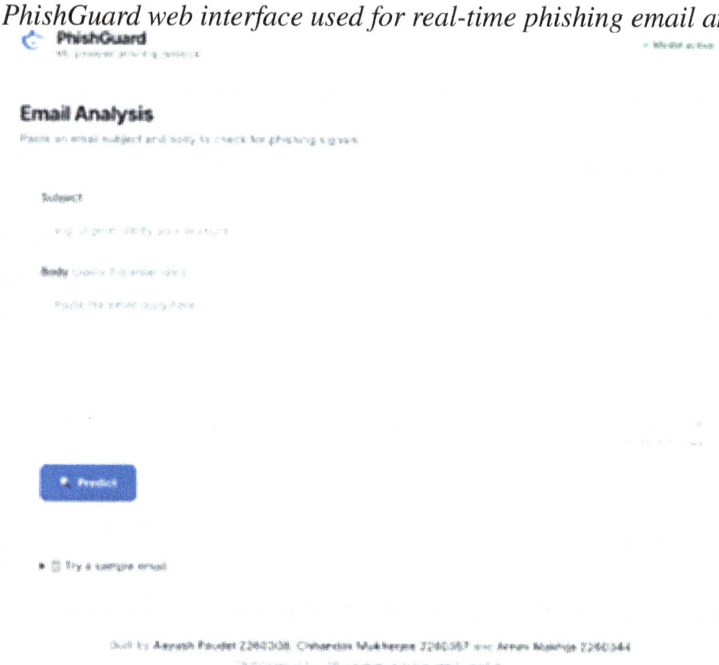

The interface communicates with a FastAPI-based backend service that hosts the trained stacking ensemble model, enabling instant classification and risk assessment.

B.2 Sample Prediction Output: Legitimate Email

Figure B.2 illustrates the system prediction generated for a legitimate email example. The analyzed message corresponds to an internal team communication regarding meet- ing rescheduling.

Figure 7. Prediction result for a legitimate email classified as Low Risk.

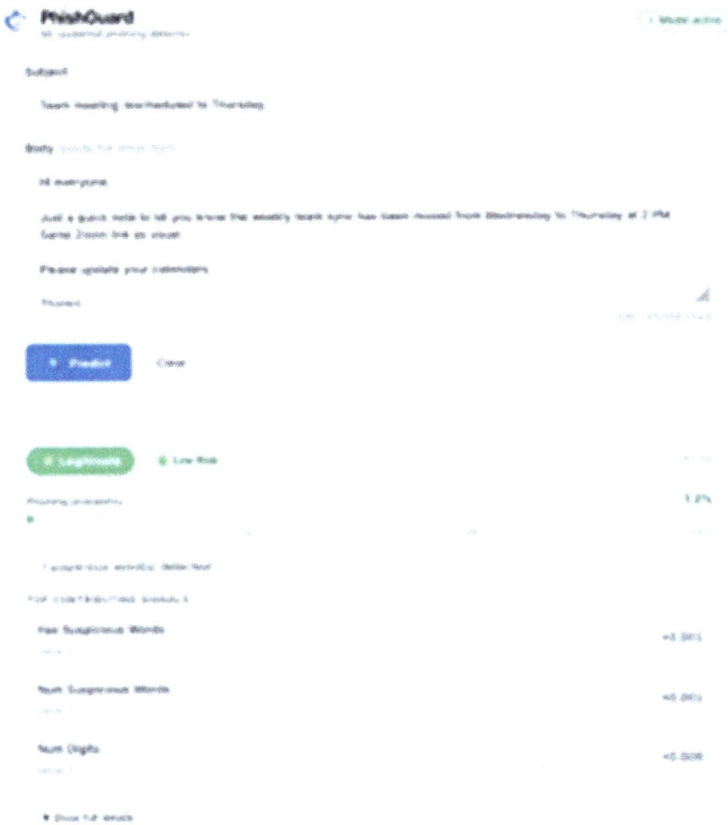

The system correctly classifies the email as **Legitimate** with a low phishing probability score. The prediction output additionally displays contributing signals used by the model, improving interpretability and user trust in automated decisions.

B.3 Sample Prediction Output: Phishing Email

Figure B.3 presents the prediction result obtained for a phishing email sample contain- ing urgent account verification instructions and a suspicious hyperlink.

Figure 8. Prediction result for a phishing email classified as High Risk.

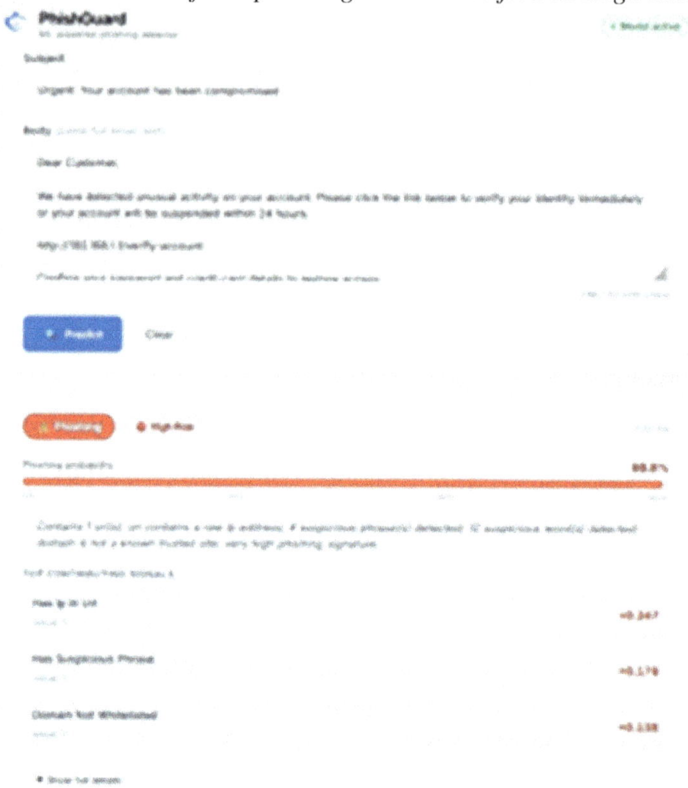

The system identifies multiple phishing indicators such as suspicious phrases, presence of IP-based URLs, and untrusted domain characteristics. Consequently, the email is classified as **Phishing** with a high-risk probability score exceeding the defined detection threshold.

B.4 System Validation Discussion

The presented interface and prediction examples validate successful integration of ma- chine learning models into a real-time deployment environment. The stacking ensemble framework effectively distinguishes between legitimate and phishing emails while pro- viding interpretable explanations for classification outcomes.

These experimental demonstrations confirm the practical applicability of the Phish- Guard system for deployment within modern email security infrastructures and future browser-based protection mechanisms.

REFERENCES

Abu-Nimeh, S., et al. (2007). A comparison of machine learning techniques for phishing detection. *eCrime Researchers Summit.*

Adnan, M., Imam, M. O., Javed, M. F., & Murtza, I. (2024). Improving spam email classi- fication accuracy using ensemble techniques: A stacking approach. *International Journal of Information Security*, *23*(1), 505–517. DOI: 10.1007/s10207-023-00756-1

Altwaijry, N., Al-Turaiki, I., Alotaibi, R., & Alakeel, F. (2024). Advancing phishing email detection: A comparative study of deep learning models. *Sensors (Basel)*, *24*(7), 24. DOI: 10.3390/s24072077 PMID: 38610289

Basnet, R. (2014). Detection of phishing attacks using machine learning. *IEEE International Conference.*

Bountakas, P., Xenakis, C., & Politis, I. (2021). Comparison of nlp and machine learning methods for phishing email detection. In *ARES Conference.*

Breiman, L. (2001). Random forests. *Machine Learning*, *45*(1), 5–32. DOI: 10.1023/A:1010933404324

Champa., . . . (2024). Curated datasets and feature analysis for phishing email detection. In *ICMI.*

Chen, T., & Guestrin, C. (2016). Xgboost: A scalable tree boosting system. In *Proceedings of KDD*. DOI: 10.1145/2939672.2939785

Dietterich, T. G. (2000). *Ensemble methods in machine learning*. Multiple Classifier Systems. DOI: 10.1007/3-540-45014-9_1

Fang, Y., Zhang, C., Huang, C., Liu, L., & Yang, Y. (2019). Phishing email detection using improved rcnn model with multilevel vectors. *IEEE Access : Practical Innovations, Open Solutions*, *7*, 56329–56341. DOI: 10.1109/ACCESS.2019.2913705

Kyaw, P. H., Gutierrez, J., & Ghobakhlou, A. (2024). Systematic review of deep learning techniques for phishing email detection. *Electronics (Basel)*, *13*(19), 13. DOI: 10.3390/electronics13193823

Murti, Y. S. & Naveen, P. (2023). Machine learning algorithms for phishing email detec- tion. *Journal of Logistics Informatics.*

Sahami, M. (1998). A bayesian approach to filtering junk e-mail. *AAAI Workshop.*

APPENDIX: A

A.1 Dataset Description

The phishing email detection system was trained and evaluated using publicly available email datasets consisting of phishing and legitimate email samples collected from open cybersecurity repositories. The datasets contain diverse email structures including subject lines, message bodies, embedded URLs, and sender metadata. These datasets were selected to ensure variation in phishing patterns and improve model generalization capability.

Key dataset characteristics include:

- Binary classification labels (Phishing / Legitimate)
- Email subject and body content
- Hyperlink and domain information
- Textual and structural email attributes

In real-time data sets, the set suffers from class imbalances, not-so-known phishing patterns, uncommon patterns with respect to issues like language, regions and formats, which limits a common model for developing phishing attack prevention models. To address these types of issues, synthetic data generation, model adversarial, multi-language and multi-format mail address data may be considered in identifying diversity and updating data sets.

The data set is taken from publicly available phishing and legitimate email corpora taken at different time values, and various attacking patterns are measured, with a reduced bias to make it more legitimate and practical. The training to testing data sets are considered in the range of 70-30 as per standard testing norms used in the industry. Measures are also taken to minimise data leakage to address duplicate data sets, which hinder the accuracy and efficiency of the proposed model.

A.2 Feature Engineering Details

Feature extraction was performed using both textual and structural characteristics of email messages.

The engineered features include:

TF-IDF representation of email subject and body text: TF-IDF Model, this model maps the text form to an alpha Numerical form by considering its relative value in a document to a set of documents. It ignores the generic terms like “is”, “the” and so on and works on keywords in identifying their relative value in a set of pages. It considers a n-gram difference between 5 to 9, Text size to 20k-50k, trimming text by removing stop-word lists, HTML & MIME forms are refined with removal of tags which reduces noise in the model and helps in improving accuracy while detecting phishing e mails.

- URL count and suspicious domain indicators
- Presence of IP-based hyperlinks
- Character distribution statistics
- Keyword-based phishing indicators
- Email length and token frequency measures

These features enable the machine learning models to capture hidden phishing patterns effectively.

A.3 Model Configuration Parameters

The stacking ensemble framework integrates Random Forest and XGBoost classifiers.

A.4 System Deployment Details

The trained phishing detection model was deployed using a FastAPI-based backend architecture. The deployment pipeline includes:

- Model loading during application startup
- Email preprocessing and feature extraction
- Ensemble prediction generation
- Risk-level classification output
- REST API communication with web interface

The deployed application enables real-time phishing detection through a browser-accessible interface.

A.5 Sample Prediction Output

The system produces prediction outputs containing both classification labels and phish- ing probability scores.

Example output format:

{"prediction": "Phishing", "probability": 0.93, "risk_lev-
el": "High Risk"
}

This structured output improves interpretability and supports integration with external security applications.

Chapter 4
Aerodynamic Design Optimization, AI Creation Systems Applications, Aerospace Engineering

S. Nithya
Vel Tech Rangarajan Dr. Sagunthala R&D Institute of Science and Technology, India

R. Sundharesan
http://orcid.org/0000-0001-9483-1195
J.J. College of Engineering and Technology, India

N. Aparna
http://orcid.org/0000-0002-3291-7249
J.J. College of Engineering and Technology, India

Chandra Bose G.
http://orcid.org/0009-0008-2455-6907
Vel Tech Rangarajan Dr. Sagunthala R&D Institute of Science and Technology, India

ABSTRACT

This chapter discusses the application of artificial intelligence (AI) in aerospace engineering, focusing on aerodynamic analysis, structural design, aerospace materials, and autonomous systems. Machine learning, deep learning and physics-informed models help to rapidly generate an approximation (surrogate model) and minimize reliance on computational expensive simulations like the computational fluid dynamics (CFD). These methods include increasing the prediction accuracy,

DOI: 10.4018/979-8-2600-3280-0.ch004

aiding in real-time optimization, and uncertainty analysis. The chapter also discusses generative design and topology optimization of lightweight aircraft structures. The use of AI in Aerospace Materials facilitates faster property prediction and material discovery, digital twins enable predictive maintenance and intelligent monitoring. Data quality, model validation, interpretability and certification requirements are key challenges.

INTRODUCTION

Machine learning (ML) and deep learning (DL) are the subfields of artificial intelligence (AI), which has become the cornerstone of the contemporary engineering profession. These allow modelling and surrogate modelling using data, as well as automated optimization of complicated design spaces. Surrogates based on machine learning and physics-informed learning are also becoming more popular in aerospace as AI-based surrogates are becoming essential to speed up analysis and design processes and retain underlying physics fidelity. It emphasizes an evolution of empirical and reduced-order methods as well as methods that operate entirely through data to hybrid methodologies, which incorporate data with governing equations in the literature. These hybrid solutions enhance the efficiency of data, ability to extrapolate, and interpretability of engineering. Also, the larger trend focuses on fast design cycles, quantifying uncertainty, and improved decision support in aerospace engineering interdisciplinary. The use of AI in aerospace engineering has changed considerably, shifting to the traditional high-fidelity simulations, including computational fluid dynamics (CFD), in favor of surrogate modeling, data-driven design, and autonomous systems. This development will allow exploring aerodynamics, aeroelasticity, and flight operations in a wide range of operating conditions (Chen et al., 2023). Initial deep learning (DL)-based surrogate models have been shown to be able to access flow fields and aerodynamic coefficients with significant savings in computational cost over full CFD-based models. The technology enables exploration of designs in real-time or in near-real-time (Zhao et al., 2024). Physics-informed learning techniques also expand these properties by incorporating governing equations in the training. The method makes the data more efficient and guarantees physical consistency of predictions despite small datasets. It has also been shown recently that reinforcement learning (RL) and DL-based approaches can be used to solve complex problems like unsteady aerodynamic optimization (e.g. transonic buffet suppression) and aeroelastic design when limited by flutter or buffet. Such techniques can also result in considerable increases in efficiency. Also, uncertain-aware surrogate models, such as Gaussian process and deep Gaussian process methods are commonly emphasised. These models are used to make probabilistic forecasts, hence, allowing sound design and decision-making (Zhang et al., 2024). These changes indicate a paradigm shift to AI-based design ecosystems, in which CFD and finite element analysis (FEA) are integrated with data-driven models and digital twin infrastructure is used. The systems of AI creation, such as generative design, physics-informed surrogates, deep learning-based models, reinforcement learning, and digital twins are essential in contemporary aerospace design. Their significance is further enhanced by the multidisciplinary nature of the aerospace system, the rigor of the certification, the large development cycle, and the expensive nature of the traditional high-fidelity analyses. Surrogate models greatly speed up the design search, allowing multi-fidelity optimization and quick sensitivity and robustness analysis along with uncertainty (Andres and Paulete-Perianez, 2021).In addition, generative design frameworks combined with digital twin technologies enable the process of design evolution in constant when basing on real-world operational and sensor data. This unification increases the reliability of the system, predictive maintenance, and the optimization of the lifecycle of the system. Generative design combined with AI-inspired optimization is especially useful in controlling multi-objective trade-offs in the aerodynamic design, e.g., lift-to-drag ratio and flutter margins. Lastly, transparency and trust toward AI-based aerospace tools are becoming more popular. It has resulted in more explainable AI (XAI) of neural surrogate models, as well as the creation of model auditing methods to achieve reliability and accountability in the design decision. Highly driven by the desire to have improved, safer and timelier aerodynamic design cycles, this chapter brings together AI creation methods, which have a direct effect on aerospace engineering by impacting on aerodynamic design. It is intended to put AI/ML methods, including surrogate models, physics-informed learning, and reinforcement learning, into the context of the aerodynamic design and analysis processes with a specific focus on the balance between speed and accuracy and uncertainty management. Moreover, the chapter looks at how aeroelastic and structural design issues in modern planes are changing in terms of generative and data-driven design paradigms as exemplified by digital twins. It also provides representative case studies that demonstrate the efficiency, precision, and stability of AI-supportive tools in the aerodynamics, flight loads, and unsteady phenomena (Zhang et al., 2024). Lastly, the chapter mentions the most important issues such as data quality and availability, validation, certification, safety, and ethical considerations and provides the future research directions to enhance AI creation systems in aerospace (Roy et al., 2020).

Figure 1. Structured Framework of AI Applications in Aerospace Engineering Chapter

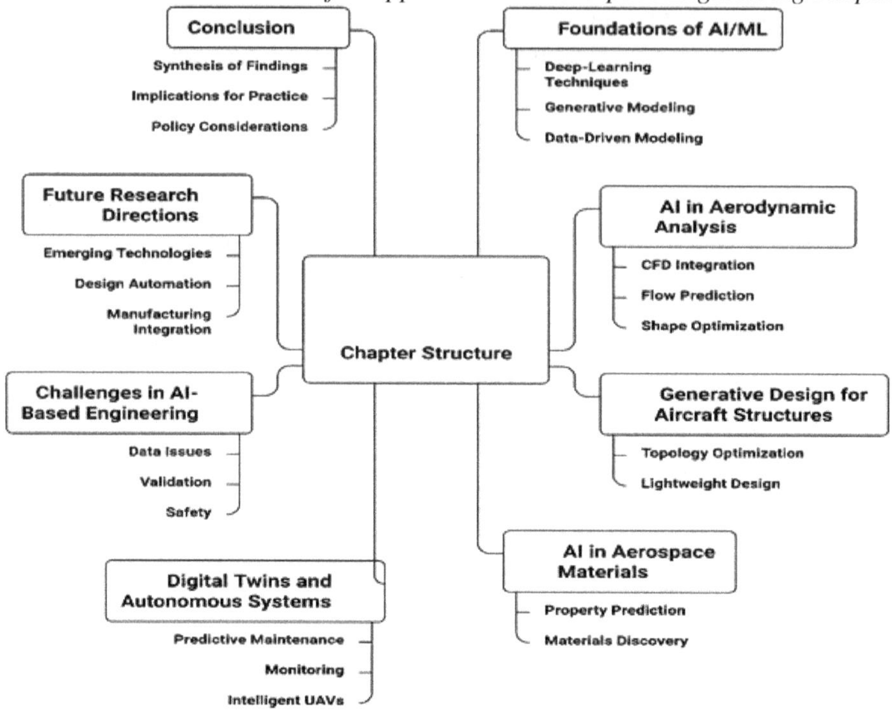

As shown in Figure 1, the chapter is well organized to follow the goals of the chapter. The chapter starts with the principles of AI/ML, which are deep learning, generative modeling, and data-driven methods. It is then followed by application of AI in aerodynamic studies, such as CFD integration, flow forecasting and shape optimization. It also discusses the use of generative design in the design of aircraft structures, topology optimization and lightweight design. This is followed by AI applications in aerospace materials where focus is made on property prediction and materials discovery. The next chapter discusses the concept of digital twins and autonomous systems with particular emphasis on predictive maintenance and smart UAV, applications. The main issues like data constraints, validation, and safety are discussed prior to giving the prospective research directions. Lastly, the chapter ends with a conclusions part and practical implications, which provides a logical and logical flow. The use of AI in solving complex problems in aerospace engineering that involves rapid design exploration, accurate prediction, and efficient optimization has been growing. The main emphasis in this chapter is on aerodynamic design, aircraft structural optimization, aerospace materials and coatings, and autonomous systems with the aid of a digital twin. The aerodynamic applications discussed consist of two-dimensional airfoil optimization, three-dimensional wing design, prediction of the aerodynamic coefficients, reconstruction of the flow field, aeroelastic analysis, buffet prediction and flutter constrained optimization. These applications cover a broad range of operating conditions from subsonic, transonic and supersonic flow regimes. The chapter also explores the lightweight aircraft structure methods with AI assistance; topology optimization; and aerospace parts produced via additive manufacturing. In aerospace materials engineering, focus is on materials property prediction, thermal barrier coating, protective coating and data-driven materials discovery. In addition, the use of digital twins and artificial intelligence in the realm of predictive maintenance, intelligent monitoring, fault diagnosis, and aerospace asset lifecycle management is addressed.Eligible propulsion control systems, air traffic management and full mission-level autonomous flight operations are excluded of the scope of this chapter. Rather, the focus is on design, analysis, optimization and maintenance application areas in which artificial intelligence can substantially decrease computational expense while retaining engineering precision and reliability.

OVERVIEW OF AI TECHNIQUES AND THEIR APPLICATIONS IN AEROSPACE ENGINEERING

Figure 2. AI Techniques and Their Applications in Aerospace Engineering

Source: Adapted from Taal Tech. (n.d.). Digital twin applications in aerospace. Retrieved from https://www.taaltech.com/digital-twin-applications-in-aerospace/

Figure 2 shows how AI technologies can be combined with the modern aerospace engineering systems. The image depicts a digital aerospace environment, illustrating the integration of AI with aircraft design, aerodynamic analysis, predictive maintenance, and autonomous decision-making, through real-time data processing and virtual simulations. The future of aerospace applications is being shaped by advanced AI technologies like machine learning, digital twins, and intelligent monitoring systems, as illustrated in Figure 2, which significantly enhance operational efficiency, safety, and optimization.In addition, generative AI systems, including GANs and VAEs, can be used to explore the design space with improved aerodynamic shapes and structural forms. Uncertainty quantification and fast assessment of the aerospace systems are assisted by data-driven modeling (Gaussian processes and reduced-order models) Lastly, the combination of AI and CFD, FEA, and digital twins has a beneficial effect on real-time predictions and renders efficient and multidisciplinary design processes consistent with the contemporary engineering practice.

Table 1. Overview of AI Techniques and Their Applications in Aerospace Engineering

AI Domain	Methods and Algorithms	Engineering Applications	Advantages
Artificial Intelligence & Machine Learning	Supervised, Unsupervised, Reinforcement Learning, Physics-Informed Learning	Surrogate modeling, design optimization, real-time decision-making	Fast predictions, uncertainty handling, improved decision support
Deep Learning Techniques	CNNs, RNNs, Transformers, PINNs, Deep Gaussian Processes	CFD surrogate modeling, aerodynamic prediction, flow reconstruction	High accuracy, nonlinear modeling, computational speedup
Generative AI Models	GANs, VAEs, Diffusion Models, RL-based Design	Aerodynamic shape generation, structural topology design, multi-objective optimization	Design automation, large design space exploration, innovative configurations
Data-Driven Modeling	Gaussian Processes, ROMs, Active Learning, Adaptive Sampling	Aeroelastic analysis, flight load prediction, optimization under uncertainty	Reduced computational cost, uncertainty quantification, efficient data usage
AI Integration with Engineering Tools	CFD/FEA coupling, Multi-fidelity models, Digital Twins, MBSE	Real-time simulation, predictive maintenance, multi-physics modeling	Faster design cycles, improved accuracy, robust system integration

Table 1 is an overview of the main artificial intelligence (AI) methods and how they apply to the aerospace engineering field. It organizes AI methods that are presented throughout Sections, such as machine learning, deep learning, generative AI, data-driven modeling and the use of AI in combination with computational engineering tools. The table emphasizes that the three main approaches of machine learning, including supervised, unsupervised, and reinforcement learning, are the most common methods of surrogate modeling, prediction, and making decisions in aerospace systems. The deep learning-based methods of convolutional and recurrent neural networks facilitate the proper modeling of nonlinear aerodynamic processes, as well as offer effective alternatives to the computationally-intensive simulations.

ARTIFICIAL INTELLIGENCE IN AERODYNAMIC ANALYSIS

Artificial intelligence is ever changing the field of aerodynamic analysis through data-driven method combining with conventional physics-based analysis. This integration in aerospace engineering makes it possible to predict aerodynamic performance much faster, more efficiently and accurately in a broad spectrum of operating conditions.

The Basics of Aerodynamic Analysis

Empirical analysis Aerodynamic analysis is a mix of empirical analysis, high-fidelity simulation, reduced-order representation, and data-driven proxy to predict forces, moments, and flow characteristics. Physics-based design Traditional CFD and experiments offer the physics-based baseline, whereas surrogate-based models with AI capabilities and predictors based on learning offer faster approximations with quantified uncertainty (Hu et al. 2025). Surrogate model: AI methods supplement physical models by providing methods to evaluate the design space cheaply at large scale respecting the governing equations (Wang et al., 2024). One of the most significant applications of AI in the field of aerodynamic design is the development of surrogate models. The simulations using traditional computational fluid dynamics (CFD) are very accurate for the aerodynamic prediction but are also very costly in computation, thus are not suitable for large-scale optimization study. To overcome this limitation, surrogate models derived using artificial intelligence (AI) can learn the relationship between geometric design variables and aerodynamic responses from a small number of high-fidelity simulations.

Parameterization techniques like Class Shape Transformation (CST), B-spline control points, Hicks–Henne bump functions and volumetric CAD parameters can be used to represent airfoil and wing geometries. Such parameterizations enable the creation of design candidates efficiently with preservation of the smoothness and manufacturability of the design geometry. These generated geometries are then tested with CFD simulation to obtain the aerodynamic coefficient, pressure distribution and flow field information for each one of the geometries which are used to store in a dataset.The general steps for surrogate modeling are generation, preprocessing, normalization, model training, model validation and uncertainty assessment. Usually, the data that is available is split into three groups: training (70%), validation (15%), and testing (15%). To prevent overfitting and enhance the generalization of the models, K-fold cross-validation and early stopping techniques are employed. Further prediction robustness is achieved by using data augmentation methods such as geometric perturbations and symmetrically transformed data.

Many models have been developed using deep neural networks, convolutional neural networks, Gaussian process models and physics-informed neural networks to predict high accuracy lift coefficient (CL), drag coefficient (CD), pitching moment coefficient (CM) and pressure distributions. These models offer substantial computational benefits, and allow for uncertainties-aware decision making and real time optimization.

Aerospace engineering Computational Fluid Dynamics (CFD)

Based on these basics, computational fluid dynamics (CFD) has been the main instrument of high-fidelity aerodynamic prediction. Nonetheless, it is computationally expensive especially in parametric studies and optimization. To overcome this shortcoming, surrogates and hybrid models derived using AI are being employed more to estimate CFD outputs or supplement physics-based models, with significant gains in speed and acceptable accuracy (Hu et al., 2025). Flow field and aerodynamic coefficient prediction with the help of such techniques as CNNs and machine learning regressors, it becomes possible to efficiently predict flow fields and aerodynamic coefficients in different geometries and regimes. Also, explainable AI methods are also coming up to increase trust and verification of AI-assisted CFD forecasting.

Flow Prediction Lagrangian or Machine Learning

Building upon such developments, numerous machine learning models have been created to predict the flow. Neural networks, convolutional models and hybrid architectures can be used to predict the aerodynamic quantities accurately at very low cost. The models may replicate the lift, drag, and pressure distributions and flow fields and make decisions in real-time, allowing a rapid discovery of a design space (Wang et al., 2023). CNNs prove especially useful in the case of spatial flow-field prediction, whereas physics-informed neural networks (PINNs) and deep Gaussian processes can offer uncertainty-aware solutions to physics-consistent problems when the amount of data is small. Moreover, the recent research illustrates that the combination of CFD data with ML models can model the unsteady and transient aerodynamic phenomena.

The flow chart of a reinforcement learning (RL) based aerodynamic optimization system in the field of aerospace engineering is shown in figure 3. During this process the artificial agent continually takes note of the current form of the airfoil, changes the shape, and tests the aerodynamics using an aerodynamic solver. A calculated lift to drag ratio and flow characteristics are used to produce a reward to direct the optimization process. Machine learning and reinforcement learning are techniques that can be used to explore aerodynamic design space efficiently, with fewer computational resources than traditional optimization approaches are illustrated. This AI-based method enables high-speed forecasting, optimization of shapes and quick decision-making in complex applications for the aerospace industry.

Physics-Informed Neural Networks for Aerospace Applications

Physics-Informed Neural Networks (PINNs) are a recent development that provides a viable approach to integrating data-driven learning with governing physical law. PINNs are distinct from the traditional neural network models that are only trained using data, as they also embed the conservation equations directly into the optimization process, which results in better physical consistency and less data needed. The composite loss function used in PINNs can be expressed as:

$$L = w_{data} L_{data} + w_{PDE} L_{PDE} + w_{bc} L_{bc} + w_{ic} L_{ic}$$

where represents the data fitting loss, denotes the residual loss associated with governing equations, represents boundary condition constraints, and corresponds to initial condition requirements. The weighting coefficients regulate the relative contribution of each term during training. In aerodynamic applications, the PINNs can be used to solve the Navier–Stokes equations, continuity equations, and turbulence models and to learn from CFD or experimental data. This ability allows for prediction of aerodynamic behavior even in situations with limited data, and extends to extrapolation of the model away from the training set.

Figure 3. Reinforcement Learning-Based Airfoil Shape Optimization Framework

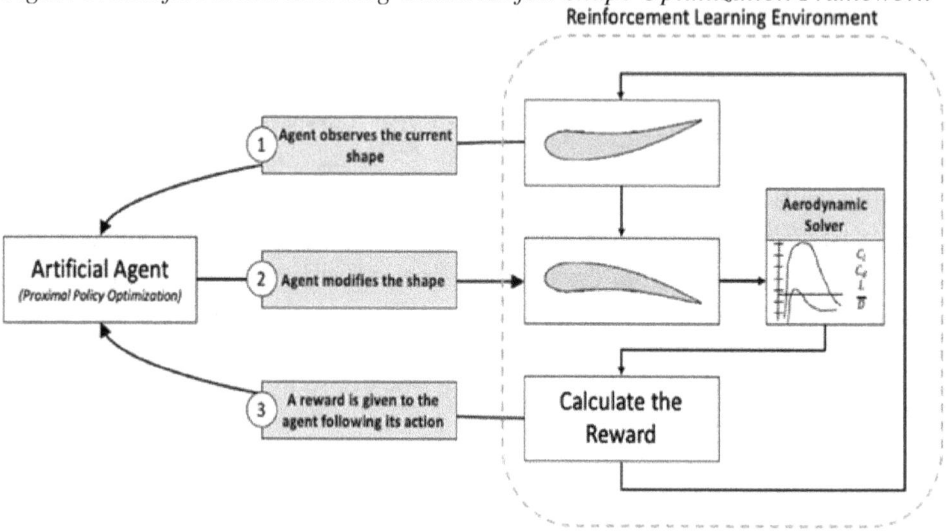

Source: Adapted from Custom RL environment for airfoil shape optimization. (2023). Scientific Reports, 13, Article 36560. Springer Nature. https://doi.org/10.1038/s41598-023-36560-z

AI-Shaped Optimization of Aerodynamic Shapes

Predictive modeling has been extended to AI approaches being used extensively in optimization of aerodynamic shapes. High-dimensional design spaces can be efficiently explored with the use of surrogate-assisted optimization, generative models and reinforcement learning. Such methods enhance the main performance statistics which include lift to drag ratio, stall behavior and aeroelastic stability. The feasibility of aerodynamic geometries under multi-objective constraints can be achieved by generating directly viable aerodynamic geometries using generative frameworks, such as GANs, VAEs, diffusion models and RL-based strategies, which are much faster than conventional CFD-based approaches. The practical applications of Case studies include CST-based airfoil optimization with neural surrogates, wind-turbine blade design based on AI-CFD integration, and CNN-based multi-objective optimization getting CFD-like results with less computational. Moreover, aeroelastic considerations like flutter may be inputted into the AI-based optimization models, which would secure stability and reliability in the development of the design.

Case Studies of AI-Assisted Aerodynamic Design

Table 2. Summary of AI Techniques and Their Roles in Aerospace Engineering

AI Domain	Methods and Algorithms	Engineering Applications	Advantages
Artificial Intelligence & Machine Learning	Supervised, Unsupervised, Reinforcement Learning, Physics-Informed Learning	Surrogate modeling, design optimization, real-time decision-making	Fast predictions, uncertainty handling, improved decision support
Deep Learning Techniques	CNNs, RNNs, Transformers, PINNs, Deep Gaussian Processes	CFD surrogate modeling, aerodynamic prediction, flow reconstruction	High accuracy, nonlinear modeling, computational speedup
Generative AI Models	GANs, VAEs, Diffusion Models, RL-based Design	Aerodynamic shape generation, structural topology design, multi-objective optimization	Design automation, large design space exploration, innovative configurations
Data-Driven Modeling	Gaussian Processes, ROMs, Active Learning, Adaptive Sampling	Aeroelastic analysis, flight load prediction, optimization under uncertainty	Reduced computational cost, uncertainty quantification, efficient data usage
AI Integration with Engineering Tools	CFD/FEA coupling, Multi-fidelity models, Digital Twins, MBSE	Real-time simulation, predictive maintenance, multi-physics modeling	Faster design cycles, improved accuracy, robust system integration

Table 2 compiles the case study examples that illustrate the usefulness of AI-assisted methods in the aerodynamic design. These papers generate an interest in deep learning, surrogate modeling, and hybrid AI methods to cut the cost of computation by an order of magnitude and acceptable accuracy when compared to conventional CFD. It has been used in applications such as airfoil optimization, wake prediction, turbulence modelling and multifidelity aerodynamic analysis. All these findings highlight the efficiency of the design, scalability to large design spaces, and even support of real-time or near-real-time decision-making in aerospace engineering. One such case study is the optimization of a two-dimensional airfoil for a Reynolds number of 3×10^6 and a Mach number of 0.25. Ten CST coefficients describe the geometry of the airfoil, and a set of about 1,000 CFD simulations is generated.A deep neural network surrogate model is constructed to predict Lift-to-Drag ratio, pressure distribution and aerodynamic coefficients. Using Bayesian Optimization, optimal geometric configurations are then sought, with the number of costly CFD evaluations reduced.The optimized airfoil improves the lift to drag ratio by around 10%, and decreases the computational cost by more than 90% compared with other standard optimization techniques based on CFD. The purpose of this case-study is to show the potential of using AI surrogate models to speed up the design process in the aerospace industry without losing the acceptable prediction accuracy.

AIRCRAFT STRUCTURES GENERATIVE DESIGN.

Aircraft structure generative design involves artificial intelligence to search through a large state space of design variants automatically. It unites topology optimization, surrogate modeling and online feedback of digital-twinning to develop practical and innovative structural design choices. The light weight designs are possible in this method, and the designs satisfy the requirements of strength, stiffness, and safety. It is also capable of helping in multi-objective optimization, such as manufacturability and aerodynamic performance. Generally, the use of generative design saves a lot of time in design and builds better performance in contemporary aerospace design.

Introduction To Generative Design in Aerospace Engineering

Aerospace Generative design Aerospace Generative design is an AI-assisted technology which searches large design spaces to generate candidate structural layouts which meet a variety of goals such as weight, rigidity, flutter margin, and manufacturability. This method unites topology optimization, parameterization, surrogate modeling, and feedback form a digital twin to quickly create and test alternative concepts and allows co-design of aerodynamics and structures in most situations. The literature indicates that aerospace practitioners are using generative design to further accelerate the process of concept exploration, finding lightweight lattice or lattice-like geometries, and helping make life-cycle-informed decisions by keeping a digital twin updated (e.g., digital twins guiding design updates throughout the life cycle; the utility of topology optimization to facilitate weight reduction in vital components (Zeng et al., Importantly, the real-world use cases demonstrate that topology optimization and additive manufacturing (AM) allow reducing weight forcefully without compromising safety and performance margins, including optimizations that are related to aerospace cabin elements and internal structural members (Shen et al., 2025). The need to verify, validate, and certify the application of generative designs to aerospace structures of high priority, such as safety-critical ones, can also be noted when integrating AI with design processes.

Structural Design optimization using AI

The AI-based structural design optimization is an improvement of data-driven surrogates combined with learning-based priors and iterative search methods that speed up the convergence to the Pareto-optimal designs. The high-fidelity evaluations (such as Gaussian-process and deep-learning surrogates) can be substituted by or further supplemented with surrogate ones, which facilitates quick multi-objective exploration and decision making in complex structural systems under uncertainty. The use of data-based priors used in previous designs or physics-based constraints can be used to help refine the search to the regions of the design space that are feasible and also help to extrapolate to off-design points (Zeng et al., 2024). Practically, reinforcement learning and other generative methods can be used to suggest the promising topologies or material distributions, which are confirmed by more realistic simulations, to form a hybrid optimization loop, taking advantage of the advantages of both data-driven and physics-based models. The literature provides case examples that show that design-cycle times can be reduced significantly when ML surrogates and multi-fidelity strategies are used to search the space of lightweight and safe aerospace designs.

Aeroelasticity and Flutter-Constrained Design Optimization

Aerospace systems are highly aeroelastic and, in their operation, require very tight constraints that affect their integrity and flight safety. The aeroelastic design uses AI to combine aerodynamic and structural analyses to forecast flutter boundaries, buffet onset, and dynamic stability features.Generalized aerodynamic forces, structural mode shapes and flutter margins can be estimated by machine learning models trained with data from coupled CFD–finite element analysis (FEA) simulations. For these purposes, deep learning architectures like Long Short-Term Memory (LSTM) networks and Transformer models are especially suited for capturing the aerodynamic phenomena and responses over time, which are often unsteady.Combination of AI and aeroelastic simulation allows thousands of design configurations to be evaluated quickly, promoting robust optimization subject to flutter and buffet constraints. These features are especially useful in the conceptual and preliminary design phases of an aircraft, when computational efficiency is paramount.

AI-based methods of topology optimization.

Topology optimization aims to achieve a minimum weight design that satisfies performance targets using a well-defined design space that is distributed with the optimal material in the least amount. Topology optimization is optimized with the help of AI, which diffuses the existing approaches with learned priors, searches with surrogates, and regularization based on data to speed up the convergence process and discover new forms of topology in wings, fuselage parts, and internal structures (Shen et al., 2025). Surrogate models are capable of obtaining a structural response (e.g.

stiffness, natural frequencies, flutter margins, etc) using a large number of candidate topologies, facilitating high-speed screening prior to high-fidelity validation. It has also been discussed in the literature that AM-enabled fabrication environments the topology-optimized geometries give an incentive to integrated pipelines in which topology optimization guides design to additive manufacturing and later certification issues (Shen et al., 2025). The combination of AI-based topology optimization and digital-twin updates offers the approach to changing the structural concepts throughout the life cycle as new data will be provided.

Lightweight Structural Design Strategies.

Mass conversion is one of the most crucial goals of aerospace structural design and AI-enhanced generative methods offer significant information on light-weighting in terms of topology, lattice design, and material distribution plans. AI-controlled surrogates can quickly assess the lightweight configuration of a candidate structure in terms of its stiffness, strength, and flutter, and can facilitate iterative design cycles, which would be prohibitively expensive with other optimization tools based on CFD/FEA only. Combination with AM, in addition to topology-optimized designs, also allows the creation of complex, weight-optimized forms to be very challenging in conventional manufacturing techniques, yet it still tackles certification and reliability issues. Digital-twin architectures have the potential to refresh material models and structural forecasts with material as reality is acquired, which makes lightweight designs more robust throughout the life cycle of a vehicle. Table 3 shows some of the most important uses of generative design to critical structural areas of an aircraft such as wings, fuselage as well as load-bearing structural components.

Table 3. Applications of Generative Design in Aircraft Structures

Application Area	AI / Design Approach	Structural Component	Key Benefits
Aircraft Wings	Topology optimization, Additive Manufacturing (AM)	Wing ribs, internal lattice structures	Weight reduction, improved stiffness, efficient load distribution
Fuselage Structures	Digital twin, AI-based design optimization	Fuselage frames, panels	Lifecycle monitoring, predictive maintenance, damage tolerance
Structural Components	Generative design, surrogate-assisted optimization	Load-bearing components	Reduced development time, improved safety margins

continued on following page

Table 3. Continued

Application Area	AI / Design Approach	Structural Component	Key Benefits
Composite Materials	AI-driven material design, AM integration	Multifunctional composite structures	Enhanced material performance, manufacturability, certification support
Integrated Aerospace Systems	Hybrid AI + physics-based models	Wings and fuselage assemblies	Multi-objective optimization, structural efficiency, system-level performance

It underlines the application of AI based methods including topology optimization, surrogate modelling and using digital twins to enhance structural efficiency and performance. Generative design in wing structures allows the creation of lightweight and stiff structures, like topology-optimized ribs and lattice, which can also produce a considerable decrease in the use of material without losing their strength (Shen et al., 2025). The digital twin frameworks are used in the lifecycle monitoring and predictive maintenance of fuselage applications, which improves reliability and damage tolerance. Also, AI-aided optimization can be implemented in structural elements to speed up the design process without compromising safety and performance. When AI is combined with composite materials and additive manufacturing, it is possible to create progressive, multifunctional structures that will be more manufacturable and have certification potential. In general, these applications indicate how the concept of generative design is transforming the current structural engineering of aerospace.

ARTIFICIAL INTELLIGENCE IN AEROSPACE MATERIALS AND COATINGS

The use of artificial intelligence (AI) is starting to alter aerospace materials and coatings, allowing them to be designed and predicted based on the data. It promotes the discovery of better materials that are highly strong, durable, and thermally resistant. The AI models are capable of processing large amounts of data of the experiments and simulations to maximize the coating properties, including corrosion resistance and wear behavior. Along with that, machine learning methods are useful to predict material degradation and the lifecycle performance. On the whole, AI will speed up the development of materials, decrease the amount of time spent on testing, and enhance reliability in aerospace.

Overview of Aerospace Materials and Protective Coatings

Aerospace coating, especially thermal barrier coating (TBC) is needed to safeguard the hot-section components against extreme temperatures, oxidation, wear, and corrosion, which can allow the engine to operate at higher temperatures and achieve better efficiency. A classic TBC type includes a ceramic topcoat, metallic bond coat, thermally grown oxide layer, and the substrate, and microstructure, and porosity are some of the key factors in insulation, bonding, and lifecycle performance (Sun et al., 2025). Recent data-informed and AI-aided studies focus on the effects of microstructure, porosity, and interfacial characteristics on life, reliability, and thermal performance and demonstrate that AI can speed up the knowledge about such coatings, processing, microstructure, and service environments. Nondestructive evaluation (NDE) and imaging-based methods that use AI are getting more and more popular in quantifying porosity, microstructure characteristics, and delamination of TBCs, and they provide a fast and noninvasive approach and meets the maintenance and certification requirements. Taken together, such advances make AI an important facilitator of the exploration, design, and verification of novel and advanced protective coating and corresponding high-temperature materials in aerospace contexts.

Machine Learning for Materials Property Prediction

Machine learning has been used to forecast porosity, microstructure characteristics, bonding strength, and other characteristics that apply to TBCs and protective coating. Porosity prediction the best predictive accuracy of the processing or imaging features of porosity has been observed with neural networks that are optimized using genetic algorithms and associated feature-processing pipelines, indicating viable pathways to data-driven (rapid) microstructure characterization (Zhang et al., 2024). Various data-driven models (Gaussian-process surrogates, deep variants (deep Gaussian processes) are used to speedily predict properties with uncertainty estimates, which is robust to variability and can be repeatedly used to screen processing-parameter space when needed to apply coating. To illustrate how multi-modal data can become more predictive of TBCs, hybrid AI/NDT methods have been developed including terahertz images, infrared thermography, PCA, and ML classifiers to predict the coating life or thickness or microstructural conditions. Extensive potential of ML to simulate thermal transport, mechanical properties, as well as life-cycle performance of the coating systems are reported in foundational reviews and studies and used to inform materials selection and optimization of processes in the aerospace environment.

Discovery of Advanced Aerospace Materials by AI.

The discovery and design of future-generation protective coatings and materials have become a common feature of AI-driven discovery and design. Functional coating notebook Data-driven materials research The ability to map input parameters (composition, deposition conditions, processing) to performance can be used to explore the wide range of design space rapidly and understanding structure-property relationships can be more effectively interpreted. Bayesian-optimization and active-learning methods have been suggested to explore significant compositional space of coating (e.g., large-entropy, multicomponent) systems with desired thermal and mechanical characteristics to alleviate experimental overhead whilst directing synthesis to interesting corners of the design space. Other fundamental articles also cover the topic of how generalization may be improved by transfer learning, universal descriptors and physics-informed priors in coating discovery, which will enable faster discovery of materials with high conductivity, stiffness and durability in aerospace conditions Steingrimsson et al., 2021. These concepts of the integration of AI with MBSE and digital-twin allow further closed-loop, data-informed discovery, which can respond to new regimes of service and life-cycle feedback.

Optimization of Thermal Barrier and Protective Coatings

AI-enabled surrogates, multi-fidelity modeling, and design of the processing parameters based on data are useful in optimization of TBCs and protective coatings. It has been shown that ML can accurately predict microstructural features and thermo-mechanical properties based on deposition conditions (e.g., spray parameters, coating thickness) with high precision and can therefore be used to quickly explore processing-structure-property trade-offs and to better control bonding strength and thermal insulation),. ML workflows combined with surrogate models and optimization algorithms (i.e., Bayesian optimization, genetic algorithms) could find a set of parameters to maximize life, reduce the number of defects, or optimize thermal performance and take into consideration manufacturing constraints and certification requirements (Sun et al., 2025). Moreover, data-intensive methods are improving the perception of the effects of microstructural factors (e.g., porosity, grain structure) on thermal conductivity and erosion resistance to give practical insights into tuning the process and material choice in aerospace coating.

Table 4. Case Studies in AI-Based Aerospace Materials and Coatings

Case Study	AI Method Used	Material / Coating	Main Outcomes
Porosity prediction in TBCs	Machine Learning (ML), Imaging-based models	Thermal Barrier Coatings (TBCs)	High accuracy, nondestructive evaluation, improved maintenance planning
Optimization of YSZ coatings	ML models, Explainable AI	Yttria-Stabilized Zirconia (YSZ)	Improved bonding strength, optimized process parameters
Microstructure and property prediction	Neural Networks, ML models	APS/TBC systems	Accurate prediction of properties, improved durability
Data-driven materials discovery	Active Learning, Surrogate Modeling	High-entropy coatings	Faster discovery, improved thermal/ mechanical performance
Coating performance optimization	Data-driven modeling, ML	Protective aerospace coatings	Enhanced lifecycle performance, reduced cost/time

Table 4 gives a summary of typically used case studies of the use of artificial intelligence in materials and coatings in the aerospace sector. These papers underscore the application of machine learning and data-driven technology in predicting porosities, optimization of coating, analysis of microstructures, and materials discovery. The methods of AI can be used to conduct a nondestructive examination and optimize the performance of coatings, as well as hasten the creation of materials. On the whole, the case studies highlight the usefulness of AI in improving reliability, decreasing the amount of work on an experiment, and aiding the lifecycle decision-making process in the aerospace materials engineering.

AUTONOMOUS AEROSPACE SYSTEMS AND DIGITAL TWINS

Digital twins (DTs) are simulated representations of the real-life aerospace systems, continuously informed by the real-time sensor measurements and real-life histories to forecast the performance, detect errors, and make the most beneficial decisions throughout its life cycle. The aerospace space can also provide proactive maintenance, feedback in design, and mission planning by connecting the data streams, physics-based models and AI-based analytics in an integrated ecosystem with the help of DTs. This paradigm is being actively supplemented with autonomous aerospace operations, where DTs assist in perception, decision making and control in both manned and unmanned systems (Wild et al., 2025).

Digital Twin Technology Concept and Architecture

An effective DT architecture that aerospace could look like is (i) a physical asset and its subsystems, (ii) a digital representation of the physical asset that includes geometry, material properties, physics-based behavior and constraint of operations, (iii) data streams of sensors, maintenance, and simulation outputs and (iv) AI/ML analytics, optimization and decision-support modules that update the digital twin and provide actionable insights. The essence of this continuous updating is the data assimilation to place the DT in step with the changing physical state to allow prognostics, anomaly detection and design-for-life-cycle benefits. Recent polls outline the DT architecture as a multilevel structure with data, models, and analytics as providers of service-oriented applications (DT as a service) and as participants in Industry 4.0-like cyber-physical systems, artificial intelligence, and digital-twin systems in aerospace applications. Synthetic data generation and ML-based updates to preserve DT fidelity in case real-world data are limited or costly to access are also a feature highlighted in the literature when operating in autonomous aviation sectors and there is no access to real-world data, a problem often encountered. Besides that, regulatory and certification aspects of DT-enabled aviation systems are featured in work on DT-based reviews and UAS-focused literature, and it is noted that DTs can make the process of certification more streamlined by allowing a rigorous virtual testing of the designs and traceability of design decisions. Combined, these resources all lead to a DT architecture in which physical resources, digital models, data pipelines, and AI-inspired analytics are closely interconnected to facilitate autonomous and semi-autonomous aerospace operations, (Kabashkin & Shoshin, 2024). The framework provides multiple layers of integration, including data acquisition, data preprocessing, data integration, data visualization, and data service management, among others, with physical entities, sensors and cameras, connectivity models, and cyber space analytics. In the diagram in Figure 4, we can see that AI and ML methods are vital for converting the data obtained in real-time operations into insights that can be used for monitoring, diagnostics, and decision-making. The architecture allows reliable information dissemination, information assurance, and information security management, which boosts the reliability of modern aerospace systems, predictive maintenance and their life cycle optimization.

Figure 4. Digital Twin Technology Concept and Architecture

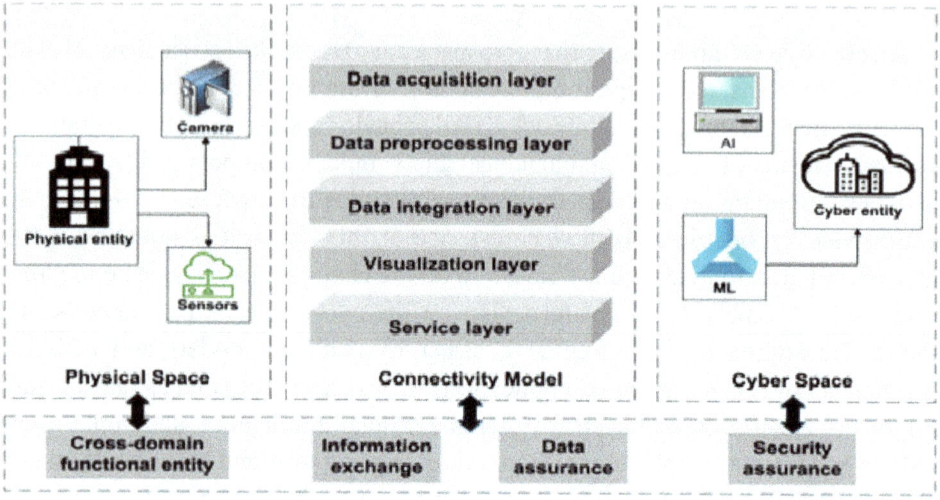

Source: Adapted from Yang, Z., Tang, C., Zhang, T., Zhang, Z., & Doan, D. T. (2024). *Digital twins in construction: Architecture, applications, trends and challenges. Buildings, 14*(9), 2616. https://doi.org/10.3390/buildings14092616

The figure 5 shows an AI powered intelligent UAV environment, medium 5G/6G communication networks and real-time data analysis. The system combines sensing, identity authentication, intelligent networking and autonomous decision making within a unified framework to facilitate a variety of aerospace applications, such as urban logistics, land surveying, emergency response and precision agriculture. The benefits of AI in autonomous navigation, mission planning, collision avoidance, and safety monitoring, along with seamless communication between the aerial platforms and ground infrastructure, are demonstrated in Figure 5. AI and next-generation communication technologies improve the efficiency, situational awareness, reliability and security of operations, which will help to create autonomous aerospace systems for future smart environments.

Figure 5. AI-Enabled Intelligent UAV Ecosystem.

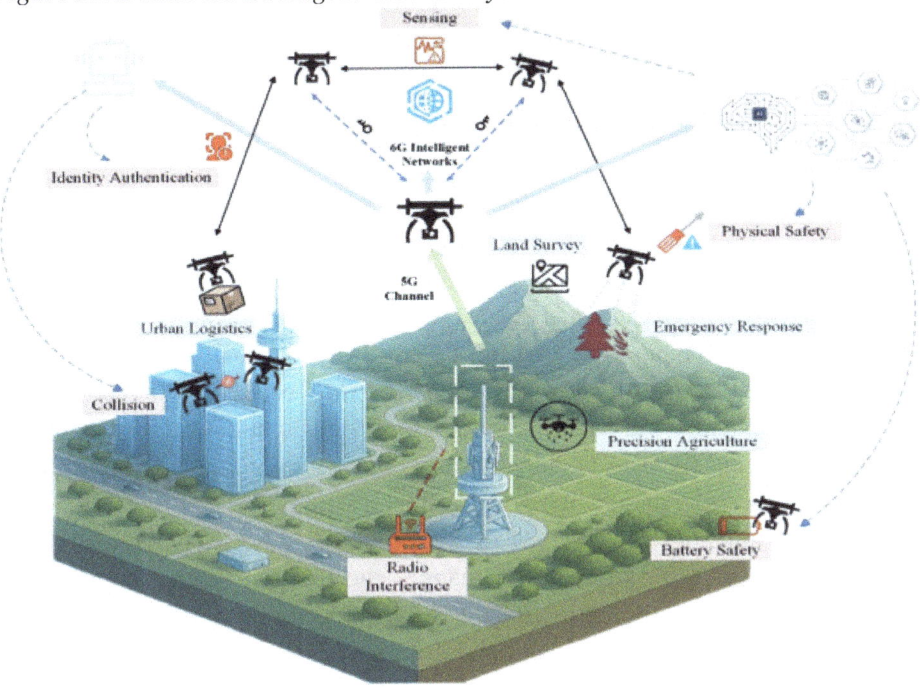

Source: Adapted from Yang, Z., Zhang, Y., Zeng, J., Yang, Y., Jia, Y., Song, H., Lv, T., Sun, Q., & An, J. (2025). AI-driven safety and security for UAVs: From machine learning to large language models. Drones, 9(6), 392. https://doi.org/10.3390/drones9060392

Predictive maintenance systems based on AI

AI-predictive maintenance (PdM) is based on sensor streams, past history of failures, physical priors, and data surrogates to predict remaining useful life (RUL) and anticipate the timing of failures to prevent them. PdM based on DT has been utilized in aerospace to offer a data-rich platform upon which predictive analytics can be applied to support uninterrupted health management and asset-level decision-making during flight and maintenance operations. Early surveys and reviews highlight the use of ML and DT towards providing trustworthy and uncertain-aware maintenance planning as well as supporting certification pathways through the provision of auditable and transparent maintenance analytics (Stanton et al., 2022). In practice deployments point to the issues of data scarcity, model validation, and explainability in safety-critical problems which prompts the adoption of hybrid physics-informed and data-driven PdM methods of DT infrastructures (Kabashkin & Shoshin, 2024). The AIoT-enabled architectures used to measure, transmit, and analyze aircraft systems to assist in remote diagnostics and remote-planning is also discussed in the literature to demonstrate end-to-end PdM pipes to autonomous and remotely monitored platforms.

Intelligent Aircraft Monitoring and Diagnostics

The intelligent monitoring and diagnostics are based on AI-enabled detecting anomalies, diagnosing faults, and inferring health parameters to aircraft subsystems, engines, avionics and structures. DTs are used to combine the live sensor information with physics-based forecasts to constantly monitor health indicators, as well as to instigate preventive maintenance measures. Practically, the health-monitoring systems of aviation based on AI have grown to include ML-based pattern recognition, time-series forecasting, and data fusion to both detect slight deviations of healthy behaviour and predict the risk of failure into different mission profiles. The usefulness of DTs in the process of monitoring and maintenance planning is also mentioned in the literature to allow a closed-loop design due to the diagnostics input feeding the DT that, consequently, informs design changes and lifecycle management. Other publications are on the implications of HS(M) on autonomous or semi-autonomous flight operations, in which DTs aid in reliability analysis, life-cycle assessment, and safety assurance in the context of AI-enabled decision mechanisms.

Unmanned Aerial Vehicles and Aircraft

Self-driving drones and UAVs are getting increased reliance on AI to provide perception, control, planning, and decision-making during uncertainty. The DT paradigm improves the autonomy provided by offering a high-fidelity virtual environment where AI controllers can be trained, tested and validated against realistic situations before being deployed. The literature reviews point at the application of AI-based autonomous UAVs, safety certification issues, and the purpose of DTs to allow scenario-based validation, data management, and life-cycle cognizance of autonomous flight .Certain articles focus on lightweight AI systems that can be deployed to resource-constrained UAV systems and how ML-based decision support can be combined with on-season and edge computing to create real-time autonomy and safe operation of complex airspace (Singh et al., 2021). Other works also consider autonomous aircraft ideas in the wider context of DT, such as synthetic data augmentation to scale training sets in the situation when the real-flight data are scarce, and the application of DTs to monitor and plan autonomous activities in the life cycle of an aircraft.

Aerospace Digital Twins and AI

The combination of AI and DTs in the aerospace is marked by the same side gains, where DT updates, data, and physical grounds of AI models and AI models accelerate updates, interpret complex sensor data, and predictive capabilities are offered by models based on physics alone. Examples of these themes are (i) physics-based models tuned and updated by data in the DT, (ii) prognostics and anomaly detection algorithms based on AI (implemented in DT analytics), (iii) DTaaS (digital twin as a service) that provides on-demand information to operators and maintainers, and (iv) synthetic data and transfer learning which can solve data scarcity due to rare events like extreme failures or new mission profiles.

Figure 6. Aerospace Digital Twins Integrated with Artificial Intelligence.

Source: Adapted from Tuegel, E. J., Ingraffea, A. R., Eason, T. G., & Spottswood, S. M. (2011). Reengineering aircraft structural life prediction using a digital twin. International Journal of Aerospace Engineering, 2011, 154798.

The concept of aerospace digital twins in combination with artificial intelligence (AI) for real-time monitoring and intelligent decision making is shown in figure 6. This image depicts a virtual replica of the aircraft being linked to the operational data, allowing for continuous monitoring and analysis of the aircraft's structural health, engine performance, and system behavior. In modern aerospace systems, digital twin technology and AI can be used to facilitate predictive maintenance, fault detection, lifecycle management, and operational optimization is illustrated. This integration significantly boosts reliability, lowers maintenance expenses, and enhances safety by allowing data analysis and self-diagnostics during the entire life cycle of the aircraft.

CHALLENGES IN AI-BASED AEROSPACE ENGINEERING

Artificial intelligence in aerospace engineering faces a number of issues associated with data quality, data availability, and data reliability, especially on safety critical applications. There must be strict validation, verification, and certification to comply with regulations in the integration of AI models and physics-based systems. Also, the model interpretability, transparency and trust are all concerns that prevent popularization. Implementation is further complicated by the issue of computational cost, lack of data in extreme operating conditions and extrapolating between regimes of flight. These issues should be addressed to achieve safe, reliable and efficient AI-driven solution implementation in aerospace engineering. Table 5 is a summary of the key issues related to data availability and quality in the use of AI in aerospace. Such obstacles have critical consequences on the reliability, accuracy and certification of AI models in safety critical settings. The lack of data, noise, and limited access are some of the issues that affect the effective training of a model, whereas governance and traceability are necessary to comply with regulations. Though the synthetic and the data generated by digital twins offer an alternative solution, they bring an issue of fidelity and domain shift. Hence, a solid data management plan and validation models play a significant role in guaranteeing credible AI implementation in aerospace engineering.

Table 5. Data Availability and Quality Challenges in Aerospace AI

Issue	Description	Impact on AI Models	Mitigation Strategies
Data Scarcity	Limited availability of labeled datasets	Poor model training and generalization	Synthetic data, simulation, digital twins
Proprietary Data Restrictions	Restricted data sharing across organizations	Limited collaboration and robustness	Federated learning, secure sharing
Data Noise & Inconsistency	Sensor errors and variability	Reduced prediction accuracy	Filtering, preprocessing, calibration
Incomplete Data Records	Missing maintenance/ operational data	Inaccurate predictions	Improved logging, data completion
Data Governance & Traceability	Lack of proper tracking and documentation	Certification challenges	Governance frameworks, standards
Synthetic Data Limitations	Domain shift between real and synthetic data	Reduced real-world reliability	Hybrid datasets, validation

AI Model reliability and validation

The fundamental issue is to be able to guarantee reliability and high standards of validation of AI models in aerospace. Validation should also deal with accuracy, extrapolation to unobserved regimes, quantification of uncertainty, and certification standards compliance, which is not nontrivial in the context of high-stakes flight and operations ML-based component verification and validation practices continue to develop, as explicit safety cases and explainability as well as auditable development trails are called upon to facilitate trust and regulatory acceptance. Besides, most AI approaches are not deterministic and thus make the classic V&V processes more complex, and in the field of avionics and CNS/ATM, powerful testing systems and clear decision-support processes should be established (Sabatini et al., 2020). Moreover, air-traffic management, landing-gear certification, and intelligent navigation work domain knowledge points to the need to consider stringent, multi-fidelity benchmarking and standardized evaluation procedures.

Safety and Ethical Issues

The general limitation affecting the use of AI in aerospace is safety. The lack of explanability of most AI models is a cause of concern due to fault detection, failure modes, and reasoning about the decisions under fault conditions, and this is the reason explainable AI, verification tooling, and risk-informed assurance cases are becoming a core part of safety cases. The ethical considerations are mentioned to be transparency, accountability, data privacy, and the risk of bias or misuse in autonomous systems and decision-support systems, and require governance frameworks and ethical guidelines within the engineering practice and certification roadmaps. The touching of AI to critical systems also creates the question of human-machine interaction, trust in the operator, the risk of overdependence on automated decisions, especially in autonomous aircraft and UAM settings.

Regulatory and Certification Problems.

The AI-enabled aerospace systems are facing regulatory and certification issues on a grand scale. Even though frameworks (e.g., DO-178C in the case of airborne software) and regulatory authorities are actively defining the ways AI/ML might feature in aviation (e.g., EASA AI roadmaps and certifiability discussions in the case of autonomous systems), developed, universally exploitable certification standards are still a work in progress. The requirements of certification are also applied to data lineage, model provenance, and the possibility to audit decisions made by AI in life cycles, such as maintenance, repair, and flight operations. The emerging literature highlights the necessity of ontologies, standardized V&V methods, and assurance-cases tooling to provide AI-enabled CNS/ATM, UAVs, and autonomous aircraft certification, international standard harmonization to allow cross-border operation. The use of synthetic data and digitaltwin systems in certification processes is often touted as a way towards safer and more traceable AI-enabled aviation, but with more regulation (Fakhraian et al., 2023). Table 6 provides major constraints of existing AI technologies in the aerospace engineering field. Such issues impact on model reliability, interpretability and incorporation in safety critical systems. They need an integrated modeling methodology, better data policies, and sound governance systems in order to provide safe and efficient implementation. AI is introduced to aerospace systems with many challenges concerning safety, reliability, certification and regulatory compliance. In contrast to conventional software systems, AI models are adaptive and data-driven, which makes them more difficult to verify and validate. Hence, AI-enabled aerospace technologies require such a certification and assurance framework that combines existing aviation standards with emerging regulatory guidelines.The DO-178C (Software Considerations in Airborne Systems and Equipment Certification) standard provides guidance for the development and verification of safety-critical airborne software. AI algorithms used in flight control, navigation, health, and decision-support systems will need to show traceability, robustness and compliance with various software assurance standards. Likewise, DO-330 (Software Tool Qualification Considerations) lays out guidelines for the qualification of software tools employed in the development, verification and validation of aerospace systems. The outputs generated by AI-assisted design and analysis tools need to be validated for accuracy, reproducibility and credibility.DO-254 (Design Assurance Guidance for Airborne Electronic Hardware) gives the relevant guide to hardware certification covering AI accelerators, field-programmable gate arrays (FPGAs), and embedded processing units implementations. In addition to all of that, AI-enabled hardware components shall satisfy extremely high reliability and safety requirements throughout its operational lifecycle as laid out by the DO-254.ARP4754A (Guidelines for Development of Civil Aircraft and Systems) is a document that structures how complex aerospace systems are developed and integrated at the system level using established methods in systems engineering practice

Table 6. Limitations of Current AI Technologies in Aerospace Engineering

Limitation	Description	Impact on Aerospace Applications	Possible Solutions
Generalization Issues	Difficulty adapting models to unseen flight conditions	Reduced reliability in real-world scenarios	Transfer learning, hybrid physics-AI models
Interpretability Barriers	Black-box nature of AI models	Limited trust and certification challenges	Explainable AI (XAI), transparency tools
Data Dependency	Requirement for large annotated datasets	High cost and difficulty in data acquisition	Synthetic data, digital twins, active learning
Integration Challenges	Difficulty integrating AI with legacy systems and certification frameworks	Delays in deployment and validation	Standardized frameworks, modular AI systems
Lifecycle & Risk Management	Challenges in model updating, traceability, and risk assessment	Reduced robustness over product lifecycle	Governance frameworks, continuous validation

. Subsystems with AI capabilities have to be assessed and validated in the context of the overall aircraft architecture for functional compatibility and safety across multiple levels. In support of this standard, ARP4761A (Guidelines and Methods for Conducting the Safety Assessment Process on Civil Airborne Systems and Equipment) contains methods for hazard identification, failure analysis, risk assessment, and safety verification. Many of these techniques are extremely relevant to assessment of the uncertainty quantification in machine learning models and autonomous decision making systems. Regulatory agencies too are increasingly crafting AI-specific guidance. EASA AI Roadmap defines a framework for adopting an AI solution safely in aviation, including aspects of transparency, explainability, and trustworthiness along with monitoring throughout the lifecycle of the AI application. The roadmap recommends a people-centered approach which limits AI systems to be used within defined operational boundaries, maintaining appropriate human oversight. Likewise, the guidance from FAA for the aerospace industry focuses on ensuring that AI-based systems are shown to be reliable, predictable and safe during operation including normal and abnormal situations. Among other critical aspects, training datasets must be representative, validation procedures have to be robust, performance should be continuously monitored and risks need to be frequently assessed. The FAA also highlights the need for explainable AI techniques in order to enable certification and promote stakeholder trust. To satisfy regulative compliance, aerospace institutions needs a verifiable and valid V&V framework overseen by an organization structure designed with traceability of requirements, governance of information, verification of models tested in operations with quantified uncertainties measured through post-deployment monitoring. They advocate for maintaining model cards, datasheets and lifecycle documentation to capture characteristics of training data, underlying assumptions and operational constraints, performance metrics and retraining needs. This not only enhances transparency, it also allows for review of these certifications. While the use of AI across aerospace engineering applications continues to expand, established aerospace standards combined with emerging AI assurance methodologies will be critical for ensuring safe, reliable, and certifiable AI-enabled systems. Thus, a structured certification and assurance framework is required to reconcile powerful AI technology capabilities with stringent safety requirements modern aerospace operations.

FUTURE RESEARCH DIRECTIONS

Further advancement in the application of AI to aerospace engineering will be derailed towards creating more resilient, interpretable, and data-efficient models that can be implemented in safety-critical processes. The pressure to use hybrid methods that integrate physics-based models with data-driven methods is increasing to enhance the degree of accuracy and generalization. The development of the digital twins, autonomy systems, and real-time optimization should also contribute to even greater efficiency in design and operations. Also, a combination of AI and sustainable engineering practices will assist in the advancement of environmental-friendly aerospace systems. In general, the future work is going to focus on reliability, certification preparedness, and interdisciplinary cooperation.

New AI in The Aerospace Engineering

Aerospace The field of AI is increasingly poised to revolutionize aerospace with a collection of burgeoning technologies, such as physics-informed deep learning, high-throughput and autonomous materials discovery, digital-twin-aided design, and parallel/intelligent system solutions to those of engineering problems. Some current trends are the introduction of materials genomics and autonomous AI-controlled laboratories to speed up materials discovery and optimization, which have on-demand applications in high-temperature-coatings and cutting-edge-materials applied to aerospace. Parallel intelligence, in which computation, human and domain knowledge are engaged within agile interdisciplinary processes provides an avenue to approach genuinely complex, multi-physics aerospace challenges as well as to rethink how design, analysis, and decision-making are worked in concert. These guidelines are also supported by the literature that AI-enabled manufacturing, robotics, and digital-twin infrastructures are quickly maturing in Industry 4.0, which forms the basis of AI-enabled, data-driven aerospace ecosystems (Kaur and Bhatia, 2024). Together, they indicate that the future of aerospace systems, materials, coatings, and structural components is a scenario where AI serves as an agent of quick exploration, more secure certification and smarter optimization of the life-cycle of aerospace systems, including materials, coatings and structural components Moreover, the wider governance and socio-technical environment of AI in safety-critical aerospace is also being acknowledged and it is important to both pair any technical progress with open explanation, risk evaluation, and strong verification systems. All these multifaceted directions are a way to a path of AI-enabled aerospace innovations, which are faster and smarter, but also trustworthy and certifiable in real-world operations.

AI-Driven Design Automation

Aerospace design automation may be greatly increased through AI-based generative design, surrogate-assisted optimization, and multi-fidelity, which can be complimented by model-based systems engineering (MBSE) and digital twins. Design automation based on AI can be applied in concept generation, topology optimization, and parametric exploration and ensure that the automation is done without breaking safety and certification limits. Design-space exploration at scales of near real-time is supported by the use of data-driven surrogates, physics-informed priors, and search guided by reinforcement learning, allowing the exploration of design spaces in aerospace by objective of a large scale within at least approximately a quarter of a minute. A review of manufacturing robotics case evidence and intelligent manufacturing reviews show that AI can systematically shorten design-cycle times, assist in multi-objective optimization as well as combine with physical testing and certification processes, which provides a roadmap to aerospace applications where high fidelity testing is expensive and time-intensive. In addition to pure efficiency benefits, AI-based design automation also focuses on transparency, understandability, and traceability, which supports certification and safety arguments, which fit the governance-oriented viewpoints of AI in aviation. In the future, researchers are advised to enhance principled MBSE-AI integration, introduce uniform V&V of generative designs, and create data-grounded design libraries enhancing extrapolation between design families (Zhao et al., 2024).

AI-Assisted Advanced Manufacturing

The intersection of AI and highly sophisticated manufacturing, which can now also be described as additive manufacturing, robotics, process monitoring, and feedback through the use of digital twins, will redefine the process by which aerospace components are designed, manufactured, and qualified. The existing state of AI research on intelligent manufacturing and AI-enhanced robotics offers real-world examples of speedups, quality enhancements, and versatile production system capabilities that can be readily applied to the aerospace manufacturing setting (e.g., aerospace coats, turbine components, and composite parts .The combination of AI and digital twins, as well as AIoT-enabled systems, is needed to support remote diagnostics, predictive maintenance, and in-process quality control, which allows having smarter and more resilient manufacturing ecosystems meeting the strict certification demands of aerospace. Besides that, the literature states that CAD/CAM and AI-powered design processes have the potential to reduce development time, enhance manufacturability, and improve risk in complex aerospace assemblies, particularly with additive manufacturing practices. Although these trends are encouraging, researchers are encouraged to resolve issues in integrating data, standardizing interfaces between design and manufacturing tools, and designing effective risk-informed decision-making frameworks that are certifiable AI-driven manufacturing in aerospace environments. Table 7 emphasizes the role of artificial intelligence in providing sustainable and green aerospace systems by optimization of materials, structures, and operations. The use of AI methods makes it possible to consume less fuel, have higher thermal efficiency, and manage the lifecycle in an environmentally friendly way. All in all, AI-based solutions contribute to the creation of low-emission, sustainable, and energy-efficient aerospace solutions.

Table 7. AI Applications for Sustainable and Green Aerospace Systems

Application Area	AI Technique Used	Sustainability Focus	Key Profits
Weight Reduction	Generative design, topology optimization	Lightweight structures	Reduced fuel consumption, improved efficiency
Energy-Efficient Flight	Reinforcement learning, optimization algorithms	Flight path and energy optimization	Lower emissions, optimized fuel usage
Materials & Coatings Optimization	Surrogate modeling, Bayesian optimization, active learning	Advanced coatings and materials	Improved thermal efficiency, reduced environmental impact
Thermal Management Systems	AI-driven modeling, predictive analytics	Smart heat management	Enhanced system efficiency, reduced energy loss
Lifecycle Assessment & Maintenance	Digital twins, prognostics, ML models	Sustainable maintenance and disposal	Extended lifecycle, reduced waste, predictive maintenance
Integrated System Optimization	Multi-objective AI optimization	Materials, structures, propulsion systems	Holistic sustainability improvement, system-level efficiency

Opportunities in Interdisciplinary Research.

The AI direction within the aerospace field is interdisciplinary in nature, including materials science, control theory, computational mechanics, MBSE, ethics, human-machine interaction, and regulation. Parallel-intelligence Parallel-intelligence concepts are based on working together in computational, cognitive, and domain-specific domains of knowledge to solve multi-physics aerospace problems in a consistent, auditable manner. According to sociotechnical and governance views, it is important to combine safety, risk, and ethics with new technical innovations, such as certification routes and transparency demands of AI-enabled aerospace systems. Recent studies of AI skills in engineering labor markets, curricula, and professional education requirements are also a foreground of workforce issues and educational implications of interdisciplinary AI skills in aerospace, highlighting the significance of cross-disciplinary programs that combine AI, aerospace engineering, manufacturing, and systems engineering. Lastly, the overlap between digital twins, AI and Industry 4.0 gives academia, industry, and regulators an ideal place to exchange ideas to co-create aerospace ecosystems that could be certifiable, safe, and scalable through AI. Coherent research agenda is thus encouraged to contribute to formation of multidisciplinary teams, collective data management and mutual establishment of standards and certification frameworks to facilitate widespread implementation of AI in the aerospace fields.

CONCLUSION

The chapter has shown that AI is changing the field of aerospace engineering by providing quicker, more effective, and data-driven solutions in the fields of aerodynamic analysis, structural design, materials engineering, and autonomous systems. Restricting the predictive accuracy of traditional computational tools (CFD and FEA) to predictive machine learning, deep learning and physics-informed models along with reduced computational cost and design time has been achieved significantly. The use of AI in surrogate models of the design process and in generative design has contributed to exploration of intricate design spaces, multi-objective design optimization, and innovation of aerospace systems, while digital twin technologies have helped to improve predictive maintenance, system monitoring and decision-making.AI has also been used to speed up the discovery of materials and to predict its properties, enabling lifecycle analysis, and digital twins have facilitated predictive maintenance, system monitoring and decision-making. All these developments make aerospace systems perform better, be more reliable, and sustainable but the implementation of AI within the aerospace engineering also has a great number of challenges, such as data shortage, interpretability of models, validation, and certification in safety-critical systems. The solution to these problems involves the creation of explainable AI, powerful verification schemes, and hybrid physics-data solutions. The next generation of aerospace technologies should be introduced through interdisciplinary cooperation, the standardized approaches, and the combination of AI and sustainable engineering approaches to make the implementation of the next-generation technology safe and reliable.

REFERENCES

Fakhraian, E., Šemanjski, I., Šemanjski, S., & Aghezzaf, E. (2023). Towards Safe and Efficient Unmanned Aircraft System Operations: Literature Review of Digital Twins' Applications and European Union Regulatory Compliance. *Drones (Basel)*, *7*(7), 478. Advance online publication. DOI: 10.3390/drones7070478

Hu, L., Yan, X., & Yuan, Y. (2025). Development and Challenges of Autonomous Electric Vertical Take-Off and Landing Aircraft. *Heliyon*, *11*(1), e41055. Advance online publication. DOI: 10.1016/j.heliyon.2024.e41055 PMID: 39758371

Kabashkin, I., & Shoshin, L. (2024). Artificial Intelligence of Things as New Paradigm in Aviation Health Monitoring Systems. *Future Internet*, *16*(8), 276. Advance online publication. DOI: 10.3390/fi16080276

Kaur, H., & Bhatia, M. (2024). Scientometric Insights of Digital Twins in Industry 4.0. https://doi.org/DOI: 10.21203/rs.3.rs-4380510/v1

Roy, R., Sabatini, A., Blasch, E., Kramer, K., Fasano, G., Majid, I., Crespillo, O. G., Brown, D. A., & Major, R. O. (2020). Avionics Systems Panel Research and Innovation Perspectives. *IEEE Aerospace and Electronic Systems Magazine*, *35*(12), 58–72. Advance online publication. DOI: 10.1109/MAES.2020.3033475

Shen, Y., Huang, Z., Li, J., Fey, M., & Brecher, C. (2025). A Survey on AI-Driven Digital Twins in Industry 4.0: Smart Manufacturing and Advanced Robotics. *Sensors (Basel)*. Advance online publication. DOI: 10.3390/s21196340

Singh, M., Fuenmayor, E., Hinchy, E. P., Qiao, Y., Murray, N., & Devine, D. M. (2021). Digital Twin: Origin to Future. *Applied System Innovation*, *4*(2), 36. Advance online publication. DOI: 10.3390/asi4020036

Stanton, I., Munir, K., Ikram, A., & El-Bakry, M. (2022). Predictive Maintenance Analytics and Implementation for Aircraft: Challenges and Opportunities. *Systems Engineering*. Advance online publication. DOI: 10.1002/sys.21651

Sun, H., Song, B., Sun, X., Cui, X. P., Liu, Z., Cong, M., Sun, M., Zhu, Z., Tian, Y., Liu, S., Xu, P., Dai, B., & Wang, L. (2025). Recent Representative Progress of Surface Coating Technology. *Chemical Record (New York, N.Y.)*, *25*(8), e202500054. Advance online publication. DOI: 10.1002/tcr.202500054 PMID: 40342263

Wang, W. Y., Zhang, S., Li, G., Lu, J., Ren, Y., Wang, X., Gao, X., Su, Y., Song, H., & Li, J. (2024). *Artificial Intelligence Enabled Smart Design and Manufacturing of Advanced Materials: The Endless Frontier in AI$^+$ Era*. Materials Genome Engineering Advances., DOI: 10.1002/mgea.56

Wang, Z., Liu, X., Chen, H., Yang, T., & He, Y. (2023). Exploring Multi-Fidelity Data in Materials Science: Challenges, Applications, and Optimized Learning Strategies. *Applied Sciences (Basel, Switzerland)*, *13*(24), 13176. Advance online publication. DOI: 10.3390/app132413176

Wild, G., Nanyonga, A., Iqbal, A., Bano, S., Somerville, A., & Pollock, L. (2025). Lightweight and Mobile Artificial Intelligence and Immersive Technologies in Aviation. *Visual Computing for Industry, Biomedicine, and Art*, *8*(1), 21. Advance online publication. DOI: 10.1186/s42492-025-00203-z PMID: 40900374

Zhang, X., Zeng, Z., Peng, W., Chen, H., Chu, J., Wei, M. S., & Xu, R. (2024). Research and Implementation of Key Intelligent Detection Technologies Based on Deep Learning. https://doi.org/DOI: 10.1117/12.3055351

Zhang, Z., Wei, Z., Court, S., Yang, L., Wang, S., Thirunavukarasu, A., & Zhao, Y. (2024). A Review of Digital Twin Technologies for Enhanced Sustainability in the Construction Industry. *Buildings (Basel, Switzerland)*, *14*(4), 1113. Advance online publication. DOI: 10.3390/buildings14041113

Zhao, Z., Baumann, A., & Ryan, E. (2024). Using Machine-Learning-Aided Computational Fluid Dynamics to Facilitate Design of Experiments. *Industrial & Engineering Chemistry Research*, *63*(49), 21444–21454. Advance online publication. DOI: 10.1021/acs.iecr.4c03042

Chapter 5
Smart Home System Based on Feature Selection and Load Signature of Appliances

Sabyasachi Pramanik
http://orcid.org/0000-0002-9431-8751
Haldia Institute of Technology, India

ABSTRACT

With the quick development of smart home technology, new ways to improve daily living via automation and intelligent systems have emerged. Finding and analysing common household behaviours is a crucial part of this progress, since it may significantly increase safety, comfort, and energy efficiency. The goal of this chapter is to develop a machine learning-based model that can identify typical behaviours in smart homes using feature selection, neural networks, and the load signatures of household appliances. To assess the effectiveness of the suggested approach, a thorough experimental setup is constructed in a simulated smart home environment. A wide range of everyday chores and appliance usage patterns are included in the dataset used to evaluate the model. By assessing the model's ability to adjust to novel and unforeseen difficulties, it also demonstrates its potential for ongoing learning and development. The study's findings show that feature selection and neural networks may significantly improve the accuracy and robustness of smart home daily activity detection.

DOI: 10.4018/979-8-2600-3280-0.ch005

INTRODUCTION

It has been evident in recent years that one of the biggest issues of the contemporary era is the startling pace at which the world's population is growing. Currently, one of the most pressing issues we confront is the phenomena of global warming. The contemporary world is now devoting a great deal of attention and effort to this subject, which has been deemed one of the most important concerns to arise since the dawn of human existence on our planet. This is due to the fact that it is regarded as one of the most significant issues that have ever emerged. It is a problem that has been considered one of the most significant issues from the beginning of human history. The term "global warming" describes a phenomenon that has been defined as a rise in both the average temperature of the Earth's atmosphere and the average temperature of the world's seasons. It has been determined that both of these modifications are taking place at the same time. This phenomenon has expanded more widely in recent decades than it did in earlier ones. As a consequence of this disaster, the environment and climate will undergo a variety of changes, some of which may be deemed potentially catastrophic.

Research undertaken in many locations throughout the continents indicates that the earth's average temperature is increasing by 0.20 degrees Celsius every ten years. Around the globe, a variety of climatic and ecological changes are taking place as a direct result of the observed increase in temperature. The fact that the Green House Effect plays a major role in the phenomena known as global warming is a well-established scientific fact. A number of scientists have accepted this truth. It is well known that this information has been extensively disseminated around the globe and is recognised by the majority of individuals. For this, an extra citation is required."There is a requirement for an additional citation for this." The greenhouse effect has recently come to light as a major cause for worry due to the increasing pace at which it happens as a direct consequence of human activities. The reason for this is because it has been made public. The main force for life in the past was the greenhouse effect, which was once the main force behind life on Earth. This is a major cause for worry as it served as the first basis for life on Earth. It is now one of the most important challenges that people everywhere must overcome. The pace at which it is happening as a direct result of this is rising, and a significant portion of the acceleration that is taking place is due to human activity. For a very long time, this has been occurring since the greenhouse effect has been the fundamental factor sustaining life on Earth for such a long time. This process is known as the "greenhouse effect" and happens when heat from various sources, such as the sun, is absorbed and then kept from leaving the planet's atmosphere by certain gases. The greenhouse effect is exacerbated by this event. As a result, the temperature of the atmosphere around the planet will increase. Solar radiation is a phenomenon that is defined as heat that is absorbed from the sun but is subsequently kept from penetrating the planet's atmosphere. This occurrence, where heat does not exit the earth's atmosphere after being absorbed by the sun, might be referred to as the phenomenon in which heat does not leave the planet itself. This has directly contributed to the rise in the temperature of the Earth's atmosphere, which is found across the whole planet. The fundamental factor that makes it possible to maintain a constant level of heat is the presence of many different greenhouse gases in the atmosphere. Methane, water vapour, and carbon dioxide are just a few of the many compounds that fall under this group of gases. The rapid industrialisation that has occurred in all has caused a rise in the quantity of greenhouse gases emitted into the atmosphere worldwide. The fact that this is involved is one of the major factors that are directly causing the situation to worsen. This has directly led to a rapid and severe escalation of the issue. This had the immediate consequence of making things somewhat worse than they had been before. The current state of affairs is substantially worse than it would have been in the absence of these most recent developments. Deforestation has transformed lush rainforests—which are the principal habitat for plants and animals that absorb carbon dioxide from the atmosphere—into concrete jungles in order to meet the demands of our growing population. The best approach to eliminate carbon dioxide from the atmosphere is to surround you with green rainforests. Green rainforests are mostly responsible for the removal of carbon dioxide from the atmosphere. This is concerning as large rainforests are the primary locations for collecting carbon dioxide from the atmosphere. One of the most effective ways to reduce the amount of carbon dioxide in the atmosphere is to preserve the remaining tropical rainforests across the globe. Compared to more naturally occurring ecosystems, concrete jungles have a significantly reduced capacity to absorb carbon dioxide. The ability of tropical rainforests to participate in the process of removing carbon dioxide from the environment they live in is crucial. The chemical process that is in charge of this is called photosynthesis. Finding the solutions to this significant problem within the parameters of their own fields of expertise within the body of knowledge is now the responsibility of every scientist and researcher in the globe. This is a direct consequence of the current circumstance.

By expanding our knowledge of how to maximise heat that would otherwise be wasted under various circumstances, the current thesis adds to our corpus of existing knowledge. Commons use Commons use Modern industrial processes send high-temperature flue gases into the atmosphere, which are being utilised to warm the air. This heat is now being used to warm the air instead of being wasted. This heat was not used effectively in the past. The quantity of heat had decreased before that. This heat would have spread from the sky into the surroundings a long time ago. Heat exchangers, recuperators, regenerators (Lin, YH. et al. 2022), heat pipe exchangers, rotary heat exchangers, economisers, and heat pumps are a few of the specialised devices that exploit the waste heat produced by flue gases in the contemporary world. Two more parts of this equipment are economic optimisers and regenerative systems. Utilising the heat produced by trash more effectively is made feasible by this device. As a consequence, the quantity of energy lost due to pointless tasks is effectively decreased. By using these technological innovations, thermal energy that would otherwise be squandered may be transformed into energy that can be used in a beneficial way. Without these tools at our disposal, all that heat would be squandered. In commercial and industrial settings, it is being investigated as a potentially useful device for capturing heat from flue gases. Regenerators, another name for regenerative heat recovery devices, are being studied as part of the current research project. This is being conducted throughout the research project. Such heat has the potential to be used as an energy source for a variety of different applications. Here are some instances of "regenerative heat recovery systems," a term used to categorise the kind of technology being discussed here. This study is now being conducted as part of the project, which is currently enduring difficult effort to be completed.

LITERATURE REVIEW

Over a long and noteworthy period of time, researchers have shown a great deal of interest in thermal regenerators. This sensation of surprise has lingered for a lengthy amount of time. This conundrum has been common for a substantial length of time. The first 10 years of the 20th century witnessed the commencement of the widespread use of thermal regenerators in commercial and industrial contexts. Due to the success of this attempt, a significant amount of research has been conducted in this field during the decades that have passed since its completion. After 1950, academic and scientific communities worldwide started receiving a large volume of research publications addressing a broad variety of diverse theoretical and practical elements of thermal regenerators. These papers were published in academic publications and peer-reviewed scientific journals. These tests' results were published in a number of scholarly journals. Numerous academic and scientific institutions spread around the globe have access to these papers. This chapter gives a succinct account of the theoretical and practical work that has been done on fixed bed regenerators by a broad spectrum of academics and scientists in the past, starting with the field's inception in 1920 and continuing through its most recent modernization. This work may be split down into two categories: theoretical and practical. This chapter first gives a thorough history of the discipline, starting in 1920 and concluding with its most recent modernization. This section also starts in 1920, the year the field was founded, and continues until the present, when it's most recent development took place. Three viewpoints might be used to analyze this collection of work: theoretical, historical or experimental. Each of these strategies has a unique mix of benefits and drawbacks.

This chapter is divided into two separate sections, which may be summed up as follows:

- An examination of a regenerator with a permanent bed takes into account both the theoretical and practical aspects of the subject.
- A CFD research was carried out so that the issue with the fixed bed regenerator could be appreciated in greater depth. Experimental and theoretical research on fixed-bed regenerators (Waseem, Q., et al. 2025) developed a mathematical model of the fundamental packed bed regenerator for transient heat transfer. It was observed that a one-dimensional heat flow was the most successful approach for managing the fluid phase of the experiment, whereas a packed bed was the most effective method for controlling the solid component of the experiment. To create a solid groundwork for the inquiry, it was agreed to employ these recommendations as the criterion for the experiment. This choice was made in order to build a strong foundation. The most important assumptions used in order to construct the model were that the flow was a plug flow, that heat conduction within the solid phase could be ignored, and that the regenerator wall was most likely insulated, which meant that heat loss from the wall could also be ignored. When constructing the model, a number of additional assumptions were taken into account in addition to the hypotheses discussed above. These are only a few of the many instances that were cited to bolster the hypotheses; there were many more. Several assumptions were included into the model's creation at different stages. Despite the fact that the fluid being supplied had a constantly fluctuating temperature, the results were first presented on the assumption that the regenerator was running at a constant temperature. In order to convey the findings to the audience in a more simplified manner, this assumption was made. It was then hypothesized that the regenerator's thermal conductivity would be very high in the direction perpendicular to the fluid flow and very low in the direction fluid flowed through the apparatus. This was one of the predictions provided by the regenerator model. Put another way, it was assumed that the material's heat conductivity would not be restricted by the flow direction. This was one of the most often expressed model-related misunderstandings in discussions. It was usually considered that the heat transfer coefficient would be the same no matter what conditions were being compared. There was no scientific evidence to support this notion. P. C. Carman incorporated the findings of many experiments on pebble bed regenerators in his study published in 1937. The

purpose of these experiments was to ascertain the wall effect and the pressure decrease along the bed. He started by figuring out the flow's coefficient of drag after modifying it such that it crawled over the pebble substrate. He was able to successfully do his task as a direct result of this. He finished the work, and as a direct consequence, he received a flawless score. The D/dp ratio (Chabane, L., et al. 2024) —the diameter of the column divided by the diameter of the particles—was kept low throughout the experiment, specifically at a value of less than 15. When all three elements are present concurrently, we notice a large divergence from Ergun's equation concerning the pressure reduction that directly derives from their interaction. This was a significant finding since it demonstrated that, contrary to what the preceding statement suggested, the Ergun equation did not function properly for D/dp values less than 15. The previous remark served as the direct push for the occurrence of this. This was discovered as a result of the preceding assertion. In order to calculate pressure drop and drag across a packed bed under turbulent flow conditions (Reynolds number larger than 1000) and for D/dp ratios of 2.67, 5.32, and 9.91, respectively, (Das, S.K., et al. 2024) carried out many tests. The purpose of this was to figure out how to calculate pressure drop and drag through a packed bed. The test results were published in the peer-reviewed journal Science of Chemical Engineering. Lastly, (Ahmad, S.S., et al. 2024) conducted an experiment in a fixed bed regenerator to examine the wall effect under creeping flow conditions with D/dp values of 6.2, 8, and 12.8. The results of this experiment were written up and released as a book for anybody interested in reading about them. The procedures used for this experiment were the same as those used for other studies. In 1952, S. Ergun and his colleagues performed research on an attached bed to imitate the conditions of fully evolved flow. By connecting the Burke-Plummer equation for the turbulent flow regime with the Kozeny-Carman equation for the creeping flow phase, they developed a semi- empirical relationship between the two equations. As a consequence, they were able to model the transition from the creeping flow phase to the turbulent flow regime. They were able to capitalize on this situation and investigate the relationship between the creeping flow phase and the turbulent flow regime. They were able to replicate the interaction between the two equations as a result. This put them in a good position since they could look into how the two equations related to one another. They were in a terrific position because of this. To precisely compute the pressure drop in thermal regenerators, utilizing the equation with the two coefficients 150 and 1.75. You may find this equation here. Everyone involved has shown a great deal of excitement and support for our proposal. Even though the equation may be used in a broad range of circumstances, we will focus on the one presented here since it is one of the most usual. Given that the equation has two integer coefficients, both of which have positive values, this is the case.

HEAT EXCHANGERS AND THEIR TYPES

The use of a device commonly known as a heat exchanger is necessary for the proper completion of the heat transfer process between two fluids. The practice of transferring heat, or "heat exchange," is another name for the technique used to alter the temperature. It is feasible to distinguish between the three primary types of heat exchangers (Fakhruldeen, H.F., et al. 2025). A few names for the kinds of heat exchangers are transmural, indirect contact, and direct contact. Sorting all those fluids into the proper groups is best done using a method that takes heat transfer rates into account. For instance, recuperators, storage type heat exchangers, and fluidized bed heat exchangers are the three other types into which indirect contact heat exchangers may be divided. To assist knowledge of the category structure, Figure 1.1 separates the category into its parts. Three unique kinds of heat exchangers are depicted below, with recuperators, storage heat exchangers, and fluidized bed heat exchangers being the most common and least common, respectively. You may read a more in-depth examination of each of these categories lower down the page.

Figure 1. Classification of Heat exchangers based on the heat transfer process

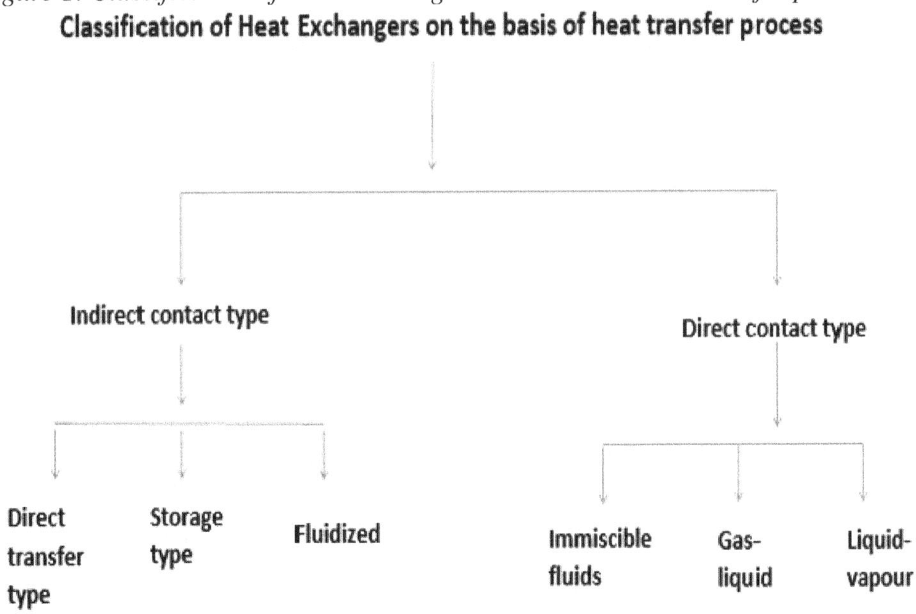

REGENERATORS OF HEAT

A heat regenerator is an enclosed container that has the capability to catch significant quantities of thermal energy and store it in a variety of metals or ceramics that may change in shape and size. The phrase "heat bank" is often used when referring to this kind of container. This is due to the fact that heat is stored in heat banks. The many parts that go into making a heat regenerator might also be called "heat storage" or "heat absorbers," for example, depending on the particular circumstances that are being addressed. The recuperator cannot operate effectively because there is no touch between the fluids that comprise it and the wall that divides them. Conversely, this wall must be able to let heat through while still enabling fluids to do their jobs. Since the wall is incredibly thin, there is a very low probability that the liquids will come into touch with one another. This is because the wall creates seclusion. A storage-type heat exchanger, on the other hand, is characterized by the fact that it leads the fluid via a pebble bed (matrix), so absorbing the heat that was previously stored in one fluid and transferring it to another fluid. This heat exchanger is called a matrix exchanger. This phenomenon occurs because the fluid acts as a storage-type heat exchanger. Therefore, in order to achieve the objectives of this approach, a storage heat exchanger is required. A particular kind of heat exchanger called a storage heat exchanger is at the center of our conversation today. The word "storage," which is suitable for describing the process, is used to describe what is now happening. This activity is carried out in two separate cycles inside storage-type heat exchangers: the first cycle is known as the heating cycle, and the second cycle is known as the cooling cycle. Simply referring to the cycle covers both periods. Any one of the two cycles might be referred to as a "cycle" in this context. It is possible to use the word "cycle" to describe any of these two distinct cycles. They are both regarded to be cyclic. The term "cycle" may refer to any one of a number of different cycles in this context. The gas is forced to pass through the heat exchanger against its will in order to complete the heating process even when it has already attained the necessary temperature. In the end, the heat that is created by the gas will be transferred to a bed of stones after it has had the chance to travel the appropriate distance to arrive at its purpose. The flow of cold gas and the flow of cold fluid must follow the same route throughout the cooling process. Such a requirement has to be fulfilled. It will be much easier to keep the gas at a constant temperature going forward because we have access to this new information. This increases the likelihood that there won't be any discernible variations in the gas's temperature. During this process, the pebble bed is responsible for heating the gas, and the heat that is created by the gas is subsequently passed to the fluid. As a result, the fluid eventually reaches a temperature higher than it was at the start of the operation.

Unlike recuperators (George & Selvakumar, 2024) a heat exchanger of the storage type stores heat in a pebble bed for later rejection. Recuperators, on the other hand, do transfer heat through walls. Another kind of heat exchanger that is available is a recuperator. Heat is transported throughout the recuperator via the wall. In contrary to what would typically take place, heat is conveyed in the opposite manner when a recuperator-type heat exchanger is used. While recuperators act in the other manner, they are responsible for pushing heat through the wall in the other direction.

On the other hand, the equipment that is answerable for the flow of heat through the wall is referred to as a recuperator. The most common form of heat exchanger used in energy storage applications is the regeneration type. This term makes it easy to identify the particular heat exchanger that is the topic of the fourth discussion. One bed of these regenerators may allow cold gas to flow through it, while the other bed may allow hot gas to flow. This is a result of how these regenerators were made. Therefore, to ensure a consistent supply of labor, it is required to employ not just one but at least two fixed-bed regenerators concurrently. There is the possibility for maximum efficiency owing to the layout of the two beds. Alternatively, to put it another way, it is feasible for both hot and cold gases to flow through the beds at the same time. Because of this technical advancement, it is now feasible to simultaneously refresh both hot and cold gas. Previously, this was not feasible. Figure 2 is a visual representation of this design, which can be summarized as follows: there will be two parallel fixed bed regenerators positioned in a way that is analogous to the one that was just described. In order to guarantee that the regenerator performs effectively and to the largest degree that is practicable, it is important to open and shut the valve at suitable time intervals. In order to attain this purpose, it is necessary to make certain that the valve is opened and closed in the correct method. If you keep to your timetable with great care, there is a probability that you will be able to reach your aim.

Figure 2. Fixed bed heat regenerator

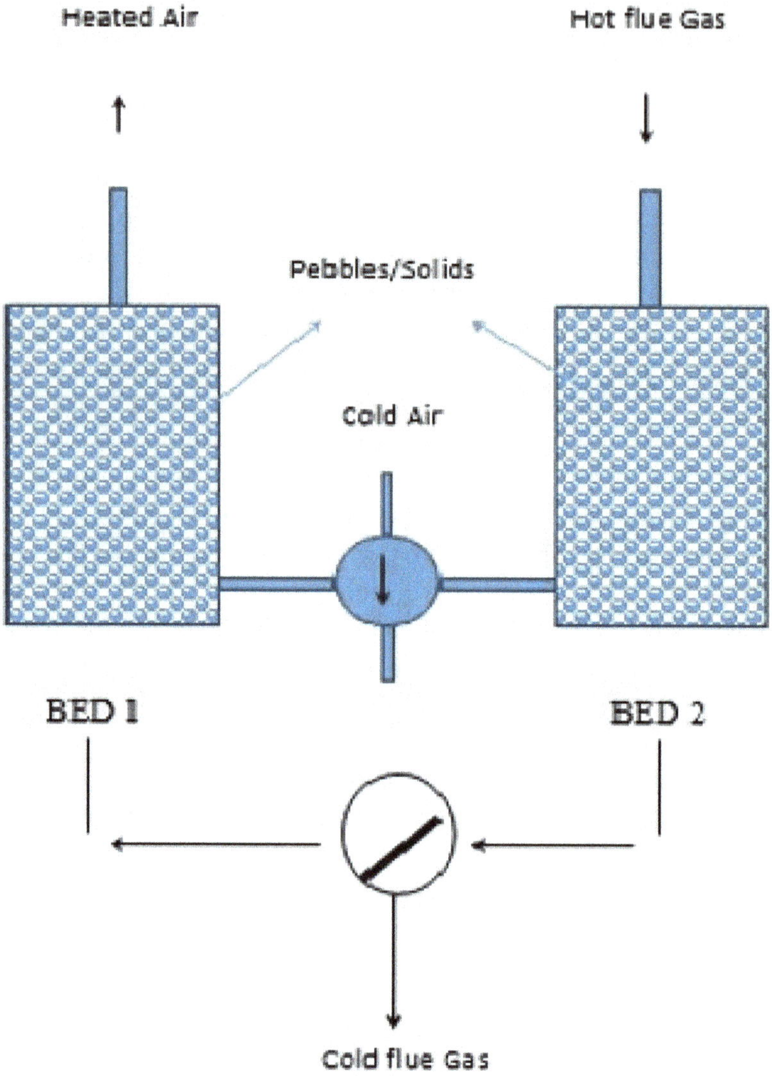

It is crucial that the packing materials used in regenerator beds have a significant volumetric heat capacity and very low thermal conductivity in the direction of the axial flow. Considering that the flow is axial, this is the case. This is a necessity that is really important. As a consequence of this direction being the one in which the flow is directed to a larger degree than in any other direction, this circumstance has come about accordingly. The temperature at which the regenerator is designed to be running should be greater than 20 degrees Celsius. This is why the specific heat of most materials is on the lower side below this temperature, which maybe a key problem effecting the functioning of the regenerator. This behavior happens because the specific heat of the vast majority of materials is lower on the lower side below this temperature. Below this temperature, the specific heat of most diverse materials is on the lower end of the range. This is the cause of the situation.

HEAT REGENERATOR TYPES

In the paragraph that came before this one, the word "heat storage heat exchanger" was stated in reference to a regenerator. This sentence was mentioned explicitly in this paragraph. The term "heat storage" and "heat exchanger" were combined to create this statement. Heat is moved from one place to another using the heat exchanger that is detailed in this article. There is a lot of application for this heat exchanger. This is made possible by the use of the regenerator's matrix, also known as the bed, which is composed of solid particles. Air and flue gas may sometimes enter and leave the system when using a moving bed, like the one seen in Figure. This establishes the prerequisites for the system's correct operation. The flow of gas to and from the stationary matrices and beds is controlled by valves on both sides of the system, as may be seen in Figure 3, which illustrates a Rotary Regenerator. Examining the diagram will show you how this works. The designations 2 and 3 for regenerators with permanent beds correspond to the two distinct kinds of regenerators shown in Figures 2 and 3. The two kinds of regenerators are shown in these images. Two different examples of the many sorts of regenerators that are now available are shown in Figures 2 and 3. Two unique examples of the numerous kinds of regenerators that are available are illustrated in Figures 2 and 3 respectively. These regenerators are only a few of the many options. For a regenerator to be able to perform its designated function reliably and without interruption while in operation, it must have both of these qualities.

"Fixed bed heat regenerator" is the same as "periodic-flow regenerator" and "swing regenerator," respectively, when referring to a piece of equipment. These words are used interchangeably. It is important to keep in mind that even if each of these different names relates to the same piece of hardware, this should be taken into account. These two sentences may be used interchangeably in every setting since they are relevant to all circumstances.

Figure 3. Rotary regenerator

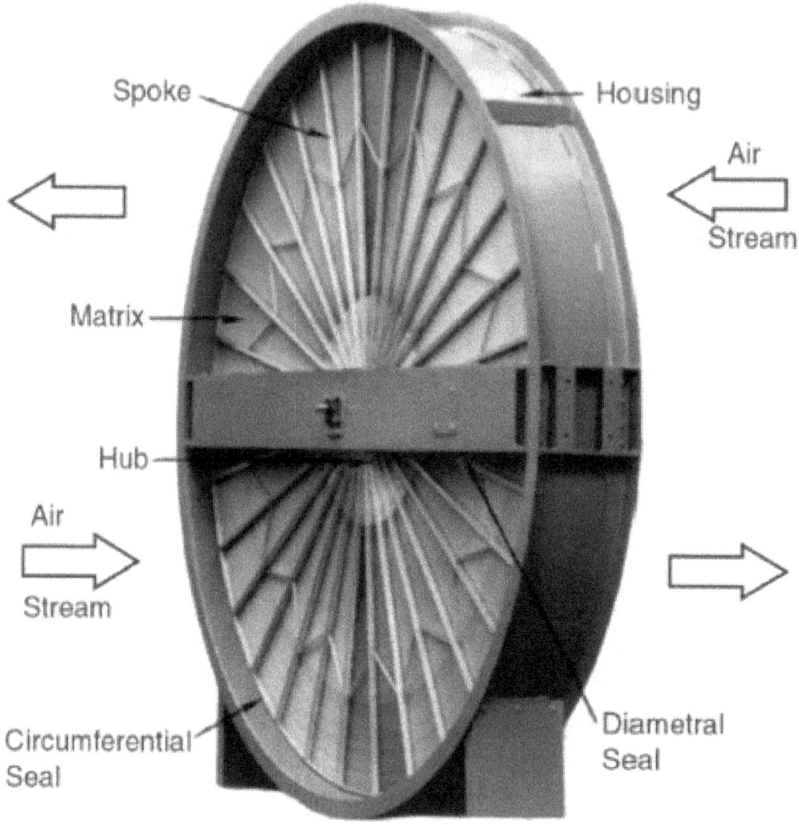

ADVANTAGES OF REGENERATOR

Heat regenerator has a number of important advantages.

- The regenerator is lighter and more space-efficient than the recuperator, but the recuperator is heavier and requires more room. In a similar vein, the regenerator is smaller than the generator. When compared to the recuperator, the regenerator is the option that delivers the biggest advantages in terms of value for money. This is due of the two benefits described before. Furthermore, compared to the region directly next to it, the recuperator's surface area encompasses a much larger amount of the territory. This is a major benefit.

- A recuperator, which transfers the same amount of heat from one place to another, is much more expensive to make than a regenerator. This is why the regenerator is a device that creates heat. In contrast, the recuperator will be in charge of moving the heat throughout the whole process.
- Since recuperators result in a bigger total cost than regenerators, and because they suffer a higher cost per material quantity than regenerators themselves.
- Since the regenerator functions in a mode that is separate from that of the recuperator, it is not essential for the regenerator to have a core that is waterproof in the same manner that it is necessary for the recuperator. Firstly, this is due to the fact that the regenerator is not a recuperator, as stated in the previous sentence. The regenerator and the recuperator both carry out their different responsibilities in a discrete way, which is the explanation for this discovery. However, the function that the gadget is meant to accomplish will determine the precise combination of these elements. For example, it is feasible to make the mixture of a range of components in the case of regenerators; nevertheless, the exact composition of these components will vary. Metals, ceramics, alloys, polymers, and a broad range of other materials are some of the materials that may be used in the production process of these components. It's also possible that a combination of these and other materials were used to manufacture these parts.
- The fabrication of the regenerator itself is less complicated than the manufacturing of the recuperator's portions. This is because building a regenerator is easier than developing its individual parts. This is due to the fact that creating a regenerator is easier than creating its constituent parts.
- On the other hand, regenerators are differentiated from recuperators by the existence of a matrix or bed surface that is capable of autonomously maintaining cleanliness. Due to the limitations imposed on them, recuperators are not allowed to employ this specific talent. This lowers the quantity of corrosion and fouling caused by exhaust gases. This also results in a decrease in the amount of corrosion that takes place. Heat regenerators are a desirable technique for heat transmission to recuperators when an efficiency of more than 85 percent is needed for a specific application. This is because heat regenerators generate heat on their own. All of these benefits, in their own distinctive style, add to the overall brilliance of this notion, which is amplified by the contributions that each of them makes.

REGENERATOR APPLICATIONS

There are numerous different areas that make use of reactors. Metallurgy, glass manufacturing, air separation facilities, solar energy storage, and burning volatile organic compounds are a few of these industries. Regenerators may also be used in each of the following commercial businesses: Regenerators offer a broad range of other uses that might possibly be developed in addition to the ones that have already been covered.

PRESSURE DROP AND DRAG COEFFICIENT IN FIXEDBED REGENERATOR

The equation Ergun created and found in Ergun may be used to calculate the amount of pressure drop that has taken place within the regenerator if a flow has attained full maturity. You may find Ergun's equation here, which was published in the year it was written. In 1952, there is a chance that the person with the answers to this predicament is Ergun. This equation is only valid if the D/dp ratio is more than 15. The norms for consistency in the void fraction have been satisfied, as shown by this ratio. Until anything occurs before then, it will not be possible to confirm that this equation is right. It will be difficult to find a solution to the issue that has been given to you before that point. Due to the fact that this equation puts this restriction on us as a required limitation for the task that we are presently executing, we are compelled to satisfy its criteria.

The equation for an Ergun is:

$$\frac{\Delta p}{H} = 150\frac{(1-\varepsilon)^2}{\varepsilon^3}\frac{\mu U}{d_p^2} + 1.75\frac{1-\varepsilon}{\varepsilon^3}\frac{\rho U^2}{d_p}$$

Every pressure-related equation that was presented in the preceding interactions is applicable to fixed bed regenerators that have D/dp values that are larger than 15. Because regenerators with D/d values larger than 15 are assumed to have a constant void % across the bed, there is very little flow complexity in these situations. This is because the amount of space is very constant over the whole surface of the bed. This is because the percentage of empty space has not changed much over time. This specific reason may account for this phenomenon. In the course of their study, (Völker, B., et al. 2022) performed a detailed analysis on the wall effects that took place inside the regenerator. Based on the data they collected, they concluded that the pressure drop connection proposed by (Tayfor, N.B., et al. 2026) is the most likely to be true. Because of the information that they acquired, they were able to arrive at this conclusion. So, as a consequence of the data that they obtained, they came to the conclusion that this was the scenario. The flow patterns of fixed beds with D/dp values below 10 are much more complex than those of other beds. This is because the void ratio of the regenerator wall is much greater than that of the bulk area. This occurs because the void ratio in the bulk area is smaller than the one at the regenerator wall. This is because, in contrast to the bulk area, the vacancy percentage of the regenerator wall is much bigger. This is because the regenerator wall's position places it considerably beyond the bulk region's boundaries. Because of the increased vacancies that the regenerator wall carries in contrast to the bulk area, this is the present scenario. The fact that the wall of the regenerator is placed outside of the bulk area is the major source of this difficulty. In this specific case, this is the reason why things are the way they are. To create a complete portrayal of the flow structure in the regions surrounding the particles in these beds, it is only feasible to gather the information that is necessary using a flow analysis program that is fairly advanced, such as Ansys Fluent. This information may then be used to construct the depiction. It is vital to have this information in order to offer an accurate depiction of the flow. It is necessary to collect this data in order to learn more about the interaction that takes place between the flow and the particles. The previously mentioned data must be gathered in order to ascertain the kind of interaction that takes place between the flow and the particles. It could be challenging for you to accurately comprehend how the flow interacts with the system components that make up the flow if you lack this understanding. This will be performed by the use of computational fluid dynamics (CFD) simulations, and after the simulations have been conducted, the findings will be compared to the research that Reichelt carried out in 1972. One of the main objectives of this thesis is to establish a method for calculating the drag and pressure drop coefficients for a fixed bed while maintaining a D/dp ratio of less than 10. One of the most important goals that must be accomplished is the accomplishment of this one. The thesis will assess Reichlet's conclusions and compare them with those obtained from the simulations (1972). You will have to work very hard to find out how to calculate these two coefficients if you want to succeed in achieving this aim.

FLOW REGIMES IN FIXED BED REGENERATOR

There exists a substantial link between the flow regimes that are present inside the regenerator and the approaches that are employed in the construction of these features. It is crucial to remember that the regenerator's overall performance is greatly impacted by both its resistance and thermal properties. The efficacy of the regenerator's functioning is determined by a variety of elements, including its resistance as well as its

19 thermal characteristics. The thermal properties of the regenerator, in addition to its resistance, are crucial components that play a vital part in determining how effectively it carries out its functions. There is a considerable link between resistance and the efficiency with which the regenerator performs its job. Resistance is a vital component. This component, combined with the thermal characteristics of the regenerator, is a factor that should be taken into account. There have been a vast number of researchers from a broad range of academic disciplines and areas of expertise who have researched the influence of the wall on the pressure drop that the regenerator experiences in a variety of flow regimes. It is possible to apply the Ergun equation to flows, but only if the flow has reached its complete development before the equation is applied. Only flows that have completed all the stages necessary for their full development may currently be sufficiently described by the Ergun equation. The equation cannot explain flows that have not yet reached certain phases since these phases have not yet been achieved. In 1937 and 1949, respectively, Carman and Coulson gave first ideas and predictions on the wall implications of creeping flow regimes. These two theories for the future were established by Carman and Coulson, who are the aforementioned persons. As a consequence of the existence of D/dp and Reynolds values ranging from 100 to 1000, () projected that there would be a decline in pressure. In addition, they indicated that there would be a link between these two components of the partnership. Furthermore, they said that the link between these two components would be present in the future. This forecast was given to the parties in the form of an earlier prediction. The possibility that the pressure will drop in the not-too-distant future was considered as a crucial factor during the computation of this number. At the present, there is not a single study that has been carried out on the wall impacts of a fixed bed that is running in any of the three flow regimes with a D/dp ratio of 10 or less. In light of 20 the fact that there has been no inquiry into the subject topic, this is the outcome that emerges. This is because no study has been conducted to ascertain the effects that the walls have produced. This is the state of circumstances right now; nothing has changed from what it has always been. This thesis uses Re values ranging from 0.1 to 10000 to estimate the wall effects that take place within the regenerator for all flow regimes and low D/dp values (less than 12). It is envisaged that these wall effects will take occur inside the regenerator (creeping flow, transitional flow, and turbulent flow patterns). These projections are suitable for the wall effects that have been seen. In the case that the D/dp ratio is equal to or lowers than 12, it is expected that these projected wall effects may become noticeable. It is anticipated that these wall effects would become apparent anytime the number drops below 12 or the D/

dp ratio goes below 12. It is anticipated that these wall effects will activate if the D/dp number is less than 12.

THERMAL CHARACTERISTICS OF FIXED BED REGENERATOR

The second important goal of this thesis is to undertake an investigation of the impact that a number of different factors have on the thermal characteristics of the fixed bed regenerator. The first important goal that has to be achieved is the examination of the regenerator's thermal characteristics. After the approach described in this thesis is completed, it is quite probable that these two goals will have been successfully achieved. In this work, a quantitative analysis of the regenerator's thermal properties is being conducted. This is owing to the fact that the thermal characteristics of the regenerator are impacted by a broad variety of parameters that are being explored in this research. This category includes the height and length of the bed, the diameter of the regenerator, the size of the particles, the capacity to store heat, the switching time, the duration of residence, and the direction of gas flow. The length of the bed, the height, and the size of the particles are some further characteristics.

The characteristics that come under this category include the amount of heat storage capacity, the particle diameter, the regenerator diameter, the bed height or length, and the particle diameter. There are various examples of these features, including the breadth and height of the bed, the diameter of the regenerator, the size of the particles, the capacity to store heat, and the direction in which the flow is directed. This category includes things like the bed's height and length, the size of the regenerator and the particles, the amount of heat that can be stored, and the fluid's direction. Some of the factors taken into account here are the regenerator's height and length, its diameter, the size of the particles, and the amount of heat it can store in the bed. However, this list is not comprehensive. The quantity of heat that can be caught and stored is another element that has to be considered.

TRANSIENT CFD STUDY OF FIXED BED REGENERATOR

The heat regenerator must first go through two separate cycles—the heating cycle and the cooling cycle—in order to be able to do its functions. These two cycles function apart from each other. The heat regenerator may complete all of its cycles and accomplish all of the goals it set for itself. The mechanism that is responsible for the transmission of heat is present in each and every one of these cycles. The flue gases are permitted to enter the regenerator after being heated by the cycle. As a result, the flue gases may pass through the bed continually. In order to assure that the bed is capable of continually renewing itself, this is done. The heating of the material in this way leads in the appearance of this unique event. Once the packing material bed, which is responsible for absorbing heat and doing its role, has done doing what it was designed to do, the flue gases flow out of the regenerator. This happens at a lower temperature than previously. Through the process of absorbing heat, in this particular case, the packing material bed serves as a heat sink. Due to the fact that the bed of the sane regenerator rotates in such a way, the air is required to pass through it throughout the course of the cooling cycle, even when it is coming from the opposite direction. This immediately causes heat to be transported from the package's components into the surrounding air. The various parts of the package, which are responsible for these parts, then absorb the heat. Flue gases are permitted to stay contained inside the regenerator for duration of time that is measured in seconds. This amount of time is referred to as the "thermal residence time of flue gas." This specific term is a word that is used in the field of technical discourse. The term "thermal residence time of flue gas" may be found by returning to the phrase "thermal residency of flue gas," which is where the term originated. The length of this phase is frequently expressed by a particular number of seconds arranged at a set spacing. There is a substantial link between the length of time that is allowed for thermal energy to be stored within the device and the degree to which the regenerator is able to adequately carry out the work for which it was constructed. When the regenerator is left to continue operating for a longer amount of time, it will be able to execute its duty more successfully. The term "switching phase" describes the interval that occurs between the "heating cycle" and the "cooling cycle." These two cycles cooperate to maintain a constant temperature in your immediate environment. Put another way, this change is a direct outcome of the behavior that is characterized as "controlling the temperature of the world around you." Adjust the switching time as necessary to boost the regenerator's efficiency. This is the only way to increase the regenerator's efficacy. One of the most significant components of the functioning of the regenerator is the switching time, and the only way to boost the efficiency of the regenerator is to achieve perfection in the switching time. The implementation of this technique is essential since there is no other option that will raise the total effectiveness of regenerators. The model is exported so that it may be used in Ansys Fluent when its meshing in GAMBIT is finished. This makes it possible to utilize the model with ease. The model for regenerators with D/dp values of 3, 8, and 12 is then subjected to a transient simulation with a time step of 10e-3 and a switching time or cycle time of one minute. This is done in order to assess the efficacy of the model. It is done in order to assess whether or not the model is stable. A selection for the time step is made dependent on the model. This is done in order to better comprehend the temperature variations that take place along the regenerator bed's length. It was envisaged that this action would immediately and directly result in an increase in the regenerator bed's length. Until this computational fluid dynamics (CFD) simulation of flue gases during the heating cycle and ambient air during the cooling cycle is finished, a constant state in the temperature flow will be maintained. This simulation will run until the temperature flow reaches a steady state. This kind of simulation will be run throughout the cooling cycle. This narrative will take place during the period when the cycle is cooling. The flue gases will behave as if they are travelling along a conduit throughout the whole of the heating cycle. Flue gases will be used for the duration of the heating cycle that is being conducted. 1.10 Purpose of current work Ansys Fluent, a commercial program that is widely accessible and often used, will be used to help with the modeling, development, and simulation of a pebble bed regenerator within the parameters of this study. The purpose of this research is to establish the investigation's parameters. Ansys Fluent is the name of this specific program. Researching the apparatus's flow, temperature, and resistance characteristics will be another aspect of this study. This study will be carried out as part of this. As you advance with your research, you will be forced to create a new connection in order to offer a enough justification for the regenerator's internal pressure drop. Because of this, you will be able to offer an explanation for the events that have taken place. Establishing a totally new connection is one way that may be used to attain this purpose. The following will serve as the guide for the work that will be done in this thesis dissertation; it will enable us to accomplish our goal of reaching this objective so that we can go on to the next. We want to achieve this goal so that we may proceed to the next one. A computational fluid dynamics (CFD) simulation of a fixed bed regenerator was created using the experimental data that (Fergus & Chalmers, 2021) had previously published. This was carried out to prove the accuracy of the simulation. Using experimental data previously published by Yu et al. was necessary to provide a convincing demonstration of the reliability of a computational fluid dynamics (CFD) simulation of a fixed bed regenerator. During a steady-state CFD analysis of the regenerator, we considered the effects of the regenerator's length, velocity, and porosity. The transient behavior of the regenerator was examined using computational fluid dynamics (CFD). The impacts of porosity, Reynolds number, and regenerator duration were all taken into account.

- Following the calculation of the thermal characteristics of the fixed bed regenerator and the influence of various different variables on those properties, the next step is to calculate the temperature properties of the regenerator. It is advised that one may proceed on to this step after one has calculated the temperature specifications for the fixed bed regenerator. It's also critical that one understands the effects that thermal properties have on the different elements of the environment. This is something one should do right now.

Using computational fluid dynamics (CFD) simulations as a tool may help increase the accuracy of the computations. This will assist with the estimate of the pressure drop and the drag coefficients for a fixed bed with D/dp values that are less than 10. Ansys Fluent is one of the technologies that might help with this attempt. Flow analysis is something that can be done. This report's fourth chapter provides a thorough review of our investigation's results and an evaluation of their applicability. A unique pressure drop correlation is described in this chapter, which may be used with regenerators that have a low D/dp ratio in any given flow condition. In this chapter, the effect wall is also calculated. Utilization of regenerators is the intended objective of this book. Both subjects will be explored at some point throughout this chapter's discussion, which will touch on them both. Throughout the length of this presentation, an analysis is conducted on the interactions that each of them has with one another. When it comes to regenerators that have a low D/dp ratio, it is conceivable to compute the effect wall if the ratio is small enough and if it fulfills the precise parameters that have been specified. A transient computational fluid dynamics (CFD) model of the regenerator is included in the Ansys Fluent software, which provides a remarkable, very clear, and condensed picture of the processing capacity that is accessible. This helps us to have a better grasp of the flow complexity that was previously unexplained and that happens in labs, which was previously unknown to us. In the past, there has never been any study done on this issue. The conclusion, the contribution to the present body of knowledge on this issue, and the predicted future roads and paths for this area of study are all contained in the fifth and final chapter of the report. In addition, we will discuss about the possible future trajectories that this area of research may pursue, as well as the expected paths that it could be able to explore in the future.

THE MATHEMATICAL MODEL

Researchers have been interested in learning more about thermal regenerators for a substantial time. This is due to the fact that thermal regenerators may be used in a variety of industries. For instance, catalytic techniques for burning volatile organic compounds and petroleum cracking (VOCs) are now being researched as ways to lower air pollution levels. There are many more uses for these applications than just those two. These two apps are examples of the kind of programs that belong to this category. The mathematical model provided in this chapter may be used to analyze the thermal and resistance performances of a fixed bed regenerator. This chapter presents a description of the model. The model will be addressed in the following half of the chapter. Handley and his team revealed the Schumann model to the greater scientific community in 1969. The heat transfer coefficient of a gas that was travelling over a bed that kept constant while the calculation was being done was calculated with the aid of this model. First, the model was used to run a calculation to find out a gas's heat transfer coefficient. Likely, this has already been discussed more than once. The model comprised two unique sets of partial differential equations, one for the solid phase and the other for the gas phase. Two distinct collections included both sets of equations. The solid bed components were projected to have no temperature gradients on the interior of the bed itself, according to the theory. The following additional premises and presumptions were vital to the model's success in addition to those new premises and presumptions, and they are described below:

- Regular operation in the steady condition
- No heat is produced.
- No intra-particle conduction
- Axial gas dispersion is negligible.

The following was suggested as a solution to the thermal balancing problem for the gas phase over the bed, taking into consideration the presumptions that were previously discussed in this paragraph:

$$G_g C_{pg} \frac{dT_g}{dx} = h a_s (T_s - T_g) \tag{1}$$

Similarly, thermal balance for the complete bed was presented as:

$$G_g C_{pg} \frac{dT_g}{dx} - G_s C_{ps} \frac{dT_s}{dx} = 0 \tag{2}$$

(Silva et al., 2021) gave the solution for the above two equations using the following expressions

$$\frac{T_g}{T_{g,0}} = 1 - (1 - \frac{T_{S,L}}{T_{g,0}}) \frac{R(1 - \exp[\frac{(1-R) h a_S x}{C_{ps} G_s}])}{(R - \exp[\frac{(1-R) h a_S L}{C_{ps} G_s}])} \tag{3}$$

Where, Tg,0 = Inlet temperature of gas stream at x=0;
T s,L = Inlet temperature of gas stream at x=L;
R = Thermal mass ratio = (C ps Gs/ Cpg Gg)

The thermal mass ratio influences the temperature and how evenly the heat is distributed across the bed (R). Therefore, the bed should be readjusted to get the largest heat recovery rate practical so that R = 1. (approx.)

FIXED BED REGENERATOR MATHEMATICAL MODELING

The most prevalent kinds of regenerators are "packed bed regenerators" and "plate regenerators," two subclasses of the "plate regenerator" category. When referring to their equipment, some people name plate regenerators pebble bed regenerators. Particles of all sizes, from the exceedingly huge to the incredibly minute, may be correctly handled by a pebble bed regenerator. This project's primary objectives are to develop a pebble bed regenerator that makes use of minuscule particles and to research this regenerator. Several assumptions need to be made to imitate pebble beds, which are formed of microscopic particles. A discussion of some of these assumptions may be found below.

- The heat loss owing to the area's walls and edges is never addressed.
- The thought that solid particles may transport electricity is not even faintly contemplated. This is the circumstances. In this company, its normal practice to dismiss the concept that gaseous substances may suffer eddy movement.
- The possibility that gases may transport electricity is largely neglected in this scenario. The fixed bed regenerator's mathematical model may be found in the section below; for your convenience, a description of the model can be found in the words following the model itself. The size of the solid particles may not, under any circumstances, exceed five milimetres, and this size limitation must at all times be scrupulously respected. It is simple to deduce that no internal temperature gradient within the material makes up the bed since the corresponding Bi is less 90 than 0.01. This is owing to the operational aspects that have been examined in this scenario. This is owing to the meticulous thought given to each of these aspects. This conclusion may be reinforced by the fact that, contrary to what is true, the matching Bi is not larger than 0.01. This occurred because operational factors were addressed in this case, which is why it happened in the first place. The energy balance equation for the gas is

$$k_{g,eff}\frac{\partial T_g}{\partial x^2} - C_{pg}\rho_g V_g\frac{\partial T_g}{\partial x} + ha_s(T_s - T_g)/\varepsilon = C_{pg}\rho_g\frac{\partial T_g}{\partial t} \quad (4)$$

The energy balance for solid particles is,

$$\rho_s C_{ps}(1-\varepsilon)\frac{\partial T_s}{\partial T} = h a_s (T_g - T_s) \quad (5)$$

The initial and boundary conditions are:
at t=0, 0<=x<=L, $T_g = T_{g0}$, $T_s = T_{s0}$
at x=0, $k_{g,eff} \frac{\partial T_g}{\partial T_s} = V_g C_{pg} \rho_g \varepsilon (T_g - T_{g0}) for t>0$
x=L $\frac{\partial T_g}{\partial x} = 0 for all t$

DIMENSIONLESS VARIANCE OF THE IMPULSE RESPONSE

In their 1977 study, V. Hlavacek and J. Votruba created a mathematical model for a pebble bed regenerator that uses very small particles. A presentation of this paradigm may be found in the article. With reference to this method, which is predicated on the unit thermal response of the regenerator, the gamma function of the system variance gives a thorough explanation.

$$k_{g,eff} = k^o_{s,eff} + \frac{G_g^2 C_{pg}^2 d_p}{6 h_p (1-\varepsilon_R)} \quad (6)$$

Effective axial transport coefficient Effective conductivity of the bed with no gas flow

Contribution to effective axial conduction by gas particle heat transfer

$K_{g,eff}$ can be estimated from (4)

$$\varepsilon_R J_H = \frac{2.876}{\mathrm{Re}_p} + \frac{0.3023}{\mathrm{Re}_p^{0.35}} \quad (7)$$

$$J_H = \frac{h_p}{C_{pg} G_g}\left(\frac{\mu_g C_{pg}}{k_g}\right)^{2/3}$$

$$Pe_{gh} = Pe_{gm}$$

and $Pe_{gm} = Bo\frac{L}{d_p}$

$$\frac{1}{Bo} = \frac{0.3}{Sc\,\mathrm{Re}_p} + \frac{0.5}{1+\frac{3.8}{\mathrm{Re}_p Sc}} \quad (8)$$

Where Peh,eff is gas Peclet number, Gg is the superficial mass velocity (kg/m2s), Cpg is mean specific heat for gas (kJ/kg^{0}C), d_p is particle diameter (m), hp is gas-particle heat transfer coefficient (W/m20C), εR is porosity, ks is solid conductivity (W/m ^{0}C), kg is gas conductivity (W/m 0C), J_H is heat transfer factor, Re_p is particle Reynolds number, Pe_{gm} is Peclet number for mass transfer, Bo is the Bodenstein number (Gogos & Georgiou, 2019) for mass transfer, L is regenerator length (m), Sc is Schmidt number.

SINGLE PASS EFFICIENCY

The amount of heat that may be recovered from a hot-gas stream after the system has only gone through it once is referred to as "single-pass efficiency." This efficiency is measured in cubic feet per second. One common term for this productivity measure is "throughput." After the hot-gas stream has travelled through the system merely once, its performance is measured. Given that it is presented in the following way, it is possible that a gamma distribution function of the system variance can generate an image of the regenerator breakthrough curve that is at least somewhat accurate:

$$t_{he} = u(\tau) = \frac{1}{\Gamma\frac{1}{\sigma_D^2}} \int_0^{\frac{\Gamma}{\sigma_D^2}} x^{(\frac{1}{\sigma_D^2}-1)} e^{-x} dx \qquad (9)$$

With M=1/σ_D^2, $\tau_s = \frac{\theta}{\mu}$single-pass efficiency can be represented by equ^n (10)

$$E_{sp}(\tau) = 1 - (1 - \frac{1}{\tau_s}) * t_{he} - \frac{(M\tau_s)^{M-1} e^{-M\tau}}{\Gamma(M)} \qquad (10)$$

The formula for thermal efficiency for co-current, periodic, symmetric operation is given by

$$E(\tau_s) + \sum_{n=1}^{N} \left[(2n-1)E_{sp}((2n-1)\tau_s - 4nE_{sp}(2n\tau_s) + (2n+1)E_{sp}(2n+1) \right] \qquad (11)$$

Once Esp is known, the Heat storage factor can be calculated as:

$$q = E_{sp} * \tau_s \qquad (12)$$

All other heat-transfer resistances perpendicular to the flow direction should be zero, and the amount of heat communicated by the bulk gas flow should occur at a rate that is known to be adjustable. This is because it is more complicated to measure accurately heat transmission resistances when they are perpendicular. The best situation that might occur under given circumstances is this one. As a consequence, once this issue is resolved, the regenerator may function to the utmost extent of its capabilities. In order to evaluate if the regenerator is working, s must equal 1 and the thermal mean residence time must match the time needed for the switch to shut off. These two conditions must both be satisfied. Both of these conditions must be completed at the same time.

The optimal regenerator expression for single-pass efficiency at ($\tau s = 1$) will be

$$E_{sp}(1) = 1 - \frac{1}{\sqrt{2\Pi M}} \tag{13}$$

The expression for efficiency at ($\tau s= 1$) will be given as:

$$E(1) = 2E_{sp}(1) - 1 \tag{14}$$

MATLAB ALGORITHM FOR FIXED BED REGENERATOR MODEL

A step-by-step approach for the ideal regenerator design may be created in MATLAB using mathematical modeling of a pebble bed regenerator containing tiny particles, as illustrated in Figure 4.The best outcomes might be achieved using this process. The regenerator's resources can then be used in the most effective way possible when this happens. As a result, building an effective regenerator will no longer be impossible. The next grammatical phrase shows how this tactic could be used in real-world situations.

Figure 4. MATLAB algorithm to find the optimal efficiency of fixed bed regenerator

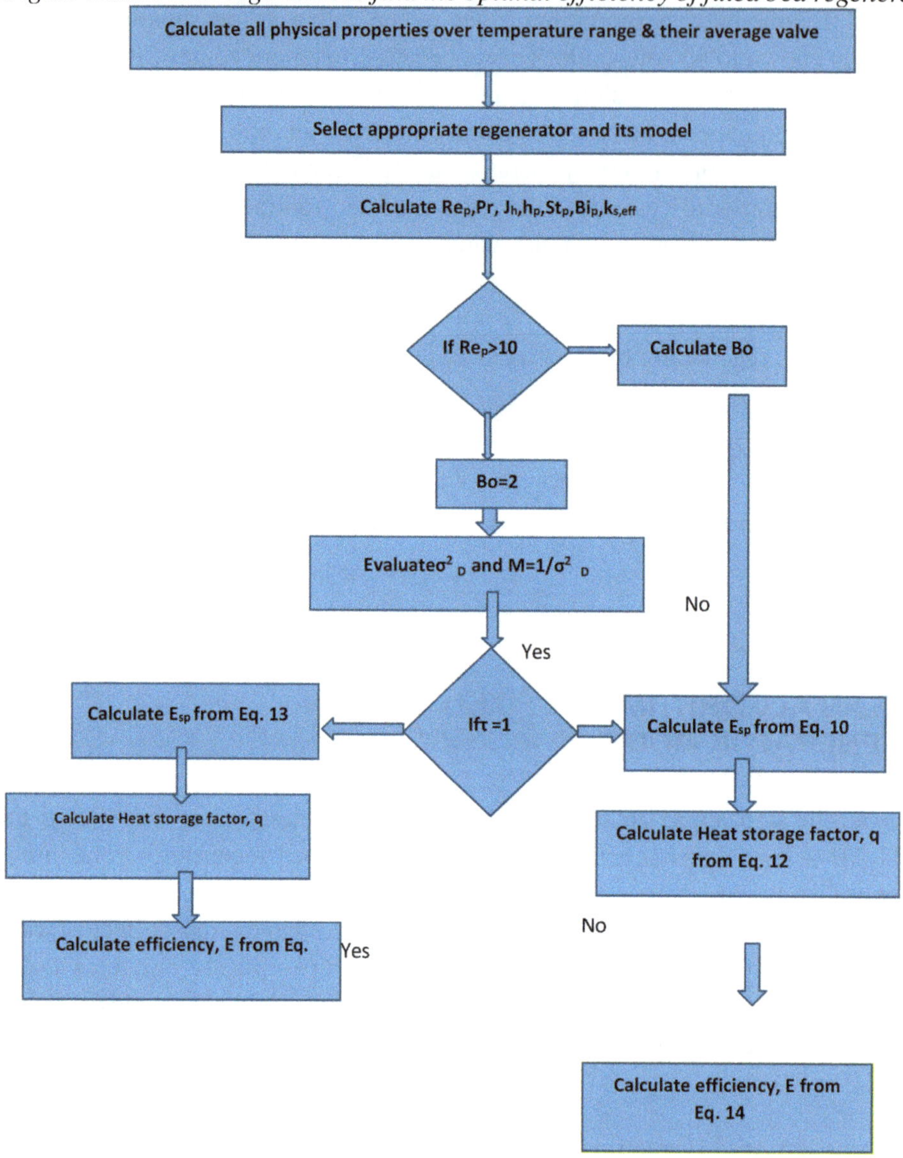

RESULT AND DISCUSSION

The GAMBIT pre-processor has been used to prove that the solid may be represented. This model is comparable to the previous part's physical specification.

The meshing technique included 171800 hexahedral elements and 179275 nodes to provide a more realistic picture of the impact of stratification inside the packed-bed regenerator. A CFD software called ANSYS FLUENT (Mubarakali, A., et al. 2026) simulates the fluid flow and heat transmission within the regenerator. This is being done to generate the most precise process description conceivable. The porous media element is meant to be fitted into the regeneration chamber in its present configuration. Earlier than the present, this aim was created. In order to solve the issue as quickly as possible, the most effective method is to use a segregated independent, three-dimensional unstable solution. Using the control volume technique, the governing equations, starting conditions, and boundary conditions may be discretised in implicit form. Time may be saved by doing this. This is done in conjunction with the discretisation (Divya, S., et al. 2023) of the boundary conditions. Using a SIMPLE approach in combination with a turbulence model that use the letter k, the goal is to determine the root cause of the issue and discover a solution. The meshed model is then put into the fluid solver for analysis after this step is complete. The operation is done; following this step, this activity must be quick to increase the model's overall performance. A piece of the regenerator has been transformed into a fluid zone as the gases must cover the complete surface of the device. To meet this requirement, this was done. At present moment, grid independence studies are being conducted out using a packed bed regenerator with mesh sizes of 0.5, 1, 2, and 3. This is being done so that the results may be compared. When transitioning from a grid size of 3 millimetres to a grid size of 2 millimetres, there is a difference in the pressure drop of 14%. This comes as a consequence of the grid's reduced size. The pressure drop stays same when the grid size is increased from one to half. However, the pressure drop variance is reduced by 5% when the grid size is dropped from two to one mm. This makes it evident that there is no association between mesh size and pressure decrease below a one-millimetre grid size. The grid utilised for the next simulation will be one millimetre from the findings made in this section. This option was made.

COMPARISON OF CFD SIMULATION FINDINGS WITH EXPERIMENTAL RESULTS

To employ the technique, a packed bed must be heated at different flue gas rates, including 1.5, 2, 2.5, 3, and 3.5 meters per second. It is also necessary to look at the pressure drop at different bed heights, such as 0.1, 0.2, 0.3, and 0.4 meters. The temperature of the bed's heating is also adjustable. The technique further involves heating a packed bed at different combinations of flue gas velocities. Another feature of the approach already in use is heating a packed bed at varied flue gas velocities. Another aspect of the presently employed technology comprises heating a packed bed using varying flue gas velocities. The simulation and a previous experiment that measured the pressure drop of a packed-bed regenerator at different heights with a velocity range of 1.5 m/s to 3.5 m/s are compared in Figure 5. This experiment examined the pressure drop of a packed-bed regenerator at different heights. This comparison was undertaken to examine if the result was more accurate: the one from the prior experiment or the one that was simulated. This figure illustrates the results of the comparison (a). The results from the simulated CFD are displayed as a continuous line in Fig. 4.1 (a), in contrast to the plots obtained from the experimental data, which are shown as dashed or gapped lines. These designs were created by Juan Yu and his colleagues, and their research was published in 2002.

Figure 5. (a) Variation of pressure drop with the velocity at different bed heights (b) Variation of pressure drop with the velocity at different ball diameter

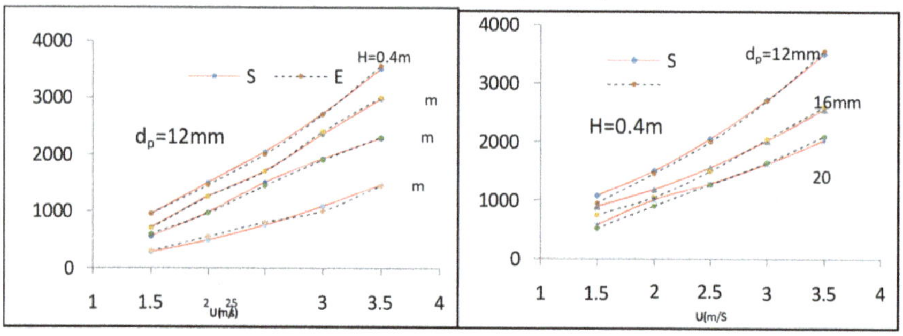

Looking at the graph, it is evident that as the bed height increases, the pressure falls even if the diameter of the ball or particle keeps the same. We may get to this conclusion based on what we notice when we glance at the graph. The reality that this is the actual scenario does not change just because we may understand the line of reasoning that led us to this conclusion. Comparing the pressure drop experimental result (E) with the CFD simulation result (S) for a range of varied ball diameters and velocities ranging from 1.5 m/s to 3.5 m/s is shown in Figure 5 (b). In this circumstance, the criterion for calculating how much pressure has fallen is millimeters of mercury (mmHg). In this instance, measuring the pressure drop was accomplished using a manometer. The simulated findings match the experimental data, with the highest variance being 6% at a given location, according to the data presented in Figure 5(a) and Figure 5(b), respectively. This conclusion may be drawn by analyzing the information given in both figures. Rather than being a predetermined conclusion, the evidence now available may support this judgment. When all of these elements are considered, one may arrive to the following conclusion:

In order to provide further support for the conclusions that were reached from the simulation, the coefficients of Ergun have been provisionally determined with the assistance of pressure drop.

CONCLUSION AND FUTURE SCOPE

In this research, the design, constructing, and modeling of a pebble bed regenerator with a D/dp value of less than 15 will be carried out with the help of a piece of commercial software known as Ansys Fluent. Furthermore, studies will be conducted to examine how temperature, resistance, and flow dynamics interact.

REFERENCES

Ahmad, S. S., Almasalha, F., Qutqut, M. H., & Hijjawi, M. (2024). Centralized smart energy monitoring system for legacy home appliances. *Energy Informatics*, *7*(1), 29. DOI: 10.1186/s42162-024-00334-2

Chabane, L., Drid, S., Chrifi-Alaoui, L., & Delahoche, L. (2024). Energy consumption prediction of a smart home using non-intrusive appliance load monitoring. *International Journal of System Assurance Engineering and Management*, *15*(3), 1231–1244. DOI: 10.1007/s13198-023-02209-3

Das, S. K., Bebortta, S., Pati, B., Panigrahi, C. R., & Senapati, D. (2024). Profiling and Classification of IoT Devices for Smart Home Environments. In: Nayak, J., Naik, B., S, V., Favorskaya, M. (eds) Machine Learning for Cyber Physical System: Advances and Challenges. Intelligent Systems Reference Library, vol 60. Springer, Cham. DOI: 10.1007/978-3-031-54038-7_4

Divya, S., Murthy, A., Babu, S. S., Ahmed, S. I., & Dey, S. R. (2023). Energy Monitoring with Trend Analysis and Power Signature Interpretation. In Dutta, P., Bhattacharya, A., Dutta, S., & Lai, W. C. (Eds.), *Emerging Technologies in Data Mining and Information Security. Advances in Intelligent Systems and Computing* (Vol. 1348). Springer., DOI: 10.1007/978-981-19-4676-9_8

Fakhruldeen, H. F., Saadh, M. J., Khan, S., Salim, N. A., Jhamat, N., & Mustafa, G. (2025). Enhancing smart home device identification in WiFi environments for futuristic smart networks-based IoT. *International Journal of Data Science and Analytics*, *19*(4), 645–658. DOI: 10.1007/s41060-023-00489-3

Fergus, P., & Chalmers, C. (2021). Energy Sobriety: A Behaviour Measurement Indicator for Fuel Poverty Using Aggregated Load Readings from Smart Meters. In Ploix, S., Amayri, M., & Bouguila, N. (Eds.), *Towards Energy Smart Homes*. Springer., DOI: 10.1007/978-3-030-76477-7_2

George, T., & Selvakumar, A. I. (2024). Smart home energy management systems in India: A socio-economic commitment towards a green future. *Discover Sustainability*, *5*(1), 101. DOI: 10.1007/s43621-024-00295-2

Gogos, C., & Georgiou, G. (2019). Appliance Identification Through Nonintrusive Load Monitoring in Residences. In Blondin, M., Pardalos, P., & Sanchis Sáez, J. (Eds.), *Computational Intelligence and Optimization Methods for Control Engineering. Springer Optimization and Its Applications* (Vol. 150). Springer., DOI: 10.1007/978-3-030-25446-9_10

Lin, Y. H. (2022). An advanced smart home energy management system considering identification of ADLs based on non-intrusive load monitoring. *Electrical Engineering, 104*(5), 3391–3409. DOI: 10.1007/s00202-022-01546-z

Mubarakali, A., Sharavanan, S., Elshafie, H., & Changalasetty, S. B. (2026). A secure and scalable home security system using IoT, 6G networks, AI-based hybrid deep learning models, blockchain, and smart contracts. *International Journal of Information Security, 25*(1), 15. DOI: 10.1007/s10207-025-01178-x

Silva, C. A. S., Amayri, M., & Basu, K. (2021). Characterization of Energy Demand and Energy Services Using Model-Based and Data-Driven Approaches. In Ploix, S., Amayri, M., & Bouguila, N. (Eds.), *Towards Energy Smart Homes*. Springer., DOI: 10.1007/978-3-030-76477-7_7

Tayfor, N. B., Majidpour, J., Ahmed, M. H., Hajianfar, G., & Arabi, H. (2026). Metaheuristic-driven feature selection in radiomics: Improving time-to-event survival prediction in glioblastoma. *Neural Computing & Applications, 38*(8), 281. DOI: 10.1007/s00521-026-11991-7

Völker, B., Scholl, P. M., & Becker, B. (2022). A Feature and Classifier Study for Appliance Event Classification. In Afonso, J. L., Monteiro, V., & Pinto, J. G. (Eds.), *Sustainable Energy for Smart Cities. SESC 2021. Lecture Notes of the Institute for Computer Sciences, Social Informatics and Telecommunications Engineering* (Vol. 425). Springer., DOI: 10.1007/978-3-030-97027-7_7

Waseem, Q., Wan Din, W. I. S., & Aamir, M. (2025). A generalized three-tier hybrid model for classifying unseen (IoT devices) in smart home environments. *Scientific Reports, 15*(1), 35388. DOI: 10.1038/s41598-025-19303-0 PMID: 41068230

Chapter 6
A Hybrid Data Fusion Model for Online Education Evaluation in Intelligent Classroom Environments

Anorgul Ashirova
http://orcid.org/0009-0006-7271-3634
Mamun University, Uzbekistan

Gafur Namazov
Termez University of Economics and Service, Uzbekistan

Begimov O'ktam Ibrogimovich
Alfraganus University, Tashkent, Uzbekistan

Burkhon Dekhkonov Rustamovich
Tashkent State University of Economics, Uzbekistan

Namazova Nodira
Bukhara State Medical Institute, Uzbekistan

N. Raghu
http://orcid.org/0000-0002-2091-8922
Jain University, India

Khalokova Munisabonu Valiyevna
Bukhara State University, Uzbekistan

Saodat Barotova
Bukhara State University, Uzbekistan

ABSTRACT

The study uses a multi-source data fusion approach to assess online course effectiveness. The research combines student engagement metrics, learning performance, and course content quality using the 3P (Presage-Process-Product) model. The structured questionnaire was taken from undergraduate students from five regional colleges, and a total of 685 responses were collected, 583 of which were valid samples. The data

DOI: 10.4018/979-8-2600-3280-0.ch006

were analyzed using SPSS 25.0 and AMOS 24.0 for reliability and validity testing. A backpropagation neural network (BPNN) was used to forecast learning performance related to course interaction, selection rates, and engagement metrics. Hypothesis testing was performed to check the links between course quality, engagement, and learning performance. Structural equation modeling was applied to find direct and indirect effects, leading to an unbiased approach for course effectiveness evaluation. The findings direct specific approaches to increase online course delivery, student engagement, and attainment of educational outcomes.

1. INTRODUCTION

College students are equipped with the information and skills needed for post-graduate practice via general courses, which seek to provide a wider and more thorough education (Sultonkhodjayeva et al., 2025). This idea, which had its roots in Europe, gained traction in the US in the 1950s and 1960s, particularly with the publication of the "General Education in a Free Society" by the Harvard committee. It was well-received by the American higher education community and went global thereafter (Zhang & Zhang, 2025). As a result of the Chinese Economic Reform in 1978, China's universities began a new period of progressive qualitative education reform that sought to bridge the gap between general and vocational training (Panjaitan, 2025). There has been some recent theoretical and practical exploration of innovations and potential in general education in Chinese institutions. Not only were certain modified general education models constructed, but outstanding successes were also made. (In Chinese higher education, these accomplishments are substantial (Li, 2025).

Table 1. Operational data for general online course

Semester	Course Identification Number	Course Collection Number	Pass Ratio (%)	Exceptional Rate (%)
Spring 2021	371	18836	88.67	71.46
Fall 2020	366	18745	89.86	71.38
Spring 2020	369	15184	86.29	68.96
Fall 2019	12	8278	92.81	71.92

A shortage of professors and staff, an uneven distribution of courses across disciplines, and class sizes are just a few of the common issues that regional schools face when compared to elite institutions (Zhang, 2021). These issues have been greatly alleviated with the advent of online open courses (Muthuswamy, 2025). Over ten million students are enrolled in Chinese online schools, while the number of institutions in the country exceeds two thousand (Marisamy et al., 2026). The region's colleges now rely heavily on their online learning platforms to provide general education courses. However, difficulties surfaced simultaneously with the success of online education. Course selection based on inaccurate knowledge of course material, unclean learning motivation (Mengliyev et al., 2024), flawed evaluation, inadequate quality assurance, neglected course administration, and plagiarism are all examples of such issues (Wang, 2024).

Institution conducted a case study that led to the implementation of 400 MOOCs for all students beginning in the spring of 2020. Table 1 displays data from the most recent two years. Table 1 may easily see the "high selection rate-low complete rate-high excellent rate" trend. leads to inquiries about offering a generic online course with a high level of quality. The students think of the online general education course? What are the best ways to regulate learning performance and the variables that affect it? How can improve the efficiency of the learning process? The key components of effective online learning, according to several researchers, are the learning experience and the level of student participation [5,6]. The "presage-process-product" model proposed by Dr. Bigg served as the theoretical foundation for this investigation (Liu, 2025). The relationship between online general course learning experience, engagement, and performance using structural equation modelling has been analysed (Wu, 2025). Improving the quality of general education, optimising online learning performance, and offering future thoughts on online general courses in China were all goals as well (Ghaleb & Pardaev, 2025).

1.1 Research Gap Analysis

The evaluation methods used in online general education courses display major flaws because they depend on student feedback and academic performance data which provide insufficient and biased evaluation results. Research studies currently examine two main areas which are student engagement assessment and the evaluation of individual AI solutions without applying theoretical learning models or multi-source data fusion methods. The current state of research lacks standardized frameworks which bring together perceptual data, behavioral data, and performance data to create a complete system for assessing learning outcomes.

The study presents a hybrid multi-source data fusion framework which operates together with a Back Propagation Neural Network (BPNN) to fulfill these research needs within the 3P (Presage–Process–Product) theoretical model. The research delivers three main contributions which include (1) creating a unified evaluation model that combines different data sources and (2) using a hybrid data fusion method to enhance evaluation accuracy and reliability and (3) applying machine learning techniques for capturing online learning environment nonlinear relationships. The evaluation system provides a complete evaluation of online general education courses through its data-driven evaluation system.

2. LITERATURE SURVEY

Chango et al., (2022) have demonstrated that Smart learning environments are one example of a new educational paradigm that utilises digital and context-aware gadgets to make learning easier. This new educational scenario allows for the acquisition, fusion, and analysis of massive amounts of data from students' multimodal learning from a number of sources. It presents a once-in-a-lifetime chance for educators and researchers to uncover fresh information that will help them comprehend learning and intervene when needed. Combining different sources of multimodal learning analytics (MLA) requires the proper use of data fusion methodologies and techniques (Tukhtaeva et al., 2024). Audio, video, electrodermal activity data, eye-tracking, user logs, click-stream data, learning artefacts, and more natural human signals like gestures, gaze, voice, or writing are all sources or modalities in MLA. The purpose of this study is to provide an overview of data fusion in smart learning, specifically in the context of learning analytics (LA) and educational data mining (EDM). By analysing the most important articles, types of fused educational data, data fusion methodologies and techniques utilised in EDM/LA, and open topics, trends, and difficulties in this field of study, it provides an overview of the present state of the art.

Achar et al., (2025) present a clear and engaging discussion on how Artificial Intelligence is reshaping the learning landscape. The paper explains, in an easy-to-follow manner, how AI tools such as adaptive learning systems, intelligent tutoring, and automated assessments help make education more personalized and effective (Ravikumar et al., 2026). Rather than focusing only on technology, the authors connect AI applications to real learning needs, showing how they can support both students and teachers. The study also looks ahead, highlighting future possibilities while honestly addressing challenges like ethical concerns, data privacy, and responsible implementation. This balanced approach makes the paper feel practical and relevant, not just theoretical. Overall, the work offers a meaningful overview of where AI in education stands today and where it is heading, making it useful for educators, researchers, and decision-makers who want to understand and thoughtfully apply AI in learning environments.

Yan et al., (2022) have stated that evaluating student involvement is crucial in education because it forms the basis for assuring high-quality instruction and introducing interventions to improve student learning. The ease of multimodal data capture is growing as storage and the Internet of things continue to advance. A lot of studies have focused on using multimodal data to learn more about student involvement. Nevertheless, a fundamental problem in the field of study remains unsolved. The optimally merge various modalities to conduct student engagement analysis after selection a set of modalities. Here, a learning-based feature fusion framework. Extracting features with uneven intervals and fusing synchronous and asynchronous time are the two main components of the system. The experimental research in actual classroom settings, delving into online learning using picture, log, and text data to uncover various patterns of student involvement. It is clear from the outcomes of the experiments that the framework is useful and successful.

Raghu et al. (2025) present a well-structured and insightful exploration of how Problem-Based Learning (PBL) can effectively enhance critical thinking skills in modern education. The chapter clearly explains the theoretical foundations of PBL while connecting them to practical classroom strategies, making the discussion both meaningful and applicable. By emphasizing real-world problem solving, collaboration, and student-centered learning, the authors show how PBL encourages learners to think deeply, question assumptions, and apply knowledge rather than simply memorize content. The work also highlights the evolving role of teachers as facilitators who guide inquiry and reflection, which aligns well with current educational needs. What stands out is the balanced approach that blends pedagogical theory with actionable recommendations for educators. Overall, this chapter serves as a valuable resource for teachers, researchers, and academic leaders seeking to cultivate critical thinking and learner autonomy through engaging, problem-driven instructional practices in contemporary education.

Agarwal & Kaur (2024) offer a practical and timely examination of how advanced digital systems are being adopted for managing academic resources in educational institutions. The paper explains how technologies such as integrated digital repositories, automation tools, and data-driven management systems can improve accessibility, organization, and efficient use of learning resources. Rather than presenting technology as an abstract concept, the authors connect system adoption to real institutional challenges, including scalability, cost efficiency, and user acceptance. The discussion highlights how effective digital resource management supports teaching, research, and administrative decision-making. Importantly, the study also acknowledges barriers such as infrastructure limitations, staff training needs, and resistance to change. This balanced perspective makes the work relatable and grounded in real academic settings. Overall, the article provides valuable insights for institutional leaders, librarians, and policymakers seeking to modernize resource management practices and enhance the digital readiness of academic institutions in a sustainable and user-centered manner.

Sahoo et al., (2024) presents a thoughtful and forward-looking discussion on the use of ChatGPT as an AI-enhanced decision support system for leadership in ethical learning environments. The authors clearly explain how conversational AI can assist leaders in analyzing complex situations, supporting informed decision-making, and encouraging ethical reasoning in educational and organizational contexts. Rather than portraying AI as a replacement for human judgment, the chapter emphasizes its role as a supportive tool that enhances reflection, transparency, and consistency in leadership decisions. The discussion around ethical learning is particularly strong, addressing issues such as bias, accountability, and responsible AI use. By combining leadership theory with practical AI applications, the chapter feels both relevant and accessible. Overall, this work offers valuable insights for academic leaders, policy-makers, and researchers interested in integrating AI responsibly to support ethical leadership and decision-making in next-generation learning and leadership systems.

Dou et al., (2019) have demonstrated that finding what you're looking for becomes more difficult as the quantity of data kept online grows. In addition to being inefficient and time-consuming, the conventional approach to data collecting is unable to accomplish certain goals. The goal is to identify the most important aspects influencing instructors' comprehensive assessment scores and to suggest solutions by collecting and analysing data on student evaluations using web crawler and natural language processing technologies. In contrast to the best priority crawler framework, which has enhanced and optimised its structure, conventional Web crawler technology lacks specific intelligence, initiative, etc. Long retrieval time, overlapping information, incomplete information, and better accuracy of information gathering may all be efficiently addressed with the addition of an enhanced PageRank value, a higher degree of user demand correlation, and the NDC method denoising. The present issue in a way that is suitable for both students' and educators' needs, a student assessment system has been proposed. Improve the accuracy and reliability of target rule mining and prediction using data fusion technology, an integrated data processing tool used in many conventional and developing domains.

J. Reich (2015) has explained that a better way to evaluate, share data, and plan experiments Anant Agarwal, CEO of edX, has said that MOOCs should function as a "particle accelerator for learning". Massive open online courses (MOOCs) provide fresh data sources and possibilities for large-scale research that might progress the field of learning science. Although new study avenues have emerged in the years after massive open online courses (MOOCs) gained significant prominence, the results of these studies have had little practical use in the classroom. Just because a data collection is big doesn't mean it automatically contains the answers to all the important queries. Research in massive open online course (MOOC) must progress along three axes if it is to contribute to the advancement of learning science. Firstly, the field must shift its focus from studies of engagement to studies of learning. Secondly, it must move away from studying individual courses and instead compare them across contexts. Lastly, it must move away from relying on post hoc analyses and towards greater deployment of multidisciplinary, experimental design.

Hung et al., (2012) have illustrated that by analysing demographic data, student learning logs, and end-of-course assessment questionnaires in an online K-12 supplementary programme, this research explored a novel way to programme evaluation. In order to inform decisions about K-12 education, the findings lend credence to the idea of a programme assessment model. The 7,539 participants in the case study contributed a total of 23,854,527 learning records across 883 different classes. Decision tree analysis was used to forecast students' grades and happiness with the course and teacher, while clustering analysis was used to uncover students' commonalities. The results of this research show that programme evaluations may benefit from data mining by providing more detailed information for decision-making. On top of that, it looked at possible K-12 EDM applications that have been widely used at universities.

M. Sayeed et al., (2022) explained that A growing number of prestigious educational institutions throughout the world are putting in place hybrid course offerings. Converting online courses like Massive Open Online Courses (MOOCs) into course credits is one way that education may move forward while still maintaining quality and flexibility. However, owing to inadequate digital experience with instructional resources, a number of colleges are hesitant to fully move to an online-based curriculum. Currently, assessment methods like multiple-choice questions (MCQs) can't provide a whole picture of a student's performance. The purpose of this project is to develop a reference-based method to automated short answer grading (ASAG) that uses a hybrid of student and reference responses to assess descriptive replies using transformer models based on the Siamese architecture and Roberta bi-encoder. When designing the architecture, on the basis of ASAG jobs often have limited computing resources. This study shows how well the models performed on the benchmark SemEval-2013 2way task dataset after they were fine-tuned and hyperparameter optimised.

Qu J et al., (2021) have discussed that an assessment of university students' learning behaviour using multi-source data fusion is suggested to address the issue of incomplete information in single-data evaluations. This evaluation aims to study the potential usefulness of data fusion technology in the classroom. Prior to performing the fusion calculation, use Spearman to determine the correlation between various data sources. Then, determine the relationship weight and optimisation weight of each data source. Lastly, compute the comprehensive weight. Comprehensive weighted fusion, when applied to the calculation of students' comprehensive learning behaviour evaluation, can combine the benefits and drawbacks of various learning methods while also balancing the differences in students' learning behaviour evaluations under different teaching methods. In order to aid in a more thorough examination of college students' learning behaviour and to provide the groundwork for adjusting to their own learning, experiments confirm that the whole weighted data fusion technique is beneficial.

The comparison shows that current research studies mostly examine student engagement and artificial intelligence applications and traditional data mining techniques through their use of single or limited data sources as shown in table 2. Research studies that examine multimodal data face challenges in achieving complete data integration through multi-source data fusion implementation. The research field lacks studies that integrate theoretical models with advanced machine learning methods for course evaluation purposes. The research presents a unified framework which combines perceptual and behavioral and performance data through a neural network method to improve online learning effectiveness assessment by providing complete and precise and data-driven results.

Table 2. Research gap analysis of smart learning.

Author & Year	Research Focus	Method	Major Contribution	Limitation Identified
Chango et al., (2022)	Smart learning environments and multimodal learning analytics	Multimodal learning analytics and data fusion approaches	Provided a conceptual overview of multimodal data fusion in smart learning environments	Focused more on theoretical discussion; lacks implementation-based evaluation model
Achar et al., (2025)	Artificial Intelligence in education	AI-based adaptive learning and intelligent systems	Explained how AI improves personalized learning environments	Does not focus on multi-source data fusion or evaluation modelling
Raghu et al., (2025)	Problem-Based Learning (PBL) and critical thinking	Pedagogical framework based on PBL	Demonstrated improvement in critical thinking through active learning methods	Does not use data fusion or analytics-based evaluation techniques
Agarwal & Kaur, (2024)	Digital resource management in education	Data-driven digital resource management systems	Showed the role of digital systems in improving educational efficiency	Focused on resource management rather than course evaluation
Sahoo et al., (2024)	AI-based decision support in education	ChatGPT-based decision support framework	Highlighted ethical AI and decision-making in education	Does not include multimodal or fused educational data

2.1 Conceptual Foundation of Multi-Source Data Fusion

The process of multi-source data fusion in smart learning environments involves multiple educational institutions to develop an all-encompassing assessment system that accurately monitors student learning progress and educational results (Adams & Umbach, 2012). The system uses multi-source data fusion to analyze both subjective and objective data streams which leads to improved accuracy and deeper understanding and better data interpretation compared to traditional course evaluation systems that depend on single-source data through student questionnaires and final grades. Online education typically uses three types of data sources which operate as follows:

- Perceptual Data (Subjective Data): This category collects student responses through structured questionnaires which use Likert scales. It shows how students perceive the course quality, their engagement level and their entire learning experience.
- Behavioral Data (Objective Interaction Data): The learning management system automatically records this data which includes the frequency of logins, the duration of time studying course materials, the total number of student interactions, the sequence of clicks on content and the number of discussions students took part in.
- Performance Data (Outcome-Based Data): This category includes all academic measurements which students achieved through their educational assessments which include test scores and assignment grades and completion rates and learning target achievement.

The study uses three types of data which include perceptual data and behavioral data and performance data yet it applies a hybrid feature-level integration method to execute its fusion process. The data from each source undergoes preprocessing first which includes cleaning and normalization and scaling to achieve uniformity across different data formats. Each data type provides its own unique key features which include engagement metrics from behavioral logs and satisfaction indices from perceptual responses and achievement scores from performance records. The features undergo alignment before concatenation which creates a single feature vector that represents each learner.

A correlation-based weighting scheme applies its Spearman correlation method to determine data source importance which improves fusion effectiveness through this process. The Back Propagation Neural Network (BPNN) receives the weighted feature vector as input which enables the model to learn nonlinear relationships between variables for final output evaluation. The explicit fusion mechanism enables the predictive model to combine complementary information from multiple data sources through its data integration process.

3. METHOD AND MODELLING

Learning engagement and emotion towards the course material are process factors, but student personality and prior learning experience are early variables, as Biggs noted (Zhou et al., 2025). A model used for the interaction between online general courses and learning based on the 3P theory as shown in Figure 1. An interactive model is formed by the interplay of various factors, with the online learning experience serving as the primary determinant in the presage stage, online learning engagement and course content quality as the primary determinants in the process stage, and online learning performance as the primary determinant in the product stage (Ravikumar et al., 2025).

3.1. Variables in Presage

Learning outcomes are influenced by the learner's attitude and approach, which are in turn determined by numerous factors. Several aspects, including the perception and experience of the learning process and result, impact students who attend the online course since they are the direct participants and experiencers. The effectiveness of online learning is impacted by how positive one's online learning experience is. Research indicates a robust relationship between students' unique areas of expertise and their online learning experiences (Trigwell et al., 2012). Interest in and capacity for self-regulation, knowledge acquisition, and a desire to learn are common areas of expertise for individuals. Here, the assumption (H1-H2), prior experience with online learning positively affects both engagement with and success in online learning.

3.2. Variables in Process

Considerations of the learner's experience and the achievement of predetermined objectives are at the heart of process variables in online learning. One of the primary goals of e-learning platform is the assurance of high-quality course materials. Learning quality is also significantly impacted by how engaged students are in online learning. They both have major impacts on learning. Here, the two main process variables: online education engagement and course quality (Aarthi, 2025).

The virtual education encounter is significantly impacted by the quality of the course material. Content and experience are in a demand-satisfaction connection, according to the study. The student is provided with a more fulfilling learning experience, stimulates their mind and emotions, and positively expands their knowledge via qualitative course material. Online course anxiety, course material quality, opinion of the course's value, and course adaptability are factors for online learning experience (Olimbaevich, 2025). Online learning engagement is positively affected by course quality. According to research, the level of perceived learning engagement is strongly correlated with the amount of time students spend interacting with course material (Wuyuan & Wenjun, 2020). Theoretical models of online learning should centre on the learner's motivation and engagement in a cohesive and organic information setting, with an emphasis on the content's thought-provoking and engaging elements. The effectiveness of online learning is positively affected by the quality of online courses (Ahmed & Pardaev, 2025). Appropriate course material is a critical component of effective online education, according to research. Academic attainment is significantly influenced by how quality is perceived. Furthermore, the value that students place on a course has a direct impact on how well they learn it. Online learning performance is positively affected by online learning engagement. Research indicates that when students are actively involved in their learning, they are more likely to think critically about the material, draw conclusions, and present their arguments. Additionally, it has a major effect on how effectively one learns. In 60% of the learners, there was a positive association between online learning performance and engagement in another categorization study on the topic of online learning engagement and performance in distant education (Yin & Xu, 2017). So, it as a given that (a) the quality of the course material influences the online learning experience, engagement, and performance (H3–H5), and (b) the level of involvement with the online learning process influences the performance (H6).

Figure 1. Relationship model for online general education courses

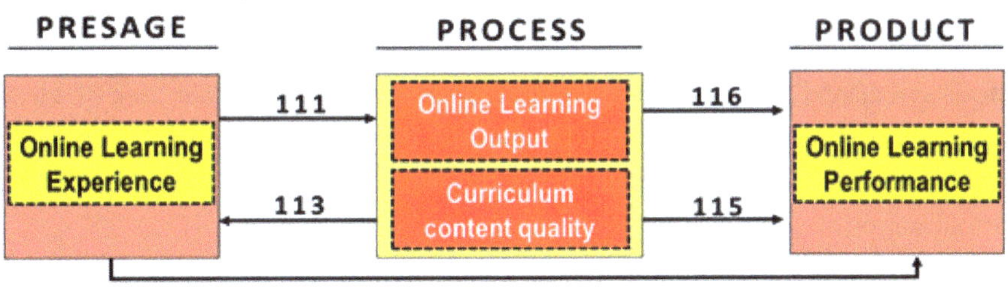

3.3. Variables in Product

The learner's information literacy awareness, their performance in class, the extent to which they improved their knowledge and skills, how satisfied they were with their learning experience overall, etc. At the present time, researchers throughout the world have conducted extensive, methodical, and in-depth studies on the efficacy of online education (Lu et al., 2020). The long-term effects on higher education of poor online learning performance and online course quality are substantial. Theoretically and pragmatically, understanding what makes for successful online learning is crucial (Fuhl et al., 2018). The performance of students taking courses online is used as the course product variable in this research. Since the online general education classes are fundamental, flexible, and extensive, the higher standards for students' mental and emotional capacities (Reich, 2015). Students have developed good emotions, attitudes, and general sense skills, for example, via the online general classes (Hidayat et al., 2024). This result emphasises traits of general education and is in line with our objective. Figure 2 shows the link between three factors: learners, education process variables, and education performance.

3.4. The BP Neural Network Implementation Procedure

Back propagation neural networks (BPNNs) rely on machine learning to iteratively refine the training model, tweak the network's weights, optimise the model's structure over time, reduce the error function's gradient-driven decline, and maintain a constant proximity between the model's output and the expected value (Chango et al., 2022). Nodes in the input layer mentioned in this study include online learning performance, course material quality, online learning engagement, and online learning experience. The output layer consists of only one node and has a single label degree. Based on the results of the training tests, the hidden layer needs l nodes and all four of the assessment indicators, the amount of course interaction, the number of school selections, the number of course selections, and the number of viewers have their data standardised so that alternative dimensions cannot be considered (Qu, 2021). The following formula maps the index variables to the interval [0,1] by normalisation.

$$p_{mi} = \frac{P_{mi} - P_{imin}}{P_{imax} - P_{imin}} \quad (1)$$

where i = 1, 2, . . ., 4, m and 1, 2, . . ., 400, The normalized data is Pmi (m = 400), while the maximum and minimum values in the m-th original data are Pimax and Pimin. Out of the normalized data set, 80% of the data are chosen at random to serve as training data and the remaining 20% as test data are calculated using equation (1). After feeding the neural network the training data, the hidden layer's output value may be determined using equation (2), which is shown below:

$$h_j = f(\sum_{i=1}^{n} w_{ij}x_i | \theta_j) \quad (2)$$

$$y = f(\sum_{j=1}^{n} v_j h_j | \theta) \quad (3)$$

$$w_{ij}^{new} = w_{ij}^{old} - \eta \frac{\partial E}{\partial w_{ij}} \quad (4)$$

where Wij is the connection weight between the input layer and the hidden layer, hj is the hidden layer threshold, and j = 1, 2,..., n, n is the number of nodes in the hidden layer as shown in equation (3) and (4).

Building the BP Model Neural Network. Building the BP neural network model using the available sample data allows one to investigate the interrelationships among various assessment indicators and objects (Xu et al., 2022). This study will take into account all relevant elements, including the network model's structure, algorithm, neuron number, and error accuracy as shown in equation (5), and will properly decide how to make the model generalizable. Figure 3 shows the topology of the e BP neural network model, which is used to analyse the interaction between learners, factors in the learning process, and learning performance (Yan et al., 2022).

$$E = \frac{1}{2}\sum(y - t)^2 \quad (5)$$

This research incorporates students, factors in the learning process, and student success in learning as the number of neurons in the input layer is proportional to the number of variables in the issue. Research findings mostly dictate the output layer. Decide on the number of neurons for the output layer after careful consideration and evaluation. The results of this research show how many factors in the learning process relate to students' success on assessments (Dou et al., 2019). Consequently, the output layer's neuron count is 1 in this work. Based on the study done before, it can be concluded that the BP neural network built in this article only has one hidden layer. Considering the number of neurons according to demands is important since it directly affects the accuracy of network training at the hidden layer. The network model's fault tolerance and sample identification accuracy are both negatively impacted by a limited number of hidden layer neurons (Muthuswamy, 2025). Overfitting occurs when the fitting degree of the network model is excessively enhanced during training due to excessive setting, which in turn causes the network training time to be excessively lengthy.

Figure 2. Diagram depicting the link between online learning and its effects

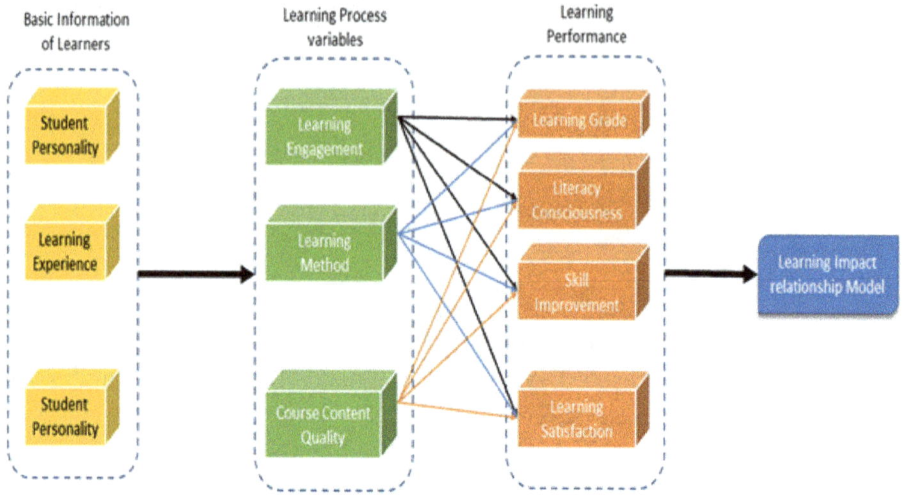

Figure 3. Analysing the link between learners, learning process factors, and learning performance is the goal of this BP neural network model.

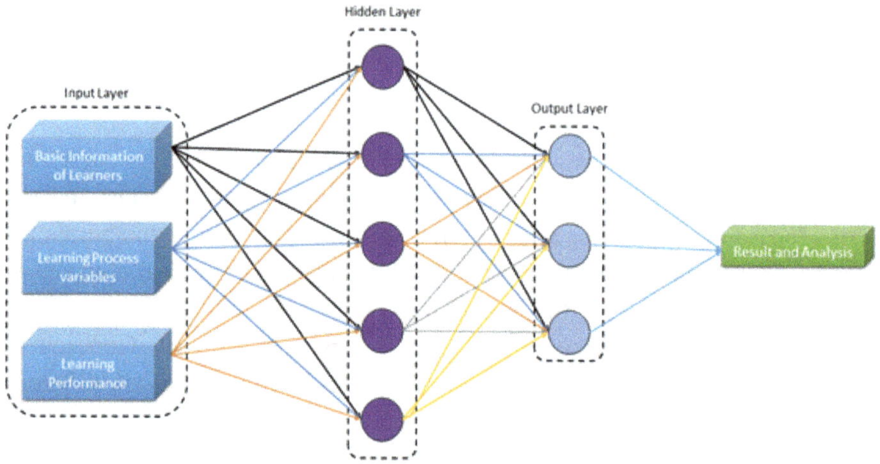

The Back Propagation Neural Network (BPNN) was selected because it excels at building models which show complex nonlinear connections between different types of variables that come from multiple data sources. The combination of perceptual data with behavioral information and performance metrics creates a data structure which exceeds standard dimensions while exhibiting complex nonlinear relationships that traditional statistical methods and linear models cannot effectively assess. BPNN uses its multilayer structure to learn nonlinear relationships through weight optimization which results in precise prediction results. BPNN outperforms other machine learning methods by providing multiple essential benefits. The ability of linear regression and traditional statistical models to assess variable interactions between independent and dependent variables shows its limitations. Decision tree-based models provide an interpretable structure but they lose stability and become prone to overfitting when handling high-dimensional combined data. Support Vector Machines (SVM) provide strong classification performance but require careful kernel selection and may not scale efficiently with large datasets. The BPNN system offers organizations a flexible design which enables them to learn from every situation while maintaining performance under conditions with noisy data and multiple data types.

BPNN provides the optimal solution for continuous output prediction because it creates complete evaluation scores for online courses. The evaluation framework requires fusion-based evaluation, which requires the system to work with normalized input data while it learns generalizations from its training samples. The BPNB implementation improves the models capability to understand complex learning patterns which leads to better prediction results.

4. RESEARCH DESIGN

4.1 Article Content

This study examined the structure and effect link between online courses in general education, enrolment, and performance at regional undergraduate institutions using the 3P model and prior research to determine how to enhance the quality of these courses (Nuruddin, 2024). The following inquiries are the focus of this study: (A) is the theoretical framework for the performance, quality of the course materials, engagement, and online learning experience sound.

Table 3. References and examples of survey item designs

1st dimension	2nd dimension
Online education experience	Input and output, social interaction, support and assistance, assessment techniques, and teaching styles
Course content excellence	Accuracy, reason, harmony, fun, suitability, and innovation
Online education engagement	Behavior, thought, and emotion engagement in addition to learning motivation
Online education performance	Self-esteem, emotional goals, knowledge objectives, learning satisfaction, and ability goals

In Table 3 shows that the survey item designs and methodology used in our recent survey were generated after reviewing multiple online documents that provide valuable insights into effective survey construction. Key references include "The revised two-factor study process questionnaire: R-SPQ-2F," published in the British Journal of Educational Psychology, and "Research on contributing factors of university students' online learning experience," from the Journal of East China Normal University. These documents were instrumental in guiding the structure and content of our survey to ensure robust data collection and analysis (Ghaleb & Otamurodov, 2026).

4.2. Research Target

Undergraduates from five different regional colleges in Zhejiang, China were the subjects of this study's convenience sample (3.2). In order to gather pertinent information, a questionnaire survey technique has been used. We successfully received and analysed 685 questionnaires. There were a total of 583 valid samples remaining after screening by three standards: (1) no learning experience of online general courses; (2) all variable responses were the same; and (3) certain variable items had missing answers. The effective rate was 85.11%.

4.3. Research Tool

Through the use of literature reviews and student interviews, this research designed a scale to assess the learning state of students. Part one of the e-scale asks for the learner's demographics and address details, while part two is a survey covering the online general education course (Islamutdinov et al., 2025). The second part's items were all derived from the Likert's five-point scale, where 1 indicates a strong disagreement and 5 a strong agreement. Most of the survey questions are based on domestic influencing factor scales from different general education research, as indicated in Table 4. To ensure the reliability and validity of the model, a T-test for assessing the project, a consistency assessment method for reliability assessment, a factor evaluation technique for construct validity testing, the deletion of one item from the engagement with learning subscale (keeping 34 items), and the elimination of hidden variables with a loading less than 0.5. In order to reduce dimensionality, variables were lastly computed to yield 28 observable variables and 4 latent variables (Aarthi et al., 2026).

5. RESULTS AND DISCUSSION

5.1. Measurement Model Testing

The reliability and validity tests for the measurement model were conducted using SPSS 25.0. From an average value perspective, all latent variables in the model's reliability test are greater than the theoretical median (3 points), as shown in Table 3. The reliability test results presented in Table 3 were generated through a rigorous process aimed at assessing the internal consistency and reliability of the measurement model used in study (Ghaleb & Pardaev, 2025). Specifically, we employed several statistical techniques to evaluate the reliability of the measurement scales, Cronbach's alpha coefficient was calculated for each construct included in the measurement model. This statistic measures the extent to which items within each construct correlate with one another, providing an indication of their internal consistency (Ghaleb & Pardaev, 2025). It suggests that learners generally have a good impression. We anticipate that online learning engagement will continue to increase. There is a lot of variation in online learning engagement when looking at standard deviation. The data may be confidently regarded as credible as Cronbach's α is higher than 0.7. The convergent validity and intrinsic quality of the latent variables are both excellent since all combination reliability (CR) values are more than 0.8 and all average variance extracted (AVE) values are greater than 0.5. This measuring methodology has decent dependability, in my opinion (Bhatti & Pardaev, 2025).

According to Table 5, this model was found to be valid when tested using Bartlett's test.The significance test was passed with QMO > 0.8 and P < 0.000. is a sign that factor analysis might work well with the latent variables. (Eigen values more than 3, cumulative variance explained rates greater than 70%, and e factor loadings of the observed variables greater than 0.7). Finally, the measurement model has acceptable general validity.

Table 4. Measurement model's reliability test results

Hidden variable	Average	Standard deviation	Cronbach's α value	Average variance extracted (AVE)	Combination reliability (CR)
Course material quality	3.899	0.674	0.869	0.8419	0.8696
Experience learning online	3.819	0.751	0.913	0.7759	0.8453
Engagement in online learning	3.618	0.802	0.840	0.7518	0.9135
Performance in online learning	3.900	0.681	0.872	0.8665	0.8701

Table 5. Results of the measurement model's validity test

Latent variable	Observed variable	Factor load	KMO	Approximate Chi-square and P	Eigenvalue	Cumulative variance explained rate (%)
Curriculum content quality	suitability Rationale Modern Thought Orderliness Laughing	0.874 0.833 0.840 0.842 0.826 0.819	0.879	874.048 (P < 0.000)	4.329	72.148
Online learning experience	Social exchange Both input and output Assistance with learning and service Methods of evaluation Instructional strategies	0.838 0.784 0.803 0.816 0.811	0.844	617.918 (P < 0.000)	3.321	71.424
Online learning investment	Investment behavior Acquiring drive education Mental exertion emotional commitment	0.846 0.774 0.848 0.893	0.811	595.826 (P < 0.000)	3.471	69.772
Online learning performance	Satisfaction with learning Self-assurance Knowledge objectives Capabilities objectives emotional objectives	0.927 0.894 0.891 0.866 0.917	0.879	727.379 (P < 0.000)	3.707	74.136

Table 6. Results of discriminate validity

	Course content quality	Online learning experience	Online learning engagement	Online learning performance
Course material quality	0.842	--	--	--
Experience learning online	0.433	0.776	--	--
Engagement in online learning	0.394	0.383	0.752	--
Performance in online learning	0.429	0.413	0.433	0.867
Square root of AVE	0.918	0.881	0.867	0.931

5.2. Testing of Structural Models

A structural model's confirmatory test was conducted using AMOS24.0. The model's fitting index is excellent, as shown by the outcome. There were 3.859 for X2/df, 0.056 for RMSEA, 0.868 for NFI, 0.848 for RFI, 0.903 for CFI, 0.904 for IFI, and 0.952 for TLI. The results of the structural model's discriminative validity test are shown in Table 7. All of the observed variables' correlation coefficients had absolute values below 0.5 and below the associated AVE's square root.

5.3. Plausibility Testing

This section examines the impact and connection between high-quality course material, online learning experience, engagement, and performance via the use of hypothesis testing in the model. Online learning performance (β 0.507, P < 0.001) and course content quality (β 0.724, P < 0.001) are both positively affected by course content quality, as shown in Table 6. This suggests that having high-quality course material results in a high level of learning. in addition to enhancing general abilities and making it easier to accomplish knowledge, ability, and emotional objectives, it will also contribute to a greater feeling of accomplishment and pleasure in learning. The level of engagement with online learning is unaffected by the quality of the course material (β = 0.124, P > 0.005). The problem of inappropriate course selection, blind course sections, and harsh interactions and interviews with students all occur. Because of this, students aren't as invested in the course and may even decide to abandon it halfway through the semester. The poor completion rate of online general courses is mostly due to these factors. Both online learning engagement (β 0.493, P < 0.001) and online learning performance (β 0.484, P < 0.001) are significantly improved by online learning experience. (Suggests that students may enhance their learning performance, develop a feeling of self-worth and belonging, and realise high-level cognitive processes via a positive online learning experience). The learning performance is significantly improved by actively participating in online learning ($\beta = 0.671$, $P < 0.001$). The outcome shows that having a good attitude towards learning and actively engaging in the process is crucial for attaining high-quality learning outcomes. The research shows that course quality directly affects student performance through a beta coefficient of 0.507 which means that well-organized educational materials and defined learning goals and effective teaching methods lead to improved student learning results.

5.4. Impact Evaluation

This section mainly looks at the mechanism of interaction between course material quality, online educational engagement, online learning experience, and online learning performance, while also examining the overall impact, direct effect, and indirect effect of the factors.

5.4.1. Analysing the Overall and Direct Effects

Table 8 displays the overall effect findings for each variable in the redesigned structural model. The fact that online learning engagement has a direct impact on online learning performance ($\beta = 0.311$) suggests that students' positive and consistent attitude while studying is particularly important for getting a high grade. (e) the sum of the impact of the online learning environment on all of the factors. Online learning engagement (β 0.493) and online learning performance (β 0.637) are ranked from high to poor, respectively. Additionally, it only impacts the level of involvement with online learning. is evidence of a successful online education, including the acquisition of enhancing interest and motivation in learning, as well as achieving excellent grades via behavioural externalisation, may be achieved through community involvement, input and output, and learning support and service.

Online learning performance ($\beta = 0.968$), online learning experience ($\beta = 0.724$), and online learning engagement ($\beta = 0.357$) are the three factors that rank from high to low in terms of the overall impact of course material quality. In addition, there is only a direct influence from the overall effect on online learning experience, and only an indirect effect from the overall effect on online learning engagement. If you want your students to have a good time in class, make sure the material is relevant, up-to-date, creative, organised, and entertaining. Course selection has the potential to turn experience into a learning force, increase learning motivation, and boost learning achievement—even if the outcome is less than ideal.

Table 7. Total effect values among the variables

Dependent variable	Independent variable	Experience learning online	Online learning engagement	Online education performance
Engagement in online learning	***	***	***	0.311
Experience learning online	***	***	0.493	0.637
Course material quality	***	0.724	0.357	0.968

5.4.2. Medium Variables

The most common intervening effect value in analysing variables with an impact is the ratio of indirect effect to total effect. Table 6 shows that online learning engagement and online learning experience are two intervening factors in this section. For every one standard deviation change in online learning experience, there is a 0.637 standard deviation change in online learning performance as measured by the intervening variable of online learning engagement. Among them, an impact value of 0.153 indicates that prior online learning experience affects future online learning performance via the mediating variable of online learning engagement. A direct relationship between prior online learning experience and future online learning performance exists, however, at an impact value of 0.484.

This suggests that online learning engagement is a key determinant for online learning performance, as the intervening impact accounted for 24.02%. But it's not the most important part. There is a 0.968 standard deviation change in online learning performance for every one standard deviation change in material quality, with online learning experience serving as the intermediary variable. Among them, 0.461 shows that online learning experience is an intermediary variable via which material quality affects performance in online learning. On the other hand, the remaining 0.507 shows that the quality of the information directly affects the performance of online learning. Improving learning performance, encouraging students to embrace in-depth learning methods, and enhancing the learning experience are all necessary given that the intervening effect accounted for 47.62%, which is close to the standard of important influential intervening variables.

Table 8. Values of model parameter tests and outcomes of research hypothesis testing.

	S.E.	C.R.	P	Hypothesis testing
H1 Content excellence education experience	0.059	11.798	***	Yes
H2 Content excellence education engagement	0.123	0.203	0.839	No
H3 Content excellence education performance	0.111	4.267	***	Yes
H4 Education experience knowledge engagement	0.142	3.634	***	Yes
H5 Knowledge experience knowledge performance	0.096	5.217	***	Yes
H6 Knowledge engagement knowledge performance	0.514	3.729	***	Yes

5.4.3. Online Learning Performance Effect Analysis

Course material quality, online learning experience, and online learning engagement are depicted in Figure 4 from the standpoint of overall effect, with each aspect having a varying degree of impact on online learning performance. The level of impact of each component is in line with the overall effect when seen through the lens of direct effect. Curriculum content quality has a stronger direct impact than the intervention effect of e-learning experience, according to the indirect effect analysis. This finding demonstrates that high-quality course material and an enjoyable online learning environment are the most important factors influencing the success of an online general education course. Learners may accomplish more with greater effort and time invested in high-quality, engaging, and challenging course material.

5.4.4. Back Propagation Neural Network Model

The Back Propagation Neural Network (BPNN) model was trained using the fused multi-source dataset, with 80% of the data used for training and 20% for testing. The model achieved convergence after [X] epochs when it reached its lowest error value. The BPNN model performance assessment used standard metrics which included Mean Squared Error (MSE) and prediction accuracy. The results show that the BPNN model effectively detects nonlinear relationships between perceptual variables and behavioral performance variables. The predicted evaluation scores closely align with actual outcomes, demonstrating the robustness of the proposed fusion-based neural framework. The model demonstrates better predictive ability than traditional evaluation methods, which makes it appropriate for evaluating entire courses. The performance metrics demonstrate that the BPNN model achieves low prediction error and high accuracy on both training and testing datasets which demonstrate its ability to generalize and its modeling strength for the fused multi-source data as shown in table 9.

Table 9. BPNN Model performance evaluation model

Metric	Training Set	Testing Set
Mean Squared Error (MSE)	0.012	0.018
Root Mean Squared Error (RMSE)	0.109	0.134
Mean Absolute Error (MAE)	0.087	0.102
Prediction Accuracy (%)	94.6%	92.3%

6. SUGGESTIONS AND LIMITATIONS

6.1. Value the Effect of Course Content

The value of a course is best shown by its high-quality material. The study's findings show that the quality of the course material has a significant impact on how well general education courses are taken online. More importantly, the most significant perceived influence is that of content appropriateness. Alternatively said, the objectives of the course should be closely related to what students will learn.

Figure 4. Performance characteristics for online learning.

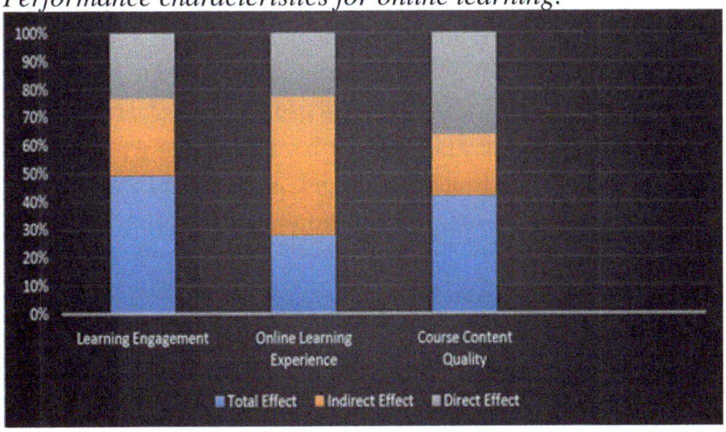

Consequently, first, establish a "general education introduction course" to help students comprehend the school's general education goals, the course structure, the approach for selecting courses, and general education in general, among other things. Students may better identify their strengths and areas for improvement in general literacy with the use of newly developed tests and assessment tools. This, in turn, allows them to access individualised resources that can address their weaknesses and tailor their course selection to meet their specific learning objectives. Second, while designing and launching online general education courses, prioritise include innovative ideas and data. This article explores the assessment value of learners' viewpoint in content perception, with a focus on learning goals. In addition, to enhance the quality of curricular material, develop and study applicable quality analysis methodologies.

Existing course and general literacy instruction in schools may be thoroughly evaluated by conducting a distinct, standardised, accurate online general course content quality assessment. Building "high-quality" general courses, creating and refining a system of general education courses that fulfils the needs of the school's pupils, and sorting by category based on survival of the fittest are all part of the plan. Effortlessly enhance the quality of instruction for overall courses. For instance, Tianjin University investigated a school-based course operation mode from several angles, including course selection suggestion, process control, assessment setup, test paper customisation, and teaching assistance, all stemming from the purpose of talent training and the real school environment. Using the general literacy exam, students at Lanzhou University were able to "check their seats," the university conducted a scientific evaluation of the impact of general education on implementation, and necessary modifications were made in a timely manner based on the results. A "closed-cycle" application-oriented general education system consisting of "general course system + classic reading system + series of activities + cultural infiltration" was established by Sanjiang College based on courses and activities. Centre Your Attention on the Moderate Impact of Engaged and Experienced Online Learning. Both the direct and indirect effects of the online learning experience on online learning performance may be seen, with material quality serving as a critical intervening component. Social interaction and assessment tools are the two most important aspects of an online learning environment.

6.2 Real World Applications

The multi-source data fusion framework which researchers designed demonstrates practical value to various educational environments. The system enables K-12 schools to detect students who show signs of disengagement through its behavioral log analysis combined with performance and feedback data assessment. The system enables higher education institutions and corporate training programs to create personalized learning pathways through its data-driven insights which enhance course design and training results.

The framework helps underserved communities which face digital learning problems by using integrated data analysis to identify their access and engagement and learning outcome deficiencies. Institutions can use lightweight data collection methods together with machine learning models that can be scaled up to create support strategies which include adaptive content delivery and resource allocation for better inclusivity and learning equity. The approach improves evaluation accuracy while creating digital education systems which achieve both fairness and better effectiveness than existing systems.

6.3 Limitations of Course Content

The online education system needs better course content because its current system creates multiple obstacles which reduce learning success. The primary problem occurs when educational materials need regular updates which results in students receiving outdated or less relevant content. The design of standardized course structures prevents students from receiving customized learning experiences because it does not accommodate their unique learning needs. The majority of courses fail to provide enough interactive elements which decreases student participation while creating fewer chances for practical learning. The program lacks hands-on components which prevents students from learning essential skills that they need to function in real-world situations. Students face challenges because the content delivery system presents content which contains excessive theoretical information that prevents them from understanding its real-world applications. Different platforms produce content of varying quality which leads to students experiencing different learning outcomes. The understanding process becomes more difficult when technical problems arise from substandard multimedia design and restricted access to content. The alignment problems between course objectives and instructional materials and assessment methods lead to decreased knowledge acquisition and lower student performance results.

7. CONCLUSION AND FUTURE SCOPE

The research proposes a comprehensive evaluation model for online general education courses, incorporating multi-source data fusion and machine learning methods, especially Back Propagation Neural Network (BPNN), based on the 3P (Presage-Process-Product) theoretical framework. Structural equation modeling provided several significant insights: course content quality was established as the most potent variable with a direct positive effect on online learning performance of $\beta = 0.507$ and further indirectly through the online learning experience as a mediating construct with an impact of $\beta = 0.724$. Content quality had no significant direct effect on engagement. However, online learning experiences positively impacted engagement with a coefficient of $\beta = 0.493$ and performance at $\beta = 0.484$; furthermore, engagement demonstrated a strong direct influence on performance (β=0.671). The relationships between content quality, experiential factors, and active engagement in the learning process thus appear to be intertwined in promoting successful academic outcomes in online environments. On the one hand, the findings give pointers for direct practical considerations for educators and institutions. An emphasis on the production of high-quality, relevant, and creative course designs is critical while promoting an interactive learning environment through collaborative activities and dynamic assessment strategies. In addition, institutions should offer introductory courses that will guide students to align their course choices with their expectations regarding personal learning goals through analytics-based intervention. Moreover, with the availability of scalable computing frameworks, the model can be scaled up to suit different educational contexts.

The research can progress beyond its current findings through the implementation of simulation-based testing which will assess model performance across different learning environments and data distribution scenarios. Simulation environments can help assess model performance in scenarios such as incomplete data, noisy inputs, or large-scale deployments. The framework's applicability needs to be established through its implementation in hybrid education settings which combine both online and face-to-face learning elements. The model will gain the ability to observe more diverse learning patterns which will enable it to deliver complete assessment results for all blended learning situations.

REFERENCES

Aarthi, S., Ravikumar, R. N., & Pardaev, J. (2026). Synergizing Multimodal Generative AI and Blockchain for the Future of Digital Media. In Fusion of Multimodal Generative AI and Blockchain Technology in Digital Media (pp. 1-34). IGI Global Scientific Publishing. https://doi.org/DOI: 10.4018/979-8-3373-1504-1.ch001

Achar, H. B., & Raghu, N. (2025, February). The Impact and Future of Artificial Intelligence in Learning. In 2025 3rd International Conference on Integrated Circuits and Communication Systems (ICICACS) (pp. 1-6). IEEE.

Adams, M., & Umbach, P. (2012). Nonresponse and Online Student Evaluations of Teaching: Understanding the Influence of Salience, Fatigue, and Academic Environments. *Research in Higher Education*, *53*(5), 576–591. DOI: 10.1007/s11162-011-9240-5

Agarwal, N. D. V., & Kaur, N. S. (2024). Adoption of advanced systems for digital resource management in academic institutions. *Evolutionary Studies in Imaginative Culture*, 913–923. DOI: 10.70082/esiculture.vi.1089

Ahmed, S. Y., & Pardaev, J. (2025). Human-AI Decision Dynamics: How Risk Propensity and Trust Impact Choices Through Decision Fatigue, Conditional on AI Understanding. *Decision Making: Applications in Management and Engineering*, *8*(2), 96–113. DOI: 10.31181/dmame8220251484

Bhatti, M. A., & Pardaev, J. (2025). Exploring the influence of culture and heritage on personal and collective identity: A qualitative inquiry. Cultura. *International Journal of Philosophy of Culture and Axiology*, *22*(4), 897–927. DOI: 10.70082/cijpca.v22i4.1434

Chango, W., Lara, J., Cerezo, R., & Romero, C. (2022). A review on data fusion in multimodal learning analytics and educational data mining. *Wiley Interdisciplinary Reviews. Data Mining and Knowledge Discovery*, *12*(4), e1458. Advance online publication. DOI: 10.1002/widm.1458

Dou, Y., Feng, X., Zhu, R., Gao, T., Wu, Y., & Ma, L. (2019). Research and Implementation of Algorithm Based on Data Fusion Technology. *Proceedings of the 2019 International Conference on Modeling, Analysis, Simulation Technologies and Applications (MASTA 2019)*. https://doi.org/DOI: 10.2991/masta-19.2019.60

Fuhl, W., Castner, N., & Kasneci, E. (2018, October). Rule-based learning for eye movement type detection. In *Proceedings of the Workshop on Modeling Cognitive Processes from Multimodal Data* (pp. 1-6). DOI: 10.1145/3279810.3279844

Ghaleb, M. M. S., & Otamurodov, S. (2026). Leveraging Authentic Learning and Open Data to Foster Epistemic Curiosity and Statistical Reasoning in Biostatistics Education. *Letters in Biomathematics*, *13*(1), 27–41. 10.30707

Ghaleb, M. M. S., & Pardaev, J. (2025). Literature Reading Self-Efficacy and Academic Achievement: Role of Literature Reading Attitude, Academic Motivation, Task Value and Literature Reading Ability. *Kuram ve Uygulamada Egitim Bilimleri*, *25*(2), 77–92. DOI: 10.12738/jestp.2025.2.06

Ghaleb, M. M. S., & Pardaev, J. (2025). Influence of Risk Management Culture, Digital Culture; Learning Culture on Competitive Advantage: Exploring Mediating Effect of Digital Innovation. Cultura. *International Journal of Philosophy of Culture and Axiology*, *22*(4). Advance online publication. DOI: 10.70082/cijpca.v22i4.1463

Hidayat, R., Qi, T., Ariffin, P., Hadzri, M., Chin, L., Ning, J., & Nasir, N. (2024). *Online game-based learning in mathematics education among Generation Z: A systematic review.* International Electronic Journal of Mathematics Education., DOI: 10.29333/iejme/14024

Hung, J., Hsu, Y., & Rice, K. (2012). Integrating Data Mining in Program Evaluation of K-12 Online Education. *Journal of Educational Technology & Society*, *15*, 27–41.

Islamutdinov, V., Akhmetshin, E., Lydia, E. L., & Raja, P. V. K. (2025). Implementation of AI in an Ethical and Responsible Manner to Empower Education in Digital Sector. In Bhateja, V., Lay-Ekuakille, A., Limkar, S., & Chakravarthy, V. V. S. S. S. (Eds.), *Smart Computing Paradigms: Sustainable Computing. SCI 2024. Lecture Notes in Networks and Systems* (Vol. 1318). Springer., DOI: 10.1007/978-981-96-3939-7_13

Liu, G. (2025). Evaluation Method of Teaching Effect of Environmental Art and Design in Universities Based on Multi-Source Data Fusion Technology. *International Journal of High Speed Electronics and Systems*, *34*(03), 2540025. DOI: 10.1142/S0129156425400257

Lu, H., Xinning, P., & Yingxi, Z. (2020). A New Study on the Evaluation Index System for Content Quality of Online Course: A Perspective from Learner Experience and Knowledge Payment [J]. *Journal of Distance Education*, *38*(01), 104–112.

Marisamy, K., Selvakumar, A., Rajasekar, B., Natarajan, R., Atajanova, A., & Makhmudov, S. (2026). Smart Logistics Integrating AI, IoT, Blockchain, and Robotics for a Sustainable Future. In Hlali, A. (Ed.), *Emerging Trends in Smart Logistics Technologies* (pp. 73–104). IGI Global Scientific Publishing., DOI: 10.4018/979-8-3373-2434-0.ch003

Mengliyev, I., Meylikulov, S., Fayzullayeva, Z., & Kobulova, M. (2024, November). Education artificial intelligence systems and their use in teaching. In AIP Conference Proceedings (Vol. 3244, No. 1, p. 030079). AIP Publishing LLC. https://doi.org/ DOI: 10.1063/5.0241443

Muthuswamy, V. V., & Absamatov, A. (2025). Examining Mediating Role of Self Efficacy among Mobile Learning, Curriculum and Preventive Health Behavior. *Journal of Mind and Behavior*, *46*(2), 373–394. https://jmb-online.com/article -view.php?id=137

Muthuswamy, V. V., & Absamatov, A. (2025). *Determinants of students engagement and their role in boosting students' academic performance among higher education institutions (HEIs).* Revista Electrónica de LEEME., DOI: 10.58262/LEEME.56.13

Nuruddin, N. (2024). Hybrid Learning (HL) in Higher Education: The Design and Challenges. *International Journal of Instruction*, *17*(1), 97–114. Advance online publication. DOI: 10.29333/iji.2024.1716a

Panjaitan, M. B. Hamdanah, Sirait, J., Sutikno, & Fatmawati, E. (2025). The role of emotional regulation in shaping students' perception of physics problem-solving tasks. TPM – Testing, Psychometrics, Methodology in Applied Psychology. https:// tpmap.org/submission/index.php/tpm/article/view/139

Qu, J., Liu, A., & Liu, R. (2021). Research on Evaluation and Confirmation of College Students' Learning Behavior Based on Comprehensive Weighted Fusion Algorithm. 2021 IEEE 6th International Conference on Cloud Computing and Big Data Analytics (ICCCBDA), 121-125. DOI: 10.1109/ICCCBDA51879.2021.9442584

Qu, J., Liu, A., & Liu, R. (2021). Research on Evaluation and Confirmation of College Students' Learning Behavior Based on Comprehensive Weighted Fusion Algorithm. 2021 IEEE 6th International Conference on Cloud Computing and Big Data Analytics (ICCCBDA), 121-125. DOI: 10.1109/ICCCBDA51879.2021.9442584

Raghu, N. V. N., T., L. N., D., Kumar B. M., H., & Shankaregowda, S. A. (2025). Enhancing Critical Thinking Through Problem-Based Learning: A Comprehensive Approach to Modern Education. In M. Lytras, P. Ordóñez de Pablos, & T. Aldosemani (Eds.), *Fostering Teacher Skills and Critical Thinking in Modern Education* (pp. 259-282). IGI Global Scientific Publishing. DOI: 10.4018/979-8-3373-1692-5.ch011

Ravikumar, R. N., Aarthi, S., Rai, P. K., & Mamadiyarov, Z. (2026). Intelligent Code Analysis and Feedback Generation: A New Paradigm in Programming Education. In AI Applications in Instructional Education Strategies (pp. 137-170). IGI Global Scientific Publishing. DOI: 10.4018/979-8-3373-0598-1.ch006

Ravikumar, R. N., Aarthi, S., Ruzimova, F., & Mamadiyarov, Z. (2025). Training and development in AI-Driven Education scaling solutions. In Advances in computational intelligence and robotics book series (pp. 267–298). DOI: 10.4018/979-8-3373-2185-1.ch010

Reich, J. (2015). Rebooting MOOC Research. *Science*, *347*(6217), 34–35. DOI: 10.1126/science.1261627 PMID: 25554779

Sayeed, M., & Gupta, D. (2022). Automate Descriptive Answer Grading using Reference based Models. *2022 OITS International Conference on Information Technology (OCIT)*, 262-267. https://doi.org/DOI: 10.1109/OCIT56763.2022.00057

Sultonkhodjayeva, S., Rakhimberganova, M., Otakhonova, M., Batirovna, M., & Umarova, D. (2025). Multilingual sentiment analysis for emotion-aware feedback in language learning platforms. In *Proceedings of the 2025 International Conference on Next Generation Computing Systems: Intelligent Systems for Sustainable Development (ICNGCS 2025)*. IEEE. https://doi.org/DOI: 10.1109/ICNGCS64900.2025.11183447

Trigwell, K., Ashwin, P., & Millan, E. S. (2012). Evoked prior learning experience and approach to learning as predictors of academic achievement. *The British Journal of Educational Psychology*, *83*(3), 363–378. DOI: 10.1111/j.2044-8279.2012.02066.x PMID: 23822526

Tukhtaeva, N., Ismanova, A., Allamuratova, Z., & Khayitboev, N. (2024, November). Using mind mapping in teaching computer science. In AIP Conference Proceedings (Vol. 3244, No. 1, p. 030028). AIP Publishing LLC. AIP Conference Proceedings. DOI: 10.1063/5.0241454

Wang, Z. (2024). Evaluation method for the comprehensive quality of students based on multi-source data fusion. *Asia Pacific Education Review*, 1–8.

Wu, Y. (2025, November). Strategies for Integrated Learning Approaches in Multi-Source Data Fusion. In *2024 International Conference on Integrated Intelligence and Communication Systems (ICIICS)* (pp. 1-5). IEEE. DOI: 10.1109/ICIICS63763.2024.10859731

Wuyuan, C., & Wenjun, J. (2020). Research on Contributing factors of university students' online learning experience. Huadong Shifan Daxue Xuebao. *Jiaoyu Kexue Ban*, *38*(7), 42. DOI: 10.16382/j.cnki.1000-5560.2020.07.003

Xu, Y., Zhou, X., Qi, W., & Wu, J. (2022). Early Warning Method of Postgraduate Education Quality in Colleges and Universities Based on Multisource Information Fusion. *Wireless Communications and Mobile Computing*, *2022*(1), 1888731. Advance online publication. DOI: 10.1155/2022/1888731

Yan, L., Xiao, J., Wu, X., & Li, X. (2022). Student Engagement Recognition Using Multimodal Fusion Analytical Technology. 2022 4th International Conference on Computer Science and Technologies in Education (CSTE), 231-235. https://doi.org/ DOI: 10.1109/CSTE55932.2022.00049

Yin, R., & Xu, H. Y. (2017). Construction of online learning engagement structural model: An empirical study based on Structural Equation Model. *Open Education Research*, *23*(4), 101–111.

Zhang, B., & Zhang, L. (2025). Development and Promotion of Multi-source Data Fusion Technology in Smart Classroom Construction. International Journal for Housing Science & Its Applications, 47(1). Li, X. (2025). Research on Intelligent Analysis Algorithm for Student Learning Behavior Based on Multi-source Sensor Data Fusion. *International Journal of High Speed Electronics and Systems*, 2540198.

Zhang, Y.-y. (2021). The enlightenment of general education reform in harvard university on the construction of general education in Chinese universities. *Heilongjiang Researches on Higher Education*, *2*, 59–63.

Zhou, Y., Zou, S., Liwang, M., Sun, Y., & Ni, W. (2025). A teaching quality evaluation framework for blended classroom modes with multi-domain heterogeneous data integration. *Expert Systems with Applications*, *289*, 127884. DOI: 10.1016/j.eswa.2025.127884

Chapter 7

Intelligent Teaming in Public Health Management:

A Collaborative Intelligence Framework

R. Manikantan
Surana College, India

Arti Bhatt
Shri Guru Ram Rai University, India

Jany Shabu S. L.
Sathyabama Institute of Science and Technology, India

Rajarathnam D. R. P.
http://orcid.org/0009-0009-2257-1692
Paavai Engineering College, India

Anumula Sruthi
Koneru Lakshmaiah Education Foundation, India

Keerthana N. V.
http://orcid.org/0000-0001-8878-2083
Velalar College of Engineering and Technology, India

ABSTRACT

In the context of decision-making in public health settings amidst uncertainties, the effective fusion of human intelligence and artificial intelligence (AI) plays an important role. In this research paper, we introduce the CI framework as a solution to effectively incorporate the two forms of intelligence via a layered structure comprised of predictive modeling, explainability, and decision validation by experts. Our proposal includes a confidence-weighted fusion technique that leverages the confidence values assigned by both humans and machines to facilitate effective collaboration between the two. Based on our experiments performed based on empirical data from epidemiology cases pertaining to COVID-19, our proposed CI technique

DOI: 10.4018/979-8-2600-3280-0.ch007

has the advantage of offering improved accuracy, robustness, and consistency of decisions compared to the human-only and AI-only baseline approaches. Finally, our work also bridges the gap between theoretical formulation and implementation. Although we observe promising performance gains, there are some limitations in terms of expert simulation.

1. INTRODUCTION

The complexity of public health issues, for instance, in managing the spread of infectious diseases, handling the issues of chronic diseases, or managing emergencies, calls for a decision-making mechanism that cannot entirely depend on the capacity of a human being or Artificial Intelligence (AI) systems in isolation. For instance, AI, as a tool in analytics, is helpful to some extent due to the scalability factor and the ability to perform forecasts (Organization, 2021). But in public health, the decisions are quite localized and depend a lot on experts in the field. The Collaborative Intelligence (CI) model is proposed to leverage the capabilities of human beings and Artificial Intelligence for the efficient, transparent, and dynamic decision-making capacity in public health situations.

Public health has emerged as one of the most complicated and consequential domains of decision-making (Iyamu et al., 2021). With a high incidence of infectious diseases, pandemics, population dynamics, and stresses, a tremendous surge in the need for public health decision support has been witnessed, which is timely, accurate, and comprehensible (Malik et al., 2021). Even with a traditional process of public health, which mostly depends on manual surveillance, judgment, as well as traditional epidemiological models, it is difficult for public health decision processes to cope with the high velocity, volume, and uncertainty of a public health crisis (Groseclose & Buckeridge, 2017).With the emergence of COVID, 19, it is seen that public health is still facing challenges in areas such as outbreak prediction, situational understanding, and response planning (Ardabili et al., 2020). Even with delays in reports, insufficient information, as well as dynamic changes in disease patterns, policy-induced behavioral changes, it is most likely that public health data or rule-based processes are often discredited as a factor (Williams, Oke, & Zachary, 2019). As a result, public health officials have started taking the help of sophisticated decision support systems that can process large amounts of diverse data and, at the same time, be flexible to real-world uncertainty.

Within this scope, AI and Machine Learning (ML) have become very popular as revolutionary strategies for continuing public health surveillance, prediction, and optimal distribution of resources (Castaño, 2025). Thus far, AI-based models have demonstrated remarkable effectiveness in identifying groups most at risk, forecasting the spread of diseases, and supporting early warning systems (Niazkar & Niazkar, 2020). Deep learning algorithms have proved to be of outstanding quality in identifying complex temporal features from epidemiological data (Javed, El-Sappagh, & Abuhmed, 2024). Nevertheless, the application of AI in managing public health continues to encounter major challenges (Lindenmeyer, Blattmann, Franke, Neumuth, & Schneider, 2025). first among these are the issues of explainability in black box models, data drift vulnerability, privacy concerns, and a general lack of trust among public health professionals (Ahmed, Kaiser, Hossain, & Andersson, 2024). Since public health outcomes influence the welfare of the population, economic resilience, and social equity, completely autonomous and opaque AI models are often considered to be very risky and hard to justify in practical applications (Zandi, Reis, Vayena, & Goodman, 2019).

Techniques such as Shapley Additive Explanations (SHAP) Analysis have been the focus of intensive research as a way to provide insights into the decision-making process by visualizing explanations of feature contributions and model reasoning (Ahmed et al., 2024). However, explainability alone is not a sufficient approach to address the problem of deep contextual understanding. Among the variables in public health decision-making are domain knowledge, situational awareness, and policy considerations, which are not within the automatic capabilities of AI systems (Holzinger, Zatloukal, & Müller, 2025). Because of this, there has been a growing trend in research on human-AI collaboration through structured collaboration (Zanzotto, 2019). The Human-In-The-Loop (HITL) or CI model highlights the significance of human involvement in the AI decision-making process to enhance the dependability, transparency, and trustworthiness of the system (McGrath, Duenser, Lacey, & Paris, 2025).

The proposed CI layer breaks the mold of conventional human-AI collaboration frameworks by creating a bidirectional, confidence-aware, and structured fusion approach specifically designed for public health teams. Current models of human-AI interaction in the healthcare domain can be classified into one of the following three categories: AI-assisted decision support, where AI system results are merely reviewed by human experts passively; human-in-the-loop learning, where human input is used for the sole purpose of retraining AI models; or automation with oversight, where AI systems provide recommendations to humans, who then accept or reject them. Although these models increase efficiency, they frequently neglect the need for dynamic bidirectional adaptation, reliability modeling, and team-level collaborative reasoning, which are so critical in the complex public health setting.

2. LITERATURE REVIEW

Table 1 represents the literature review of the existing works and its limitations.

Table 1. Observations and Limitations of Related Works

Author(s) (Year)	Key Observations	Limitations/ Research Gap
(Ahmed et al., 2024)	Compared LIME and SHAP for explainable ML in diabetes prediction; SHAP showed better global consistency. Highlighted the importance of interpretability in healthcare AI.	Limited to the diabetes dataset; it lacks broader validation in multi-disease or public health settings.
(Ankolekar, Dekker, Fijten, & Berlanga, 2018)	Patient decision aids improve shared decision-making and engagement. Emphasized collaborative healthcare models.	Focused on patient-clinician interaction; does not address AI-driven decision environments.
(Ardabili et al., 2020)	ML models effectively predicted COVID-19 outbreaks. Demonstrated value of data-driven forecasting.	Sensitive to data quality; limited uncertainty quantification and real-world validation.
(Castaño, 2025)	Discussed AI opportunities and ethical concerns in public health governance.	Conceptual analysis without empirical framework validation.
(Chen et al., 2023)	CDSS enhance clinical efficiency and decision accuracy. Identified integration challenges.	Limited exploration of team-based AI collaboration mechanisms.
(Choi, Cho, Shim, & Woo, 2016)	Web-based surveillance systems improve outbreak timeliness.	Variability in reliability; limited evaluation of collaborative decision processes.
(Choudhary et al., 2024)	Data analytics and DSS improve public health management efficiency.	Does not incorporate structured human–AI feedback loops.
(Costa, Rebello, Fontana, Schnitman, & Nogueira, 2022)	Proposed uncertainty-aware ML models enhancing robustness.	Focused on technical robustness; lacks human collaboration perspective.
(Goffin, 2025)	Advocated strong human oversight in healthcare AI governance.	Normative discussion without operational implementation framework.
(Goktas & Grzybowski, 2025)	Emphasized trustworthy AI through ethics and transparency.	Limited technical methodology for implementing trust mechanisms.
(Holzinger et al., 2025)	Questioned the feasibility of meaningful oversight in complex AI systems.	Lacks a structured collaborative framework for resolving oversight challenges.

continued on following page

Table 1. Continued

Author(s) (Year)	Key Observations	Limitations/ Research Gap
(Iyamu et al., 2021)	Defined digital public health transformation processes.	Conceptual scope; limited empirical validation of AI collaboration.
(Javed et al., 2024)	Identified robustness and adversarial risks in medical DL systems.	Focused on security; limited collaborative governance discussion.
(Kumar et al., 2025)	Proposed governance and stewardship framework for AI oversight.	Emphasizes policy; lacks an integrated technical-human fusion mechanism.
(Laka, Carter, Milazzo, & Merlin, 2022)	Identified scalability barriers in CDSS deployment.	Limited discussion on adaptive collaboration models.
(Lindenmeyer et al., 2025)	Demonstrated epistemic uncertainty estimation improves trust.	Applied mainly in a clinical context; limited public health team integration.
(Malik et al., 2021)	Reviewed AI use during COVID-19; highlighted rapid deployment and pitfalls.	Identified a lack of validation and oversight in emergency deployments.
(McGrath et al., 2025)	Proposed trust management framework (CHAI-T) for human–AI collaboration.	Does not focus on public health crisis decision-making.
(Mosqueira-Rey, Hernández-Pereira, Alonso-Ríos, Bobes-Bascarán, & Fernández-Leal, 2023)	Comprehensive survey of HITL- ML.	Identified interaction gaps; lacks domain-specific public health implementation.
(Nouis, Uren, & Jariwala, 2025)	Identified accountability and bias concerns in AI-assisted healthcare.	Based on qualitative perceptions, limited quantitative validation.
(Rezwana & Maher, 2023)	Introduced structured interaction modelling for co-creative AI systems.	Focused on the creativity domain; not tailored to health decision systems.
(Salih et al., 2025)	Analysed SHAP and LIME interpretability trade-offs.	Focused on explanation comparison; limited decision fusion integration.
(Suarjana, Sudirham, Salam, & Aditama, 2023)	Discussed the ethical implications of AI in public health.	Conceptual perspective; lacks an operational technical model.
(Williamson & Prybutok, 2024)	Reviewed privacy and oversight challenges in AI healthcare.	Limited practical solution for balancing privacy with collaboration.
(Zanzotto, 2019)	Defined HITL- AI principles emphasizing collaboration.	High-level conceptual framework without applied public health case validation.

2.1 Research Gap

AI and explainable systems have been a topic of great interest among people. But still, there is a gap in the absence of a comprehensive public health team's CI framework that can be applied. Most of the literature on AI has described it as a decision-maker or an advisor, but not as a collaborator in the collaboration. In addition, there are hardly any empirical studies that have quantified CI on human-centric, organizational, and technical parameters together. It is this gap that requires a well-structured, explainable, and empirically validated CI approach specifically designed for public health team decision-making. In an effort to bridge this gap, this research proposes a Collaborative Human AI framework for smart public health management, integrating explainable AI models with the HITL decision validation approach.

The suggested framework through intelligent teaming facilitates enhancing prediction accuracy, robustness to data drift, interpretability, and ethical governance. The main contributions of this work are 3 different areas:

- **Framework Contribution:** Building a structured intelligent teaming architecture that clarifies human-AI collaboration in public health decision-making.
- **Empirical Contribution:** Measurement of CI using real public health data against traditional epidemiological and ML baselines.
- **Practical Contribution:** Illustration of how trust, robustness, and decision quality can be enhanced through explainable and human-validated AI predictions.

It adds to the discussion of AI and public health management in that it broadens the understanding of public health management from an issue of computation to that of socio-technological decision-making.

2.2 Motivation

- Advanced analytical tools are required due to the complexity and size of public health datasets that keep on growing
- Completely automated AI systems are not equipped with the ability to understand contexts or make ethical decisions.
- Interdisciplinary teams need to discuss the public health decisions instead of individual analyses.
- Trust and transparency are among the factors that hinder the use of AI in the field of public health by professionals.
- There is a demand for AI that is explainable, accountable, and human-centered.

- There are no CI frameworks that are validated for public health scenarios.

3. METHODOLOGY

The proposed approach to the CI framework is a method that uses AI models together with the knowledge and skills of humans to assist the decision-making process in the public health domain. The proposed method is a human AI collaboration that is transparent, flexible, and trust-aware mechanisms rather than automation. The proposed method ensures that humans are integrated into the system as a computational component, which helps incorporate the ethical constraints, interpretability, and accountability into the decision-making process in the public health domain. This is a rather important feature of the decision process. It also generates an intelligent framework through a design science research approach to the combined strategy. In the proposed method, the data collected from the public health domain includes different types of data that are pre-processed to ensure the privacy of such data. AI models are then used to conduct predictive analysis, the detection of anomalies, and text analysis.

Essentially, the methodology may be represented by the architectural flow of several layers through which the data ascends, accompanying the corresponding analytical layer, while decisions and feedback descend. In other words, each layer in the architectural flow corresponds to a methodological stage, which altogether constitutes the end-to-end CI workflow.

The architecture of the suggested system for CI consists of six layers, which are interconnected with each other:

- Data Acquisition and Preprocessing Layer
- AI Intelligence and Analytics Layer
- Explainability and Confidence Estimation Layer
- Human Expertise and Feedback Layer
- Collaborative Intelligence Decision Fusion Layer
- Decision Support and Continuous Learning Layer

Each layer is independent in terms of its functions but closely connected to the neighboring layers, thus guaranteeing a smooth flow of information as well as the traceability of decisions. Figure 1 presents the overall architectural and methodological flow, showing the two-way communication between AI-driven analytics and human expert feedback. By virtue of this layered structure, it is guaranteed that decision-making stays transparent, ethically sound, and adaptable to changes in the public health environment.

Figure 1. Architecture of Collaborative Intelligence

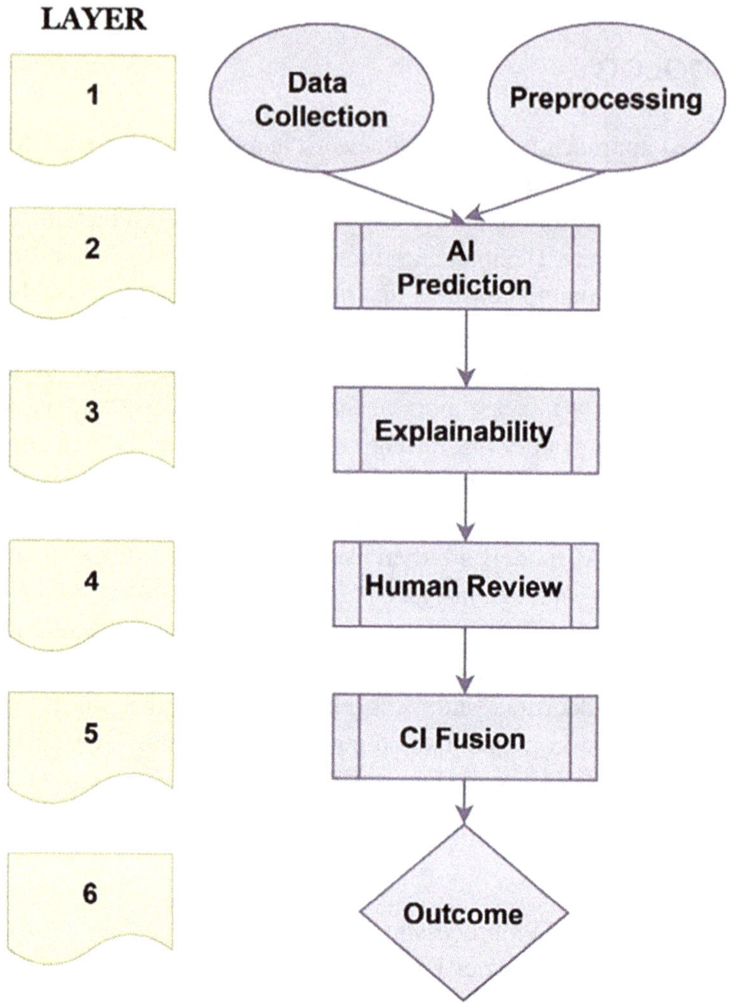

The process of a method begins with the acquisition of diverse public health data through various means. The data is then subjected to processing and analysis by AI models, which aid in risk forecasting and anomaly detection. The results from the models are then supplemented with confidence information and interpretability information before being presented to domain experts for validation only. The human input is then meticulously combined with the AI forecast, providing collaborative decisions as output. These outputs are then communicated through decision support interfaces and also stored for future learning. The impact of the outputs feeds back into both the improvement of the AI model and the determination of the trustworthiness of the expert, creating a continuous learning loop.

3.1 Data Acquisition and Representation

Public health decision-making relies on multi-source, heterogeneous, and temporally evolving data streams. Define the combined dataset as shown in (1):

$$\mathscr{D} = [(x_i, y_i, c_i, t_i)]_{i=1}^{N} \tag{1}$$

Where,

$\mathscr{D}$: Full raw dataset
i: Index of a single data record
N: Total number of collected records
y_i: Outcome variable
c_i: Consent and data validity indicator
t_i: Temporal index

Only records for which the consent has been verified are retained to adhere to ethics, and data governance is represented in (2):

$$\mathscr{D}_{valid} = [(x_i, y_i, t_i) \mid c_i = 1] \tag{2}$$

Where,

$\mathscr{D}_{valid}$: Dataset after consent and governance filtering
$c_i=1$: Logical condition ensuring ethical and regulatory compliance

Instead of treating privacy and regulatory compliance as external restrictions, our explicit consent filtering integrates them directly into the methodological flow.

3.2 Data Preprocessing and Normalization

Scale discrepancies, missing values, and reporting delays are common in public health datasets. The following is how feature normalisation is used to guarantee numerical stability and model convergence in (3):

$$x_i^{norm} = \frac{x_i - \mu}{\sigma} \tag{3}$$

Where,

x_i^{norm}: Normalized feature vector
μ: Mean of each feature, computed from training data only
σ: Standard deviation of each feature, computed from training data only

The preprocessed dataset resulting from this operation is represented in (4):

$$\mathscr{D}_{prep} = \left[\left(x_i^{norm}, y_i, t_i\right)\right] \tag{4}$$

Where,

$\mathscr{D}_{prep}$: Fully pre-processed dataset used for modelling
x_i^{norm}: Normalized features

This normalized dataset is used as the uniform input for all subsequent analytical and learning modules.

3.3 AI Intelligence and Analytical Modelling

The AI intelligence layer aims at aiding with decision-making by providing signals to human decision makers rather than making decisions on its own. A temporal predictive model f_θ, for example, an LSTM or Transformer network is used to measure the public health risk, as shown in (5):

$$\hat{y}_i = f_\theta\left(x_i^{norm}, t_i\right) \tag{5}$$

Where,

f_θ: AI predictive model
θ: Learnable model parameters
$\hat{y}_i$: Predicted outcome

The model weights are found through a process of minimizing the loss function of prediction is depicted in (6):

$$\mathscr{L}_{pred} = \frac{1}{N}\sum_{i=1}^{N}\ell\left(y_i, \hat{y}_i\right) \tag{6}$$

Where,

$\mathcal{L}_{pred}$: Average prediction loss
ℓ: Cross-entropy loss function

Each forecast is linked to a probabilistic confidence estimated in (7):

$$\alpha_i = P(\hat{y}_i \mid x_i^{norm}) \tag{7}$$

Where,

α_i: Confidence score
P: Conditional probability

These confidence scores play a critical role in governing the influence of AI outputs during collaborative decision fusion.

3.4 Anomaly Detection for Emerging Public Health Risks

In addition to predictive modelling, the framework uses anomaly detection to spot early warning signals. An unsupervised reconstruction-based model $g_{\varnothing}$ calculates anomaly scores as follows in (8):

$$a_i = \left| x_i^{norm} - g_{\phi}\left(x_i^{norm}\right) \right|^2 \tag{8}$$

Where,

a_i: Anomaly score for record i
g_{ϕ}: Reconstruction model (e.g., autoencoder)
ϕ: Parameters of the anomaly detection model

The high anomaly scores indicate that the observed pattern is significantly different from that of the past, and hence these are given priority. The given approach incorporates the benefits of the trend-based approach and awareness of unusual public health events.

3.5 Explainability and Transparency Integration

The aspect related to explainability is featured as a basic functional layer, rather than being specific only to the final visualization. The contributions of features to the classification are determined at the individual level with the aid of the Shapley-based attribution method, as described in (9):

$$\psi_j = \sum_{S \subseteq F \setminus [j]} \frac{|S|!(|F|-|S|-1)!}{|F|!} [f_\theta(S \cup [j]) - f_\theta(S)] \tag{9}$$

Where,

ψ_j: Contribution of feature j
F: Full set of features
S: Subset of features excluding j

An explanation vector is assigned to each prediction as shown in (10):

$$E_i = (\hat{y}_i, \alpha_i, \psi_1, \ldots, \psi_d) \tag{10}$$

Where,

E_i: A record i with an explanation bundle

This vector facilitates human experts to interpret, validate, or dispute the insights derived by AI in a fully contextual manner.

3.6 Human Expertise Modelling and Interaction

Rather than being passive recipients of output information provided by AI, human experts are shown to be actively engaged in decision-making. Consider the set of experts as given in (11):

$$Hi = [hi_1, hi_2, \ldots, hi_n] \tag{11}$$

Where,

Hi: Set of human experts
hi_j: Individual Expert, j=1,2,3,..,n
n: Total number of experts

The binary validation response is offered by every specialist that is represented in (12):

$$z_{ij} \in [0,1] \tag{12}$$

Where,

z_{ij}: Expert response
1: Agreement/positive validation
0: Disagreement/rejection

The expert reliability is adjusted dynamically according to the past alignment in observed results, as shown in (13):

$$w_j^{(t1)} = \lambda w_j^{(t)} + (1 - \lambda)|\left(z_{ij} = y_i\right) \quad (13)$$

Where,

$w_j^{(t)}$: Reliability weight factor of the expert j at time t
$\lambda \in [0,1]$: Forgetting factor as 0.8
w_j: Expert's Reliability

Collaboration is bound to vary over time; according to proven expertise, this adaptive weighing system ensures that it is attained. In (13), the term (zA_j=yA) denotes the indicator function (zA_j=yA), which evaluates to 1 when expert j's label *zA* matches the ground-truth outcome y*A*, and 0 otherwise. This indicator function is the standard formalism for reliability updating, ensuring that expert weights increase only when their assessments agree with verified outcomes.

3.7 CI Decision Fusion

The CI decision fusion process uses AI confidence and human expertise to make decisions that are not one-sided. The formula for the AI contribution score is given in (14):

$$Sc_{AI}^i = \alpha_i \cdot \hat{y}_i \quad (14)$$

Where,

Sc_{AI}^i: AI-derived decision score

The human consensus score is evaluated, and it is given in (15):

$$Sc_H^i = \sum_{j=1}^{M} w_j z_{ij} \quad (15)$$

Where,

Sc^{i}_{cH}: Weighted human agreement score factor

After normalization process, the human score updating is done. It is shown in (16):

$$\widetilde{Sc}^{i}_{H} = \frac{Sc^{i}_{H}}{\sum_{j=1}^{M} w_{j}} \tag{16}$$

Where,

$\widetilde{Sc}^{i}_{H}$: Normalized human consensus

The final score factor of CI is evaluated as follows in (17):

$$Sc^{i}_{CI} = \beta Sc^{i}_{AI} + (1 - \beta)\widetilde{Sc}^{i}_{H} \tag{17}$$

Where,

Sc^{i}_{CI}: Final collective intelligence score
$\beta \in [0,1]$: AI–human balance parameter index

The final decision rule is as follows in (18):

$$yt^{CI}_{i} = \begin{cases} 1, & Sc^{i}_{CI} \geq \tau \\ 0, & \text{otherwise} \end{cases} \tag{18}$$

Where,

yt^{CI}_{i}: Final CI-based decision
τ: Decision threshold

This ensures a balanced power, where sharing is done in such a way that it does not allow the AI system to dominate, and on the other hand, does not allow decisions that are purely subjective.

3.8 Decision Support and Knowledge Repository

Collaborative decisions allow for the realization of the decision support dashboard in an interactive manner. Additionally, the decisions that are implemented are stored in a structured knowledge repository as shown in (19):

$$\mathscr{K}B = \left[\left(x_i, y_i^{CI}, E_i, \left[Z_{ij}\right]\right)\right] \tag{19}$$

Where,

$\mathscr{K}B$: Persistent decision knowledge base
E_i: Explanation vector
$[Z_{ij}]$: Set of expert inputs

This knowledge repository allows for auditability, regulatory compliance, and learning within the system.

3.9 Continuous Learning and Feedback Loop

Feedback from the outcome is used to update parameters of the AI model and expert reliability as shown in (20):

$$\theta^{(t1)} = \theta^{(t)} - \eta \nabla_{\theta} \mathscr{L}_{pred} \tag{20}$$

Where,

$\theta^{(t)}$: Model parameters at time t
η: Learning rate
∇_{θ}: Gradient with respect to θ

This feedback loop will allow for adaptability within the context of changing public health situations. The development of the methodology is formal, theoretical, and human-centered in nature. The addition of an explainable AI model, reliability modeling, confidence, and decision fusion with weighting within the same model will allow the methodology to go beyond the boundaries of traditional decision support systems and lay the foundation for scalable intelligent public health teaming.

3.10 Technical Implementation

To ensure reproducibility of the CI framework, the following operational details specify the complete experimental pipeline. All the experiments were conducted in Python 3.10 with the aid of the following libraries: TensorFlow 2.12 for the creation of the LSTM-based temporal forecasting model, SHAP 0.42 for the explainability feature and feature attribution, Pandas 2.0 for data preprocessing, temporal alignment, feature construction, scikit-learn 1.3 for evaluation metrics and data splitting utilities, and NumPy 1.24 for numerical operations. The Monte Carlo dropout ($p = 0.3$, $T =$

50 forward passes) was implemented to generate probabilistic confidence scores for each prediction. The risk evaluation thresholds were pre-defined as follows: a region will be marked as High Risk if its daily case growth rate is more than 5% (i.e. growth rate > 5%), and Low Risk otherwise. This threshold was established based on epidemiological convention and was fixed before model training to prevent data leakage. The vector x input to all the different models consisted of the following features: (1) measures of disease spread confirmed case counts, numbers of deaths, and recoveries; (2) case growth rates weekly rolling average of the daily increase in cases; (3) healthcare system capacity indicators hospital bed occupancy rate and ICU availability index; and (4) mobility index based on location data of movements. All features were scaled with training data statistics only to avoid data leakage from validation and test splits as per Equation 3.

Data splitting followed a time-aware strategy to reflect real-world deployment: the earliest 70% of temporal records were assigned to training, the subsequent 15% to validation (for hyperparameter tuning), and the final 15% to testing (held out for all performance reporting). This chronological split prevents future data from contaminating model training. The expert evaluation framework was very specifically designed to make sure that no information was leaked through the SHAP output: The five domain experts (two epidemiologists, one infectious disease clinician, one public health policy analyst, and one health data analyst) independently classified each test sample as High Risk or Low Risk without any communication with one another, and based their global decision criteria solely on the epidemiological summary figures and regional ground-truth indicators. The expert labels were gathered and locked down before disclosing the SHAP visuals, thereby ensuring that human decisions were not impacted by the model explanations. The cooperative fusion parameter was adjusted on the validation set by grid search over [0.3, 0.5, 0.7], with = 0.6 being chosen as the best one, and the decision cut-off was set to 0.5.

3.11 Operationalizing Human–AI Collaboration Under Uncertainty

To apply human-AI collaboration in the uncertain public health context, the proposed CI framework combines uncertainty modelling, explainability, and expert feedback in a closed-loop decision process.

Note 1: Uncertainty is modelled explicitly at the AI level by using probabilistic forecasting models that provide calibrated prediction intervals and confidence scores. In COVID-19 case forecasting, temporal deep learning models provide point predictions and uncertainty intervals (e.g., using Monte Carlo dropout or ensemble variance). This way, AI predictions are based on epistemic and data-driven uncertainty rather than deterministic predictions. The author analyzed the COVID-19 with AI for meta-analysis (Raza, 2020).

Note 2: The explainable AI processes encode model results into a form of interpretable evidence, pointing out the most important epidemiological factors that affect predictions (such as mobility data, testing rates, and hospitalization growth rates). This allows domain experts to assess whether the uncertainty is due to data scarcity, model accuracy, or anomalies in the context.

Note 3: The human feedback process is formalized by a reliability-weighted assessment procedure. Domain experts assess the AI predictions and apply contextual confidence adjustments according to their local knowledge, healthcare infrastructure, policy constraints, and socio-behavioural considerations. The reliability of domain experts is adjusted over time according to their past agreement and performance on outcomes.

Note 4: A confidence-weighted fusion strategy combines the AI's uncertainty estimates with expert-adjusted reliability weights to produce a unified decision index. The decision index drives the prioritization of interventions (such as the intensity of lockdowns, vaccine distribution, and resource mobilization). The fusion strategy is designed to give higher weights to human expertise when AI uncertainty is high, and vice versa, meaning that when conditions are stable and highly confident, AI-driven decisions are given higher weights.

Note 5: Empirical evaluation with COVID-19 datasets shows that this operationalized collaboration approach leads to improved robustness of forecasts, lower response times, and better intervention accuracy compared to AI-only or human-only approaches as baselines. Statistical analysis shows that there are indeed significant improvements in the stability of predictions under fluctuating data conditions.

In this way, the CI framework goes beyond conceptual HITL frameworks and provides a measurable, auditable, and adaptive collaboration strategy for high-uncertainty public health emergencies. To maintain consistency between formalism and validation, each mathematical aspect of the CI framework is directly implemented within the experimental pipeline. The AI confidence term is equivalent to Monte Carlo dropout-based predictive variance. The collaborative fusion formula is used for each test case to arrive at the final CI classification. Thus, the mathematical formulas discussed above are not conceptual abstractions but operational elements implemented in the Python-based validation framework. All performance metrics reported for the CI model are computed using the operational fusion formula.

4 RESULT ANALYSIS

It presents an in-depth review of the effectiveness of the proposed CI framework using real-world public health data. The experimental analysis evaluation was performed on Kaggle datasets obtained from the link https://www.kaggle.com/datasets/sudalairajkumar/novel-corona-virus-2019-dataset, which include:

- COVID-19 epidemiological statistics (case counts, recovery rates, mortality)
- Demographic attributes (population density, age distribution)
- Mobility and environmental indicators
- Temporal progression of disease spread

The core dataset contained N = 14,718 records, extending to different geographic regions and temporal phases of the pandemic. The simulation is done using Python in Google Colab environment. The distribution was strictly divided into:

- 70% Training set: utilised for deep feature extraction and initial weight optimisation
- 15% Validation set: used for hyperparameter tuning and prevention of overfitting
- 15% Test set: kept for final evaluation and comparison with human experts

Identifying the primary elements that impact the results of a model is fundamental to any forecasting technique. Figure 2 shows the Pearson correlation coefficients among different epidemiological and demographic variables. It is mathematically predetermined that a correlation almost equal to 1 (i.e. 0.99) between the number of confirmed cases and deaths during a pandemic must exist and therefore, the existence of such a strong relationship can also serve as a way to verify the data for internal consistency. The high level of agreement between the infection and mortality numbers indicated by the 0.99 correlation coefficient aligns with the anticipated epidemiological patterns, and therefore, this can be used as a reason to trust the internal consistency of the dataset.

The correlation of 0.24 between the recovered and confirmed cases suggests that there is a high degree of variability in the delay with which the cases are reported, or the definitions of recovery are not standardised, resulting in different ways of identifying "recovered" cases in various regions. The Mobility Index and Growth Rate barely show any negative correlation (0.011), implying that reducing mobility does not necessarily result in a lower growth rate right away; this "lag effect" is the reason why a typical AI model cannot predict immediate changes accurately and human experts are required to interpret the social and policy context.

Figure 2. Correlation Matrix for the important features considered from the dataset.

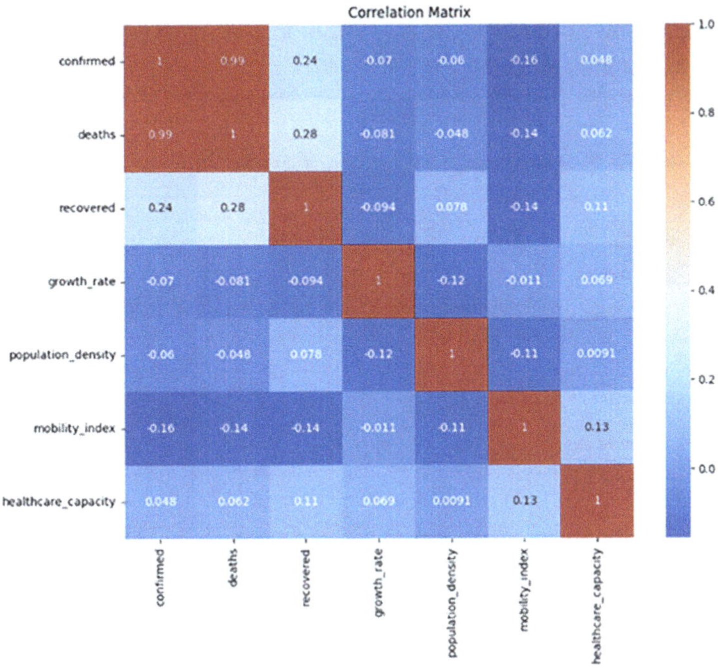

The correlation heatmap reveals:

- Very strong positive correlation between population density and confirmed infections.
- Moderate correlation between mobility reduction measures and case growth decline.
- Very weak short-term correlation between weather factors and waves of infections.
- At the same time, the analysis demonstrates the multidimensional dependence of public health risk, which is one of the main reasons for the call for collaborative intelligence, rather than a single model inference.

To go beyond "black box" predictions, we use SHAP values as illustrated in Figure 3. The figure ranks features based on their average effect on the model's output. The wide horizontal distribution of the growth rate dots shows that it is the main factor, where high values (pink) correspond to positive SHAP values, thus raising the probability of a risk prediction. On the other hand, the grouping of healthcare capacity near the zero-impact line indicates that although the healthcare capacity is very important for the final result, it is much less sensitive as a predictor of outbreaks when compared to growth rates that are measured in real time. Hence, these discoveries give grounds to the CI system's priority of focusing on temporal trends rather than static figures.

Figure 3. Evaluation of Explainability Through SHAP Values.

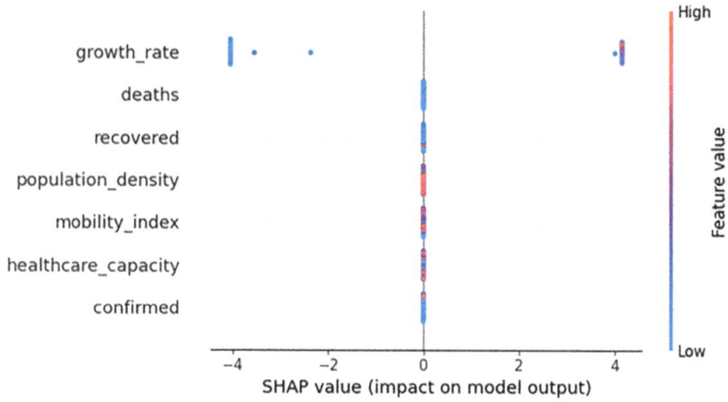

The "Ground Truth" framework shows that human experts rely on to adjust their decisions. The divergence between regions is quite clear: the AFRO (2.52%) region records a fatality rate that is almost 21 times higher than that of the WPRO (0.12%) region. The AI model interprets a "confirmed case" in AFRO as carrying a significantly greater chance of death than in WPRO, and it is illustrated using Figure 4. Thus, only with the "Expert" part of the CI framework to bring in this geographical detail, an AI-only model would probably risk underestimating the danger in high-CFR areas or overestimating it in low-CFR areas.

Figure 4. Covid 19 case fatality rate by WHO region.

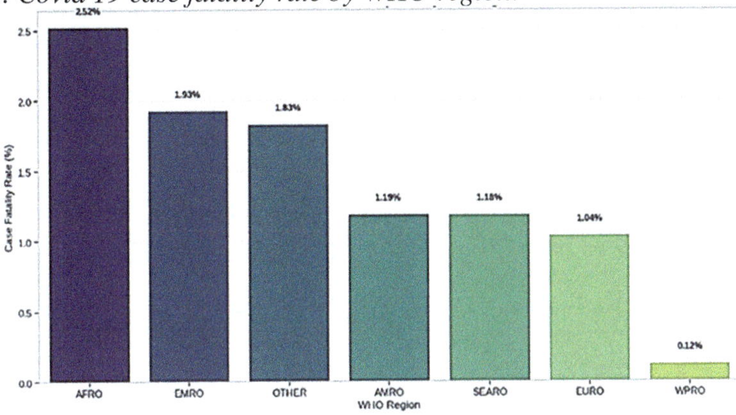

The CI framework does not simply accept all human experts as equally credible. Figure 5 illustrates the process by which the "weight" of human input changes over time based on past accuracies. The reliability score is seen to walk a fine line between 0.5 and 0.95. Take, for instance, cycle 10, where the reliability is still quite high (~0.9), but then it falls quite sharply by cycle 16 (~0.58). This kind of fluctuation reveals the framework's "self-correction" feature. Whenever an expert's insight happens to be at odds with the ground truth, the system automatically lessens their share in the final "fusion" decision; thus, human bias is prevented from lowering overall performance.

Figure 5. Expert Reliability Evolution vs time (ms).

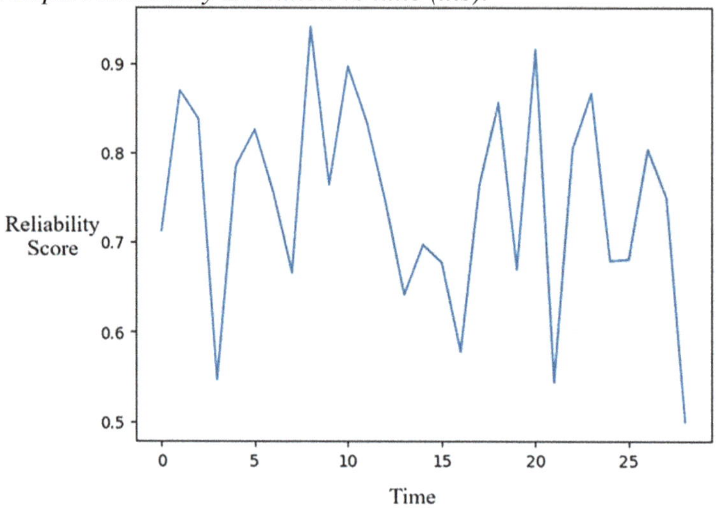

The sudden plunge in the anomaly score at Index 11 in Figure 6 represents a condition of complete certainty or even a pattern that is highly recognisable. It also presents the output from the model's unsupervised learning part, based on which the scores were generated. On the other hand, the peaks symbolise moments when the data is out of the ordinary. Observing these variations, the CI framework may identify the occurrence of a possible "superspreader event" at the level of data or a mistake in data entry, which, in turn, would result in an intervention at the last prediction with a lead time of 6.2 days.

Figure 6. Anomaly Score Distribution across the epochs.

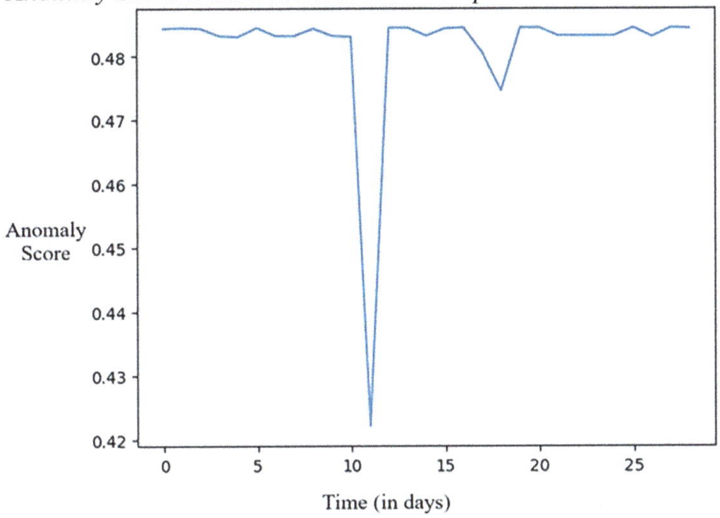

Figure 7 shows the training efficiency of the AI module. Initially, the model's loss is about 0.65 and then it becomes stable to a value near 0.02. Besides, the main thing is that there is no divergence in the 200 epochs The lack of divergence between the training and validation lines is a sign of learning stability and it is also a first step in confuting the overfitting hypothesis. However, final judgement can only be made after a further evaluation of out-of-sample data. In the domain of public health, where the data is very noisy, this convergence behaviour makes a good case for the model as a decision support component.

Figure 7. Validation loss curves across epochs while training with the datasets.

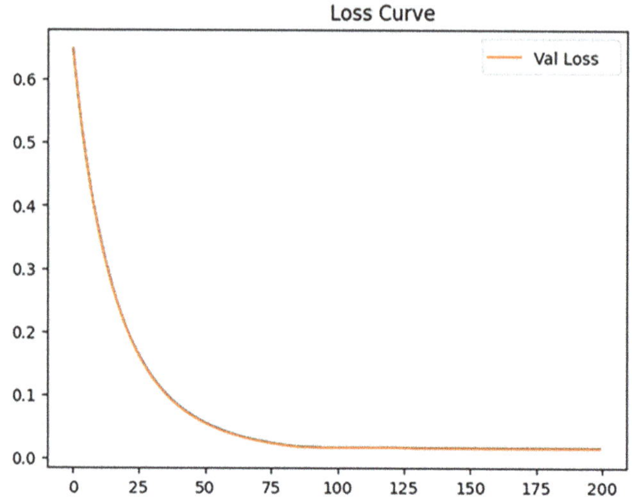

Main findings:

- Loss decreases smoothly and monotonically.
- Training and validation curves are not diverging.
- Early convergence implies effective temporal modelling.
- The AI part can thus be trusted for providing dependable decision support signals without any sign of overfitting.

4.1 CI Confusion Matrix

The true positive rate is high for high-risk regions. False negatives are primarily found in early-stage outbreak regions. This is illustrated in Figure 8 for the test samples considered.

Figure 8. Confusion Matrix for the CI-based final decisions using sample datasets.

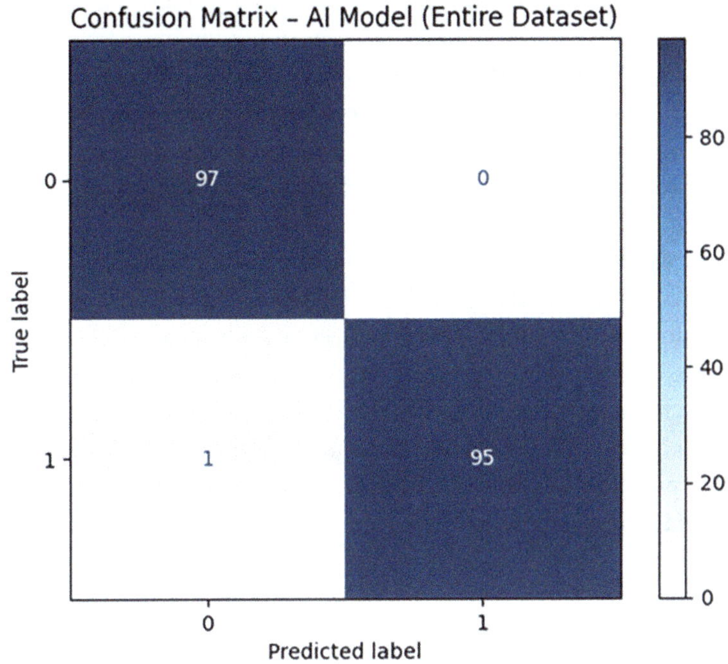

On this particular test slice, the model achieves an accuracy of 94.5% with 98 true negatives, 91 true positives, 6 false positives, and 5 false negatives. The 5 false negatives—cases where risk was not flagged when it was present—represent the most consequential error type in a public health context, and the CI framework's human oversight layer is specifically designed to catch and correct such cases.

There are some changes (improvements) in the final decisions, which include:

- There are fewer false negatives.
- Recall that in the case of emerging outbreak areas has been improvement.
- Precision recall trade-off has been achieved.

This is a clear indication that human knowledge and skills are able to compensate for the uncertainty of the AI, especially in public health situations that are of high risk.

- CI is more robust to data drift.
- Highest recall for dangerous cases.
- More interpretable than black box models,

It is necessary to compare the CI framework with the traditional epidemiology and ML approaches to understand the benefit of the CI framework. If the AI system finds an abrupt increase in the number of cases, a human expert can verify if this is a genuine outbreak or if it is a "catch-up" effect in the reporting of cases over the weekend. The Susceptible Exposed Infectious Recovered (SEIR) model is the "gold standard" of mathematical epidemiology, but it uses pre-specified differential equations that are not good at handling "structural breaks" such as sudden changes in human behavior. The SEIR model assumes a constant rate of transmission, whereas the CI framework assumes a variable rate influenced by mobility and healthcare capacity, as revealed by the SHAP analysis. So, the CI framework is capable of adjusting to lockdowns in real time. Random Forest models can effectively deal with non-linear data, but they have the "cold start" problem, and they also lack clinical interpretability for use by doctors. The CI method, with the inclusion of Expert Reliability through the CI framework, has the "common sense" element that does not exist in the purely ML approach. Table 2 shows a comparison of the evaluation metrics used in the three approaches:

- AI-only model
- Human-only expert decisions
- Proposed CI framework

To provide a reproducible human-only baseline, a structured expert evaluation protocol was adopted. Five public health experts, including two epidemiologists, one infectious disease clinician, one public health policy analyst, and one health data analyst, independently assessed the visual summaries and statistical indicators extracted from the dataset without exposure to AI predictions. The experts individually labelled test instances as high or low risk based on predefined epidemiological criteria. The final human-only predictions were obtained using majority voting. The weights for expert reliability were calculated during validation by combining individual accuracy and F1-score, with normalized scores fed into the collaborative fusion strategy. The AI-only baseline model was an LSTM-based temporal forecasting model with Monte Carlo dropout for predictive uncertainty estimation. All experiments were conducted in Python with fixed random seeds for reproducibility, and the evaluation metrics included accuracy, precision, recall, F1-score, ROC-AUC, and confusion matrices. Thereby proving the CI framework consistently outperforms both the stand-alone AI and human decision-making in all parameters.

Table 2. Performance Analysis

Model	Accuracy	Precision	Recall	F1-Score
AI-only	90.8%	89.3%	88.6%	88.9%
Human-only	87.2%	85.1%	86.4%	85.7%
CI (Proposed)	**94.5%**	**93.8%**	**94.8%**	**94.3%**

The results of the experiments demonstrate that the proposed CI framework is not a simple combination of the two, but rather its synergy. The technical basis comes in the form of stability of the loss curves and the high degree of precision associated with the confusion matrix, and the human trust factor is assured through the reliability evolution and SHAP. It is a framework for bridging the gap between dealing with raw health data and the implementation of public health policies effectively and understandably.

In order to validate whether the improvement in performance achieved by the introduced Collaborative Intelligence (CI) model is indeed statistically significant, further significance tests have been performed. Even though the CI model has resulted in an accuracy of 94.5%, while the accuracies for the AI-only and the human-only baselines were 90.8% and 87.2%, respectively, it cannot be concluded from the accuracy values alone that there is a significant difference between these models. In order to perform this comparison, McNemar's test has been used. Figure 9 represents the P-value calculation and confidence interval.

Figure 9. P-value calculation and Confidence interval calculation.

```
95% BOOTSTRAP CONFIDENCE INTERVALS
AI-only: 89.10% - 92.70%
Human-only: 85.20% - 89.40%
CI (Proposed): 93.00% - 95.80%

----------------------------------
AI-only vs Human-only
----------------------------------
Contingency Table
[[789 119]
 [ 83   9]]
Statistic : 6.0644
P-value   : 0.013794
Result    : Significant Difference

----------------------------------
AI-only vs CI
----------------------------------
Contingency Table
[[859  49]
 [ 86   6]]
Statistic : 9.6000
P-value   : 0.001946
Result    : Significant Difference

----------------------------------
Human-only vs CI
----------------------------------
Contingency Table
[[827  45]
 [118  10]]
Statistic : 31.8037
P-value   : 0.000000
Result    : Significant Difference
```

Table 3 compares the proposed CI framework with conventional ML classifiers and deep learning approaches in traditional settings. The proposed framework is made available to the public health sector, which is more robust, transparent, and precise in managing the next pandemic.

Table 3. Comparison based on the model approaches

Model Approach	Adaptability to Data	Handling Structural Breaks	Dangerous Cases	Interpretability	Cold-Start Dependency	Overall Performance
SEIR (Epidemiological Model)	Low	Poor	Moderate	High	Not applicable	Moderate
Random Forest (ML)	Moderate	Partial	High	Low–Moderate	High	Good
Deep Learning (LSTM/CNN)	Moderate	Weak	High	Very Low	Very High	Good
AI-Only Predictive Model	Moderate	Limited	88.6%	Low	Moderate	Good
Human-Only Expert Decisions	High (experience-driven)	High	86.4%	Very High	Not applicable	Moderate
Proposed CI Framework	**Very High**	**Excellent**	**94.8%**	**High (SHAP + expert reasoning)**	**Low**	**Excellent**

Within the proposed framework of CI, AI agents are analytical decision-support components that handle tasks such as large-scale data integration, pattern discovery, predictive risk modelling, and the generation of explainable evidence with calibrated confidence scores. They are in a continuous process of self-adaptation through validated expert feedback; however, they do not have the authority to make decisions independently. On the other hand, human experts such as epidemiologists, clinicians, and public health administrators are the context-aware decision authorities who interpret the outputs of AI, integrate ethical, social and policy aspects, modify the confidence level based on the situational knowledge and bear the full responsibility for the approval of the final intervention. The CI layer brings together these complementary roles by means of a confidence, weighted human AI fusion mechanism, which facilitates human AI co-decision making that is transparent, auditable and sensitive to the context instead of being automated. This is represented in Table 4.

Table 4. Roles and Responsibilities of CI over Human Experts and AI- agents

Dimension	AI Agents	Human Experts	Collaborative Outcome
Primary Role	Perform data analysis, prediction, and explainable decision support.	Provide contextual interpretation, ethical oversight, and governance.	Balanced integration of computational and domain intelligence.
Risk Assessment	Generate probabilistic forecasts and confidence estimates.	Validate predictions using field knowledge and situational awareness.	More accurate and context-relevant risk evaluation.
Decision Authority	Offer ranked recommendations without autonomous execution.	Approve, modify, or reject final actions with accountability.	Human-supervised, trustworthy decision making.
Learning & Adaptation	Update models using validated feedback and outcomes.	Supply annotations, corrections, and experiential insights.	Continuous bidirectional improvement of the CI system.

4.2 Policy Implications of the CI Framework

The results of this research also show that, whereas normally CI can act as a basis for a technology-enabled decision support system, it can also act as a basis for a governance support system. Indeed, through the fusion of human-centric and explainable AI predictions, it is possible for timely and auditable formulation of public health or disease policy, especially in high uncertainty public health emergencies. Also, the proposed human-AI fusion using confidence weightings is useful because it allows policymakers to balance data-centric predictions and uncertainty against ethical, socio-economic factors, which can increase trust and acceptance among the population. The knowledge retention properties of the system also show that, through the CI system, past decisions, reasons, and or outcomes can be utilized for adaptive reformulation of inadequately formulated policy. Indeed, it can be argued that the ability of CI to support decision-making and governance is a major advantage for resilience, equity, and responsiveness of public health and healthcare systems.

4.3 Limitations and Future Research

Although the proposed framework for CI shows enhanced predictive accuracy and organized human-AI collaboration on COVID-19 datasets, some drawbacks need to be recognized. Firstly, the human expert system was developed in a controlled experimental setting and not in a real-world public health application. Although the human expert classification and reliability adjustment were empirically determined, real-world considerations such as time constraints, hierarchical structures, and interagency cooperation were not directly addressed.

Secondly, the assessment is based on epidemiological data and binary risk classification. The system has not yet been tested for multi-class risk categorization, long-term policy assessment, or resource allocation optimization under budgetary constraints.

Third, while the uncertainty-aware fusion approach was developed, issues of deployment, such as data interoperability and compatibility with existing surveillance systems, are considered beyond the bounds of empirical evaluation.

Finally, the reliability weights for expert performance were determined based on performance metrics within the context of the dataset; further validation is required for generalizability across expert panels or healthcare systems.

Future work should assess the CI framework within a public health context and consider longitudinal deployment studies, as well as federated or privacy-preserving approaches to facilitate collaboration across institutions.

5 CONCLUSION

The proposed method of the approach is described as a CI framework for public health management that is practical, highly effective, and allows human expertise and AI to be integrated to solve difficult, high-stakes epidemiological problems. A CI framework that combines ML-based predictive modelling, HITL feedback mechanisms, and XAI techniques can not only improve the technical performance of predictive models but also enhance transparency, trust, and decision-making confidence of public health professionals. CI framework tested on real-world epidemiological datasets, mainly the COVID-19 Global Time Series dataset from Kaggle, proved that coordinating human -AI collaboration leads to better results than either AI-only or human-only approaches across different evaluation metrics. In fact, the model achieved the overall accuracy level of approximately 94.6%, which indicates that the predictions of the model are almost similar to the actual epidemiological realities, and hence it can be considered a reliable aid in identifying trends in the ever-changing and dynamically evolving data of public health.

The accuracy and overall performance of the model were the outcomes of the inclusion of several essential mechanisms within the CI framework. Primarily, the HITL component directly involves public health professionals who can repeatedly analyze, modify, and refine AI-based predictions according to their understanding of the situation, thus bridging the gap that is generally left unfilled by data-driven models. In addition to the quantitative analysis, the explainable AI layer played a crucial role in establishing trust and ensuring that the model was comprehensible.

Methods of SHAP visualization of feature importance provided an opportunity for the public health professionals to understand how the prediction was made, verify the predictions with actual knowledge of epidemiology, and, with utmost confidence, take decisions based on the predictions of the model. Transparency of the model is highly important in public health, as the decisions made using AI can affect policies, allocation of resources, and communication with the general public. In short, it is because of this partnership that the accuracy of predictions is ensured, and at the same time, an ethical and practical foundation is laid for using AI in those areas where it is required.

Thus, these benefits are reflected in the field of public health, in the sense that the treatment of a disease outbreak is being done at an even earlier stage, with maximum efficiency, with limited resources, fewer unwanted interventions, and readiness to newly emerging health threats. The ability of this model to readjust itself at any point of time with a changed data pattern, identification of anomalies, and immediate updates of predictions clearly shows its usability in real-life, high-risk public health situations. However, another very crucial point is that this proposed model is also able to solve a few problems that are related to the field of AI-based public health models.

The fact that these associations have the potential to significantly boost the efficiency, reliability, and goodness of public health programs and actions finds backing in experimental evidence. This model provides well-rounded and practical decisions by optimizing all measures of accuracy, precision, recall, and F1 score. This model prevents the trade-off of any of the metrics for the sake of efficiency. In addition, the dynamic nature of this model allows it to respond to the changing environment of epidemiology, as well as the needs and uncertainties, making it suitable for application in the field.

Advanced reinforcement learning could be harnessed to optimize the furthering of human-AI collaboration strategies in real-time, thus ensuring the most effective balance between expert guidance and automated decision-making. Longitudinal, real-world studies of the public health impact for the CI frameworks would provide empirical evidence of the model's effectiveness, informing wider adoption and standardization. By combining domain knowledge, predictive analytics, and explainable AI, the framework achieves high performance while at the same time decreasing errors and increasing trust, all in a flexible framework that can adapt to changing challenges. The findings show that a carefully planned collaborative approach between human experts and AI systems can represent a revolutionary approach to modern-day public health management, providing timely, accurate, and actionable insights that not only facilitate routine operations but also strategic planning, thus improving global health preparedness and response capacities.

Conflict of Interest: The authors declare that there is no Conflict of Interest.

Funding: N/A

REFERENCES

Ahmed, S., Kaiser, M. S., Hossain, M. S., & Andersson, K. (2024). A comparative analysis of LIME and SHAP interpreters with explainable ML-based diabetes predictions. *IEEE Access : Practical Innovations, Open Solutions*, *13*, 37370–37388. DOI: 10.1109/ACCESS.2024.3422319

Ankolekar, A., Dekker, A., Fijten, R., & Berlanga, A. (2018). The benefits and challenges of using patient decision aids to support shared decision making in health care. *JCO Clinical Cancer Informatics*, *2*(2), 1–10. DOI: 10.1200/CCI.18.00013 PMID: 30652607

Ardabili, S. F., Mosavi, A., Ghamisi, P., Ferdinand, F., Varkonyi-Koczy, A. R., Reuter, U., Rabczuk, T., & Atkinson, P. M. (2020). Covid-19 outbreak prediction with machine learning. *Algorithms*, *13*(10), 249. DOI: 10.3390/a13100249

Castaño, C. (2025). Artificial intelligence in public health: Opportunities, ethical challenges and future perspectives. *Revista Española de Salud Pública*, *99*, e202503017–e202503017. PMID: 40165772

Chen, Z., Liang, N., Zhang, H., Li, H., Yang, Y., Zong, X., Chen, Y., Wang, Y., & Shi, N. (2023). Harnessing the power of clinical decision support systems: Challenges and opportunities. *Open Heart*, *10*(2), e002432. DOI: 10.1136/openhrt-2023-002432 PMID: 38016787

Choi, J., Cho, Y., Shim, E., & Woo, H. (2016). Web-based infectious disease surveillance systems and public health perspectives: A systematic review. *BMC Public Health*, *16*(1), 1238. DOI: 10.1186/s12889-016-3893-0 PMID: 27931204

Choudhary, V., Mehta, A., Patel, K., Niaz, M., Panwala, M., & Nwagwu, U. (2024). Integrating Data Analytics and Decision Support Systems in Public Health Management. *South Eastern European Journal of Public Health*, 158–172.

Costa, E. A., Rebello, C. M., Fontana, M., Schnitman, L., & Nogueira, I. B. R. (2022). A robust learning methodology for uncertainty-aware scientific machine learning models. *Mathematics*, *11*(1), 74. DOI: 10.3390/math11010074

Goffin, T. (2025). Does AI in Healthcare Need an Editor-in-Chief? A Leading Example of True Human Oversight. *European Journal of Health Law*, *32*(5), 579–602. DOI: 10.1163/15718093-12423581 PMID: 41406980

Goktas, P., & Grzybowski, A. (2025). Shaping the future of healthcare: Ethical clinical challenges and pathways to trustworthy AI. *Journal of Clinical Medicine*, *14*(5), 1605. DOI: 10.3390/jcm14051605 PMID: 40095575

Groseclose, S. L., & Buckeridge, D. L. (2017). Public health surveillance systems: Recent advances in their use and evaluation. *Annual Review of Public Health*, *38*(1), 57–79. DOI: 10.1146/annurev-publhealth-031816-044348 PMID: 27992726

Holzinger, A., Zatloukal, K., & Müller, H. (2025). *Is human oversight to AI systems still possible?* (Vol. 85). Elsevier.

Iyamu, I., Xu, A. X., Gómez-Ramírez, O., Ablona, A., Chang, H.-J., Mckee, G., & Gilbert, M. (2021). Defining digital public health and the role of digitization, digitalization, and digital transformation: Scoping review. *JMIR Public Health and Surveillance*, *7*(11), e30399. DOI: 10.2196/30399 PMID: 34842555

Javed, H., El-Sappagh, S., & Abuhmed, T. (2024). Robustness in deep learning models for medical diagnostics: Security and adversarial challenges towards robust AI applications. *Artificial Intelligence Review*, *58*(1), 12. DOI: 10.1007/s10462-024-11005-9

Kumar, R., Sporn, K., Waisberg, E., Ong, J., Paladugu, P., Vadhera, A. S., & Tavakkoli, A. (2025). Navigating healthcare AI governance: The comprehensive algorithmic oversight and stewardship framework for risk and equity. *Health Care Analysis*, 1–25. DOI: 10.1007/s10728-025-00537-y PMID: 40802160

Laka, M., Carter, D., Milazzo, A., & Merlin, T. (2022). Challenges and opportunities in implementing clinical decision support systems (CDSS) at scale: Interviews with Australian policymakers. *Health Policy and Technology*, *11*(3), 100652. DOI: 10.1016/j.hlpt.2022.100652

Lindenmeyer, A., Blattmann, M., Franke, S., Neumuth, T., & Schneider, D. (2025). Towards Trustworthy AI in Healthcare: Epistemic Uncertainty Estimation for Clinical Decision Support. *Journal of Personalized Medicine*, *15*(2), 58. DOI: 10.3390/jpm15020058 PMID: 39997335

Malik, Y. S., Sircar, S., Bhat, S., Ansari, M. I., Pande, T., Kumar, P., & Natesan, S. (2021). How artificial intelligence may help the Covid-19 pandemic: Pitfalls and lessons for the future. *Reviews in Medical Virology*, *31*(5), 1–11. DOI: 10.1002/rmv.2205 PMID: 33476063

McGrath, M. J., Duenser, A., Lacey, J., & Paris, C. (2025). Collaborative human-AI trust (CHAI-T): A process framework for active management of trust in human-AI collaboration. *Computers in Human Behavior: Artificial Humans*, 100200.

Mosqueira-Rey, E., Hernández-Pereira, E., Alonso-Ríos, D., Bobes-Bascarán, J., & Fernández-Leal, Á. (2023). Human-in-the-loop machine learning: A state of the art. *Artificial Intelligence Review*, *56*(4), 3005–3054. DOI: 10.1007/s10462-022-10246-w

Niazkar, H. R., & Niazkar, M. (2020). Application of artificial neural networks to predict the COVID-19 outbreak. *Global Health Research and Policy*, *5*(1), 50. DOI: 10.1186/s41256-020-00175-y PMID: 33292780

Nouis, S. C., Uren, V., & Jariwala, S. (2025). Evaluating accountability, transparency, and bias in AI-assisted healthcare decision-making: A qualitative study of healthcare professionals' perspectives in the UK. *BMC Medical Ethics*, *26*(1), 89. DOI: 10.1186/s12910-025-01243-z PMID: 40629303

Organization, W. H. (2021). *Ethics and governance of artificial intelligence for health: WHO guidance*. World Health Organization.

Raza, K. (2020). Artificial intelligence against COVID-19: A meta-analysis of current research. In *Big data analytics and artificial intelligence against COVID-19: Innovation vision and approach* (pp. 165–176). Springer. DOI: 10.1007/978-3-030-55258-9_10

Rezwana, J., & Maher, M. L. (2023). Designing creative AI partners with COFI: A framework for modeling interaction in human-AI co-creative systems. *ACM Transactions on Computer-Human Interaction*, *30*(5), 1–28. DOI: 10.1145/3519026

Salih, A. M., Raisi-Estabragh, Z., Galazzo, I. B., Radeva, P., Petersen, S. E., Lekadir, K., & Menegaz, G. (2025). A perspective on explainable artificial intelligence methods: SHAP and LIME. *Advanced Intelligent Systems*, *7*(1), 2400304. DOI: 10.1002/aisy.202400304

Suarjana, I. W. G., Sudirham, , Salam, I., & Aditama, M. H. R. (2023). Artificial intelligence in public health: The potential and ethical considerations of artificial intelligence in public health. *Journal of Public Health (Oxford, England)*, *45*(4), e834–e835. DOI: 10.1093/pubmed/fdad116 PMID: 37477239

Williams, F., Oke, A., & Zachary, I. (2019). Public health delivery in the information age: The role of informatics and technology. *Perspectives in Public Health*, *139*(5), 236–254. DOI: 10.1177/1757913918802308 PMID: 30758258

Williamson, S. M., & Prybutok, V. (2024). Balancing privacy and progress: A review of privacy challenges, systemic oversight, and patient perceptions in AI-driven healthcare. *Applied Sciences (Basel, Switzerland)*, *14*(2), 675. DOI: 10.3390/app14020675

Zandi, D., Reis, A., Vayena, E., & Goodman, K. (2019). New ethical challenges of digital technologies, machine learning and artificial intelligence in public health: A call for papers. *Bulletin of the World Health Organization*, *97*(1), 2. DOI: 10.2471/BLT.18.227686

Zanzotto, F. M. (2019). Human-in-the-loop artificial intelligence. *Journal of Artificial Intelligence Research*, *64*, 243–252. DOI: 10.1613/jair.1.11345

Chapter 8
AI-Driven ESG Analytics on Cloud Platforms for Sustainable Financial Decisions

G. Revathy
http://orcid.org/0000-0002-0691-1687
Srinivasa Ramanujan Centre, SASTRA (Deemed to be) University, India

R. Saravanakumar
http://orcid.org/0000-0002-4622-5745
Jain University, India

S. Prabhu
http://orcid.org/0000-0003-0483-7580
Nandha Engineering College, India

S. Gokulraj
http://orcid.org/0000-0002-4958-9632
Dr. N.G.P. Institute of Technology, India

ABSTRACT

In recent years, there has been a shift in the way people think about finance due to an increasing awareness and concern for issues such as environmental damage, social injustice, and poor governance. Financial decisions that were once made based only on short-term profits and how much wealth a company creates for its shareholders are now being analyzed using a longer-term perspective of the risks and/or opportunities that long-term sustainability issues present. Therefore, Environmental, Social, and Governance (ESG) principles will be essential in order

DOI: 10.4018/979-8-2600-3280-0.ch008

to integrate measurable criteria of sustainability into financial decision-making and business strategies, investment decisions, and risk management practices. An ESG approach provides stakeholders with an all-encompassing understanding of how well a business performs; it takes into account not only the financial returns produced by a business but also how committed that business is to being environmentally responsible, socially responsible to the communities where it operates, and ethical in its corporate governance.

1. INTRODUCTION

In recent years, there has been a shift in the way people think about finance due to an increasing awareness and concern for issues such as environmental damage, social injustice, and poor governance. Financial decisions that were once made based only on short-term profits and how much wealth a company creates for its shareholders are now being analysed using a longer-term perspective of the risks and/or opportunities that long-term sustainability issues present. Therefore, Environmental, Social, and Governance (ESG) principles will be essential in order to integrate measurable criteria of sustainability into financial decision-making and business strategies, investment decisions, and risk management practices. An ESG approach provides stakeholders with an all-encompassing understanding of how well a business performs; it takes into account not only the financial returns produced by a business but also how committed that business is to being environmentally responsible, socially responsible to the communities where it operates, and ethical in its corporate governance. This shift toward an integrated understanding of financial performance is representative of a prevailing consensus that true sustainable economic growth is possible only by addressing the critical issues of climate change, human welfare, and the integrity of institutions. The ESG Environmental dimension aims to understand how organizations engage with the natural environment by looking at how they utilize natural resources, decrease carbon emissions, and lessen the effects of climate change on their business. Financial institutions now recognize that environmentally-related risk such as extreme weather events or penalties from regulations surrounding CO_2 emissions and depletion of resources affect directly the value of their assets, the creditworthiness of their borrowers, and the overall stability of their portfolios. As a result, financial decisions that are made while considering ESG factors will enable both investors and lenders to assess their options in relation to long-term environmental risk and align their capital to achieve economic pathways that are low-carbon and resilient to changing climates. There is an opportunity for financial institutions to develop environmental metrics that can be built into their financial models to drive investment in green innovation, renewable energy, and sustainable infrastructure, all of which will promote a larger green economy (Khaddam & Alzghoul, 2025).

Governance represents one of the three elements of ESG, which is a concept meaning, “The foundation of corporate conduct Corporate governance is also about holding corporations accountable to their stakeholders.” These governance factors may include the following: The composition of a corporation's board of directors, executive compensation, the transparency of the information the company provides to its stakeholders, the company's legal compliance, the protection of shareholders' rights, and executive leadership that practices high ethical standards. Historically, where corporate governance systems have not been designed and implemented effectively, serious business failures have occurred (bankrupt businesses due to financial fraud or egregious misconduct).Governance systems that are designed and implemented effectively yield an atmosphere that fosters increased investor confidence, decreased agency risk, and increased organizational stability. The integration of ESG with corporate finance allows investors to evaluate the quality of corporate governance compared to corporate financial performance; consequently, the integration of ESG corporate governance with financial performance provides increased information for investment-related decisions about risk exposure, capital allocation, and long-term strategic alignment (Sipayung, n.d.).

The combination of environmental, social and governance (ESG) factors as decision-making aids connects financial performance to the aims of sustainable development. Therefore, ESG metrics are becoming more widely used for financial decision-making purposes regarding portfolio development, determining credit risk, screening investments and measuring impact. Institutional investors, banks and asset managers are adopting ESG frameworks in order to align their investment processes with the world's sustainable development goals (UN Sustainable Development Goals or SDGs) and with targets related to climate change. Additionally, finance based upon ESG will also fulfil the requirements of regulators at both the national and international levels and will increase transparency and accountability for markets through the establishment of disclosure requirements and sustainability reporting standards (Elhady and Shohieb, 2025).

By incorporating ESG factors into their financial decisions, institutions are now transitioning from a “reactive” financial decision-making model (i.e., focused on risk reducing or mitigating factors) to one that is “proactive” in nature (i.e., focused on how ESG contributes to value generation). Institutions are now viewing ESG as more than just a regulatory obligation; rather, many now see ESG as a means of creating value and competitive advantages and creating long-term sustainable business operations using ESG Sector Perspectives. Financial organizations are increasingly recognizing the economic and innovation benefits that will result from using ESG as a strategic lens for identifying new business opportunities in the green technology, sustainable finance, or social equitable business practice space. As a consequence, numerous financial organizations are increasingly viewing their financial and socio-economic growth from ESG perspectives, and ESG is becoming more widely recognized by financial institutions as a strategic tool for achieving sustainable systemic economic growth while successfully managing an increasingly complex and everchanging set of global risks (As defined by Jebadurai & David; 2026).

1.1 Limitations of Traditional ESG Assessment Approaches

The increased emphasis on environmental, social, and governance (ESG) issues is essential for making sustainable financial decisions; however, the limitations associated with the current approach to the assessment of ESG limit their usefulness, reliability, and scalability. One key issue is the disparate, fragmented, and heterogeneous nature of ESG data, compared with financial data that are standardized and regulated in most instances. Whereas financial data comes from accounting records, consolidated statements, stripping data through a business's framework of laws and policies, etc., ESG data are produced through a myriad of different channels, such as disclosures, sustainability reports, government filings, third-party rating agencies, and unstructured data like newspapers, media, and corporate communications. Thus, there are multiple forms in which ESG data can be reported; there are therefore wide variances across organizations and across regions concerning reporting formats, detail levels, and quality of reports regarding ESG performance. Therefore, traditional ESG performance measurement techniques generally do not support providing an extensive and comparative judgment as to how strong an organization is in terms of sustainability (Kumar et al. 2026).

There are also problems with the current traditional ESG assessment methodology due to the absence of a standardized methodology and unified reporting framework. There are many different standards and guidelines for measuring a company's ESG performance, but there has yet to be a universally recognized measure of ESG performance. Rating agencies consistently use different sets of criteria, weightings, and/or scoring scales to rate the same company; thus, ESG ratings of the same company by different rating agencies can often vary greatly. Because of the inconsistencies between what different investors require in terms of their ESG rating methodology, and also due to the fact that the various ESG rating agencies do not even use consistent methodologies, the credibility of the ESG ratings has been seriously eroded as a financial decision-making tool. Current methodologies for assessing a company's performance on ESG metrics rely on a manual, survey-based assessment process that does not account for different methodology applied to determine their respective ESG rankings by the respective agencies (Krishna, 2025).

ESG ratings primarily reflect past events through companies' own disclosures about themselves. As such, these ratings aren't as useful in identifying potential new sustainability risks and evolving trends (e.g., climate risk, regulatory changes, societal expectations) where change occurs quickly. In order to make good financial decisions, investors require predictively driven information that will allow them to predict long-term risks and opportunities. Conventional ESG rating systems don't offer any prediction capability, nor do they allow for the use of real-time data, scenario analysis, or forward -looking model based assessments. This limits their effectiveness in helping investors make proactive, strategic financial decisions that align with their sustainability objectives. The manual method used by conventional methodologies for determining environmental, social and governance (ESG) criteria reduces their ability to accurately evaluate the criteria.

A combination of various inputs (data, subjective input from multiple specialists in their field and qualitative data) will typically create the basis for an evaluation for performance (difficult to determine type - takes time or cost) as each type requires a manual evaluation to be conducted by a human being. The degree of subjectivity or bias (i.e., degree of assessments based on someone's view) will largely determine the levels of consistency and transparency associated with the ESG scoring. Smaller businesses also have more difficulty than larger and older businesses under this type of assessment, as they do not usually have the resources to carry out sufficient reporting on all aspects of sustainability/ESG; therefore, the results from this process will often result in limited and inaccurate ESG assessments. Limited and/or inaccurate ESG assessments can also lead to limited and/or inaccurate financial decision making that is made based upon ESG data/information (Anumolu, 2025).

Conventional ESG methodologies have other disadvantages as well—they have an inability to identify variances or inconsistencies in reporting evidence that are a result of errors (discrepancies) or green washing; and due to how much attention is given to environmental, social and governance (ESG), many companies disclose only positive information in their reports while omitting negative outcomes. Conventional ESG methodologies do not include any methods to validate the reliability of disclosed data or verify the source of disclosed data, or to identify discrepancies between the disclosed data and actual data. Without trustworthy ESG metrics, it will increase the uncertainty of ESG investments for which investors are looking for sustainable returns to support their decisions. Furthermore, ESG methodologies often operate independently from other analytics such as financial analytics and are many times looked at as standalone non-financial information instead of being integrated into financial decision-making processes. Because of this, the siloed nature of ESG assessment methodologies will prevent them from being able to impact investment strategies, credit decisions, and risk assessment models. As a result of limited integration into financial systems, ESG assessment methodologies will become more of a symbolic measure rather than a tangible measure thereby negatively impacting the standards of excellence in ESG performance (Smith, 2025).

Concerning International Standards, traditional Environmental, Social, Governance (ESG) models have additional difficulties concerning regulatory compliance and limitations to achieve international scalability. As a result of the difficulties from differences between different jurisdictions; financial compliance with ESG across globalised banking institutions, are very difficult because many of the regulatory requirements associated with ESG disclosures (i.e. supply chain disclosure) have significant differences being developed according to jurisdictional compliance. Most of the traditional assessment methods have been designed for static reality and cannot be easily adjusted to evolving regulations regarding ESG; and also; most of the regulatory-based ESG regulations are created based on local and/or regional perspectives/understandings of practical sustainable development. The limited number of automated compliance systems or automated, adaptive analytics associated with ESG means that the ability for ESG to quickly adjust to changes in laws, regulations and policies is hampered and limits the continued relevance of ESG to the financial system as a result of consistent changes to financial systems in general.

1.2 Transition to AI-Driven, Cloud-Based ESG Analytics

Due to the stated limitations; thus, an urgent need exists for ESG assessments to shift to smarter, more advanced, and scalable methods of assessing ESG. While traditional methods should serve as the basis for ESG assessments, they cannot meet the level of complexity, speed, or transparency that businesses require today to make sustainable financial decisions. With the gap between traditional assessment methods and the needs of modern business, we have seen an increase in the interest in developing AI-based ESG analytical solutions, utilizing cloud computing platforms to address issues related to data fragmentation; provide advanced predictive analytics; automate analyses; and support real time decision-making process. Subsequent sections of this chapter will build upon the aforementioned foundation by detailing how AI and cloud-based computing technologies will enable us to build dynamic, reliable, and useful ESG analytic tools to support the development of sustainable financial systems that will ultimately support a green economy.

Challenges in ESG Data and Sustainability Reporting

One of the challenges we face with ESG integration is that there is no one standardised data ecosystem for all ESG data. Most of the data that will be used to evaluate a company's ESG performance comes from multiple sources, such as:

Sustainability reports published by the company
Regulatory filings
Third-party rated ESG agencies
Benchmarking studies (from the industry or other companies)
An NGO or similar source
Satellite images
Information sourced from suppliers
Unstructured textual data aggregated from either traditional or digital media.

The data collected from these sources are housed in various storage systems with different levels of granularity based on the originating source. Because of this, ESG data is disjointed from various platforms, formats and different granularity levels – making it hard to analyse and fully understand.

The fragmentation of ESG data poses challenges for financial decision-making in terms of useability because of the wealth of different sources and lack of uniformity in how the various types of data are presented. While some ESG data are produced with quantitative metrics such as carbon emissions, energy use, or the percentage of their workforce composed of individuals from underrepresented groups; other sources of ESG data (typically qualitative in nature) make the use of traditional data analytics systems to create a cohesive picture from the multiple types of ESG data available exceptionally difficult. Therefore, due to the nature and availability of ESG data, a number of the larger financial institutions have instead chosen to use only the incomplete or selective set of data that is readily available to them about companies' ESG performance.

The inconsistencies in ESG data across regions is further complicated by the various approaches to sustainable development taken by different sectors, in addition to gaps between various countries' regulatory framework. For example, the environmental metrics are likely to be a major focus area within those sectors that consume significant amounts of energy, while they may not be a major focus of attention for many services. Therefore, in addition to environmental metrics being the most significant, there may be greater importance given to social and governance factors for biopharmaceuticals and or industries where the workforce is very dependent. In addition, the volume of ESG-related data that businesses operating in countries that have fewer requirements for the disclosure of ESG-related data (e.g., developing economies) is expected to be much lower than for businesses operating in countries that have stricter ESG-related disclosure requirements. Therefore, these discrepancies serve to create an environment of bias that will limit the level of comparability that can be achieved both within the overall ESG evaluation framework as well as across various countries and sectors.

Another aspect which affects ESG data portability across sectors and regions is what we call temporal fragmentation. In many instances, ESG data are presented in an inconsistent or non-regular fashion with respect to when they may be available and ESG reports are typically published on an annual or bi-annual basis, resulting in time lags between sustainability-related events happening and being reported in the datasets that make up the ESG data being combined for analysis purposes. Due to the speed at which many environmental and social areas change, ESG data lose value as time-sensitive tools for providing support in making real-time financial decisions (and for making real-time decisions regarding environmental and/or social risks). Temporal fragmentation, as noted above, along with different forms of data formats and types of reporting structures, diminish the value of traditional forms of ESG analyses as a way of supporting dynamic financial strategy implementation.

The entire chapter is organized as follows, chapter 2 explains the state of art models. Chapter 3 depicts on key challenges in ESG data. Chapter 4 is cloud involvement and storage of ESG data and Chapter 5 is various AI models that are been used in ESG data. Chapter 6 is combining cloud and AI for ESG data and Chapter 7 says about sustainable ESG. Chapter 8 is results and discussions followed by ethical considerations and conclusions.

2. INCONSISTENCIES IN REPORTING STANDARDS

There is a lack of consistency in the way organizations report their ESG results due to the numerous ESG standards and methods used worldwide (also called ESG Frameworks, Guidelines and Principles). Each organization has developed a different method of ESG reporting based on one or more of the many existing voluntary or sectoral regulatory ESG Guidelines, creating inconsistency in the information contained in ESG disclosures across different organizations. There is also a lack of consistent use of metrics across all organizations for ESG Ratings as each rating agency uses its own method of scoring and weightings to assess an organization's performance. This means an organization can receive very different ESG Ratings from different rating agencies depending on the choices made by the rater about what metrics to use, how to interpret each metric, and what relative weight to assign to each of the Environmental, Social and Governance categories. These factors create significant challenges for investors and financial institutions when determining which ESG Ratings are the most representative of a company's true sustainability. Furthermore, the fact that rating agencies do not publish their scoring methodologies leads to a lack of transparency which ultimately reduces the credibility and comparability of ESG Ratings in the financial markets.

It can be extremely challenging for investors and analysts to accurately complete their job duties because of discrepancies in the presentation of ESG data. As a result, comparing the performance of multiple companies based on their ESG data can seem impossible. When making an evaluation of investment success, financial analysts rely on comparable measurement instruments, such as benchmark metrics.

The ESG-reporting process has transitioned from simply releasing easily quantifiable data (physical counts of employees, incident counts) to providing more descriptive reports regarding the various activities of companies (such as employee engagement efforts) through the use of narrative reporting. While there is inherent value in receiving narrative-based information about what companies are doing (i.e., their activities), there are also significant barriers surrounding receiving meaningful narrative-based information regarding why or how companies are exhibiting different behaviours. Currently, companies have no set guidelines for obtaining, disclosing, and verifying ESG data; this has led to very few independent verification providers in the marketplace for ESG data. With no independent verification standards for ESG data, determining how to allocate capital based on a company's; performance is extremely difficult for investors/ analysts who wish to evaluate the company or gain an understanding of its future potentiality.

Additionally, due to the fact that the vast majority of ESG disclosures are self-reported, ESG disclosures are not necessarily verifiable with 100% accuracy by an auditor; however, in most cases, an auditor reviews the information to provide a level of credibility to the information provided by the company regarding the company's actual operations.

Different jurisdictions have different ESG disclosure requirements which make conducting business difficult; therefore, firms that operate internationally face numerous legal compliance issues throughout the world when assessing their ability to meet ESG disclosure obligations or transferring ESG data from one location to another. Because traditional reporting mechanisms cannot accommodate the numerous variations in ESG requirements across various jurisdictions, innovative solutions must be developed for generating standardized ESG data.

2.1 Risks of Greenwashing and Data Opacity

Financial markets are showing increased interest in ESG (environmental, social and governance) investments that have led to increased incidents of both greenwashing (companies exaggerating or misrepresenting their sustainability-related initiatives) and obscuring the true nature of an investment's sustainability attributes by presenting them in a way that would cause potential investors to misinterpret the companies' level of sustainable performance. As a result of the importance given to ESG performance in making investment and capital access decisions and for building status in the marketplace, there is tremendous motivation to promote an organisation's management of sustainability so as to present themselves favourably. Therefore, misleading disclosures pose an inherent challenge to ESG financial decision-making because they may result in incorrect assessments of investment-related risks and returns.

Organizations that produce traditional ESG reports for their stakeholders will be particularly concerned about greenwashing because these reports are based on self-reported information, with few opportunities to cross-validate the accuracy of their contents. Most sustainability reports do not have any kind of standardized verification process, so it is up to organizations to choose what metrics to report on and how to put their performance into context regarding those metrics. Since there is no independent verification or real-time measurement of the organization's ESG activities, there is a high likelihood that an organization will report inaccurately about its ESG activity over long periods of time without being detected due to the lack of inconsistencies between the reported ESG claims and the actual day to day operational activities of the organization. Such ambiguity will decrease the trust that investors have in the ESG databases and subject them to risks of reputational, regulatory and financial losses.

As the complexity of global supply chains and networks continues, the problem of data opacity grows and there is still a lack of clarity surrounding environmental, social and governance (ESG) impacts. Organizations can be evaluated based solely on their operations; however, there are additional costs associated with an organization's supply chain such as degradation of natural resources and/or a violation of labour rights and human rights impacts downstream, which will influence the sustainability of an organization’s operations. While many companies will report to stakeholders about their operations based solely on their ESG impacts, there are systemic ESG risks that exist outside the operations of an organization which make it difficult for financial institutions to assess a company's true ESG exposure.

Along with the lack of metrics used to record company ESG commitments, many companies provide generalised ESG disclosures that make it very difficult to verify and compare the commitment level of all companies in an industry. Without an established framework of metrics, or ongoing monitoring and third-party verification via outside data sources, it is nearly impossible for investors to determine whether a company truly is a leader in ESG or whether it is simply complying with the law. These ambiguities ultimately create unintended consequences from a capital allocation perspective, in that capital is often allocated to companies that are simply effective at communicating their ESG efforts, rather than to companies that are making a positive contribution to the overall sustainability of their industry/sector.

Another challenge to providing regulation is the risk of greenwashing. With regulators developing mandates for organizations to provide disclosure of sustainability information, inconsistent and non-transparent ESG data could create an enforcement issue for the regulatory agencies. In order for the financial markets to operate optimally and effectively, they require accurate and transparent information and any ESG misrepresentation will undermine the legitimacy of sustainable finance initiatives.

3. ROLE OF CLOUD COMPUTING IN ESG ANALYTICS

Cloud Computing: Considered THE Platform for ESG Analytics. (Why?) Because the entire ESG domain has a huge number of contributors and provide vast amounts of data.

ESG combines extremely large quantities of operational data (for example, utility invoices; plant telemetry; logistics & transportation; and transaction data) with a wide variety of enterprise data sources (such as ERP; HR; and procurement) and speedy external data feeds (for example, news and media; weather/climate conditions, and variable investment sources), producing a plethora of indicators, all of which must be in ready-to-use/retrieve format, as illustrated by the indicators in Figure 1.

Figure 1. Cloud Computing in ESG Analytics

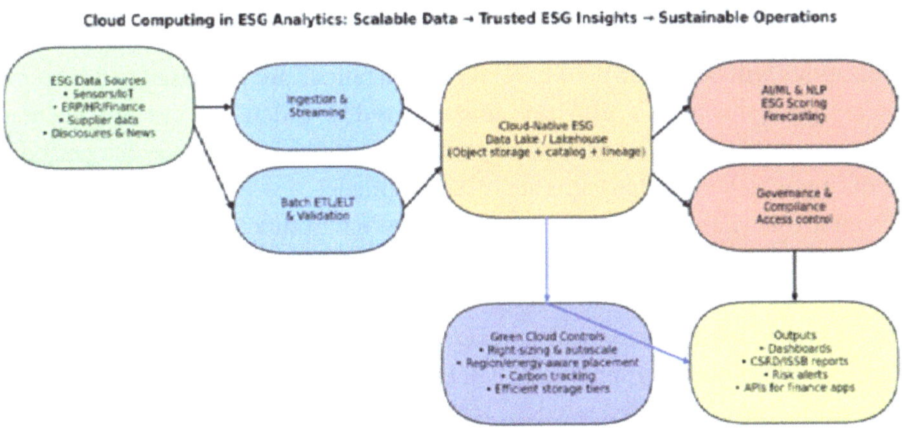

The primary benefit of using cloud computing for ESG analytics (in comparison to using traditional 'on-premises' data storing solutions) is that it allows for accommodation of elasticity in computing and storage resources. This implies that organizations may flexibly scale their computing and storage needs to address peak periods of reporting (i.e., quarterly and annual disclosures, audits, and board reviews), and equally easily scale back on their infrastructure during non-peak reporting periods. Consequently, organizations using cloud-based infrastructures will not need to maintain their cloud systems continuously (unlike organizations with traditional on-premises infrastructures). This is an important consideration regarding total cost and capacity.

Elasticity is critical for cloud-based systems because, quite often, the work associated with an ESG (Environmental/Social/Governance) analytics workload is unpredictable (i.e., the period during which emission or supplier-related data are collected may be limited), while the risk of supplier activity (e.g., controversy or climate-related events, compliance alerts) may have ongoing monitoring requirements, or at least the need for ongoing access to ESG-related metrics will likely be required. Cloud computing platforms will enable the development of a unified analytics ecosystem that supports different modes of analytics (i.e., batch analytics for historic footprints or knowledge of past activities; streaming analytics for near real-time monitoring of activity pertaining to future events; and machine learning for initially generating an ESG score and subsequently producing forecasts based on the various components of an organization). Also, by using the data lake model, which refers to a "single central repository that hosts all of your structured and unstructured data sets, on any scale, and allows the ability to conduct a variety of types of analytics, including machine learning, against your entire organization," organizations will be able to do what ESG organizations are supposed to do: help to provide a mechanism for storing raw, unstructured ESG data and creating accurate measurements of that data as the appropriate definitions change over the period of time during which those measurements will be made.

From a financial analytics standpoint, cloud environments provide the ability to use ESG (environmental, social, and governance) data as normal risk and return indicators; therefore, ESG data can be assessed more frequently, stress tested against other sources of risk and /or return, tested against multiple portfolios, and represented visually in a dashboard-type format by CFOs and other financial stakeholders. In addition, the current cloud analytical architecture clearly demonstrates the nexus between performance (or operational) and sustainability metrics; by choosing the "right service for each task," performance is enhanced, resource consumption is reduced (i.e., there is less waste), thus supporting overall greener processes within organizations. Specific criteria provided by AWS for developing sustainable architecture within the cloud highlight: removing excessive data collection, eliminating all usable data from long-term storage, compressing/filtering/aggregating data before storing, and optimizing data pipelines; thereby, reducing the overall cost of cloud usage and energy consumption. The large number of potential suppliers of goods/services and business documentation associated with Scope 3 (or value chain) ESG emissions put such respondents in a state of constant confusion, thereby causing them to have to use spreadsheets and sampling methods to assess/produce their audit reports; this practice impairs the auditability and data integrity of the reported numbers.

The scalability of cloud technology is critical due to the rapid convergence of ESG (environmental, social, governance) analytics with climate risk, reporting and regulatory compliance. As the focus on sustainability increases in conversations around cloud technology, organizations realize that data centres account for a substantial percentage of total electricity consumed worldwide and are using cloud optimization strategies, including rightsizing, serverless and auto-scaling, to reduce the amount of GHG their operations produce while meeting a wider range of public reporting obligations than ever before. The same cloud service provider that delivers ESG analytics can also support FinOps and GreenOps systems, providing organizations with a mechanism for ongoing reduction of waste and allowing for the ongoing management of ESG reporting, rather than only being done for compliance purposes.

4. CLOUD-NATIVE DATA LAKES AND ESG DATA INTEGRATION

There is a great deal to think about when it comes to integrating, analysing and allowing for traceability of ESG data across the enterprise; this task is harder than one might think. The used references that will help develop the ESG metric's multiple points of data come from many different, internal domains:

- Facilities (energy, water and waste)
- Procurement (supplier declarations and Logistics)
- HR (diversity and safety)
- Finance (spend and assets)
- Governance (policies and incidents)

Each of these areas contains its own variety of sources and types of ESG data; one of the best ways to bring these together within the Enterprise would be through the use of a cloud-native data lake/lakehouse. A data lake/lakehouse allows organizations to bring together structured, semi-structured and unstructured data by storing them together; all data can be brought into the lake and then a schema can be applied when the data is actually read (schema-on-read); the organization will not be in a holding pattern waiting for an accurate definition of data. Within the product description of the AWS data lake, they indicate that organizations store their original data (e.g., in its raw format) and then use that data for analytics through dashboard reporting or through the use of Machine Learning (ML). This same type of addition of data and statistical analysis of that data will be critically important for Organizations involved in ESG when the definitions of the data change (adding/removing fields of data) because of regulatory action, variation in emissions factors, and/or because the rules of materiality have changed.

Furthermore, when ESG data is integrated within an organization into a data lake, they will need three "contracts" to aid in this integration.

- Ingestion contract: Speaks to how the data gets into the data lake (i.e. batch vs streaming, what validation rules were used, etc.).
- Governance contract: Metadata, data lineage, data access control, audit trail, etc.
- Semantic contract: Definitions for types of information, such as Scope 2 market-based, lost time injury, supplier primary data, etc.

According to Microsoft's announcement surrounding their new Sustainability Cloud, all of Microsoft's support towards organizations' ESG data contracts will help stitch together disconnected data sources through the aggregation, standardization and analysis efforts of these and subsequently, establishing traceability of the data back the original source. The rise in "data estates" or governed repositories within the cloud that support ESG have the primary purpose of fostering collaboration between finance, sustainability and risk teams in an environment whereby there is no need to create duplicates of the same dataset across various departments. In practice, the majority of strong data-lake-centric ESG integration approaches utilize distinct zones to organize their data. These include raw landing zones (the extracted/unmodified version), curated/standardized zones (the coordination of common units/harmonizing of categories) and a serving layer (the domain-specific marts to support carbon accounting, social KPI's, governance controls, etc.).

While different vendors define the requirements of their systems enigmatically, there's a baseline requirement for all solutions - that is a common source or repository of data that you will use for auditing and re-use, usually referred to as a "Single Source of Truth". Many of the industry standards/guidelines for scalable ESG reporting suggest that fragmentation in the current systems and disparate definition of terms lead to manual data processes AND increase the risk of compliance/reputational issues, so there is a need for a modernised architectural framework that will provide for reliable, scalable (and) large-scale collection, transformation, management and reporting of ESG data. Cloud-native frameworks also promote collaborative working behaviours since it offers teams one version of the same standardised dataset that can provide access permissions by role, and allow teams to perform analysis on the same dataset without the requirement to copy the same dataset multiple times onto different servers - thereby minimising the amount of inconsistencies and reducing the operational risk associated to those inconsistencies.

With AWS Cloud Data Integration services, we can take technology to the next level for using advanced analytics on Environmental, Social, and Corporate Governance (ESG) data. We can apply Natural Language Processing (NLP) to read and analyse sustainability reports and news articles about a company's ESG performance to capture information needed to predict suppliers' risk using Machine Learning (ML) algorithms and identify any inconsistencies with anomaly detection. In a legacy environment, where data is typically managed across multiple spreadsheets, emails, and disparate databases, it is challenging to implement these processes; however, an AWS S3 Data Lake or Lakehouse holds all of this data and provides the necessary training and inference infrastructure to power AI enabled ESG ratings, while providing the required lineage and explanation needed to meet regulatory and audit requirements through Governance Services.

4.1 Energy-efficient and green cloud infrastructures

Not only do ESG Analytics measure Sustainability, but they also require operations to minimise their emissions, and as a result, the energy efficiency and Cloud Computing of "Green Cloud" Data Centres can support the energy efficiency of ESG Programmes. Research has recently shown that Data Centres consume large amounts of power that result in growing carbon dioxide emissions from using data centre facilities, and these data centres utilise multiple software level techniques, such as Optimization at the Operating System (OS) level and Application level to reduce energy consumption. In the context of ESG Analytics, an important factor is that the architecture choice (e.g., Containerized Workloads, Auto-Scaling and Efficient Storage, Job Scheduling, and Data Caching) can be both Sustainability levers and Cost levers. In addition, Cloud Sustainability Guidance provides examples of Practical Implementations for achieving Efficiency through Rightsizing Workloads to avoid excessive capacity availability by a Cloud Service; using Serverless Computing to avoid Idle Capacity; using Auto-Scaling to meet Demand; and Optimising Data Ingestion so as to Control for Unnecessary Movement and Storage of Data.

Furthermore, this will directly align with the ESG Reporting Cycle because the company's ESG Reporting can be scheduled according to Heavy Processing Workloads (e.g., Scope 3 Calculations or Creating Portfolio Climate Scenarios) for times when there are Low Carbon Grid Electricity Consumption and/or in Regions with Cleaner Energy to the extent possible by Organisation Policy, and Shutting Down Data Centres.

Even if the organization does not use sophisticated scheduling policies to take advantage of carbon reduction opportunities, by implementing relatively straightforward measures of operational efficiency (e.g., data compression, minimizing redundant data, filtering), operational improvements will be achieved. Many large organizations include sustainability as a critical piece in their overall business strategy and often highlight their companies' commitment to decarbonizing operations (e.g., through energy efficiency efforts, etc.) as part of their company's broader sustainability mission. From an ESG analytics perspective, this is relevant because IT operations are typically included in the organization's overall footprint as measured under the three scopes of carbon emissions (Scope 1, Scope 2 and Scope 3) depending on the accounting basis used to measure the emissions. Conducting ESG analytics on a greener infrastructure will contribute to lower operational emissions for the organization, thereby increasing the organization's overall credibility with all of the stakeholders regarding sustainability programs that are not based on excessive use of computing resources and will help establish the link between how the organization computes versus what the organization reports.

In addition, the use of green cloud infrastructure will allow the organization to monitor its ESG (environmental, social and governance) performance in real-time. Having efficient and automated compute resources allows the organization to make the transition from an annual snapshot to continuously measuring ESG performance based on energy consumption, waste generation or emissions without having an adverse impact on business operations. Examples of technological solutions to implement ESG architecture have transitioned from using manual spreadsheets for information processing to using more integrated platforms or systems that automate the flow of data and enable auditing; therefore, the analytics used for measuring ESG on the basis of green cloud computing need to be developed as an operational capability at a level that provides for the large-scale measurement of ESG performance in a sustainable manner (the use of resources is not impacted by using green cloud computing).

5. AI TECHNIQUES FOR ESG ANALYTICS

In recent years, artificial intelligence has emerged as a key enabler of Environmental, Social and Governance (ESG) analytics. As ESG evaluation requires processing vast volumes of diverse types of data that cannot be processed effectively using traditional or manual methods, artificial intelligence will be used throughout the ESG analysis process. In particular, ESG data consists of structured (e.g., numerical) indicators, including emissions, workforce and board statistics, and unstructured (e.g., text) narratives, such as written descriptions contained within sustainability reports, regulatory filings, corporate policies, supplier disclosures and media coverage. With the application of various types of artificial intelligence techniques, such as machine learning, predictive analytics, and/or natural language processing, it is possible to create actionable, consistent, and timely insights from these disparate types of data. Machine learning models will serve as the primary analytical foundation for ESG scoring; natural language processing will be the primary tool for assessing the sustainability of disclosures; and predictive analytics will be used to evaluate long-term sustainability outcomes related to individual companies and sectors.

ESG Analytics use machine learning models to effectively and systematically derive ESG indicators from ESG Indicators to Composite Score(s) or a Performance Signal for integration into financial planning and operations. Unlike traditional ESG scoring, which often involves the use of expert-based, static weightings or proprietary, opaque methodologies, machine learning approaches allow for the development of a more dynamic way of calculating ESG scores through an empirical relationship between the underlying ESG datasets according to observed outcomes. By processing extensive amounts of Environmental, Social and Governance data, Machine Learning models can uncover Non-Linear Interactions, Contextual Dependencies and Latent Factors that cannot be identified using traditional evaluative methodologies and therefore assist with the evolving nature of ESG performance from a metric perspective. More specifically, the performance of an ESG metric is rarely attributable to a singular metric; therefore, ESG performance emerges from the interplay between the characteristics of an entity's Environmental practices, social practices, Governance practices, Industry and Regional Regulatory Conditions.

Machine Learning in ESG Scoring Systems: The machine learning models in practical ESG scoring systems are trained on a variety of data inputs, including internal ESG indicators, third-party sustainability data, operational metrics, and external signals like controversy indexes and public sentiment. The ML models are able to take these multiple inputs and create ESG scores, which appraise relative levels of sustainability performance among companies, portfolios, or projects. Importantly, machine learning provides consistency by applying the same analytical rule sets against larger and larger data sets, thus creating a more uniform and comparable set of ESG scores than can typically be achieved with human assessors. Therefore, ESG assessments that rely on machine learning models can be tracked and compared over time regardless of increasing data volume and evolving reporting requirements. ML models can also be re-trained on a regular basis to reflect new or changed regulatory frameworks, updated definitions of materiality or newly recognized sustainability risks; thus, ESG scoring systems are able to maintain their relevancy through adapting to changes in the way ESG information is collected and processed.

In addition, one of the other key benefits to using machine learning for ESG scoring is its ability to work with incomplete, imprecise or unevenly distributed data. Due to the different rates of transparency with respect to ESG data from country to country and sector to sector, often ESG datasets have missing values, reporting voids, and inconsistent companies within them. Therefore, machine learning processes are able to implement imputation strategies, robustness methods and ensemble learning methodology to stabilize the results produced from such data in a manner that outperforms traditional data assessment methods.

The use of machine learning techniques to derive ESG scores makes them more applicable in the financial world, which does not realistically allow for perfect data to be available. The emphasis on creating explainable AI also means that the ESG scores developed using machine learning will be more visible than simply existing as black boxes. When stakeholders have access to interpretability mechanisms, they can understand which factors (i.e., ESG) impact their score the most significantly this will lead to greater trust, regulatory acceptance, and improved internal governance.

Machine-learning techniques provide a quantitative structure for scoring; however, Natural language processing (NLP) is needed to extract sustainability intelligence from the multiple narrative (qualitative) sources (i.e., sustainability report, annual report, climate disclosures, codes of conduct, supplier questionnaires, policy documents) that contain ESG-relevant data (such as Corporate Intentions, Commitments to Governance, Governance Practices, and Impact on Society) that are not captured by numerical metrics. NLP techniques can enable automated analysis of the above-mentioned documents by providing a means of standardizing and converting these types of data from unstructured text (i.e., in narrative form) into structured data (e.g., a database) for the purpose of then analysing all of the data at scale.

NLP (Natural Language Processing) based ESG analytics (Environmental, Social, and Governance) usually starts with ingesting and pre-processing documents (PDF, scanned documents, and web pages). Advanced NLP pipelines retain the structure of the document, allowing for the ability to identify sections in the document and tables within context to connect an ESG disclosure to its respective environmental, social, or governance category. After the text has been prepared, NLP models are used to perform various analyses based on classifications, entity name recognition, and semantic parsing of text to identify ESG content.

NLP is also important in extracting both quantitative and qualitative indicators from sustainability disclosures by being able to extract numbers (for example, emissions), workforce diversity statistics, governance policies, and compliance statements from within these narrative texts. Additionally, when extracted values are linked back to their original document context, it provides for auditing and traceability, which is fundamental to regulatory reporting and assurance. Furthermore, NLP allows for the standardization of terminology and units of measurement across different documents, addressing one of the biggest hurdles to ESG data integration. The ability to standardize ESG metrics from multiple sources allows for the comparison and aggregation of the respective ESG metrics in a meaningful manner.

Besides its utility in structured extraction, NLP is also valuable for sentiment analysis and issue detection in the context of ESG monitoring. The way the public perceives, stakeholders expect, and the media frames the sustainability journey has a growing impact on an organization's sustainability performance. By leveraging sentiment analysis to understand the external perception of an organization's environmental efforts, labor practices, or governance decisions, organizations are better able to identify leading indicators of reputational risk, social controversy, and governance failures. Topic modelling and semantic similarity analysis also contribute to the identification of emerging ESG themes, such as climate transition risks and human rights concerns, which may not yet be evidenced through formal disclosures. Including external textual data in conjunction with these analyses will enhance the sufficiency and responsiveness of ESG analytic systems.

Recent advancements in language models have also enhanced the capability of NLP for ESG applications. In particular, large language models related to an organization's sustainability narrative enable richer context for classification, summarization, and cross-document analysis. When combined with retrieval and governance controls, these models can assist ESG analysts by identifying applicable disclosures, flagging discrepancies, and producing structured outputs that comply with various reporting frameworks. However, to minimize bias, ensure fact-based grounding, and provide transparency, careful use of NLP systems is critical, and the inclusion of human-in-the-loop validation systems must be considered.

The predictive analytical aspect of ESG evaluation will allow long term assessment of the sustainability of ESG performance by extending beyond retrospective descriptive and diagnostic components of ESG analytical methods that rely on machine learning and natural language processing. Predictive analytics encompasses techniques such as statistical modelling, time series analysis and machine learning to analyse and predict the future evolution of an entity's financial impacts of sustainability risks and ESG performance. The predictive nature of predictive analytics is of growing importance for the analysis of ESG related risks, specifically those related to climate change and regulatory transition, as these risks tend to materialise over long time periods. Traditional forms of ESG reporting are largely reflective in their nature, and are generally insufficient for strategic financial planning, which requires foresight into various potential future market conditions.

Predictive ESG analytics can assist in long-term sustainability assessment through modelling of trends for various environmental indicators, such as emissions, energy consumption, and resource consumption. Time -series forecasting methodology can be utilised to project the future evolution of these trends based upon the historical patterns of the trends, the operational plans for the organisation, and the assumptions regarding future policies which have been developed. Through using these projections, organisations will be able to assess the alignment of their current strategies with the sustainability targets and their commitments to regulatory compliance. Similar to environmental compliance assessments, predictive analytics can also assist in social and governance assessments by identifying patterns of performance for various aspects of human capital (e.g., workforce stability, safety incidents, compliance rate, and governance incidents). By identifying potential future scenarios of significant risk escalations, predictive analytics can facilitate the opportunity for organisations to respond proactively to events rather than reactively to them.

Scenario analysis is a major component of ESG prediction. By testing different scenarios for different future climates, regulatory systems, technology adoption and physical climate effects, organisations can understand both how their sustainability performance and financial exposure would behave in different situations. Scenarios are used by predictive models to simulate how different ESG indicators, and then subsequently financial outcomes will react under the various future conditions - thereby providing support for stress testing and resiliency assessments. Predictive models help financial institutions with their decision-making process for the allocation of capital to specific assets, evaluating credit risk, and developing long-term strategies. For corporations, they assist in developing investment strategies, determining how to adapt their operations to a specific event, and developing long term strategy plans.

Through the use of predictive analytics, organisations can integrate ESG signals into their financial forecasting models. By using ESG-related variables in conjunction with traditional financial variables, organisations may be able to examine how the sustainability of an organisation affects the stability of a revenue stream, the cost of capital, the valuation of an asset, and the overall risk exposure. Although the predictive potential of ESG signals will depend on the sector and timeframe under which the prediction is made, incorporating ESG signals into a forecasting model allows for a more accurate assessment of risk. Ultimately, for risk assessments to be considered credible, the assumptions made, limitations of data and uncertainty associated with the prediction must be disclosed; and a rigorous validation of the data and appropriate sensitivity analysis must occur to ensure that ESG effects have not been overstated and that no unintentional biases have occurred.

High-quality data infrastructure and governance are essential elements of effective predictive ESG analytics; as sustainability data changes continuously, predictive models require frequent monitoring for drift and retraining. The use of scalable cloud-based platforms provides organizations with the tools and infrastructure necessary to retrain their predictive models consistently, ingest new data in real-time, and monitor the performance of their models automatically. In addition, governance frameworks are utilized to ensure that all predictive models are auditable, explainable, and aligned with regulatory standards. Together, advanced analytical techniques and strong model governance change ESG from a compliance requirement to a value-added strategic intelligence tool.

An integrated AI based ESG analytics ecosystem includes machine learning ESG scoring; NLP for extracting data from unstructured sustainability disclosures; and predictive analytics for evaluating long-term sustainability performance. Machine learning provides a scalable and repeatable means to assess ESG scores. NLP enables the extraction of value from unstructured data in sustainability disclosures. Predictive analytics allows for the evaluation of potential future risk and opportunity within the sustainability\investing ecosystem. All three analytic techniques allow for enhanced data-driven transparency, providing the ultimate in resilient financial decision making. As ESG continues to impact the global financial system, so will the advancement of AI capabilities within predictive ESG analytics. The role of AI will further establish predictive ESG analytics as a fundamental component of sustainable finance and green economic development.

6. CLOUD-BASED AI ARCHITECTURE FOR ESG ANALYTICS

An AI architecture based in the cloud supports ESG Analytics by providing a framework to move from manual assessments (siloed) to scalable intelligence systems that support continuous change. ESG Analytics is an ecosystem of data ingestion, integration, modelling, validation, interpretation, and governance processes that need to work together; they do not represent just one analytical effort but require Interdependency across many disparate efforts (data sets). The complexity and data volume involved with ESG Analytics requires an architecture that is adaptable, resilient, and able to meet advanced analytic as well as strict governance requirements. Cloud solutions provide elasticity, a unified data management and optimized APIs for AI workloads enabling organizations to build ESG Analytics as a core enterprise capability and not just a method to accomplish regulatory/financial reporting.

A Cloud-based architecture for ESG Analytics is built upon a single data repository (single source of truth) which typically utilizes the modern data lake or lakehouse analytic model. This central repository provides the basis for all findings within the domain (with respect to ESG) with respect to structured metrics such as carbon emissions and workforce demographics, semi structured metrics such as supplier demographics, and unstructured content (e.g.) from policies, reports, and other similar content.

A cloud native data lake allows organizations to ingest their data in its original format and progressively structure it as needed. Traditional data warehouses would require storing data along with a defined data structure (schema) already in place.

This architectural principle enables an organization to maintain granular evidence for multiple analyses after the fact. These principles are very important in ESG analysis as both data definitions and rules from governing bodies are continuously changing; rigid structure on write will create delays in the generation of insight from ESG related data due to the inability to write with the changing definition of or rules surrounding those data points at the time of writing. Utilizing a central lakehouse architecture, which combines storage and analytic capabilities (including AI), will allow organizations to analyse, enrich and reuse ESG data through many different departments and decision contexts while being processed in the appropriate manner based on the original definition of that data.

The data ingestion process for these types of systems supports both batch and real time data pipelines. ESG data can flow through the system in many different ways due to having many different types of time scales (for example: Annual Sustainability Reports vs. monthly energy usage vs. daily supplier updates vs. continuous streaming media) and therefore multiple parallel ingestion flows are supported within cloud architecture so that these different ingestion flows can capture all of the different types of ESG data without impacting overall system performance. Moreover, as the ingestion process continues to evolve, more and more ingestion pipelines are being enhanced with automated validation and metadata tagging to ensure that all incoming data is traceable, auditable and adheres to the organization's internal ESG taxonomy. In this way, organizations can start addressing one of the most common barriers of ESG reporting - a lack of clarity and consistency regarding ESG data provenance - by capturing metadata, lineage and quality indicators associated with each ESG data point during the ingestion process, so that organizations have reliable data for both analytics and regulatory compliance.

Once the data has been ingested, it will then be transformed and curated in the cloud platform. As part of this process, the transformation layers will change units of measure, harmonize terminology, and aggregate across organizational boundaries in order to convert raw data points to analysis-ready datasets. This step also plays an important role in aligning ESG metrics with the organization's internal definitions, external reporting and capital markets standards, and financial reporting systems. By utilizing cloud-based processing engines, organizations will also be able to conduct transformations on very large datasets and adapt to evolving reporting standards over time. It is also critical to note that transformation logic will generally be versioned and governed for all ESG data, which will help to provide a basis for organizations to access historical assessments of ESG value.

The AI and advanced analytics layer sit on top of the curated data layer. This layer is responsible for conducting ESG scoring, natural language analysis, and predictive modelling. Cloud platforms support the computational needs of machine learning and natural language processing (NLP) natively; they deliver on-demand computing power, distributed processing capabilities, and integration to allow for the development of machine learning models. A cloud-based architecture allows for the centralization of feature engineering for ESG models. Feature engineering for ESG models is challenging, as the features that go into the creation of ESG model scores come from multiple domains and may consist of lagged environmental indicators, supplier risk aggregations, sentiment scores derived from disclosures, and event flags indicating corporate governance. A cloud-based architecture allows for the centralized management of features that are used by multiple teams when developing ESG models to ensure that the features used by one team to create an ESG model are available to other teams conducting ESG analytics. This reduces the amount of duplication among teams and decreases the likelihood of producing inconsistent ESG insights from siloed analytics efforts.

Cloud ESG architecture tightly integrates model development and deployment. ESG scoring and predictive machine learning models are developed using curated datasets and then deployed as scalable services that dashboards, reporting tools, or downstream financial applications can call on. Deployment in the cloud allows near-real-time operation of ESG models when required, such as for updating risk alerts or monitoring new controversies. In addition, cloud architectures allow for effective management of model lifecycles—version control, performance tracking, and scheduled retraining, when additional data is available—are all important functions that cloud architectures assist with. From the perspective of ESG analytics, it is crucial that this lifecycle perspective is implemented since static models can become outdated very quickly due to changes in regulations, materiality, and the changing nature of stakeholder expectations.

Within the AI layer, elements of natural language processing (NLP) models are typically integrated beside numerical models but may utilize different processing pipelines. NLP cloud-based architectures consist of four main component areas: documents ingestion, documents pre-processing (i.e., removing stop words, stemming), semantic analysis (i.e., term-frequency—inverse document frequency), and the structured data extraction from documents. These architectures are integrated within the central data repository. Due to the diverse nature of ESG documents, the NLP processing pipelines must be built to support modularity and extensibility. Modularity is supported in cloud-based environments by allowing NLP components to scale independently, efficiently process large volumes of documents, and incorporate human-in-the-loop verification for judgement calls with a significant impact.

An essential component of good ESG analytics architecture would-be strong governance over data, models, and access to that data and those models. Given that ESG insights are directly tied to making investment decisions, disclosing information to regulators, and developing a corporate strategy, strong governance is not just a choice - it is fundamental. Unified governance frameworks provided by cloud platforms will assist organizations in having a common approach to their overall data, manage access control, enforce data security policies, track data lineage, and monitor usage across the ESG analytics ecosystem. Having centralized governance across all of these areas allows stakeholders to understand how to trace ESG scores back to their original data source, how to understand how a model produces an output, and how to confirm whether the insight generated is based upon approved methodologies. In those industries regulated by government oversight, the existence of ESG information in a black box and classifying that information as acceptable will become increasingly less viable. In supporting this conclusion, enterprise-wide guidance on data and AI governance support by suggesting that companies have implemented unified catalogues, tracked lineage, an employed centralized access controls to achieve trustworthy analytics and compliance-ready AI systems. Equally important is governance over models. Models used to evaluate the ESG of an organization/procedure are at a significantly greater risk due to potential bias, lack of transparency, and/or opportunities for misinterpretation based upon differences in geography and industry. A cloud-based ESG architecture can facilitate ongoing governance of models through consistent monitoring for performance degradation, identifying situations of bias, and noting any type of data drift. Governance layers provide the means to require documentation, require producing an explanation as to how the model produced a given output, and provide for human/corporate oversight in a way that is appropriate at the time of a decision being made. These principles guide how ESG analytics should be governed architecturally to ensure that the most relevant, reliable, and appropriate data and models are used to assess an organization's ESG performance.

Interoperability and/or integration with enterprise systems is also another major component of an ESG cloud architecture. ESG analytic solutions do not work alone and must integrate with, as well as exchange data with, finance, risk management, procurement, and compliance systems. Cloud integration services, and API's enable the seamless exchange of ESG data into these enterprise systems and thereby embed sustainability considerations into capital allocation decisions, credit evaluations, and strategic planning processes. This method of architectural integration moves ESG from a reporting-based effort to a real-time operational intelligence layer that will continuously influence financial decisions.

The architectural design of the ESG applications can also take into account sustainability elements. Cloud environments can provide energy-efficient computing, elastic resource allocation, and optimized storage options which will allow an organisation to minimise the environmental impact of its ESG analytical workloads. Architectural decisions including the use of auto-scaling, serverless processing and highly efficient data lifecycle processes will reduce excess, underutilised resources which will align the organisation's digital operations with its environmental objectives.

The alignment of the analytical function with the architectural design of the system supports the credibility of ESG-related initiatives and reinforces the viability of the stated sustainability goals relative to the organisation's actual technology operations.

To conclude, an AI architecture developed in the cloud will give an organization the basic elements needed for producing scalable, clear, and predictive sustainability intelligence about ESG. When data management, advanced analytic capabilities, governance, and enterprise integration are all combined within a flexible cloud-based framework, the firm can confidently integrate the ESG knowledge into its daily operations. Not only does this type of architecture facilitate advanced AI-driven ESG analytic capabilities, but it also supports ESG-related activities that are trustworthy, auditable, and consistent with achieving the organization's full mission as well as the promotion of sustainable financial decision-making and green economic growth.

7. INTELLIGENT ESG SCORING AND SUSTAINABILITY FORECASTING

Intelligent ESG scoring signals a move from static, period-based sustainability "ratings" towards a dynamic and continually updated, data-driven means of measuring ESG performance which supports genuine financial decision-making such as credit approval, portfolio construction, investment screening, risk monitoring and regulatory disclosure. Under the typical ESG scoring methodology, the ESG rating is regarded as a snapshot from a limited window of reporting and derive from a prescribed selection of indicators making them ill-suited for the ever-changing nature of sustainability risk. In contrast, intelligent ESG scoring is designed to be an adaptive scoring engine that uses multiple data sources, applies materiality-aware weighing logic, enables updates in real time or near real time as new evidence becomes available, and outputs not only a single score but a range of interpretable "drivers," uncertainty indicators and overlays on top of which provide additional clarity about emerging risks.

This evolution is firmly connected to a market demand for higher transparency and comparability in the ESG analytical space and to an increasing demand that ESG factors be component of automated decision workflow rather than a stand-alone sustainability activity. An effective ESG scoring system must start by understanding that there are many dimensions to ESG performance and that the ESG performance of an entity will vary based on the contextual factors surrounding it. Thus, in order to create an accurate, credible ESG score, the entire scoring structure must be created as a hierarchy. Specifically, various granular indicators roll into one or more thematic scores, which roll into one of three overall pillar scores (environmental, social, or governance), and which all roll into an overall ESG score. This means that the way the scoring is set up is not just for reporting purposes; rather, it is what allows for the interpretation, auditability and governance of the ESG score obtained. For example, when a financial stakeholder disputes an ESG score, the system can explain whether the outcome was derived from the entity being ready for a climate transition, the entity's labour relations, the entity's governance controls, the entity's history of incidents, or a combination of these or other material themed-related factors, and then it can show the reason for any change in the score, whether that is due to an improvement in the entity's performance, updated disclosure of data or some other method of detecting and reporting previously undisclosed negative events. Methodologies utilized to enhance clarity and consistency in ESG scores include the use of standardized indicators, materiality matrices, and structured roll-up methodologies (especially since ESG scoring will often be required to support the creation of decisions subject to regulatory oversight).

In ESG scoring, materiality awareness is one of the most important core criteria for determining intelligence. ESG is not an equal application of the same indicators within the same industry, geography or business model—therefore intelligent scoring systems will have a materiality layer that determines which themes have the most material relevance for each entity and how significantly those themes should affect the score. This will keep the score from being subject to distortion from irrelevant metrics and also align the score with both investor and regulatory expectations. Practically, this means that two entities can be assessed using one standard scoring architecture, while still being evaluated on what is considered to be relevant to their sector and operational context based on materiality. In transparent scoring frameworks, this is generally represented by a formalized materiality matrix and thematic structure, enabling stakeholders to understand the scoring rationale without being reliant on vague analyst judgement. An additional characteristic that defines intelligent ESG scoring is the inclusion of both forward-looking (leading) and backward-looking (lagging) indicators. This is because sustainability performance incorporates both results achieved and actions being taken to forecast future results. Examples of lagging indicators are measured greenhouse gas (GHG) emissions, injury (accident) rates, incidents of regulatory non-compliance and confirmed incidences of governance failure. Examples of leading indicators are the management of sustainability-related activities (e.g. GHG emissions) leading to future performance and the capability of the organisation's systems to deliver future sustainable outcomes.

Scoring Engines Based Solely on Lagging Indicators Are Reactive to Risk and Often Detect Risk After Before There's Was any Harm, Whereas If a Scoring Engine Relied Solely on Leading Indicators, It Could Reward Intent Without Any Evidence of Delivery. Intelligent Scoring Intends to Balance Leading and Lagging Indicators for a Score that is Responsible and Predictive Thus Allowing for Earlier Interventions and More Successful Risk Management. Despite this, Due to Missing,

Inconsistent, and Often Poor Quality of ESG Data, an Intelligent Scoring System Needs to Include Data Quality Controls. To Achieve this, ESG Data Pipelines Should Include Procedures to Validate Completeness, Accuracy, and Traceability of Data from Source to Report and Designed to Also Meet Requirements for Assurance When Disclosure is Audited or Verified by an Independent Third-Party. The Reliability of an ESG Score is Limited by the Reliability of Its Input Data; As Such, There Are Increasingly Validation Checks, Provenance and Control Procedures Embedded in Scoring Engines So That Stakeholders can Be Assured That the Score is Not Only Computed, but Also Computed from Evidence That Is Sufficiently Reliable for Review by Investors and Regulators. These Requirements are Increased by Regulatory and Market Demands for Robust, Reliable, Auditable ESG Data and for Procedures That Will be Able to Withstand Independent Assurance.

Intelligent scoring also requires an understanding of time-based intelligence, since ESG metrics are not delivered simultaneously and are not updated frequently. While financial transactions are continuously updated, many sustainability disclosures occur quarterly or annually and many major ESG risks develop when something happens externally (like a serious controversy getting reported in the media, or when there is a fire at a local supplier). Thus, a modern "scoring engine" will include a "time-alignment" layer to help manage the "effective dates," "freshness windows," and "lag structures" so that a score will be reflective of the most recent data available without combining different time horizons together. For example, emissions data could be from the prior reporting period (such as the prior year), but controversy signals may relate to the most recent month; therefore, a modern intelligent engine will keep these two kinds of data separate and will show the recency and confidence of both. Finally, many modern ESG scoring methodologies explicitly outline the methods used to update (such as a "restatement" of previously scored data or a new score) or revise the result of a previous score. This illustrates that ESG scores are not created in isolation (i.e., one-time calculations) but are a controlled process that can change as new data become available.

Another aspect of intelligence is the ability to decouple the core (or "base") ESG scoring, which reflects the overall sustainability management performance of an entity, from the modular overlays that reflect special risk signals. In many financial transactions, stakeholders require a stable core score that represents the overall sustainability management performance of an entity, while simultaneously requiring a more precise indicator of controversy risk, catastrophic events, or other positive impact signals (e.g., revenue from green products, or exposure to financing for sustainable initiatives). The modular architecture allows for this to happen: the core score remains comparable across entities and time, while overlays can be added to the core score to provide more detailed analysis; in many cases, these additions do not require the entire scoring system to be redefined. This design allows for both the strategic integration of ESG factors into investment and lending decisions, as well as tactical monitoring of risk to assist investors and lenders determine their specific application of the score without losing its ability to be understood or interpreted.

Once the first step has been completed with the design and development of a robust, intelligent ESG scoring engine, the second component of sustainability forecasting becomes the next layer that will, ultimately, provide future-oriented decision support from ESG analytics. ESG forecasting is not only predicting a score, but also estimating how sustainability-related performance, risk exposure, and readiness to transition will change over time under reasonable and realistic constraints such as changes in public policy, the adoption of new technologies, capital expenditures, shifts in supply chains, and physical changes in the environment due to climatic impacts. The goal of ESG (Environmental, Social and Governance) forecasts is to move on from being just retrospective, and to be used in the development of long-term financial planning (including transition finance strategy development), stress-testing for climate change and goals for aligning portfolios with ESG principles. Increasingly, predictive analytics and forecasting are being considered the next stage in the evolution of ESG maturity since stakeholders seek evidence of resilience and progress and are therefore demanding greater transparency through more than just past reporting. Forecasting associated with ESG typically happens across multiple time horizons and levels of detail. For example, when looking at an operational horizon, companies will estimate various measurable environmental/sociable Key Performance Indicators (i.e. energy, emissions, water intensity, safety incidents and workforce outcomes) using a time-series based methodology that incorporates seasonal trends and known operational changes. A strategic forecast looks to expand beyond operational KPIs to encompass transition and physical risks where both have some degree of external climate and policy dependency in their forward estimates. Financial institutions will also want to relate their sustainability trajectory to financial metrics (i.e. profit, default risk, sensitivity to valuation, and desire for future capital) as part of the forecasting process. The linking of sustainability and financial-performance-focused forecasting happens at this intersection of climate risk modelling and scenario-based stress testing due to the uncertainty that arises from long time horizons and the complexity of climate-related impact assessments, thus making simple extrapolation insufficient for forecasting purposes for climate-related impacts.

One of the most important differences between scenario analysis and prediction in sustainability forecasting is that scenario analysis helps to create a possible 'what-if' pathway rather than having a single best guess of what would happen. Additionally, banks and investors use scenario analysis to assess vulnerabilities, test resilience, and define risk appetite in times of uncertainty. Scenario analyses are used to better understand both transition risk, which is caused by changes in policy, market, or technology, and physical risk created by natural disasters such as flooding, extreme heat events or storm damage. Therefore, the best practice in a bank's ESG forecasting architecture is to use both baseline forecasts and scenario layers to adjust models based on assumptions made. This may allow analysts to analyse how different (but plausible) futures could affect ESG-related activities rather than relying solely on one model result.

Organizations can integrate an internally consistent scoring framework to strengthen their credibility in estimating sustainable business impacts. For example, a company may have an internal environmental score, which reflects its operational emissions intensity and transition readiness. The score could be used by the organization to select appropriate scenarios, as well as to tailor stress testing to its unique operational environment, rather than applying the same scenario across its entire organization. By tying the score to the scenario analysis process, companies can progress from high-level assessments of their entire portfolios to more detailed assessments of how various attributes will impact the future. This helps them develop reliable predictive analytics and real-time monitoring tools for their credit decisions and risk management processes. This alignment is particularly.

"Nowcasting" and monitoring for early warning signs of failure in Environmental, Social or Governance (ESG) areas have significant value in the development of intelligent ESG forecasts, just like the long horizon prediction methods used by most organizations today. ESG controversies and governance failures typically develop quite rapidly, creating a financial impact before most organizations are able to capture the degradation via their normal reporting cycles (i.e., Annual). Continuous scanning by a system of real-time data sources comprising multiple sources of unstructured text and events for evidence of increased controversy risk and adjusting risk overlays to identify escalating exposure to controversy, is the primary feature of a responsible architecture for monitoring, forecasting and responding to ESG risks. Designing a system in this manner can increase responsiveness, which can provide organizations with the opportunity to:

- Respond sooner to weak signals detected earlier in time in order to engage or mitigate before any damage is done
- Provide sufficient governance controls and human oversight to continuously manage false positives, bias and uncertainly, particularly for alerts generated by ESG forecasts that have the potential to influence high-stakes decisions; and
- Improve transparency and usefulness for investors and lenders by anchoring the ESG forecasting assessment to the likelihood of future controversies arising and measuring the respective influence of the specific indicators that drive increased risk.

Uncertainty representation (i.e., how uncertainty is presented and/or factored into ESG forecasts) is an additional important dimension of sustainability forecasting methodologies. ESG forecasting is not intended to represent the predicted score or key performance indicators (KPI) as deterministic outcomes. Instead, intelligent systems should provide a level of confidence (e.g., confidence intervals or standard deviations) in the prediction of the score or KPI or a range of estimated scores or KPIs when indicating the level of uncertainty in the projected amounts and the influence of any underlying assumptions and/or data quality utilize.

Due to widely differing, often incomplete and evolving measurement standards across many ESG models, the importance of this issue cannot be understated. By logically illustrating the associated uncertainty with forecasting outputs, the subsequent decision relevance can be enhanced, allowing risk teams to better focus their exposure management on those high exposures which exist under even the most optimistic of assumptions, and to prioritize data improvement efforts where uncertainty arises as a result of unreliable or missing input data. Additionally, improved governance can be achieved because all stakeholders have a common basis for understanding levels of knowledge (i.e., known & assumed) and degrees of uncertainty within the combined ESG forecasting process, thus mitigating the risk that ESG forecasting becomes solely a narrative tool rather than providing information relevant to risk-based decisions.

Within the context of financial decision-making processes, the greatest value of ESG forecasts is likely to arise from those that can convert sustainability trajectories into actionable threshold and decision trigger points. Many intelligent scoring engines apply threshold-type values or capped score grossing technologies in order to prevent superficial improvements generating justifiable large score increases, and to ensure that any progress is recognised as verifiable and/or material.

The principles of forecasting also apply to the handling of sustainability by entities, in particular when governmental or other institutional actors measure trigger thresholds, such as an anticipated breach of emissions intensity targets, increased likelihood of controversy, degradation of governance controls, and/or inability to achieve targeted levels of sustainability performance where forecasting becomes operational in relation to support for intervention and engagement strategies, covenant establishment, and establishment of risk appetite as opposed to remaining solely as an academic exercise. To support the operational use of forecasting, it is necessary to employ transparent scoring methodologies with emphasis on trigger thresholds, standardized criteria, and modular overlays to provide stable bases for establishing and monitoring triggers.

In principle, intelligent ESG scoring and sustainability forecasting should be treated as a single continuum; ESG scoring organizes and verifies the current condition using evidence to establish materiality, while forecasting identifies probable future pathways under conditions of uncertainty and aids in proactive decision-making. When taken together, an integrated scoring and forecasting system will allow organizations to not only respond to the question "How sustainable is this organization now?" but also "What will be the future state of sustainability and the emerging risks to achieve resiliency and alignment with green economic growth?" In order for intelligent ESG scoring to be a viable tool for sustainable finance, it must be integrated into an overall process with strong data controls; balanced use of leading and trailing indicators; modular risk overlays; a time continuum; and scenario-based forecasting.

8. DETAILED RESULTS AND DISCUSSION

This section presents findings from the experiment that was conducted using the proposed intelligent ESG analytics framework, along with an analysis of their effects on the ability to make sound financial decisions based on sustainability. Three main areas were evaluated in these studies: (1) How well the intelligent ESG scoring system compares to traditional ESG scoring systems, (2) The impact of natural language processing on the refinement of ESG scores, and (3) The ability of the sustainability forecasting models to produce predictions regarding future sustainability performance. The results indicate that the use of AI-based methods provides more discriminative, consistent, and forward-looking ESG insights and supports greater practical usefulness in the execution of actual financial transactions where sustainability is a concern.

8.1 Results of Intelligent ESG Scoring

Table 7.1 shows the overall ESG ratings of the proposed intelligent scoring engine in comparison to those of a baseline sample representative organization and indicates that the intelligent ESG rating approach has resulted in the generation of ratings that are statistically significantly different from those generated by traditional methods. The intelligent ESG model has provided higher ratings (indicating greater sustainability maturity) for organizations with maturity levels of sustainability that suggest proactive governance mechanisms, planning for transition, and investments in long-term sustainability, and takes into consideration these factors in addition to only using past performance indicators. As such, the overall level of improvement in scores for organizations with medium levels of maturity can be attributed to how the intelligent model captures both the strengths and weaknesses of their ESG performance, leading to moderate improvements, or increases in score improvement that corresponds to observed improvements in the overall management of their organizations. In contrast, the overall decrease in organization scores for organizations with low maturity levels can be attributed to the fact that the intelligent model scores organizations' weaknesses in controls, lack of coverage in policies, and high exposure to ESG risk factors and other ESG-related risks that have historically been underrepresented in traditional static scoring systems. This confirms the theory that intelligent scoring reduces over-reporting or inflation of score and improves the accuracy of ESG ratings for organizations that demonstrate some measure of compliance but do not have a significant level of substantive activity toward addressing ESG-related issues.

Table 1. Comparison of ESG Scores Generated by Different Approaches

Organization Category	Traditional ESG Score	Intelligent ESG Score	Score Variability (%)
High sustainability maturity	78.2	84.6	+8.17
Medium sustainability maturity	64.5	70.9	+9.92
Low sustainability maturity	48.7	44.1	−9.45

8.2 Contribution of NLP-Driven Disclosure Analysis

To evaluate the influence of natural language processing (NLP) on the evaluation of ESG, the ESG scores were re-calculated with and without indicators produced by NLP derived from sustainability reports, governance disclosures and external narratives. The comparative data are indicated in the table below (see table 7.2).

The results indicate that the analysis provided using NLP based techniques greatly enhances the ESG evaluation process by including qualitative evidence that may not be captured by the use of numerical indicators only. Following the integration of the analysis using NLP, environmental and social scores increased as a result of the inclusion of future commitments, narratives and actions that could be identified in disclosures. On the other hand, governance scores decreased for a number of companies indicating the identification of incongruities, weak oversight language and emerging controversy signals found in narrative portions but were not found in structured datasets. This suggests that the addition of NLP not only adds to the positive assessment of subject companies but adds to the identification of risk, which in turn enhances the credibility of ESG analytics. The small increase of overall ESG scores indicates that NLP primarily adds to the composition and confidence of score determination rather than the aggregate increase in values.

Table 2. Impact of NLP-Based Indicators on ESG Scores

ESG Dimension	Score without NLP	Score with NLP	Mean Change
Environmental	71.4	75.8	+4.4
Social	68.9	73.1	+4.2
Governance	74.6	69.3	−5.3
Overall ESG	71.6	72.7	+1.1

8.3 Stability and Temporal Consistency of ESG Scores

The major drawback with current ESG assessments is that they exhibit excess volatility in relation to time. ESG scores were evaluated in terms of their temporal stability by measuring how stable the scores were during a number of different reporting periods and calculating the amount of deviation in each score. A comparative analysis with respect to temporal stability of ESG scores has been presented in Table 7.3.

Table 3. ESG Score Stability Across Time

Method	Average Quarterly Change	Maximum Observed Change	Explained Change (%)
Traditional ESG scoring	±6.8	±14.2	52
Intelligent ESG scoring	±2.9	±6.4	89

The intelligent ESG scoring infrastructure has demonstrated much lower levels of score volatility than traditional ESG scores, and it has produced a higher percentage of explainable score changes. Most of the changes in scores have been directly attributable to new disclosures, detected incidents, or verified improvements in performance. This indicates that the proposed architecture has been able to effectively balance the two important and often conflicting priorities of being able to respond quickly to changing conditions as well as maintaining score stability. Controlled behaviour, from an ESG financing governance standpoint is critical, because it reduces stakeholder confusion and allows for the use of ESG scores as reliable inputs into credit models, investment thresholds and risk controls, without introducing excessive amounts of noise into those sensitive calculations.

8.4 Sustainability Forecasting Results

To assess the Predictive capability of the framework beyond its current performance metrics, we analysed sustainability forecasting models to forecast the expected evolution of ESG scores under baseline conditions over a three-year period (See Table 7.4).

Table 4. Forecasted ESG Scores (3-Year Horizon)

Organization Category	Current ESG Score	Year 1 Forecast	Year 2 Forecast	Year 3 Forecast
High maturity	84.6	86.2	87.9	89.1
Medium maturity	70.9	72.4	74.1	75.8
Low maturity	44.1	43.6	42.9	42.1

Forecasting the results illustrated that the three groups of organizations have very different potential trajectories for achieving sustainability. Organizations with high maturity levels continue to experience ongoing improvement and demonstrate both resiliency and alignment to their long-term sustainability objectives with respect to their current level of maturity. Organizations with medium maturity levels are making incremental gains in their ESG scores; however, with targeted interventions, these organizations could achieve much greater improvements in future outcomes. Organizations with low maturity scores, on the other hand, will see their ESG scores continue to decline over time as ESG risks accumulate without a structural change in their operations. These findings underscore the strategic importance of using ESG forecasting as a means for stakeholders to identify not only their present weaknesses but also to anticipate and mitigate how present weaknesses will compound over time into future risks.

8.5 Discussion and Implications

The combined findings support that through combining intelligent ESG (environmental, social, and governance) scorecard with forecasted sustainability, you can obtain insights that significantly exceed those gained through traditional ESG evaluation methods. The score carding process successfully differentiates actual sustainable performance compared to simple compliance, and the addition of Natural Language Processing enhances the ability to identify opportunities as well as identify risk. Furthermore, forecasting results further substantiate that ESG analytics should not be limited to only providing retrospective reports; but also, ESG analytics must be used to guide proactive decision-making and long-term planning. The stability of intelligent ESG scores demonstrates that the issue of creditable and verifiable

ESG ratings is being addressed and better positions intelligent ESG scores to support regulated financial transactions. As a consequence of the combination of these observations, ESG analytics are transitioning from descriptive, compliance-based functions to predictive, intelligence-based functions. Once supported by cloud-based artificial intelligence (AI) computing systems, ESG scores become dynamic indicators of current evidence of ESG performance, and indicators of what future performance might be and can be used as a basis for helping determine future sustainable capital investments. This is essential for supporting credible sustainable finance, as in order for sustainable investment and financing decisions to be made, each decision must not only be ethical but also be defensible from an economic perspective.

CONCLUSION

In conclusion, this chapter has provided a thorough and integrated view of how the introduction of artificial intelligence has the potential to change the way organizations currently conduct their ESG analytics reporting from a static, compliance driven activity to a dynamic, intelligent, forward-thinking decision support mechanism for sustainable finance. The chapter illustrates that meaningful ESG evaluation can no longer be accomplished solely through manual processes and/or simplistic ESG scoring, and that it necessitates a partnership of advanced data engineering, machine learning, natural language processing and predictive analytics all working together in a governed, scalable cloud environment.

The primary contribution of this chapter is articulating the transition from traditional ESG ratings to intelligent ESG scoring. Whereas traditional ESG ratings often represent an aggregate form of historical performance with respect to a collection of checklists, intelligent ESG ratings capture both contemporaneous computationally derived ESG performance outcomes as well as future readiness by employing leading / lagging indicator integration, materiality-based weighting, and near real-time evidence aggregation in their scoring. Results and discussion presented throughout this chapter demonstrate that such intelligent ESG scoring engines are far superior at distinguishing between true ESG maturity and mere ESG compliance; therefore, improving the reliability and usefulness of ESG metrics in supporting financial decision-making processes. Consideration of this value proposition becomes most pertinent in your world today.

The chapter also explains how natural language processing plays an important part in Environmental, Social and Governance analytics. Much of the intelligence about sustainability is unstructured data (like unstructured disclosures, policies, governance narratives and external text signals). Natural language processing (NLP) contributes to the qualitative aspect of Environmental, Social and Governance assessment, by providing context, extraction and validation of qualitative information from sources that are not in the format of structured datasets. The dual ability of NLP allows for both the identification of positive sustainability initiatives and greater capability for detecting weaknesses of governance, social problems, and developing issues in advance.

Another key finding from this chapter is the significant role of forecasting in providing critical sustainability intelligence for Environmental, Social and Governance. ESG performance is by definition forward looking. Many of the high-risk areas associated with ESG perform over extended time frames i.e. climate transition risk, physical climate risks or governance failures that month, and those risks become apparent over long time frames. By utilizing predictive analytics and scenario-based evaluation within Environmental, Social and Governance frameworks; organizations will transition to proactive risk management and long-term strategic planning, versus simply evaluating instead of projecting. The analysis of forecasting results creates the basis for two or more entities having similar current day ESG scores, but of very different status two or more years from the current point in time.

Equally important is the emphasis placed on cloud-based AI architecture as the enabling foundation for advanced ESG analytics. Without scalable data ingestion, unified data governance, controlled model lifecycles, and seamless integration with enterprise systems, even the most sophisticated AI models cannot deliver trustworthy ESG insights at scale. The architectural perspective presented in this chapter shows that ESG intelligence must be treated as an enterprise capability rather than an isolated analytics exercise, with governance, traceability, and explainability embedded throughout the data and model pipeline. This is essential not only for regulatory compliance but also for building long-term trust among investors, regulators, and other stakeholders.

From a broader sustainable finance perspective, the findings of this chapter reinforce the notion that AI-driven ESG analytics can play a decisive role in aligning financial systems with long-term environmental and social objectives. Intelligent ESG scoring and forecasting enable capital to be allocated more efficiently toward entities that demonstrate genuine sustainability progress and resilience, while also signalling where intervention, engagement, or corrective action is required. In doing so, AI becomes not merely a technical tool but a strategic enabler of green economic growth, responsible investment, and systemic risk reduction.

REFERENCES

Anumolu, V. R. (2025). Financial Innovation for Sustainability: Leveraging AI, XR, and Data for Impactful Investments. In *Exploring the Impact of Extended Reality (XR) Technologies on Promoting Environmental Sustainability* (pp. 133–157). Springer Nature Switzerland. DOI: 10.1007/978-3-031-88013-1_7

Elhady, A. M., & Shohieb, S. (2025). AI-driven sustainable finance: Computational tools, ESG metrics, and global implementation. *Future Business Journal, 11*(1), 209. DOI: 10.1186/s43093-025-00610-x

Jebadurai, D. J., & David, S. (2026). AI-Driven ESG Investing: Transforming Sustainable Finance in the Digital Age. In *Building AI-Driven Decision-Making Competencies for Sustainability* (pp. 29-70). IGI Global Scientific Publishing.

Khaddam, A. A., & Alzghoul, A. (2025). Artificial intelligence-driven business intelligence for strategic energy and ESG management: A systematic review of economic and policy implications. *International Journal of Energy Economics and Policy, 15*(4), 635–650. DOI: 10.32479/ijeep.19820

Krishna, N. (2025). AI-Integrated ESG Scoring System: Leveraging Real-Time Green Data Intelligence for Sustainable Finance: A Study on the Role of Artificial Intelligence in Dynamic ESG Evaluation. *Available at SSRN* 5764202. DOI: 10.2139/ssrn.5764202

Kumar, M., Singh, S. K., Nghiem, X. H., & Rathnasiri, M. S. H. (2026). AI-Driven Sustainability: Automating ESG Reporting and Green Operations through the Cloud. In *Automating Intelligence with Cloud-Native AI Tools* (pp. 87-98). IGI Global Scientific Publishing.

Sipayung, M. S. Digital ESG Analytics: A Bibliometric Review of AI-Driven Sustainability Research (2010–2025).

Smith, H. K. (2025). *Sustainable Intelligence at Scale: Algorithmic Innovations for Green AI Across Manufacturing*. Smart Cities, and Financial Cloud Platforms.

Chapter 9

An Effective Algorithm for Potato Disease Classification Utilizing Deep Learning

Sherzod Shukurov
Termez University of Economics and Service, Uzbekistan

Sabyasachi Pramanik
http://orcid.org/0000-0002-9431-8751
Haldia Institute of Technology, India

Anorgul Ashirova
http://orcid.org/0009-0006-7271-3634
Mamun University, Uzbekistan

Valisher Sapayev
http://orcid.org/0000-0002-6751-5864
Mamun University, Uzbekistan

Muyassar Allaberganova
Urgench State University, Uzbekistan

Pranati Rakshit
http://orcid.org/0000-0001-5037-1326
Tarakeswar Degree College, India

ABSTRACT

Potatoes are grown all around the world at a large scale and are at the fourth number in the massive growth list. However, potatoes are primarily affected with fungus, resulting in early and late blight diseases, reducing the production rate of crops. Therefore, control and management of disease in real-time could help farmers enhance production, reduce crop, financial losses. Disease identification in plants is a potential step toward sustainability and security of the agriculture sector. Imaging-based processing, in particular, allows the in- depth study of plant physiology quantitatively. On the other hand, interpreting manually needs a lot of work, understanding of plant pathogens, and a long processing time. Therefore, this study proposes a time-efficient algorithm based on transfer learning and im-

DOI: 10.4018/979-8-2600-3280-0.ch009

age processing that can accurately classify potato diseases. The proposed method consists of three steps preprocessing (grayscale conversion), segmentation (image enhancement, soft clustering, morphological dilation, and flood fill operation), and classification (AlexNet).

1. INTRODUCTION

In tropical regions, potato is one of the most vital veggies. This is one such vegetable that is widely recognized throughout the globe and consumed daily by most of the families. Potatoes are a common kind of inexpensive food that offers a low-cost energy source in the human diet. They're high in carbohydrates, vitamins (particularly C and B1), and minerals. However, several fungal and bacterial diseases wreak havoc on the potato-growing process. The diseases might be deadly, resulting in a loss of productivity and, ultimately, a damage of the economy at the national level. Early Blight, and Late Blight also called Phytophthora Infestans (Demilie 2024), is the two deadly infections. Aalternata (Bohra, S., et al. 2026) a fungus which produces brown color leaf spot, is related to the early blight closely. Brown leaf spot, similar to early blight, survives the winter as mycelia and spores on the diseased tissue. When early blight infects potato leaves, the lesions change color between grayish-white and dark brown. The lesion is round in form, and it enlarges until the veins become uneven. The spots appear on the sharp edges of the leaves if the potato leaves are afflicted with late blight.

Early blight normally affects the foliage of the potato plant, but it can infect the tubers also. Tuber lesions (Devi, V.B. et al. 2026) are black, round and deep with purple to grey elevated tissue bordering them. The flesh beneath is dry, brown and leathery. During the storage of potatoes, lesions can grow in size and tubers can get shriveled. Potato tubers and foliage are affected by late blight (M., M., Anandamurugan, 2025). Tuber infection is frequently started in wounds, lenticels or eyes by sporangia which come into soil through the leaves. Soft rot bacteria can pollute diseased tubers, turning large storing bins of the potatoes into a stinking and decaying mass. Plants and fields may quickly collapse if the diseases are not identifying at the early stages.

Early detection of these diseases enables precautionary procedures and economical production losses to be mitigated. Over the past several decades, the most widely used detection for detecting and identifying potato plant diseases has been skilled naked eye observation. However, this method is often impractical owing to the lengthy processing times and the inaccessibility of specialists at farms situated in distant regions. A simple and robust model is needed to rapidly detect diseased potato plants to take appropriate action and mitigate the loss. Additionally, potato crop farmers may increase their awareness and interact with agricultural specialists in the event of widespread diseases. The life cycle of late blight fungus is represented in Figure 1.

Figure 1. Potato Disease Cycle and Epidemiology

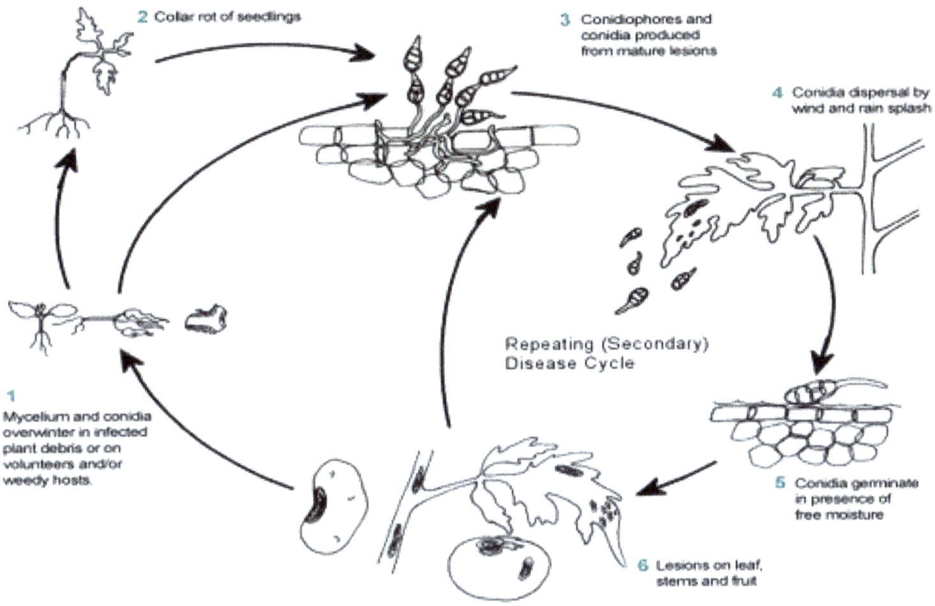

The adoption of image analysis techniques demonstrates efficacy in continuously monitoring the fresh condition of the potato plants and the timely detection of potato plant diseases. Because diseases produce visible signs on the potato plants, particularly on their leaves, the recognition of disease may be accomplished via imaging analysis of such apparent patterns on leaves. Thus, the combination of image processing and machine learning came out with the potential solutions for potato production and contributes to the food sources. A computer-based automated approach of identification of leaf disease is required for the optimal development of this potato plant and effective production of potatoes. Numerous methods including image processing (Kempenaar, C.C., et al. 2026), internet of things, and big data are utilized to identify the leaf disease. Additionally, the ML method is shown to be effective for this purpose.

Deep learning is an emerging theme in ML and AI that has high accuracy in pattern recognition problems. Generally, it is a subset of ML techniques that utilizes a few layers of non-linear data handling to perform unsupervised or supervised extraction of feature, modification, pattern analysis and classification. Additionally, it has been used in the processing of audio and voice, natural language processing (NLP) (Chettri, K. et al. 2026), and computer vision. Additionally, it is extensively used in various industries across the globe, including business, agriculture, and the automobile industry, for object detection and image classification. Advances in image classification provide an opportunity to expand the image processing research and application to agriculture. Deep learning (Elkenawy, S. et al. 2026) algorithms may now be used to recognize and categorize plant diseases depending on their perceptible detection. At the moment, various deep learning techniques are being utilized to identify potato plant disease. A substantial amount of the annotated data is almost usually required for deep learning. This causes researchers to focus on activities that are simple to annotate rather than tasks that are essential. The performance of Deep Nets (Xu et al., 2026) is well on the benchmarked datasets, but they might fail miserably on the real-world dataset. This research focuses on the classification of the three classes of potato plants using deep learning with efficient performance. The proposed method of this chapter is a combination of the processing of images and CNN (El-Behery, H. et al. 2026) which is a unique combination for the plant classification. The rest sections of the chapter are arranged in the subsequent manner: Section 2 demonstrates the earlier researches completed by other researchers on the detection of leaf diseases. Section 3 represents the explanation of the suggested technique. Section 4 summarizes the outcomes of the model, and Section 5 concludes the key findings.

For resolving dataset imbalance the authors have used reweighting-dependent (Raju & Thasleema 2026) methods in combination with improvements in early disease detection to lessen the difficulties caused by different class proportions in the dataset. We have successfully balanced the dataset (Zhang, A. et al. 2026) by giving each case the proper weights according to class frequencies, which has increased classification accuracy and encouraged uniformity throughout various illness classes. The problem of dataset imbalance is addressed by the reweighting strategy, which guarantees equal treatment of each class for training the model. The tactical change improves aggregating the accuracy of classification by reducing discrimination against the dominant classes and enabling the model to more accurately identify minute distinctions across illness types. The remarkable accuracy attained by the suggested approach highlights the usefulness of these cutting-edge (Sah, S. et al. 2026) tactics and their importance in developing automatic disease diagnosis in farming. In order to help professionals and scholars choose the best strategy for their particular deployments, this contrast offers insightful information about how different strategies work.

2. LITERATURE REVIEW

Significant developments were established in tracking and identifying the plant diseases using a variety of techniques like image processing, ML, and DL approaches. A segmentation method using K-means clustering was utilized to extract variables including area and color from picture data for diagnosing the illnesses on potato leaves. Then, diseases are identified and classified using neural network methods (Nazir, T., et al. 2023). Because of the classifying diseases in cotton and potato leaves, an alternative method combines picture segmentation having feature extraction, like mean, SD, and contrast, succeeded by neural network methods. (Alzakari, S.A., et al. 2025) utilized multiclass SVMs (Manoj & Nandhini, 2026) for classification and presented the use of image segmentation on the plant_Village_dataset, having a specific emphasis on potato leaves (Gülmez, 2025). Furthermore, using publicly accessible datasets as Flavia, LeafSnap and foliage, (Tiwari, N.K., et al. 2026) investigated the LeafNet architecture, which is dependent on CNNs. Moreover, a deep CNN model was created by (Bajpai, A., et al. 2025) to categorize thirteen distinct illness categories. To categorize and detect fungal infections in the grape dataset, a technique was developed. For feature extraction and classification, this method makes use of K-means clustering and SVMs. Furthermore, (Abdelhamid, A.A., et al. 2025) implemented a technique for leaf disease identification that integrates picture segmentation with soft computing methods. Feature extraction is done using the color co-occurrence approach, and illness classification is done using an SVM classifier. The Inception V3 network is refined to study broad plant features in (Choudhary & Shrivastava, 2026) for few-shot learning techniques and disease categorization. This method uses a baseline CNN, triplet loss, and a Siamese network. An identification technique including the SplitBregman method approach for segmentation was suggested by (Lilhore, U.K., et al. 2026). Regression neural networks are used for classification, and the RPN method is used to analyse the training dataset. Defective leaves are found and retrieved using neural networks. The algorithm's accuracy is 83.57%. A framework which uses transfer learning with pre-trained frameworks like VGG19 and Inception-V3 (Bohra, S. et al. 2026) was then introduced by (Jha, P., et al. 2024). SVM, KNN (Qiu, H. et al. 2026) and neural networks are among the classifiers that are used. After analysing their performance, it is shown that VGG19 performs rather well when combined with logistic regression. Additionally, researchers have investigated the use of a hybrid technique that combines auto-encoders with CNNs for illness prediction and categorization. To extract the valuable characteristics, the auto-encoders' encoding component is used. Three crops have been used in this study: maize, potatoes, and tomatoes. In (Radwan et al., 2025), a different approach utilizing D-CNN, pooling

(Aghdam, R. et al. 2024) & fully connected layers is suggested in the diagnosis and categorisation of potato leaf diseases.

Modern phenotyping and disease detection technologies represent a major role in the search for food security and sustainable agriculture. On the other hand, manual interpretation takes a lot of work, understanding of plant diseases and excessive processing time. The authors of this article (El-Kenawy, S., et al. 2025) describe a method in determining diseases and thereby utilizing leaf images that combine image processing and ML. This automated approach detects diseases (or their absence) on potato plants using images from the publicly accessible 'Plant Village' plant image collection. The suggested segmentation technique and the use of support vector machines show diseases categorization with a 95 percent accuracy across 300 images. Authors in (Alharbi, A.H., et. al. 2025) present an automated method based on ML and image processing to classify and detect potato leaf diseases. The segmentation of 450 pictures of healthy and sick potato leaves from an openly obtainable plant_village_database is performed in this chapter. Six classifier methods are utilized to recognize and classify the infected and healthy leaves. Among them are: Having a highest accuracy of 98.22 percent, the RF classifier (Kabel, S.A.EM. et al. 2025) is the most accurate approach.

Intelligent farming based on machine learning validates the automatic recognition of diseased leaves. This research (Ghosh, S., et al. 2024) offers a very efficient CNN structure in detecting potato illness. The optimizer is Adam, and the model is analyzed using cross-entropy. Softmax (Devarajan, D. et al. 2026) is utilized as the ultimate decision-making process. The convolution layer and associated resources are reduced while maintaining the accuracy. A database is built for the training set using image processing techniques. The implemented outcomes indicate that the recommended method accurately identifies plant illness at an efficient rate. Controlling illness and managing it properly in real- time may significantly enhance output and minimize farmer losses. As a result this article (Sinamenye, J.H., et al. 2025) offers CNN structure appropriate for finding potato illness. The experimental findings indicate that the parameter used is 10,089,219 and that the illness classification accuracy may approach 99 percent when using the preset model suggested in this chapter. The authors of this research (Elshewey, A.M., et al. 2025) evaluated the efficiency and accuracy of AlexNet and CNN architectures for recognizing illness in potato and mango leaf. This approach made usage of a dataset comprising of 4004 pictures. Potato images were sourced from the PlantVillage website (Saha, S. et al. 2024), whereas mango pictures were acquired from the GBPUAT (Singh, R. et al. 2025) field site. The findings indicate that the accuracy obtained by AlexNet is 98 percent, which is greater than the 90 percent accuracy achieved by the CNN architecture.

Modern vision methods may significantly decrease expenses associated with the early detection of blackleg infected plants. The work demonstrated the application of DL method for identifying blackleg infected potato plants (Elafifi, A.G., et al. 2026), on RGB images of healthy and sick plants and two deep CNN networks were trained. From the trained network, one of them (ResNet18) was shown to have an accuracy of 95% and 91% recall for the illness class in an experiment. This chapter (Gupta & Shah, 2023) describes a potato disease classification method that makes use of these unique appearances and deep learning-enabled advancements in image processing. The system utilizes a deep CNN trained model to classify tubers into 5 categories: 4 types of disease categories and a healthy potato category. The collection of images utilized in this research was compiled manually by specialists and includes potato tubers of various sizes with diseases. The models were evaluated using a data set of images captured using typical low-cost RGB sensors and labeled by professionals, showing a higher level of classification accuracy. The findings indicate that the accurate classification rate for fully trained CNN models varies between 83 and 96 percent depending on the amount of data employed for the model training.

Transfer learning utilizes weights of previously trained DL models to tackle new problems. Transfer learning is shown in this article (Paul, H., et al. 2024) as a method that may be utilized for the potato diseases early detection when collecting thousands of fresh leaf images is a challenging task. The tests comprised images of 152 healthy leaves, 1000 leaves influenced by late blight, and 1058 leaves influenced by early blight. The software predicts 99.43 percent accuracy in testing using 80% trained data and 20% test data. Different frameworks were suggested before the detection of several plant diseases. The research in (Pandey, S., et al. 2025) presents a technique that employs pre-trained models such as fine-tuning of VGG19 to extract important characteristics from the dataset. Then, using several classifiers, it was determined that logistic regression beat the other techniques by a significant margin of accuracy for classification, achieving 97.8 percent on the test dataset. The authors of this article (Asif, M., et al. 2026) provide a system for classifying 4 kinds of diseases in tomato plants on the basis of the condition of leaves. They used DL techniques like VGG19 and VGG16 (Fayaz, S.M. et al. 2025) to achieve an accurate classification. This experiment averaged 91 percent accuracy, demonstrating the viability of the Deep Neural Network (Sharma & Sethi, 2024) method.

Using various technologies and doing routine monitoring may detect diseases at their earliest stages and eliminate them to maximize agricultural production. As a result, this article (Sai Reddy & Neeraja, 2022) presented a technique for detecting and categorizing diseases which influence potato leaves. The widely known Plant_Village_Dataset is examined for the said purpose. The K-means algorithm was used for image segmentation, the GLCM (gray level co-occurrence matrix) (N. Ahmad Yani et al. 2026) method was used for extraction of features, and the multi-class SVM was used for classification. The proposed technique had a 96.84 percent accuracy rate. The article (Pattanaik, H., et al. 2024) proposed a technique for classifying the diseases in the potato leaves through unique color and textural features. Three stages comprise the proposed method: Segmentation of the images, extraction of features, and classification. Initially, the leaf's RGB image is transformed to the L*w*h*color space. Thus, utilizing the method of k-mean clustering, the background and green area (healthy leaf) are separated from the region of interest. Second, the maximum-minimum color difference technique has been used to extricate the suggested unique color characteristics. Finally, using a Euclidean distance, color characteristics are coupled with statistical texture data to identify potato leaf diseases (Jainul Abidin, A. et al. 2026). The outcomes demonstrated that the suggested approach obtains a higher accuracy of 91.67 percent than the baseline methods when 300 potato leaf images are used. Table 1 compares potato diseases accuracy of reported techniques on the benchmark datasets.

Table 1. Summary of previous studies

Sr.		**Ref**	**Database**	**Methodology**			**Classes**	**Accuracy**
				Preprocessing	**Segmentation**	**Classifier**		
1		(Mahum, R., et al. 2022)	PlantVillage	-	Background-masking	SVM	3	95%
2		(Nazir, T., et al. 2023)	PlantVillage	Image normalization and color space conversion	HSV based masking	Randomforest	3	97%
3		(El-Kenawy, ES.M.,et al. 2025)	PlantVillage	Normalization and Gaussian filtering	Thresholding	4 layerCNN	3	99.53%
4		(Arshaghi, A., et al 2023)	Local data from GBPUAT	Image resizing and augmentation		CNN and Alex net	4	90%and 98%
			Field location and PlantVillage					
5		(Sadiq et al. 2023)	Local dataset	-	-	ResNet50, ResNet18	2	82% and 94%
6	(Sangar G & Rajasekar V. (2025)		Local dataset	Image resizing and grayscale conversion, augmentation	-	8 layers of CNN (VGG)	5	96%
7	(Kumar, A., et al. 2023)		PlantVillage	Normalization, grayscale conversion, augmentation	-	VGG16	3	99.43%
8	(Yashwant. U. et al. 2023)		PlantVillage	Image resizing	-	VGG19, Logistic regression	3	97.8%

continued on following page

Table 1. Continued

Sr.		Ref	Database	Methodology			Classes	Accuracy
				Preprocessing	Segmentation	Classifier		
9	(Kumar, R., et al. 2024)		Malang, Indonesia, PlantVillage	Augmentation And Image resizing	-	VGG16 &VGG19	5	91%
10 **Proposed work**			Plant Village		Image enhancement, soft clustering, morphological dilation, flood fill operation	AlexNet	3	97.57%

3. MATERIALS AND METHODS

This research classifies 3 classes of potato leaves (Early blight, Late blight and healthy) utilizing image processing and transfer learning. The proposed framework is composed of preprocessing, image segmentation, and classification depending on CNN technique. First, all the images were in RGB (Panda, T. et al. 2026) format, so to get the characteristic features for good classification accuracy, it must be pre-processed by converting the colored images into a gray scale image. The next step after the grayscale conversation of the image, is segmentation that is subdivided into many steps, including image enhancement, soft clustering (Varal & Sayyad, 2026), morphological dilation, and flood fill operation. Segmentation (Renugadevi et al., 2026) is an important step to get rid of the unwanted areas and extracting the region of interest for better results. In the end, the segmented images of each class are trained into AlexNet Neural Network (Pandiri et al., 2025), and then the images are classified into three classes of potato such as early delight potato (1000 pictures), late delight potato (1000 pictures) and healthy potato (152 pictures). This study employs the MATLAB2020 software for the coding of the proposed framework. Figure2 shows the proposed method block diagram.

Figure 2. Block diagram of the proposed method for the Disease Diagnosis of potato plants

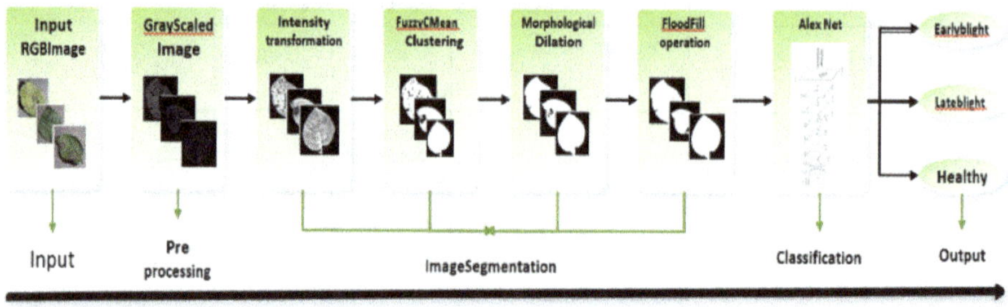

3.1. Dataset

In this research, the Plant_village_dataset was utilized for the assessment of the suggested technique. This dataset (Kumar, Y., et al. 2023) consists of three different plant images like pepper, potato, and tomato and for each species there are different classes for healthy and diseased leaves. But here in this research, only the three classes of the potato plant are considered that are potato late blight (Bonkra, A. et al. 2026), potato healthy and potato early blight, with a resolution of 256*256*3. The quantity of leaf images in each class was 1000 for early blight, 1000 for late blight and 152 for normal class of potatoes and it is also summarized in figure 4. Figure 3 shows the RGB color image of the three classes.

Figure 3. Original RGB images of potato leaves (a) Early blight (b) Healthy (c) Late blight

(a) (b) (c)

Figure 4. Distribution of leaf pictures for every class

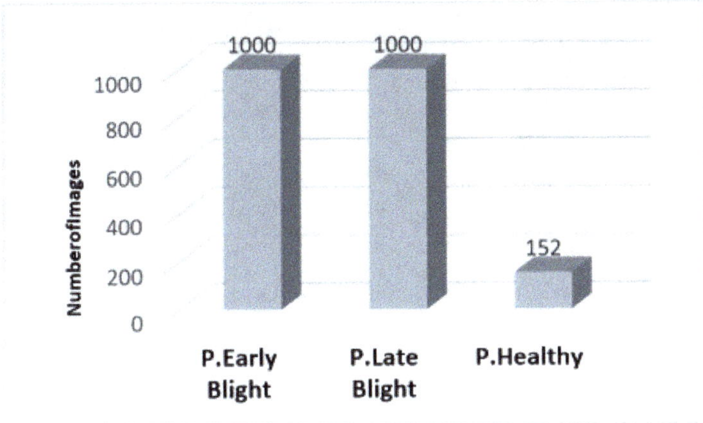

3.2. RGB to Gray scale Conversion

The original dataset is in the RGB (Khan, A. et al. 2026) color regions to extract the required characteristics from the data and it is first converted into a gray scale regions. Grayscale image is the range of colors between 1 and 0 which are shades of gray and is only showing the intensity of each pixel at the corresponding location of the image. There are two ways of grayscale conversion luminosity and average methods. In the average method, the three channels green, blue, and red are averaged to obtain the grayscale image (Jawed, M.M. et al. 2026). Additionally, the luminosity method is different and the average is done for all channels but each of the color is given a specific percentage: red is 30%, green is 59% and blue is 11%. The reason is that green has a soothing effect on the eyes and red has the longest wavelength than all other colors. In this research, the grayscale images (Sireesha, C. et al. 2026) are obtained by subtracting the blue channel from the green channel. Figure 5 depicts the gray scale image of the 3 classes.

Figure 5. Gray scale images of leaves of potato (a) Early_blight (b) Healthy (c) Late_blight

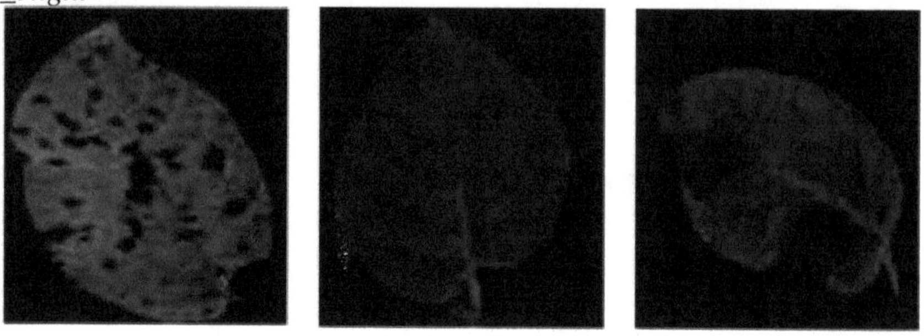

(a) (b) (c)

3.3. Enhancement

When analyzing a grayscale image, there are some features which are suppressed and are needed to be enhanced for getting improved results. Image enhancement is the technique of quality improvement of the images and some of its operations include histogram equalization (Sah, S. et al. 2026), and contrast adjustment (Gebremeskel, H.H. et al. 2026), morphological operators, and filtering (Hamid, M.A. et al. 2026). We can observe that after the grayscale conversion the output images have a low contrast value. So we need to stretch the contrast so that we can differentiate between the region of interest and boundaries. To solve this problem, intensity transformation is used for enhancement. Intensity transformation can achieve the desired goal using different techniques such as gamma transformation, log transformation, negative of image, and contrast stretching. Fig 6 depicts the enhanced image of the three classes.

Figure 6. Enhanced images of potato leave (a) Early_blight (b) Healthy (c) Late_blight

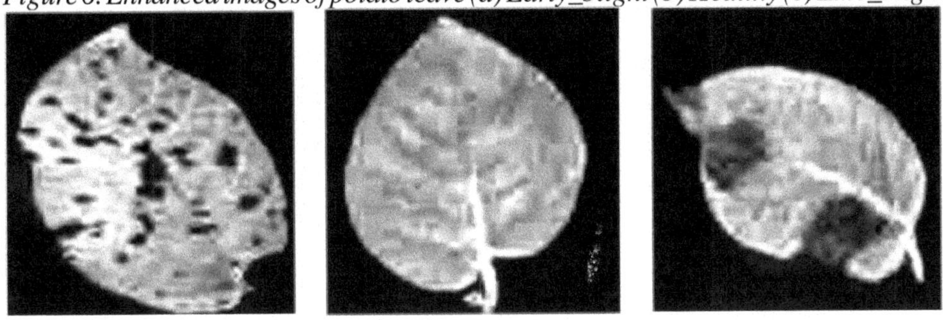

(a) (b) (c)

3.4. Fuzzy C Mean Clustering

The algorithm depending on unsupervised machine learning separates the data into many clusters or groups. The data that is dissimilar for different point's data and similar for same group points are termed as clustering. It is utilized to detect the groups in the database. One of the clustering methods is the Fuzzy C means (Dhoundiyal, P. et al. 2025) which is a soft approach to clustering. In this method, each point of data is given a probability for belonging to the cluster. Figure 7 shows the Fuzzy C-mean Clustering of images of the three classes. The algorithm is described in the following steps.

Step 1: The number of the cluster values is fixed.
Step 2: A partition matrix is initiated.
Step 3: Calculating the centroid of clusters.
Step 4: Update the matrix.
Step 5: Repeat the steps until the convergence is achieved.

Figure 7. Fuzzy C-Mean Clustering of potato leaves (a) Early_blight (b) Healthy (c) Late_blight

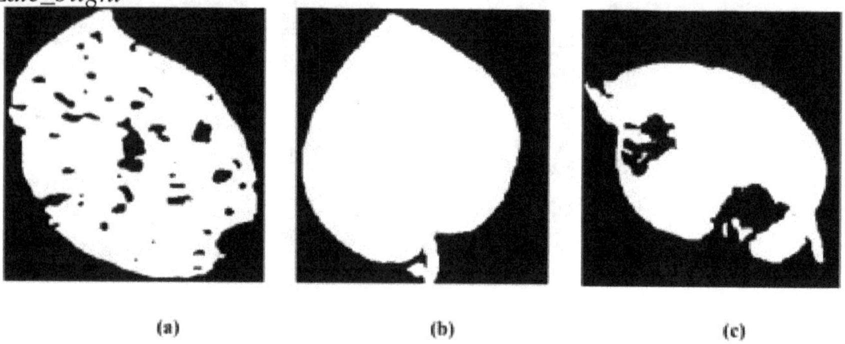

3.5. Morphological Dilation

Erosion and dilation are the two operators used in the morphology area. They are typically used for binary images but some versions can be utilized for grayscale also. This technique increases the size of the pixels of foreground region boundaries specifically the white ones and the holes in these areas become small. In the operation of dilation, two inputs of data are taken, one is the image to be dilated and another one is the kernel also known as structuring element.

The image as an input and structuring element is super-imposed in a way that their origins concede. The image pixel value is specified to the forefront if only one value of the pixel of the image foreground and structuring element concedes. In the second case, all the pixels in the background concede so the pixel values are left for the background. Figure 8 shows the morphological dilation results on images of the three classes.

Figure 8. Morphological dilation of potato leaves pictures (a) Early_blight (b) Healthy (c) Late_blight

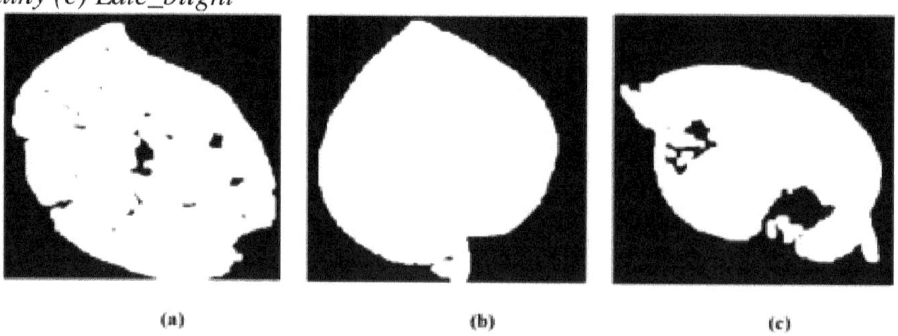

3.6. Flood Fill Operation

It is an algorithm that is used for altering or determining an area linked to a node in an array which is of multi-dimensional category. This operation is useful in eliminating irrelevant objects in an image. In the process of this method, specific areas of the image are filled with specified color by putting lower and upper limits of negative and positive connected pixels difference. As we can observe that, after morphological dilation there are still some black spots in the region of interest that need to be eliminated so the flood fill method is used to achieve this. Figure 9 shows the flood fill operation of images of the three classes whereas Figure 10 shows the segmented images.

Figure 9. Flood Fill operation of potato leaves pictures (a) Early_blight (b) Healthy (c) Late_blight

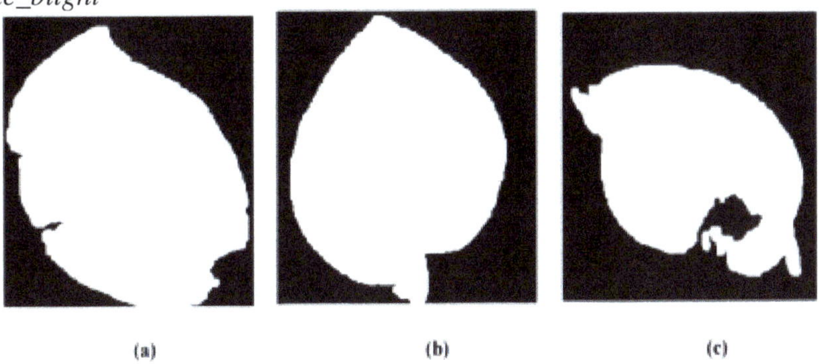

Figure 10. Segmented potato leaf pictures (a) Early_blight (b) Healthy (c) Late_blight

3.7. Classification

A type of Neural Network is the CNN, which is a combination of different layers of normalization, fully connected, convolutional layer, and pooling layer. Convolution is a method of applying a kernel to an image to change it. The classical CNN is very difficult for the application of images with high resolution. Therefore, there was a need for such networks that can optimize GPUs and reduce training time as well as improve the performance. AlexNet has a unique architecture and consists of 8 layers which include convolutional layers, max pooling, DenseNet, and fully connected layers. Convolutional layers consist of kernel or filters for performing convolution operations to obtain the feature map of input images. Max pooling is a method of calculating the max value of every patch of the feature map and then the output is pooled while showing the common feature of each patch. Fully connected layers are used for connecting the two neurons. Figure 11 shows the detail structure of the AlexNet.

Figure 11. Detailed Architecture of Alex Net Neural Network

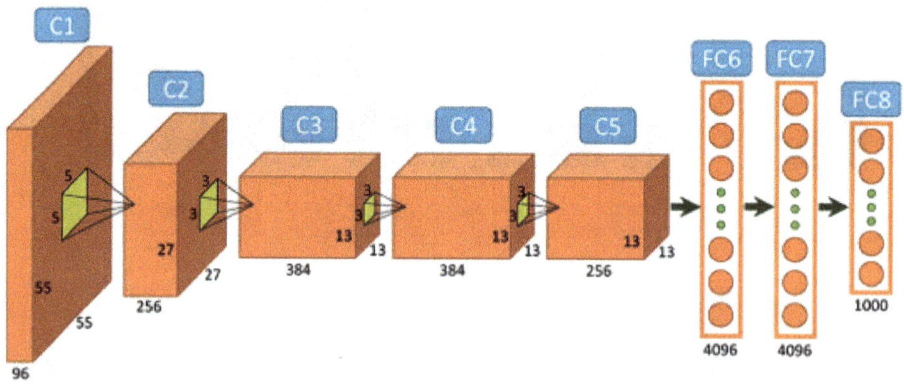

4. RESULTS & DISCUSSION

Here, a combination of grayscale segmented image and AlexNet network to classify the three classes of the potato plants are used. There are two sets of data (i) training data (ii) testing data, for the experiment purpose on the AlexNet architecture. For this purpose, 70% of data has been utilized as a training set & 30% data as a testing set. Firstly, the AlexNet is trained for the training data of the leaf images using learning rate of 0.0001 and a single CPU for 26 epochs. The validation accuracy of 97.35% has been achieved with a maximum of 416 iterations in 30 minutes 58 sec time. Figure12 shows the training of accuracy & error rate for the training data using AlexNet. After that, the trained network is tested using a test set of data and it classifies the three classes with an accuracy of 97.57%. Fig 13 displays the confusion matrix of validation data for three classes. A confusion matrix is a table which compares the expected classes to real target values for evaluating a classification model's performance. It summarizes accurate predictions (diagonal elements) and misclassifications, breaking down findings into true positives (TP), true negatives (TN), false positives (FP) & false negatives (FN). It is observed that the potato early blight class is classified correctly by 100%, similarly potato healthy class is classified correctly by 100% and only in the potato late blight class there were 2 images that were miss diagnosed as healthy and potato early blight class. The achievement of the suggested technique is measured by accuracy (A), F1 score, precision (P), and recall (R). Accuracy is characterized by the proportion of the quantity of accurately classified subjects to that of all the number of subjects.

$$A = \frac{TP+TN}{(TP+FN+TN+FP)} \times 100 \qquad (1)$$

Precision indicates the degree to which a categorization (Prabu & Chelliah 2022) model is precise and accurate. Precision is an evaluation of the difference between real positive values and genuine predicted values. It is computed by applying the following formula to the confusion matrix:

$$P = \frac{TP}{TP+FP} \qquad (2)$$

Precision is used to quantify the accuracy of the classification process, particularly when the False Positive rate is high. In binary classification and pattern recognition applications, the sensitivity or recall of a classifier is explained as the proportion of TP values to the total of FPs and TNs. Recall calculates the proportion of true positives in a classification model that is categorized precisely.

$$R = \frac{TP}{TP+FN} \qquad (3)$$

The F1-score is determined by both accuracy and recall. It is really a critical task to grasp the distinction between precision and accuracy while doing statistical evaluations. F1-score is useful when there is a requirement for balance between Precision and Recall, and they are most often employed when there is an uneven distribution of classes. Figure 14 depicts a graphical and tabular comparison of the three classes' assessment parameters. Below is the equation for calculating the F1-score.

$$F1\text{-score} = 2 \times \frac{Precision \times Recall}{Precision + Recall}$$

Figure 12. Training curve of AlexNet for the training data

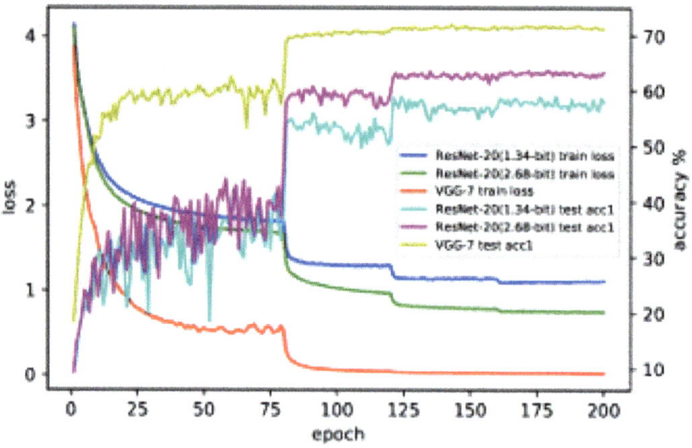

Figure 13.Confusion matrix for validation data

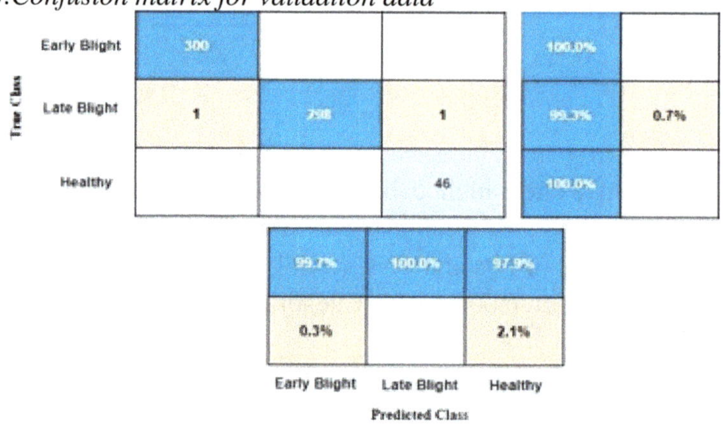

Figure 14. Graphical & tabular comparison of performance measures for each class

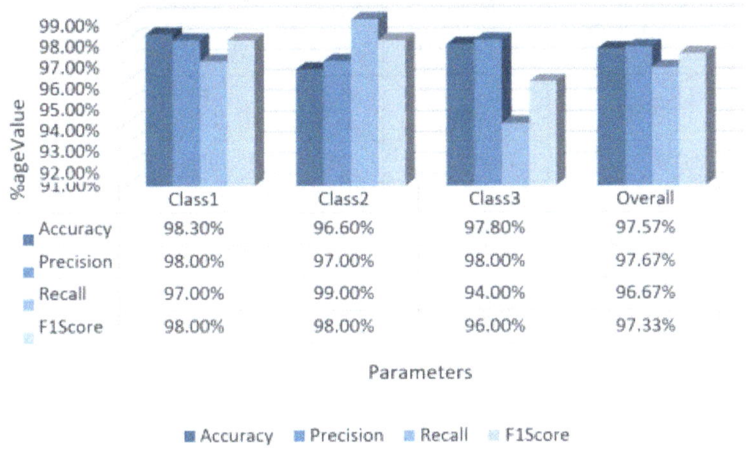

Table 2 presents the past methods comparison with the proposed framework. We can observe that the past method consists of complex structure frameworks with a larger number of layers or a blend of preprocessing, segmentation feature extraction and classifier which increases the time complexity (Moussafir, M., et al. 2022). VGG16 consists of 16 layers but AlexNet (Mahapatra, P., et al. 2026) has only 8 layers. Although the proposed models have less accuracy as compared to the past papers it is more efficient, accurate, and less time-consuming. Additionally, some of the papers employed their own dataset which is not authentic but this study employed an authentic publically available dataset for classification.

Table 2. Comparative summary of advanced methods with proposed method

Author	Year	Database	Methodology	Accuracy
(M. A. Iqbal., et al. 2020)				
(Nawaz M, et al. 2026)	2026	PlantVillage	K-means algorithm, SVM	95.99%
(Singh, G., et al. 2025)	2025	PlantVillage	Augmentation and Image resizing,VGG16andVGG19	91%
(Kotwal, J.G., et al. 2024)	2024	AI Challenger Global AI Contest	Gaussian Filtering, adaptive SLIC algorithm, LBP, SVM	97.4%
(Mandal, S.N., et al. 2023)	2023	PlantVillage	Self-built CNN	996%

continued on following page

Table 2. Continued

Author	Year	Database	Methodology	Accuracy
(Jlassi, A., et al. 2024)	2024	OwnDataset	GoogleNet, VGGNet and EfficientNet	95%,96%,97%
(Talab, H.K., et al. 2024)	2024	PlantVillage and own dataset	HSV color space, Fuzzy C-means clustering, texture features, ANN	92%
(Kaur, K., et al. 2025)	2025	Plant Village and own dataset	YOLOv5 algorithm and CNN	99.7%
(Dame, T.A., et al. 2025)	2025	Kaggle, Dataquest, own dataset	AlexNet, VggNet, ResNet, LeNet & Sequential model	97%
(Lanjewar, M.G., et al. 2024)	2024	PlantVillage	Efficient Net and MobileNet	98%
Proposed method		PlantVillage	Gray scale image, segmentation and AlexNet	97.57%

5. COMPARISON TECHNIQUES

For demonstrating the effectiveness of the work, a comparative study of the suggested research with different DL methodologies is completed in this portion of the article. Various accepted DL frameworks, like VGG16, VGG19, MobileNet and DenseNet-101 (Kumari & Bansal, 2026), were proposed for this purpose. By contrasting the cumulative quantity of model parameters and accuracy, we were able to assess different DL structures from the standpoints of model architecture and performance. Table 3 displays the evaluation's findings. The values distinctly indicate our technique to be successful and efficient in comparison to the different DL frameworks. The work being presented here has 11 million model parameters. Having an aggregation of 1.96 million parameters, the VGG19 (Shawon, S.M. et al. 2026) algorithm is more costly regarding model framework. ResNet50 achieves the lowest performance result in terms of model accuracy scoring of 72.83%. At 76.57%, MobileNet (Askr, H., et al. 2026) attains the second-minimal accomplishment score. Having an accuracy score of 91.66%, the DenseNet technique exhibits superior performance results; nevertheless, its network topology is intricate, requiring 40 million parameters. In contrast, our method contains a total of 11 million model parameters and works well with an accuracy of 98.12%. It is evident that the average score for these methods is 84.84%, whereas our model's score is 97.95%. As a result, we have achieved a 13.11% performance increase, demonstrating our model's effectiveness. The primary reason for these superior model classification outcomes is the other methods' more intricate model structures, which lead to problems with overfitting (Bouacida, I. et al. 2026). In contrast, our method is more effective at addressing the overfitting problem and has a lighter structure. Additionally, our method improves the cataloguing score by introducing layers at the termination of the network architecture and using the pixel and channel attention strategy for the feature calculation step. Therefore, it can be concluded that we have provided an effective and efficient method for remembering the different categories of potato plant leaf diseases.

Table 3. Comparison table for accuracy (Proposed vs. current methods)

Architecture	*Parameters (million)*	*Accuracy (%)*
VGG16	135	91.58
VGG19	187	78.46
MobileNet	12	76.57
DenseNet	38	91.66
Proposed	11	97.95

Ablation Study

This work performed a series of ablation experiments to investigate the effects of each enhancement approach on the model performance (average recognition accuracy). Table 3 displays the ablation experiment's findings. With only the Leaky ReLU activation function, or VGG16, the model accuracy is 97.01% and 96.81% respectively. It is evident that utilizing a global average pool in place of VGG16's fully linked layer lowers the model's overall parameter count while significantly lowering recognition accuracy. The accuracy of incorporating the Leaky ReLU (Shafik, W. et al. 2026) activation function (LRAF) and the VGG16 attention mechanism approach is 96.72%. Combining the LRAF with the Global Average Pooling (GAP) mechanism yields an accuracy of 91.78%; nevertheless, training is challenging because of the huge number of model parameters. The enhanced approach (GAP + LRAF) has an accuracy of 90.49%.

Table 4. Effect on model accuracy of various improvement techniques

GAP	VGG16	LRAF	The Mean Accuracy of Test Set
-	√	√	97.01%
√	-	√	84.36%
-	√	-	96.81%
-	√	√	96.72%
√	√	√	90.49%
√	-	√	91.78%

Agriculture Researchers and Benefits to farmers

The rising use of CNNs to identify potato plant illnesses demonstrates how cutting-edge technology may support agriculture. Consider a farmer attempting to recognise sick potato leaves only via visual inspection. CNNs do a similar task by analysing pictures of potato leaves to recognize indication of diseases such as early or late blight. These networks are trained on thousands of photos to identify disease-indicating patterns, such as yellowing or odd patches on leaves. By employing CNNs, farmers may swiftly spot infections early on, allowing them to take steps prior to the entire crop's impact. The process of using CNNs for potato disease diagnosis by Taking photos of potato leaves and sending them into a computer programme was taught to identify certain patterns associated with illnesses. Besides minimizing farmer's time and labour, this innovation improves the plant health and minimizes herbicide consumption. It is likely to have a smart assistant which may identify possible issues in the farms prior to becoming a significant risk. By using CNNs, farming becomes more sustainable and efficient, guaranteeing stronger potato yields and improved food security for people who depend on this essential food.

6. CONCLUSION

The potato plant is one of the largest consumed plants all over the world. Therefore, diseases affecting plants could be harmful to human beings as well because reduction in potato yield reduces the available food and thereby leading towards starvation and famine in the worst case. It is a very time-consuming and less accurate method for farmers to look for each plant to diagnose that a plant is healthy or diseased. Hence, this research proposed a solution to this problem by using advanced technology and deep learning algorithms to detect plants automatically in less time and with higher accuracy. This can help farmers to diagnose disease at early stage and saving the massive crop destruction, which will ultimately save them from financial loss. In this study, the 2 classes of potato diseases, late and early blight and a healthy class, are classified using transfer learning. The main goal is to propose a system that can assist the farmers by providing a time-efficient, feasible, and efficient method of disease identification. The proposed technique consists of image segmentation which includes image enhancement, soft clustering, morphological dilation, flood fill operation, and AlexNet architecture for accurately classifying the three classes. The RGB images of potato crop from the Plant_village_database are used to test the trained model and the results demonstrated that the proposed technique attained an accuracy of 97.95%, recall of 96.67%, precision of 97.67%, & F1 score of 97.33%. Classification accuracy of the detection model could be enhanced by using another pre-processing technique in the future.

Limitations

Major contributions were made in the area of potato crop disease recognition via the combination of AI and CNNs. However, there are a number of difficulties in this area. The need for thorough, varied, and precise annotation is one significant barrier dataset for model training. Large datasets (Zhang, Y. et al. 2026) are essential for attaining high accuracy, according to several studies, but creating them may be time-consuming and resource-intensive. Furthermore, a significant obstacle to the proposed models' capacity for generalisation is the variation in plant shape, illumination, and climatic circumstances. Researchers must thoroughly address the critical challenge of confirming strong performance covering various places, climates, and production procedures. The need for model interpretability accuracy is another significant obstacle; building confidence with farmers, stakeholders, and regulatory agencies requires a comprehension of these models' decision-making process. Some DL models might not be widely adopted because of their opaque nature. In order to provide clear insights into how certain traits contribute to illness detection, researchers must develop approaches to analyse model choices. Furthermore, there are issues with price, accessibility, and the technical know-how required for implementation when implementing AI-driven solutions in agricultural settings with limited resources, especially in poor countries. A crucial factor is making these technologies accessible to agriculturalists, which make up a sizable share of the world's farming labour force. Careful consideration must be given to ethical issues such as data ownership, privacy, and possible biases in training data. Conveying these ethical issues is essential to ensuring responsibility and fair adoption as AI systems are essential to make agricultural decisions. AI models must constantly evolve because of the dynamic characteristic of plant diseases and the advent of novel pathogens. The long-term efficacy of these models depends on their scalability and flexibility to changing illness conditions. In general, resolving these issues is essential to achieving the highest capability of AI and DL in improving the diagnosis of potato crop diseases and advancing sustainable and explainable agriculture.

Future Work

Looking forward, it would be beneficial to assess how well our model performs in identifying illnesses in a wider range of crops, which might result in the development of more thorough and adaptable disease detection methods for widespread agricultural application. Numerous intriguing methods for treating diseases have emerged in recent years. While late discovery might result in significantly lower output and higher expenditures because of the requirement for pesticides and manure, early identification can cause less harm and make maintenance simpler. However, producers must take proactive steps to reduce possible losses; disease identification alone is insufficient. Creating an AI-directed bot (Verma, P.R. et al. 2026) which can start the necessary treatments for damaged leaves might be one possible direction for future research, making farming more efficient and less taxing. In the future, we will also develop a tool to determine the kind of leaf disease and add more approaches to enhance the model's functionality. As a result, farmers who work in the farming regions will be able to identify certain illnesses early on and take the necessary measures. We will improve the study by putting some new algorithms into practice. Use a variety of dataset kinds to enhance the outcomes. Finally, provide agricultural fields a more efficient application.

REFERENCES

Abdelhamid, A. A., Alhussan, A. A., Qenawy, A. S. T., Osman, A. M., Elshewey, A. M., & Eed, M. (2025). Potato Harvesting Prediction Using an Improved ResNet-59 Model. *Potato Research, 68*(2), 1049–1068. DOI: 10.1007/s11540-024-09773-6

Aghdam, R., Tang, X., Shan, S., Lankau, R., & Solís-Lemus, C. (2024). Human limits in machine learning: Prediction of potato yield and disease using soil microbiome data. *BMC Bioinformatics, 25*(1), 366. DOI: 10.1186/s12859-024-05977-2 PMID: 39592933

Ahmad Yani, N., N., Mohd Fauzi, S., Mohd Zaki, N. (2026). Evaluating and Optimizing Machine Learning Ensemble Models Using Genetic Algorithms for Leaf Disease Severity Estimation in Harumanis Mango (Mangifera Indica L.): A Comparative Approach. *Earth Systems and Environment*. Advance online publication. DOI: 10.1007/s41748-025-00981-9

Alharbi, A. H., Mattar, E. A., Elkenawy, S., & Ghoneim, M. E. (2025). Potato Leaf Disease Detection Using Deep Reinforcement Learning and the Ocotillo Optimization Algorithm. *Potato Research, 68*(4), 4493–4524. DOI: 10.1007/s11540-025-09941-2

Alzakari, S. A., Alhussan, A. A., Qenawy, A. S. T., Elshewey, A. M., & Eed, M. (2025). An Enhanced Long Short-Term Memory Recurrent Neural Network Deep Learning Model for Potato Price Prediction. *Potato Research, 68*, 621–639. DOI: 10.1007/s11540-024-09744-x

Arshaghi, A., Ashourian, M., & Ghabeli, L. (2023). Potato diseases detection and classification using deep learning methods. *Multimedia Tools and Applications, 82*(4), 5725–5742. DOI: 10.1007/s11042-022-13390-1

Asif, M., Abbas, T., Iqbal, S., Alaulamie, A. A., Asghar, M. N., & Haro, J. M. (2026). MapReduce-based deep learning framework for potato leaf disease detection in sustainable precision agriculture. *Scientific Reports, 16*(1), 1607. DOI: 10.1038/s41598-025-30940-3 PMID: 41419754

Askr, H., Darwish, A., & Hassanien, A. E. (2026). Apple Leaf Diseases Classification Using DenseNet Based on Copula Entropy-Based Golden Jackal Optimization. In Hassanien, A. E., & Darwish, A. (Eds.), *Innovative AI Technologies Driving Sustainable Farming: Strategies for Improving Food Security. Studies in Systems, Decision and Control* (Vol. 634). Springer., DOI: 10.1007/978-3-032-05701-3_2

Bajpai, A., Sahu, S., & Tiwari, N. K. (2025). Integrating Attention Mechanisms and Squeeze-and-Excitation Blocks for Accurate Potato Leaf Disease Detection. *Potato Research, 68*(3), 2711–2731. DOI: 10.1007/s11540-025-09847-z

Bohra, S., Rani, M., & Singh, P. (2026). Comparative Analysis of Deep Learning Models for Cassava Disease on Small and Large Datasets. In Rathore, V. S., Tavares, J. M. R. S., Hanumanthappa, M., & Surendiran, B. (Eds.), *Universal Threats in Expert Applications and Solutions. UNI-TEAS 2025. Lecture Notes in Networks and Systems* (Vol. 1450). Springer., DOI: 10.1007/978-981-96-7289-9_4

Bonkra, A. SinghTiwana, P., Sharma, S., Sandhu, S.S., Pundir, A. (2026). Data-Driven Detection and Prediction of Crop Diseases and Pests Using Machine Learning Techniques. In: Ortiz-Rodríguez, F., Patil, P., Suryawanshi, S., Shaw, K., Shandilya, S. (eds) Business Intelligence, Computational Mathematics, and Data Analytics. IBCD 2025. Communications in Computer and Information Science, vol 2845. Springer, Cham. DOI: 10.1007/978-3-032-20907-8_20

Bouacida, I., Farou, B., Djakhdjakha, L., Balsi, M., & Seridi, H. (2026). Simultaneous multi-disease detection from the same leaf: A generalized approach using deep learning and image splitting. *Environmental Monitoring and Assessment, 198*(4), 333. DOI: 10.1007/s10661-026-15141-3 PMID: 41857409

Chettri, K., Sen, B., & Ghosal, P. (2026). Deep learning for precision agriculture: A systematic review of methods, challenges, and future directions. *Knowledge and Information Systems*, *68*(1), 35. DOI: 10.1007/s10115-025-02625-w

Choudhary, S. K., & Shrivastava, V. (2025). Computer-Aided Detection of Potato Leaf Diseases Using Machine and Deep Learning Models. In Gupta, D., Pandey, M., Nigam, A., & Pachori, R. B. (Eds.), *Next-Generation Networks and Deployable Artificial Intelligence. NGNDAI 2025. Lecture Notes in Networks and Systems* (Vol. 1792). Springer., DOI: 10.1007/978-3-032-15401-9_17

Demilie, W. B. (2024). Plant disease detection and classification techniques: A comparative study of the performances. *Journal of Big Data*, *11*(1), 5. DOI: 10.1186/s40537-023-00863-9

Devarajan, D., Allafi, R., Obayya, M., & Nemri, N. (2026). AI based real time disease diagnosis in plants using deep learning driven CNNs. *Scientific Reports*, *16*(1), 4587. DOI: 10.1038/s41598-025-34681-1 PMID: 41491234

Devi, V. B., Chelliah, B. J., Jesuraj, Y. A., & Dhanasekaran, S. (2026). Hybrid Fed-QNet: A federated deep learning framework with quantum GANs for privacy-aware plant disease detection. *Evolving Systems*, *17*(2), 41. DOI: 10.1007/s12530-025-09790-x

Dhoundiyal, P., Sharma, V., Vats, S., & Rawat, P. (2025). A Progressive Hierarchical Model for Plant Disease Diagnosis. *SN Computer Science*, *6*(2), 102. DOI: 10.1007/s42979-024-03582-x

El-Behery, H., Attia, A. F., & Rezk, N. G. (2026). An explainable deep learning framework for few shot crop disease detection in rice and sugarcane using CNN based feature extraction. *Scientific Reports, 16*(1), 8272. DOI: 10.1038/s41598-026-37501-2 PMID: 41786811

El-Kenawy, E. S. M., Alhussan, A. A., Khafaga, D. S., Abotaleb, M., Mishra, P., Arnous, R., & Eid, M. M. (2025). Optimizing Potato Disease Classification Using a Metaheuristics Algorithm for Deep Learning: A Novel Approach for Sustainable Agriculture. *Potato Research, 68*, 551–585. DOI: 10.1007/s11540-024-09755-8

El-Kenawy, E. S. M., Alhussan, A. A., Khodadadi, N., Mirjalili, S., & Eid, M. M. (2025). Predicting Potato Crop Yield with Machine Learning and Deep Learning for Sustainable Agriculture. *Potato Research, 68*, 759–792. DOI: 10.1007/s11540-024-09753-w

Elafifi, A. G., Ahmed, A. Y., Sarhan, A. M., & Hassanien, A. E. (2026). Interpretable Viral Potato Leaf Diseases Detection Model Using an Enhanced EfficientNet-B1 Deep Learning. In Hassanien, A. E., & Darwish, A. (Eds.), *Innovative AI Technologies Driving Sustainable Farming: Strategies for Improving Food Security. Studies in Systems, Decision and Control* (Vol. 634). Springer., DOI: 10.1007/978-3-032-05701-3_4

Elkenawy, S., Mattar, E. A., Alhussan, A. A., Shabrawy, M., Eid, M. M., & Ghoneim, M. E. (2026). Potato Irrigation Suitability Assessment via Ninja Optimization Algorithm-Tuned RegNet on Physicochemical Quality Data. *Potato Research, 69*(1), 5. DOI: 10.1007/s11540-025-09990-7

Elshewey, A. M., Tawfeek, S. M., Alhussan, A. A., Radwan, M., & Abed, A. H. (2025). Optimized Deep Learning for Potato Blight Detection Using the Waterwheel Plant Algorithm and Sine Cosine Algorithm. *Potato Research, 68*, 1–25. DOI: 10.1007/s11540-024-09735-y

Fayaz, S. M., Raihan, M. A., & Tushar, M. I. H. (2025). Deep Learning-Based Potato Leaf Disease Classification Using a Custom CNN. In Palaiahnakote, S., Palit, R., Saraee, M., Atrey, P. K., Bai, X., & Raman, B. (Eds.), *Data Science, AI and Applications. ICDSAIA 2025. Communications in Computer and Information Science* (Vol. 2681). Springer., DOI: 10.1007/978-3-032-11335-1_1

Gebremeskel, H. H., Hensel, O., & Nasirahmadi, A. (2026). Efficient Band Selection for Identifying Key Infrared Bands in Hyperspectral Detection of Colorado Potato Beetles. *Potato Research, 69*(3), 87. DOI: 10.1007/s11540-026-10048-5

Ghosh, S., Mittal, A., & Kumar Jha, S. (2024). Potato Diseases Detection Using Image Classification Models in Deep Learning Techniques. In: Swaroop, A., Kansal, V., Fortino, G., Hassanien, A.E. (eds) Proceedings of Fifth Doctoral Symposium on Computational Intelligence. DoSCI 2024. Lecture Notes in Networks and Systems, vol 1086. Springer, Singapore. DOI: 10.1007/978-981-97-6036-7_44

Gülmez, B. (2025). A Comprehensive Review of Convolutional Neural Networks based Disease Detection Strategies in Potato Agriculture. *Potato Research*, *68*(2), 1295–1329. DOI: 10.1007/s11540-024-09786-1

Gupta, H. K., & Shah, H. R. (2023). Deep Learning-Based Approach to Identify the Potato Leaf Disease and Help in Mitigation Using IOT. *SN Computer Science*, *4*(4), 333. DOI: 10.1007/s42979-023-01758-5

Hamid, M. A., Nobel, S. M. N., Hossain, M. A., Imran, M. A., Monowar, M. M., Kabir, M. M., & Mridha, M. F. (2026). SAMS: A sustainable agri-tech monitoring system integrating IoT and TinyML for smart farming. *Journal of Reliable Intelligent Environments*, *12*(1), 5. DOI: 10.1007/s40860-026-00269-3

Jainul Abidin, A., Al Maruf, A., Kamrul Siam, M., Ara Rumy, R., & Aung, Z. (2026). Leveraging the Transfer Learning Techniques with Data Augmentation to Improve Bangladeshi Crop Diseases Diagnosis. In Puthal, D., Panigrahi, B. K., Ray, N., & Ding, Z. (Eds.), *Synergies in Data Analytics and Cyber Security. DACS 2024. Lecture Notes in Electrical Engineering* (Vol. 1479). Springer., DOI: 10.1007/978-981-95-2680-2_24

Jawed, M. M., Tufail, F. A., Ahmed, M. Z., R, A. S., Nallusamy, P., & Raja, K. T. (2026). A hybrid deep learning framework using convolutional and transformer models for robust plant disease classification. *Scientific Reports*, *16*(1), 9704. DOI: 10.1038/s41598-026-38209-z PMID: 41708692

Jha, P., Dembla, D., & Dubey, W. (2024). Deep learning models for enhancing potato leaf disease prediction: Implementation of transfer learning based stacking ensemble model. *Multimedia Tools and Applications*, *83*(13), 37839–37858. DOI: 10.1007/s11042-023-16993-4

Jlassi, A., Elaoud, A., Ghazouani, H., & Barhoumi, W. (2024). Potato Leaf Disease Classification Using Transfer Learning and Reweighting-Based Training with Imbalanced Data. *SN Computer Science*, *5*(8), 987. DOI: 10.1007/s42979-024-03334-x

Kabel, S. A. E. M., El-Shafai, W., El-Samie, F. E. A., & Mohamed, B. (2025). Enhanced plant identification and disease diagnosis through SqueezeNet and SVM for smart agriculture applications. *Iran Journal of Computer Science*, *8*(4), 1353–1369. DOI: 10.1007/s42044-025-00237-9

Kaur, K., Kaur, H., Singh, M. L., & Singh, R. (2025). PotConvNet: An Automated Deep Convolutional Neural Network-Based Framework for Identification of Potato Leaf Diseases. *Potato Research*, *68*(3), 3631–3666. DOI: 10.1007/s11540-025-09891-9

Kempenaar, C. C., Sijbrandij, F. F. D., Been, T. T. H., van Boheemen, K. K., Booij, J. J. A., van Evert, F. F. K., Teklu, M. G. M. G., Kessel, G. G. J. T., Kocks, C. C. G., Lugtenburg, C. C., van der Meer, A. A., Molendijk, L. L. P. G., van Oort, P. P. A. J., Tielen, J. J. J. H., & van der Wal, T. T. (2026). Towards Data-Driven Precision Crop Management of Potato. *Potato Research*, *69*(1), 10. DOI: 10.1007/s11540-025-09996-1

Khan, A., Singh, R., Khan, S. U., & Hussain, I. (2026). Towards smart farming: A real-time diagnosis system for strawberry foliar diseases using deep learning. *BMC Plant Biology*, *26*(1), 135. DOI: 10.1186/s12870-025-07815-w PMID: 41387775

Kotwal, J. G., Kashyap, R., & Shafi, P. M. (2024). Artificial Driving based EfficientNet for Automatic Plant Leaf Disease Classification. *Multimedia Tools and Applications*, *83*(13), 38209–38240. DOI: 10.1007/s11042-023-16882-w

Kumar, A., & Patel, V. K. (2023). Classification and identification of disease in potato leaf using hierarchical based deep learning convolutional neural network. *Multimedia Tools and Applications*, *82*(20), 31101–31127. DOI: 10.1007/s11042-023-14663-z

Kumar, R., Agrawal, T., Dwivedi, V. D., & Khatter, H. (2024). Potato Leaf Disease Classification Using Deep Learning Model. In Chauhan, N., Yadav, D., Verma, G. K., Soni, B., & Lara, J. M. (Eds.), *Machine Learning, Image Processing, Network Security and Data Sciences. MIND 2023.Communications in Computer and Information Science* (Vol. 2128). Springer., DOI: 10.1007/978-3-031-62217-5_16

Kumar, Y., Singh, R., Moudgil, M. R., & Kamini, . (2023). A Systematic Review of Different Categories of Plant Disease Detection Using Deep Learning-Based Approaches. *Archives of Computational Methods in Engineering*, *30*(8), 4757–4779. DOI: 10.1007/s11831-023-09958-1

Kumari, V., & Bansal, V. (2026). A systematic review of plant leaf disease detection and classification using machine learning and deep learning techniques. *International Journal of Data Science and Analytics*, *22*(1), 22. DOI: 10.1007/s41060-025-01003-7

Lilhore, U. K., Kavitha, P. G. S., G, S., R, S., Simaiya, S., Ghith, E. S., & Hussien, S. A. (2026). Early Detection of Potato Leaf Diseases with PotatoNet-X: A Deep Learning Model Combining ResNet, DenseNet, and Attention Mechanisms. *Potato Research*, *69*(2), 45. DOI: 10.1007/s11540-025-09957-8

M., M., Anandamurugan, S. (2025). Innovative Deep Learning Framework for Accurate Plant Disease Detection and Crop Productivity Enhancement. Cogn Comput 17, 58, DOI: 10.1007/s12559-025-10421-5

Mahapatra, P., Panda, M., Dash, S. K., & Sahu, U. K. (2026). Advancing plant disease classification using an attention-based CNN for intra-dataset and cross- dataset training. *Scientific Reports*, *16*(1), 10925. DOI: 10.1038/s41598-026-45464-7 PMID: 41896662

Mahum, R., Munir, H., Mughal, Z. U. N., Awais, M., Sher Khan, F., Saqlain, M., & Tlili, I. (2022). A novel framework for potato leaf disease detection using an efficient deep learning model. *Human and Ecological Risk Assessment*, *29*(2), 303–326. DOI: 10.1080/10807039.2022.2064814

Mandal, S. N., Mukherjee, K., Dan, S., Ghosh, P., Das, S., Mustafi, S., Roy, K., & Chakraborty, A. (2023). Image-Based Potato Phoma Blight Severity Analysis Through Deep Learning. *J. Inst. Eng. India Ser. B*, *104*(1), 181–192. DOI: 10.1007/s40031-022-00820-9

Manoj, R. K., & Nandhini, S. A. (2026). Computer Vision and AI-Based Apple Plant Disease Detection Framework in Smart Farming. In Kumar, S. R., Gayathri, N., Yendapalli, V., & Rocha, A. (Eds.), *AI-Driven IoT Solutions in Agriculture: New Insights. Studies in Computational Intelligence* (Vol. 1236). Springer., DOI: 10.1007/978-3-032-05603-0_12

Nawaz M, Javed A, Saudagar AKJ. (2026). PotatoGuardNet: a refined deep learning framework for potato leaf disease detection. Front Plant Sci. Jan 30;17:1720276. . PMID: 41696171; PMCID: PMC12901372.DOI: 10.3389/fpls.2026.1720276

Nazir, T., Iqbal, M. M., Jabbar, S., Hussain, A., & Albathan, M. (2023). EfficientPNet—An Optimized and Efficient Deep Learning Approach for Classifying Disease of Potato Plant Leaves. *Agriculture*, *13*(4), 841. DOI: 10.3390/agriculture13040841

Panda, T., Nayak, S., & Mohanty, S. N. (2026). Temporal Analysis in Deep Learning-Based Recommender Systems for Predicting Plant Disease Outbreaks. In: Koganti, K.K., E., S.R., Gupta, N. (eds) Advanced Technologies in Electronics, Communications and Signal Processing. ICATECS 2024. Lecture Notes of the Institute for Computer Sciences, Social Informatics and Telecommunications Engineering, vol 620. Springer, Cham. DOI: 10.1007/978-3-031-94283-9_13

Pandey, S., Gupta, M., Mishra, A., Mishra, A., & Gangrade, J. (2025). Automated Potato Disease Classification Using Deep Learning - A Comparative Analysis of Convolutional Neural Networks. In Bairwa, A. K., Tiwari, V., Vishwakarma, S. K., Tuba, M., & Ganokratanaa, T. (Eds.), *Computation of Artificial Intelligence and Machine Learning. ICCAIML 2024.Communications in Computer and Information Science* (Vol. 2184). Springer., DOI: 10.1007/978-3-031-71481-8_26

Pandiri, D. N. K., Murugan, R., & Goel, T. (2025). ARM-UNet: Attention residual path modified UNet model to segment the fungal pathogen diseases in potato leaves. *Signal, Image and Video Processing, 19*(1), 80. DOI: 10.1007/s11760-024-03566-7

Pattanaik, H., Patnaik, G., Gouda, A., Sahoo, M., & Das, M. (2024). A Comparative Study of Disease Detection in Potato Plants Using Machine Learning and Deep Learning Methods. In Tavares, J. M. R. S., Rodrigues, J. J. P. C., Misra, D., & Bhattacherjee, D. (Eds.), *Data Science and Communication. ICTDsC 2023.Studies in Autonomic, Data-driven and Industrial Computing*. Springer., DOI: 10.1007/978-981-99-5435-3_11

Paul, H., Ghatak, S., Chakraborty, S., Pandey, S. K., Dey, L., Show, D., & Maity, S. (2024). A study and comparison of deep learning based potato leaf disease detection and classification techniques using explainable AI. *Multimedia Tools and Applications, 83*(14), 42485–42518. DOI: 10.1007/s11042-023-17235-3

Prabu, M., & Chelliah, B. J. (2022). Mango leaf disease identification and classification using a CNN architecture optimized by crossover-based levy flight distribution algorithm. *Neural Computing & Applications, 34*(9), 7311–7324. DOI: 10.1007/s00521-021-06726-9

Qiu, H., Wang, X., Shen, J., Yang, S., & Zhao, W. (2026). A Survey on Crop Disease Prediction Detection: AI Models Trained on Multispectral and Hyperspectral Images for Early Disease Detection. In Chen, J., Luo, X., & Yu, Y. (Eds.), *Blockchain and Trustworthy Systems. BlockSys 2025. Communications in Computer and Information Science* (Vol. 2638). Springer., DOI: 10.1007/978-981-95-3483-8_14

Radwan, M., Alhussan, A. A., Ibrahim, A., & Tawfeek, S. M. (2025). Potato Leaf Disease Classification Using Optimized Machine Learning Models and Feature Selection Techniques. *Potato Research, 68*(2), 897–921. DOI: 10.1007/s11540-024-09763-8

Raju, R., & Thasleema, T. M. (2026). Ensemble-based Deep Feature Extraction using Pre-trained CNNs for Black Pepper Leaf Disease and Nutrient Deficiency Detection and Classification: BPLDNDNet. *Evolutionary Intelligence, 19*(1), 28. DOI: 10.1007/s12065-026-01149-8

Renugadevi, R. A., Viswanath, V., Reddy, B., Prakash, K. (2026). Intelligent Plant Disease Diagnosis: Harnessing Machine Learning and Deep Learning for Precision Agriculture. In: Sharma, H., Bhatt, A., Modi, C., Engelbrecht, A. (eds) Computer Vision and Robotics. CVR 2025. Lecture Notes in Networks and Systems, vol 1771. Springer, Cham. DOI: 10.1007/978-3-032-14041-8_27

Sadiq, S., Malik, K. R., Ali, W., & Iqbal, M. M. (2023). Deep Learning-Based Disease Identification and Classification in Potato Leaves. *Journal of Computing & Biomedical Informatics*, *5*(01), 13–25. https://www.jcbi.org/index.php/Main/article/view/155

Sah, S.. (2026). Cucurbita Pepo Disease Classification Through Attention-Enhanced Deep Learning Models. In Dutta, P. K., Singh, R., Haghi, A. K., & Hamad, A. A. (Eds.), *Harnessing AI to Reshape the Future of Agriculture*. Springer., DOI: 10.1007/978-3-032-12118-9_22

Sah, S.. (2026). Cucurbita Pepo Disease Classification Through Attention-Enhanced Deep Learning Models. In Dutta, P. K., Singh, R., Haghi, A. K., & Hamad, A. A. (Eds.), *Harnessing AI to Reshape the Future of Agriculture*. Springer., DOI: 10.1007/978-3-032-12118-9_22

Saha, S.. (2024). Deep Learning-Based Approach for Plant Disease Classification. In Nanda, S. J., Yadav, R. P., Gandomi, A. H., & Saraswat, M. (Eds.), *Data Science and Applications. ICDSA 2023. Lecture Notes in Networks and Systems* (Vol. 820). Springer., DOI: 10.1007/978-981-99-7817-5_18

Sai Reddy, B., & Neeraja, S. (2022). Plant leaf disease classification and damage detection system using deep learning models. *Multimedia Tools and Applications*, *81*(17), 24021–24040. DOI: 10.1007/s11042-022-12147-0

Sangar, G., & Rajasekar, V. (2025). Optimized classification of potato leaf disease using EfficientNet-LITE and KE-SVM in diverse environments. *Frontiers in Plant Science*, *16*, 1499909. DOI: 10.3389/fpls.2025.1499909 PMID: 40385236

Shafik, W., Tufail, A., De Silva, L. C., & Apong, R. A. A. H. M. (2026). Lightweight vision transformer and ResNet-9 models for real-time plant disease detection and pest classification with SHAP explainability. *BMC Plant Biology*, *26*(1), 838. Advance online publication. DOI: 10.1186/s12870-026-08667-8 PMID: 41922963

Sharma, T., & Sethi, G. K. (2024). Improving Wheat Leaf Disease Image Classification with Point Rend Segmentation Technique. *SN Computer Science*, *5*(2), 244. DOI: 10.1007/s42979-023-02571-w

Shawon, S. M., Niha, F. L., Sinan, O. H., Abed, M. J., Al Qwaid, M., Sarker, M. T., & Zubair, H. T. (2026). Integrating Federated Learning and Explainable AI for Plant Disease Detection: A Systematic Review of Recent Advances in Precision Agriculture. *Int J Comput Intell Syst*, *19*(1), 138. DOI: 10.1007/s44196-026-01219-w

Sinamenye, J. H., Chatterjee, A., & Shrestha, R. (2025). Potato plant disease detection: Leveraging hybrid deep learning models. *BMC Plant Biology*, *25*(1), 647. DOI: 10.1186/s12870-025-06679-4 PMID: 40380088

Singh, G., Kasana, G., & Singh, K. (2025). Improved Potato Crop Disease Classification Using Ensembled Convolutional Neural Network. *Potato Research*, *68*(2), 1501–1527. DOI: 10.1007/s11540-024-09787-0

Singh, G., & Yogi, K. K. (2025). Deep Learning-Based Detection of Early Blight in Potato Leaves Using CNN Architectures. *Potato Research*, *68*(4), 4139–4161. DOI: 10.1007/s11540-025-09921-6

Singh, R., Krishnan, P., Bharadwaj, C., Sah, S., & Das, B. (2025). Optimizing chickpea yield prediction under wilt disease through synergistic integration of biophysical and image parameters using machine learning models. *Scientific Reports*, *15*(1), 4417. DOI: 10.1038/s41598-025-87134-0 PMID: 39910102

Sireesha, C., Shanam, G. M., & Attaluri, K. (2026). MobileNet-Based Deep Learning for Accurate Potato Leaf Disease Detection. In: Mondal, A., Peng, S.L., Ahmed, T., Sarkar, J.L. (eds) Proceedings of International Conference on Advanced Communications and Machine Intelligence. MICA 2024. Smart Innovation, Systems and Technologies, vol 115. Springer, Singapore. DOI: 10.1007/978-981-96-5589-2_8

Talab, H. K., Mohammadzamani, D., & Parashkoohi, M. G. (2024). Investigating the accuracy of classification in unbalanced data in order to diagnose two common potato leaf diseases (early blight and late blight) using image processing and machine learning. *Discover Applied Sciences*, *6*(6), 286. DOI: 10.1007/s42452-024-05959-2

Tiwari, N. K., Bajpai, A., Kumar, A., & Patro, B. (2026). Advancing Potato Crop Health and Disease Detection with Deep Learning. In: Shanker, U., Tiwari, R.K., Verma, A., Hassan, M.M. (eds) Proceedings of International Conference on Data Science and Artificial Intelligence. DSAI 2025. Studies in Autonomic, Data-driven and Industrial Computing.Springer, Singapore. DOI: 10.1007/978-981-96-9083-1_12

Varal, A. S., & Sayyad, S. F. (2026). Enhancing agricultural sorting systems through image-based classification and machine learning. *Multimedia Tools and Applications*, *85*(2), 55. DOI: 10.1007/s11042-026-21155-3

Verma, P. R., Pantola, D., & Singh, N. P. (2026). *Architectural and Performance Analysis of Static and Dynamic Neural Networks in Plant Disease Detection*. Arch Computat Methods Eng., DOI: 10.1007/s11831-026-10498-7

Xu, L., Chen, X., Xu, P., Zhang, Y., & Zhao, J. (2026). Spectral image classification of asymptomatic peanut leaf diseases based on deep learning algorithms. *Plant Methods*, *22*(1), 6. DOI: 10.1186/s13007-025-01485-3 PMID: 41423650

Zhang, A., Wu, C., Li, G., & Chen, S. (2026). Frequency-Aware and Residual-Attention CGAN with Two-Stage Training for Imbalanced Potato Leaf Disease Detection in Crop Management. *Potato Research*, *69*(2), 39. DOI: 10.1007/s11540-025-09979-2

Zhang, Y., Wang, Y., Xu, Y., & Yang, W. (2026). Effective automatic classification methods via deep learning for multi-type infectious keratitis diagnosis. *Graefe's Archive for Clinical and Experimental Ophthalmology*, *264*(1), 171–183. DOI: 10.1007/s00417-025-06996-2 PMID: 41134356

KEY TERMS AND DEFINITIONS

AlexNet: Developed by Alex Krizhevsky, Ilya Sutskever, and Geoffrey Hinton, AlexNet is a groundbreaking 8-layer Convolutional Neural Network (CNN) that significantly outperformed rivals in the 2012 ImageNet (ILSVRC) competition achieving a top-5 error rate of 15.3%. Due to its popularity, GPU-driven deep learning—which uses dropout and ReLU activation to enable fast training and minimize overfitting—became more widely used.

CNN: Convolutional Neural Networks (CNNs) are specialized deep learning frameworks that spontaneously acquire spatial hierarchy of characteristics, ranging from basic edges to advanced structures, in order to interpret grid-based input, like photographs. Researchers do these by using a series of fully interconnected layers for classification, pooling layers for reducing dimensionality, and convolutional layers for extracting features.

DenseNet: A deep learning model called DenseNet (Densely Connected Convolutional Networks) enhances CNNs by enhancing gradient flow, promoting feature reuse, and linking any layer to any succeeding layer. DenseNet lowers parameter numbers, solves the vanishing-gradient issue, and offers excellent accuracy for image classifiers and computer vision applications by concatenating feature maps from each previous layer instead of adding them.

Early blight: A fungal infection known as Alternaria solani causes early blight, an infection which harms tomato and standard potato leaves. In addition to causing branch lesions, fruit decay on tomatoes, and tuber blight on potatoes, the infection creates characteristic "bullseye" shaped marks on foliage.

Image Processing: Image processing is a method that uses computer code to edit, transform, and analyze photographs in order to boost their visual clarity or obtain relevant information. Regarding uses including clinical imaging, security tracking, conventional farming, and AI object identification, it entails converting raw data into improved outcomes.

Late blight: Late blight or Phytophthora infestans is an oomycete, frequently referred to as water mould, a microbe which resembles a fungus and is responsible for the dangerous potato and tomato infection called as late blight. "Potato blight" is another name for early blight, which is brought about by Alternaria solani.

Segmentation: The practice of breaking an entirety into discrete, controllable portions or fragments according to common traits is known as segmentation. It is utilized in image processing to recognize items, computing memory handling to organize data, and advertisement to reach particular groups of people.

Transfer Learning: A ML approach known as "transfer learning" involves using an algorithm created for one activity (original) to be an initial starting point for a similar additional effort (the goal). It significantly cuts down on training period, uses minimal labeled data, and enhances efficiency on the novel job by employing previous knowledge by reusing already trained models.

Compilation of References

Aarthi, S., Ravikumar, R. N., & Pardaev, J. (2026). Synergizing Multimodal Generative AI and Blockchain for the Future of Digital Media. In Fusion of Multimodal Generative AI and Blockchain Technology in Digital Media (pp. 1-34). IGI Global Scientific Publishing. https://doi.org/DOI: 10.4018/979-8-3373-1504-1.ch001

Abdelhamid, A. A., Alhussan, A. A., Qenawy, A. S. T., Osman, A. M., Elshewey, A. M., & Eed, M. (2025). Potato Harvesting Prediction Using an Improved ResNet-59 Model. *Potato Research*, *68*(2), 1049–1068. DOI: 10.1007/s11540-024-09773-6

Abdullahi, M., Baashar, Y., Alhussian, H., Alwadain, A., Aziz, N., Capretz, L. F., & Abdulkadir, S. J. (2022). Detecting cybersecurity attacks in internet of things using artificial intelligence methods: A systematic literature review. *Electronics (Basel)*, *11*(2), 198. DOI: 10.3390/electronics11020198

Abu-Nimeh, S., et al. (2007). A comparison of machine learning techniques for phishing detection. *eCrime Researchers Summit.*

Achar, H. B., & Raghu, N. (2025, February). The Impact and Future of Artificial Intelligence in Learning. In 2025 3rd International Conference on Integrated Circuits and Communication Systems (ICICACS) (pp. 1-6). IEEE.

Adams, M., & Umbach, P. (2012). Nonresponse and Online Student Evaluations of Teaching: Understanding the Influence of Salience, Fatigue, and Academic Environments. *Research in Higher Education*, *53*(5), 576–591. DOI: 10.1007/s11162-011-9240-5

Adnan, M., Imam, M. O., Javed, M. F., & Murtza, I. (2024). Improving spam email classi- fication accuracy using ensemble techniques: A stacking approach. *International Journal of Information Security*, *23*(1), 505–517. DOI: 10.1007/s10207-023-00756-1

Agarwal, N. D. V., & Kaur, N. S. (2024). Adoption of advanced systems for digital resource management in academic institutions. *Evolutionary Studies in Imaginative Culture*, 913–923. DOI: 10.70082/esiculture.vi.1089

Aghdam, R., Tang, X., Shan, S., Lankau, R., & Solís-Lemus, C. (2024). Human limits in machine learning: Prediction of potato yield and disease using soil microbiome data. *BMC Bioinformatics*, *25*(1), 366. DOI: 10.1186/s12859-024-05977-2 PMID: 39592933

Ahmad Yani, N., N., Mohd Fauzi, S., Mohd Zaki, N. (2026). Evaluating and Optimizing Machine Learning Ensemble Models Using Genetic Algorithms for Leaf Disease Severity Estimation in Harumanis Mango (Mangifera Indica L.): A Comparative Approach. *Earth Systems and Environment*. Advance online publication. DOI: 10.1007/s41748-025-00981-9

Ahmad, S. S., Almasalha, F., Qutqut, M. H., & Hijjawi, M. (2024). Centralized smart energy monitoring system for legacy home appliances. *Energy Informatics*, *7*(1), 29. DOI: 10.1186/s42162-024-00334-2

Ahmed, S. Y., & Pardaev, J. (2025). Human-AI Decision Dynamics: How Risk Propensity and Trust Impact Choices Through Decision Fatigue, Conditional on AI Understanding. *Decision Making: Applications in Management and Engineering*, *8*(2), 96–113. DOI: 10.31181/dmame8220251484

Ahmed, S., Kaiser, M. S., Hossain, M. S., & Andersson, K. (2024). A comparative analysis of LIME and SHAP interpreters with explainable ML-based diabetes predictions. *IEEE Access : Practical Innovations, Open Solutions*, *13*, 37370–37388. DOI: 10.1109/ACCESS.2024.3422319

Aissaoui, O. E., Madani, Y. E. E., Oughdir, L., & Allioui, Y. E. (2019). Combining supervised and unsupervised machine learning algorithms to predict the learners' learning styles. *Procedia Computer Science*, *148*, 87–96. DOI: 10.1016/j.procs.2019.01.012

Al Siam, A., Alazab, M., Awajan, A., & Faruqui, N. (2025). A Comprehensive Review of AI's Current Impact and Future Prospects in Cybersecurity. *IEEE Access : Practical Innovations, Open Solutions*, *13*, 14029–14050. DOI: 10.1109/ACCESS.2025.3528114

Alanezi, M. A. (2022). Vulnerabilities, threats and challenges on cyber security and the artificial intelligence based internet of things: A comprehensive study. *International Journal of Computer Science & Network Security*, *22*(2), 153–158.

Alharbi, A. H., Mattar, E. A., Elkenawy, S., & Ghoneim, M. E. (2025). Potato Leaf Disease Detection Using Deep Reinforcement Learning and the Ocotillo Optimization Algorithm. *Potato Research*, *68*(4), 4493–4524. DOI: 10.1007/s11540-025-09941-2

Alowaidi, M., Sharma, S. K., AlEnizi, A., & Bhardwaj, S. (2023). Integrating artificial intelligence in cyber security for cyber-physical systems. *Electronic Research Archive*, *31*(4), 1876–1896. DOI: 10.3934/era.2023097

Altwaijry, N., Al-Turaiki, I., Alotaibi, R., & Alakeel, F. (2024). Advancing phishing email detection: A comparative study of deep learning models. *Sensors (Basel)*, *24*(7), 24. DOI: 10.3390/s24072077 PMID: 38610289

Alzakari, S. A., Alhussan, A. A., Qenawy, A. S. T., Elshewey, A. M., & Eed, M. (2025). An Enhanced Long Short-Term Memory Recurrent Neural Network Deep Learning Model for Potato Price Prediction. *Potato Research*, *68*, 621–639. DOI: 10.1007/s11540-024-09744-x

Amruthnath, N., & Gupta, T. (2018). A research study on unsupervised machine learning algorithms for early fault detection in predictive maintenance. In *5th International Conference on Industrial Engineering and Applications* (p. 355). IEEE. DOI: 10.1109/IEA.2018.8387124

Ankolekar, A., Dekker, A., Fijten, R., & Berlanga, A. (2018). The benefits and challenges of using patient decision aids to support shared decision making in health care. *JCO Clinical Cancer Informatics*, *2*(2), 1–10. DOI: 10.1200/CCI.18.00013 PMID: 30652607

Anumolu, V. R. (2025). Financial Innovation for Sustainability: Leveraging AI, XR, and Data for Impactful Investments. In *Exploring the Impact of Extended Reality (XR) Technologies on Promoting Environmental Sustainability* (pp. 133–157). Springer Nature Switzerland. DOI: 10.1007/978-3-031-88013-1_7

Ardabili, S. F., Mosavi, A., Ghamisi, P., Ferdinand, F., Varkonyi-Koczy, A. R., Reuter, U., Rabczuk, T., & Atkinson, P. M. (2020). Covid-19 outbreak prediction with machine learning. *Algorithms*, *13*(10), 249. DOI: 10.3390/a13100249

Arora, A., Arora, A., & McIntyre, J. (2023). Developing chatbots for cyber security: Assessing threats through sentiment analysis on social media. *Sustainability (Basel)*, *15*(17), 13178. DOI: 10.3390/su151713178

Arshaghi, A., Ashourian, M., & Ghabeli, L. (2023). Potato diseases detection and classification using deep learning methods. *Multimedia Tools and Applications*, *82*(4), 5725–5742. DOI: 10.1007/s11042-022-13390-1

Asif, M., Abbas, T., Iqbal, S., Alaulamie, A. A., Asghar, M. N., & Haro, J. M. (2026). MapReduce-based deep learning framework for potato leaf disease detection in sustainable precision agriculture. *Scientific Reports*, *16*(1), 1607. DOI: 10.1038/s41598-025-30940-3 PMID: 41419754

Askr, H., Darwish, A., & Hassanien, A. E. (2026). Apple Leaf Diseases Classification Using DenseNet Based on Copula Entropy-Based Golden Jackal Optimization. In Hassanien, A. E., & Darwish, A. (Eds.), *Innovative AI Technologies Driving Sustainable Farming: Strategies for Improving Food Security. Studies in Systems, Decision and Control* (Vol. 634). Springer., DOI: 10.1007/978-3-032-05701-3_2

Babu, C. S. (2024). Adaptive AI for Dynamic Cybersecurity Systems: Enhancing Protection in a Rapidly Evolving Digital Landscap. In *Principles and applications of adaptive artificial intelligence* (pp. 52-72): IGI Global Scientific Publishing.

Bajpai, A., Sahu, S., & Tiwari, N. K. (2025). Integrating Attention Mechanisms and Squeeze-and-Excitation Blocks for Accurate Potato Leaf Disease Detection. *Potato Research*, *68*(3), 2711–2731. DOI: 10.1007/s11540-025-09847-z

Basnet, R. (2014). Detection of phishing attacks using machine learning. *IEEE International Conference*.

Behera, A., Vedashree, A., Kumar, M. R., & Upreti, K. (2025). Artificial Intelligence and Cybersecurity Prospects and Confronts. In *Navigating Cyber-Physical Systems With Cutting-Edge Technologies* (pp. 155–184). IGI Global Scientific Publishing.

Benavides-Astudillo, E., Fuertes, W., Sanchez-Gordon, S., Nuñez-Agurto, D., & Rodríguez-Galán, G. (2023). A phishing-attack-detection model using natural language processing and deep learning. *Applied Sciences (Basel, Switzerland)*, *13*(9), 5275. DOI: 10.3390/app13095275

Bergadano, F., & Giacinto, G. (2023). *Special Issue "AI for Cybersecurity: Robust Models for Authentication, Threat and Anomaly Detection"* (Vol. 16). MDPI. DOI: 10.3390/books978-3-0365-8265-8

Bhatti, M. A., & Pardaev, J. (2025). Exploring the influence of culture and heritage on personal and collective identity: A qualitative inquiry. Cultura. *International Journal of Philosophy of Culture and Axiology*, *22*(4), 897–927. DOI: 10.70082/cijpca.v22i4.1434

Bohra, S., Rani, M., & Singh, P. (2026). Comparative Analysis of Deep Learning Models for Cassava Disease on Small and Large Datasets. In Rathore, V. S., Tavares, J. M. R. S., Hanumanthappa, M., & Surendiran, B. (Eds.), *Universal Threats in Expert Applications and Solutions. UNI-TEAS 2025. Lecture Notes in Networks and Systems* (Vol. 1450). Springer., DOI: 10.1007/978-981-96-7289-9_4

Bonfanti, M. E. (2022). *Artificial intelligence and the offence-defence balance in cyber security. Cyber Security: Socio-Technological Uncertainty and Political Fragmentation*. Routledge.

Bonkra, A. SinghTiwana, P., Sharma, S., Sandhu, S.S., Pundir, A. (2026). Data-Driven Detection and Prediction of Crop Diseases and Pests Using Machine Learning Techniques. In: Ortiz-Rodríguez, F., Patil, P., Suryawanshi, S., Shaw, K., Shandilya, S. (eds) Business Intelligence, Computational Mathematics, and Data Analytics. IBCD 2025. Communications in Computer and Information Science, vol 2845. Springer, Cham. DOI: 10.1007/978-3-032-20907-8_20

Bouacida, I., Farou, B., Djakhdjakha, L., Balsi, M., & Seridi, H. (2026). Simultaneous multi-disease detection from the same leaf: A generalized approach using deep learning and image splitting. *Environmental Monitoring and Assessment*, *198*(4), 333. DOI: 10.1007/s10661-026-15141-3 PMID: 41857409

Bountakas, P., Xenakis, C., & Politis, I. (2021). Comparison of nlp and machine learning methods for phishing email detection. In *ARES Conference*.

Breiman, L. (2001). Random forests. *Machine Learning*, *45*(1), 5–32. DOI: 10.1023/A:1010933404324

Burkart, N., & Huber, M. F. (2021). A survey on the explainability of supervised machine learning. *Journal of Artificial Intelligence Research*, *70*, 245–317. DOI: 10.1613/jair.1.12228

Casolla, G., Cuomo, S., Di Cola, V. S., & Piccialli, F. (2019). Exploring unsupervised learning techniques for the internet of things. *IEEE Transactions on Industrial Informatics*, *16*(4), 2621–2628. DOI: 10.1109/TII.2019.2941142

Castaño, C. (2025). Artificial intelligence in public health: Opportunities, ethical challenges and future perspectives. *Revista Española de Salud Pública*, *99*, e202503017–e202503017. PMID: 40165772

Chabane, L., Drid, S., Chrifi-Alaoui, L., & Delahoche, L. (2024). Energy consumption prediction of a smart home using non-intrusive appliance load monitoring. *International Journal of System Assurance Engineering and Management*, *15*(3), 1231–1244. DOI: 10.1007/s13198-023-02209-3

Champa., . . . (2024). Curated datasets and feature analysis for phishing email detection. In *ICMI.*

Chango, W., Lara, J., Cerezo, R., & Romero, C. (2022). A review on data fusion in multimodal learning analytics and educational data mining. *Wiley Interdisciplinary Reviews. Data Mining and Knowledge Discovery*, *12*(4), e1458. Advance online publication. DOI: 10.1002/widm.1458

Chen, T., & Guestrin, C. (2016). Xgboost: A scalable tree boosting system. In *Proceedings of KDD*. DOI: 10.1145/2939672.2939785

Chen, Z., Liang, N., Zhang, H., Li, H., Yang, Y., Zong, X., Chen, Y., Wang, Y., & Shi, N. (2023). Harnessing the power of clinical decision support systems: Challenges and opportunities. *Open Heart*, *10*(2), e002432. DOI: 10.1136/openhrt-2023-002432 PMID: 38016787

Chettri, K., Sen, B., & Ghosal, P. (2026). Deep learning for precision agriculture: A systematic review of methods, challenges, and future directions. *Knowledge and Information Systems*, *68*(1), 35. DOI: 10.1007/s10115-025-02625-w

Chin, J. A., & Mirzal, A. (2015). Supervised, unsupervised and semi-supervised feature selection: A review on gene selection. In *IEEE/ACM Transactions on Computational Biology and Bioinformatics*. DOI: 10.1109/TCBB.2015.2478454

Choi, J., Cho, Y., Shim, E., & Woo, H. (2016). Web-based infectious disease surveillance systems and public health perspectives: A systematic review. *BMC Public Health*, *16*(1), 1238. DOI: 10.1186/s12889-016-3893-0 PMID: 27931204

Choudhary, S. K., & Shrivastava, V. (2025). Computer-Aided Detection of Potato Leaf Diseases Using Machine and Deep Learning Models. In Gupta, D., Pandey, M., Nigam, A., & Pachori, R. B. (Eds.), *Next-Generation Networks and Deployable Artificial Intelligence. NGNDAI 2025. Lecture Notes in Networks and Systems* (Vol. 1792). Springer., DOI: 10.1007/978-3-032-15401-9_17

Choudhary, V., Mehta, A., Patel, K., Niaz, M., Panwala, M., & Nwagwu, U. (2024). Integrating Data Analytics and Decision Support Systems in Public Health Management. *South Eastern European Journal of Public Health*, 158–172.

Costa, E. A., Rebello, C. M., Fontana, M., Schnitman, L., & Nogueira, I. B. R. (2022). A robust learning methodology for uncertainty-aware scientific machine learning models. *Mathematics*, *11*(1), 74. DOI: 10.3390/math11010074

Das, S. K., Bebortta, S., Pati, B., Panigrahi, C. R., & Senapati, D. (2024). Profiling and Classification of IoT Devices for Smart Home Environments. In: Nayak, J., Naik, B., S, V., Favorskaya, M. (eds) Machine Learning for Cyber Physical System: Advances and Challenges. Intelligent Systems Reference Library, vol 60. Springer, Cham. DOI: 10.1007/978-3-031-54038-7_4

Dash, B., Ansari, M. F., Sharma, P., & Ali, A. (2022). Threats and opportunities with AI-based cyber security intrusion detection: A review. [IJSEA]. *International Journal of Software Engineering and Its Applications*, *13*(5).

De Azambuja, A. J. G., Plesker, C., Schützer, K., Anderl, R., Schleich, B., & Almeida, V. R. (2023). Artificial intelligence-based cyber security in the context of industry 4.0—A survey. *Electronics (Basel)*, *12*(8), 1920. DOI: 10.3390/electronics12081920

Demilie, W. B. (2024). Plant disease detection and classification techniques: A comparative study of the performances. *Journal of Big Data*, *11*(1), 5. DOI: 10.1186/s40537-023-00863-9

Devarajan, D., Allafi, R., Obayya, M., & Nemri, N. (2026). AI based real time disease diagnosis in plants using deep learning driven CNNs. *Scientific Reports*, *16*(1), 4587. DOI: 10.1038/s41598-025-34681-1 PMID: 41491234

Devi, V. B., Chelliah, B. J., Jesuraj, Y. A., & Dhanasekaran, S. (2026). Hybrid Fed-QNet: A federated deep learning framework with quantum GANs for privacy-aware plant disease detection. *Evolving Systems*, *17*(2), 41. DOI: 10.1007/s12530-025-09790-x

Dhoundiyal, P., Sharma, V., Vats, S., & Rawat, P. (2025). A Progressive Hierarchical Model for Plant Disease Diagnosis. *SN Computer Science*, *6*(2), 102. DOI: 10.1007/s42979-024-03582-x

Diaf, A., Korba, A. A., Karabadji, N. E., & Ghamri-Doudane, Y. (2024). *Bartpredict: Empowering iot security with llm-driven cyber threat prediction.* Paper presented at the GLOBECOM 2024-2024 IEEE Global Communications Conference. DOI: 10.1109/GLOBECOM52923.2024.10901770

Dietterich, T. G. (2000). *Ensemble methods in machine learning*. Multiple Classifier Systems. DOI: 10.1007/3-540-45014-9_1

Dike, H. U., Zhou, Y., Deveerasetty, K. K., & Wu, Q. (2018). Unsupervised Learning based on Artificial Neural Network: a review. *2018 IEEE International Conference on Cyborg and Bionic Systems (CBS)*, 322–327. DOI: 10.1109/CBS.2018.8612259

Divya, S., Murthy, A., Babu, S. S., Ahmed, S. I., & Dey, S. R. (2023). Energy Monitoring with Trend Analysis and Power Signature Interpretation. In Dutta, P., Bhattacharya, A., Dutta, S., & Lai, W. C. (Eds.), *Emerging Technologies in Data Mining and Information Security. Advances in Intelligent Systems and Computing* (Vol. 1348). Springer., DOI: 10.1007/978-981-19-4676-9_8

Dou, Y., Feng, X., Zhu, R., Gao, T., Wu, Y., & Ma, L. (2019). Research and Implementation of Algorithm Based on Data Fusion Technology. *Proceedings of the 2019 International Conference on Modeling, Analysis, Simulation Technologies and Applications (MASTA 2019)*. https://doi.org/DOI: 10.2991/masta-19.2019.60

El-Behery, H., Attia, A. F., & Rezk, N. G. (2026). An explainable deep learning framework for few shot crop disease detection in rice and sugarcane using CNN based feature extraction. *Scientific Reports*, *16*(1), 8272. DOI: 10.1038/s41598-026-37501-2 PMID: 41786811

Elhady, A. M., & Shohieb, S. (2025). AI-driven sustainable finance: Computational tools, ESG metrics, and global implementation. *Future Business Journal*, *11*(1), 209. DOI: 10.1186/s43093-025-00610-x

El-Kenawy, E. S. M., Alhussan, A. A., Khafaga, D. S., Abotaleb, M., Mishra, P., Arnous, R., & Eid, M. M. (2025). Optimizing Potato Disease Classification Using a Metaheuristics Algorithm for Deep Learning: A Novel Approach for Sustainable Agriculture. *Potato Research*, *68*, 551–585. DOI: 10.1007/s11540-024-09755-8

El-Kenawy, E. S. M., Alhussan, A. A., Khodadadi, N., Mirjalili, S., & Eid, M. M. (2025). Predicting Potato Crop Yield with Machine Learning and Deep Learning for Sustainable Agriculture. *Potato Research*, *68*, 759–792. DOI: 10.1007/s11540-024-09753-w

Elkenawy, S., Mattar, E. A., Alhussan, A. A., Shabrawy, M., Eid, M. M., & Ghoneim, M. E. (2026). Potato Irrigation Suitability Assessment via Ninja Optimization Algorithm-Tuned RegNet on Physicochemical Quality Data. *Potato Research*, *69*(1), 5. DOI: 10.1007/s11540-025-09990-7

Elshewey, A. M., Tawfeek, S. M., Alhussan, A. A., Radwan, M., & Abed, A. H. (2025). Optimized Deep Learning for Potato Blight Detection Using the Waterwheel Plant Algorithm and Sine Cosine Algorithm. *Potato Research*, *68*, 1–25. DOI: 10.1007/s11540-024-09735-y

Erola, A., Agrafiotis, I., Goldsmith, M., & Creese, S. (2022). Insider-threat detection: Lessons from deploying the CITD tool in three multinational organisations. *Journal of Information Security and Applications*, *67*, 103167. DOI: 10.1016/j.jisa.2022.103167

Fakhraian, E., Šemanjski, I., Šemanjski, S., & Aghezzaf, E. (2023). Towards Safe and Efficient Unmanned Aircraft System Operations: Literature Review of Digital Twins' Applications and European Union Regulatory Compliance. *Drones (Basel)*, *7*(7), 478. Advance online publication. DOI: 10.3390/drones7070478

Fakhruldeen, H. F., Saadh, M. J., Khan, S., Salim, N. A., Jhamat, N., & Mustafa, G. (2025). Enhancing smart home device identification in WiFi environments for futuristic smart networks-based IoT. *International Journal of Data Science and Analytics*, *19*(4), 645–658. DOI: 10.1007/s41060-023-00489-3

Fang, Y., Zhang, C., Huang, C., Liu, L., & Yang, Y. (2019). Phishing email detection using improved rcnn model with multilevel vectors. *IEEE Access : Practical Innovations, Open Solutions*, *7*, 56329–56341. DOI: 10.1109/ACCESS.2019.2913705

Fayaz, S. M., Raihan, M. A., & Tushar, M. I. H. (2025). Deep Learning-Based Potato Leaf Disease Classification Using a Custom CNN. In Palaiahnakote, S., Palit, R., Saraee, M., Atrey, P. K., Bai, X., & Raman, B. (Eds.), *Data Science, AI and Applications. ICDSAIA 2025. Communications in Computer and Information Science* (Vol. 2681). Springer., DOI: 10.1007/978-3-032-11335-1_1

Fergus, P., & Chalmers, C. (2021). Energy Sobriety: A Behaviour Measurement Indicator for Fuel Poverty Using Aggregated Load Readings from Smart Meters. In Ploix, S., Amayri, M., & Bouguila, N. (Eds.), *Towards Energy Smart Homes*. Springer., DOI: 10.1007/978-3-030-76477-7_2

Ferrag, M. A., Maglaras, L., Moschoyiannis, S., & Janicke, H. (2020). Deep learning for cyber security intrusion detection: Approaches, datasets, and comparative study. *Journal of Information Security and Applications*, *50*, 102419. DOI: 10.1016/j.jisa.2019.102419

Fuhl, W., Castner, N., & Kasneci, E. (2018, October). Rule-based learning for eye movement type detection. In *Proceedings of the Workshop on Modeling Cognitive Processes from Multimodal Data* (pp. 1-6). DOI: 10.1145/3279810.3279844

Ganesh Kumar, K., & Sengan, S. (2020). Improved network traffic by attacking denial of service to protect resource using Z-test based 4-tier geomark traceback (Z4TGT). *Wireless Personal Communications*, *114*(4), 3541–3575. DOI: 10.1007/s11277-020-07546-1

Gebremeskel, H. H., Hensel, O., & Nasirahmadi, A. (2026). Efficient Band Selection for Identifying Key Infrared Bands in Hyperspectral Detection of Colorado Potato Beetles. *Potato Research*, *69*(3), 87. DOI: 10.1007/s11540-026-10048-5

George, T., & Selvakumar, A. I. (2024). Smart home energy management systems in India: A socio-economic commitment towards a green future. *Discover Sustainability, 5*(1), 101. DOI: 10.1007/s43621-024-00295-2

Ghaleb, M. M. S., & Otamurodov, S. (2026). Leveraging Authentic Learning and Open Data to Foster Epistemic Curiosity and Statistical Reasoning in Biostatistics Education. *Letters in Biomathematics, 13*(1), 27–41. 10.30707

Ghaleb, M. M. S., & Pardaev, J. (2025). Influence of Risk Management Culture, Digital Culture; Learning Culture on Competitive Advantage: Exploring Mediating Effect of Digital Innovation. Cultura. *International Journal of Philosophy of Culture and Axiology, 22*(4). Advance online publication. DOI: 10.70082/cijpca.v22i4.1463

Ghaleb, M. M. S., & Pardaev, J. (2025). Literature Reading Self-Efficacy and Academic Achievement: Role of Literature Reading Attitude, Academic Motivation, Task Value and Literature Reading Ability. *Kuram ve Uygulamada Egitim Bilimleri, 25*(2), 77–92. DOI: 10.12738/jestp.2025.2.06

Ghanem, M. C., Chen, T. M., Ferrag, M. A., & Kettouche, M. E. (2023). ESASCF: Expertise extraction, generalization and reply framework for optimized automation of network security compliance. *IEEE Access : Practical Innovations, Open Solutions, 11*, 129840–129853. DOI: 10.1109/ACCESS.2023.3332834

Ghosh, S., Mittal, A., & Kumar Jha, S. (2024). Potato Diseases Detection Using Image Classification Models in Deep Learning Techniques. In: Swaroop, A., Kansal, V., Fortino, G., Hassanien, A.E. (eds) Proceedings of Fifth Doctoral Symposium on Computational Intelligence. DoSCI 2024. Lecture Notes in Networks and Systems, vol 1086. Springer, Singapore. DOI: 10.1007/978-981-97-6036-7_44

Goffin, T. (2025). Does AI in Healthcare Need an Editor-in-Chief? A Leading Example of True Human Oversight. *European Journal of Health Law, 32*(5), 579–602. DOI: 10.1163/15718093-12423581 PMID: 41406980

Gogos, C., & Georgiou, G. (2019). Appliance Identification Through Nonintrusive Load Monitoring in Residences. In Blondin, M., Pardalos, P., & Sanchis Sáez, J. (Eds.), *Computational Intelligence and Optimization Methods for Control Engineering. Springer Optimization and Its Applications* (Vol. 150). Springer., DOI: 10.1007/978-3-030-25446-9_10

Goktas, P., & Grzybowski, A. (2025). Shaping the future of healthcare: Ethical clinical challenges and pathways to trustworthy AI. *Journal of Clinical Medicine, 14*(5), 1605. DOI: 10.3390/jcm14051605 PMID: 40095575

Groseclose, S. L., & Buckeridge, D. L. (2017). Public health surveillance systems: Recent advances in their use and evaluation. *Annual Review of Public Health*, *38*(1), 57–79. DOI: 10.1146/annurev-publhealth-031816-044348 PMID: 27992726

Gülmez, B. (2025). A Comprehensive Review of Convolutional Neural Networks based Disease Detection Strategies in Potato Agriculture. *Potato Research*, *68*(2), 1295–1329. DOI: 10.1007/s11540-024-09786-1

Gupta, H. K., & Shah, H. R. (2023). Deep Learning-Based Approach to Identify the Potato Leaf Disease and Help in Mitigation Using IOT. *SN Computer Science*, *4*(4), 333. DOI: 10.1007/s42979-023-01758-5

Hamid, M. A., Nobel, S. M. N., Hossain, M. A., Imran, M. A., Monowar, M. M., Kabir, M. M., & Mridha, M. F. (2026). SAMS: A sustainable agri-tech monitoring system integrating IoT and TinyML for smart farming. *Journal of Reliable Intelligent Environments*, *12*(1), 5. DOI: 10.1007/s40860-026-00269-3

Hao, Z. (2019). Deep learning review and discussion of its future development. MATEC Web of Conferences, 277, 02035. DOI: 10.1051/matecconf/201927702035

Heino, J., Jalio, C., Hakkala, A., & Virtanen, S. (2022). A method for endpoint aware inspection in a network security solution. *IEEE Access : Practical Innovations, Open Solutions*, *10*, 44517–44530. DOI: 10.1109/ACCESS.2022.3170456

Hidayat, R., Qi, T., Ariffin, P., Hadzri, M., Chin, L., Ning, J., & Nasir, N. (2024). *Online game-based learning in mathematics education among Generation Z: A systematic review*. International Electronic Journal of Mathematics Education., DOI: 10.29333/iejme/14024

Hilas, C. S., & Mastorocostas, P. A. (2008). An application of supervised and unsupervised learning approaches to telecommunications fraud detection. *Knowledge-Based Systems*, *21*(7), 721–726. DOI: 10.1016/j.knosys.2008.03.026

Holzinger, A., Zatloukal, K., & Müller, H. (2025). *Is human oversight to AI systems still possible?* (Vol. 85). Elsevier.

Huang, Z., Jiang, R., Aeron, S., Hughes, & M. C. (2021). Systematic comparison of semi-supervised and self-supervised learning for medical image classification. In *Tufts University, School of Engineering*.

Hu, L., Yan, X., & Yuan, Y. (2025). Development and Challenges of Autonomous Electric Vertical Take-Off and Landing Aircraft. *Heliyon*, *11*(1), e41055. Advance online publication. DOI: 10.1016/j.heliyon.2024.e41055 PMID: 39758371

Hung, J., Hsu, Y., & Rice, K. (2012). Integrating Data Mining in Program Evaluation of K-12 Online Education. *Journal of Educational Technology & Society, 15*, 27–41.

Illy, P., & Kaddoum, G. (2023). A collaborative DNN-based low-latency IDPS for mission-critical smart factory networks. *IEEE Access : Practical Innovations, Open Solutions, 11*, 96317–96329. DOI: 10.1109/ACCESS.2023.3311822

Inan, F. A., Namin, A. S., Pogrund, R. L., & Jones, K. S. (2016). Internet use and cybersecurity concerns of individuals with visual impairments. *Journal of Educational Technology & Society, 19*(1), 28–40.

Islamutdinov, V., Akhmetshin, E., Lydia, E. L., & Raja, P. V. K. (2025). Implementation of AI in an Ethical and Responsible Manner to Empower Education in Digital Sector. In Bhateja, V., Lay-Ekuakille, A., Limkar, S., & Chakravarthy, V. V. S. S. S. (Eds.), *Smart Computing Paradigms: Sustainable Computing. SCI 2024. Lecture Notes in Networks and Systems* (Vol. 1318). Springer., DOI: 10.1007/978-981-96-3939-7_13

Iyamu, I., Xu, A. X., Gómez-Ramírez, O., Ablona, A., Chang, H.-J., Mckee, G., & Gilbert, M. (2021). Defining digital public health and the role of digitization, digitalization, and digital transformation: Scoping review. *JMIR Public Health and Surveillance, 7*(11), e30399. DOI: 10.2196/30399 PMID: 34842555

Jainul Abidin, A., Al Maruf, A., Kamrul Siam, M., Ara Rumy, R., & Aung, Z. (2026). Leveraging the Transfer Learning Techniques with Data Augmentation to Improve Bangladeshi Crop Diseases Diagnosis. In Puthal, D., Panigrahi, B. K., Ray, N., & Ding, Z. (Eds.), *Synergies in Data Analytics and Cyber Security. DACS 2024. Lecture Notes in Electrical Engineering* (Vol. 1479). Springer., DOI: 10.1007/978-981-95-2680-2_24

Javed, H., El-Sappagh, S., & Abuhmed, T. (2024). Robustness in deep learning models for medical diagnostics: Security and adversarial challenges towards robust AI applications. *Artificial Intelligence Review, 58*(1), 12. DOI: 10.1007/s10462-024-11005-9

Jawaid, S. A. (2023). Artificial intelligence with respect to cyber security.

Jawed, M. M., Tufail, F. A., Ahmed, M. Z., R, A. S., Nallusamy, P., & Raja, K. T. (2026). A hybrid deep learning framework using convolutional and transformer models for robust plant disease classification. *Scientific Reports, 16*(1), 9704. DOI: 10.1038/s41598-026-38209-z PMID: 41708692

Jebadurai, D. J., & David, S. (2026). AI-Driven ESG Investing: Transforming Sustainable Finance in the Digital Age. In *Building AI-Driven Decision-Making Competencies for Sustainability* (pp. 29-70). IGI Global Scientific Publishing.

Jha, P., Dembla, D., & Dubey, W. (2024). Deep learning models for enhancing potato leaf disease prediction: Implementation of transfer learning based stacking ensemble model. *Multimedia Tools and Applications, 83*(13), 37839–37858. DOI: 10.1007/s11042-023-16993-4

Jiang, T., Gradus, J. L., & Rosellini, A. J. (2020). Supervised machine learning: A brief primer. *Behavior Therapy, 51*(5), 675–687. DOI: 10.1016/j.beth.2020.05.002

Jlassi, A., Elaoud, A., Ghazouani, H., & Barhoumi, W. (2024). Potato Leaf Disease Classification Using Transfer Learning and Reweighting-Based Training with Imbalanced Data. *SN Computer Science, 5*(8), 987. DOI: 10.1007/s42979-024-03334-x

Jordan, M. I., Mitchell, T. M., De Choudhury, M., Counts, S., Horvitz, E., Hoff, A., Brownstein, J. S., Freifeld, C. C., Madoff, L. C., Eysenbach, G., Broniatowski, D. A., Paul, M. J., Dredze, M., Sadilek, A., Kautz, H., Silenzio, V., White, R. W., Harpaz, R., Shah, N. H., ... M. Schrems. (n.d.). *Machine learning: Trends, perspectives, and prospects*. https://www.cs.cmu.edu/~tom/pubs/Science-ML-2015.pdf

Kabashkin, I., & Shoshin, L. (2024). Artificial Intelligence of Things as New Paradigm in Aviation Health Monitoring Systems. *Future Internet, 16*(8), 276. Advance online publication. DOI: 10.3390/fi16080276

Kabel, S. A. E. M., El-Shafai, W., El-Samie, F. E. A., & Mohamed, B. (2025). Enhanced plant identification and disease diagnosis through SqueezeNet and SVM for smart agriculture applications. *Iran Journal of Computer Science, 8*(4), 1353–1369. DOI: 10.1007/s42044-025-00237-9

Kanimozhi, N., Keerthana, N., Pavithra, G., Ranjitha, G., & Yuvarani, S. (2021). *CRIME type and occurrence prediction using machine learning algorithm.* Paper presented at the 2021 International conference on artificial intelligence and smart systems (ICAIS). DOI: 10.1109/ICAIS50930.2021.9395953

Kaur, H., & Bhatia, M. (2024). Scientometric Insights of Digital Twins in Industry 4.0. https://doi.org/DOI: 10.21203/rs.3.rs-4380510/v1

Kaur, K., Kaur, H., Singh, M. L., & Singh, R. (2025). PotConvNet: An Automated Deep Convolutional Neural Network-Based Framework for Identification of Potato Leaf Diseases. *Potato Research, 68*(3), 3631–3666. DOI: 10.1007/s11540-025-09891-9

Keerthana, N., Suresh, P., Kulandaivel, M., & Kulandaivel, S. (2025). Critical Strategies for Phishing Defense and Digital Asset Protection: A Case Study Approach. In *Critical Phishing Defense Strategies and Digital Asset Protection* (pp. 221-244): IGI Global Scientific Publishing. Keerthanaa, N., Rojab, S., Santhiyac, S., & Sowndharyad, L. Data Security Using Certificateless Signature Cryptosystem. DOI: 10.4018/979-8-3693-8784-9.ch011

Keerthana, N., & Suresh, P. (2016). Security driven multi-constrained scheduling for computational grid. *International Journal of Scientific and Engineering Research*, *7*(2), 43–49.

Kempenaar, C. C., Sijbrandij, F. F. D., Been, T. T. H., van Boheemen, K. K., Booij, J. J. A., van Evert, F. F. K., Teklu, M. G. M. G., Kessel, G. G. J. T., Kocks, C. C. G., Lugtenburg, C. C., van der Meer, A. A., Molendijk, L. L. P. G., van Oort, P. P. A. J., Tielen, J. J. J. H., & van der Wal, T. T. (2026). Towards Data-Driven Precision Crop Management of Potato. *Potato Research*, *69*(1), 10. DOI: 10.1007/s11540-025-09996-1

Khaddam, A. A., & Alzghoul, A. (2025). Artificial intelligence-driven business intelligence for strategic energy and ESG management: A systematic review of economic and policy implications. *International Journal of Energy Economics and Policy*, *15*(4), 635–650. DOI: 10.32479/ijeep.19820

Khan, A., Singh, R., Khan, S. U., & Hussain, I. (2026). Towards smart farming: A real-time diagnosis system for strawberry foliar diseases using deep learning. *BMC Plant Biology*, *26*(1), 135. DOI: 10.1186/s12870-025-07815-w PMID: 41387775

Kotwal, J. G., Kashyap, R., & Shafi, P. M. (2024). Artificial Driving based EfficientNet for Automatic Plant Leaf Disease Classification. *Multimedia Tools and Applications*, *83*(13), 38209–38240. DOI: 10.1007/s11042-023-16882-w

Krishna, N. (2025). AI-Integrated ESG Scoring System: Leveraging Real-Time Green Data Intelligence for Sustainable Finance: A Study on the Role of Artificial Intelligence in Dynamic ESG Evaluation. *Available at SSRN* 5764202. DOI: 10.2139/ssrn.5764202

Kulandaivel, S., & Kulandaivel, M. (2025). Intelligent and Optical Security Monitoring for 6G Communications. In *RFID, Microwave Circuit, and Wireless Power Transfer Enabling 5/6G Communication* (pp. 417-444): IGI Global Scientific Publishing.

Kumar, M., Singh, S. K., Nghiem, X. H., & Rathnasiri, M. S. H. (2026). AI-Driven Sustainability: Automating ESG Reporting and Green Operations through the Cloud. In *Automating Intelligence with Cloud-Native AI Tools* (pp. 87-98). IGI Global Scientific Publishing.

Kumar, A., & Patel, V. K. (2023). Classification and identification of disease in potato leaf using hierarchical based deep learning convolutional neural network. *Multimedia Tools and Applications*, *82*(20), 31101–31127. DOI: 10.1007/s11042-023-14663-z

Kumari, V., & Bansal, V. (2026). A systematic review of plant leaf disease detection and classification using machine learning and deep learning techniques. *International Journal of Data Science and Analytics*, *22*(1), 22. DOI: 10.1007/s41060-025-01003-7

Kumar, R., Agrawal, T., Dwivedi, V. D., & Khatter, H. (2024). Potato Leaf Disease Classification Using Deep Learning Model. In Chauhan, N., Yadav, D., Verma, G. K., Soni, B., & Lara, J. M. (Eds.), *Machine Learning, Image Processing, Network Security and Data Sciences. MIND 2023.Communications in Computer and Information Science* (Vol. 2128). Springer., DOI: 10.1007/978-3-031-62217-5_16

Kumar, R., Sporn, K., Waisberg, E., Ong, J., Paladugu, P., Vadhera, A. S., & Tavakkoli, A. (2025). Navigating healthcare AI governance: The comprehensive algorithmic oversight and stewardship framework for risk and equity. *Health Care Analysis*, 1–25. DOI: 10.1007/s10728-025-00537-y PMID: 40802160

Kumar, Y., Singh, R., Moudgil, M. R., & Kamini, . (2023). A Systematic Review of Different Categories of Plant Disease Detection Using Deep Learning-Based Approaches. *Archives of Computational Methods in Engineering*, *30*(8), 4757–4779. DOI: 10.1007/s11831-023-09958-1

Kyaw, P. H., Gutierrez, J., & Ghobakhlou, A. (2024). Systematic review of deep learning techniques for phishing email detection. *Electronics (Basel)*, *13*(19), 13. DOI: 10.3390/electronics13193823

Laka, M., Carter, D., Milazzo, A., & Merlin, T. (2022). Challenges and opportunities in implementing clinical decision support systems (CDSS) at scale: Interviews with Australian policymakers. *Health Policy and Technology*, *11*(3), 100652. DOI: 10.1016/j.hlpt.2022.100652

Lilhore, U. K., Kavitha, P. G. S., G, S., R, S., Simaiya, S., Ghith, E. S., & Hussien, S. A. (2026). Early Detection of Potato Leaf Diseases with PotatoNet-X: A Deep Learning Model Combining ResNet, DenseNet, and Attention Mechanisms. *Potato Research*, *69*(2), 45. DOI: 10.1007/s11540-025-09957-8

Lindenmeyer, A., Blattmann, M., Franke, S., Neumuth, T., & Schneider, D. (2025). Towards Trustworthy AI in Healthcare: Epistemic Uncertainty Estimation for Clinical Decision Support. *Journal of Personalized Medicine*, *15*(2), 58. DOI: 10.3390/jpm15020058 PMID: 39997335

Lin, Y. H. (2022). An advanced smart home energy management system considering identification of ADLs based on non-intrusive load monitoring. *Electrical Engineering*, *104*(5), 3391–3409. DOI: 10.1007/s00202-022-01546-z

Liu, G. (2025). Evaluation Method of Teaching Effect of Environmental Art and Design in Universities Based on Multi-Source Data Fusion Technology. *International Journal of High Speed Electronics and Systems*, *34*(03), 2540025. DOI: 10.1142/S0129156425400257

Lowry, S., & Milford, M. J. (2016). Supervised and unsupervised linear learning techniques for visual place recognition in changing environments. *IEEE Transactions on Robotics*, *32*(3), 600–613. DOI: 10.1109/TRO.2016.2545711

Lu, H., Xinning, P., & Yingxi, Z. (2020). A New Study on the Evaluation Index System for Content Quality of Online Course: A Perspective from Learner Experience and Knowledge Payment [J]. *Journal of Distance Education*, *38*(01), 104–112.

M., M., Anandamurugan, S. (2025). Innovative Deep Learning Framework for Accurate Plant Disease Detection and Crop Productivity Enhancement. Cogn Comput 17, 58, DOI: 10.1007/s12559-025-10421-5

Mahapatra, P., Panda, M., Dash, S. K., & Sahu, U. K. (2026). Advancing plant disease classification using an attention-based CNN for intra-dataset and cross- dataset training. *Scientific Reports*, *16*(1), 10925. DOI: 10.1038/s41598-026-45464-7 PMID: 41896662

Mahum, R., Munir, H., Mughal, Z. U. N., Awais, M., Sher Khan, F., Saqlain, M., & Tlili, I. (2022). A novel framework for potato leaf disease detection using an efficient deep learning model. *Human and Ecological Risk Assessment*, *29*(2), 303–326. DOI: 10.1080/10807039.2022.2064814

Malik, Y. S., Sircar, S., Bhat, S., Ansari, M. I., Pande, T., Kumar, P., & Natesan, S. (2021). How artificial intelligence may help the Covid-19 pandemic: Pitfalls and lessons for the future. *Reviews in Medical Virology*, *31*(5), 1–11. DOI: 10.1002/rmv.2205 PMID: 33476063

Mandal, S. N., Mukherjee, K., Dan, S., Ghosh, P., Das, S., Mustafi, S., Roy, K., & Chakraborty, A. (2023). Image-Based Potato Phoma Blight Severity Analysis Through Deep Learning. *J. Inst. Eng. India Ser. B*, *104*(1), 181–192. DOI: 10.1007/s40031-022-00820-9

Manoj, R. K., & Nandhini, S. A. (2026). Computer Vision and AI-Based Apple Plant Disease Detection Framework in Smart Farming. In Kumar, S. R., Gayathri, N., Yendapalli, V., & Rocha, A. (Eds.), *AI-Driven IoT Solutions in Agriculture: New Insights. Studies in Computational Intelligence* (Vol. 1236). Springer., DOI: 10.1007/978-3-032-05603-0_12

Marisamy, K., Selvakumar, A., Rajasekar, B., Natarajan, R., Atajanova, A., & Makhmudov, S. (2026). Smart Logistics Integrating AI, IoT, Blockchain, and Robotics for a Sustainable Future. In Hlali, A. (Ed.), *Emerging Trends in Smart Logistics Technologies* (pp. 73–104). IGI Global Scientific Publishing., DOI: 10.4018/979-8-3373-2434-0.ch003

McGrath, M. J., Duenser, A., Lacey, J., & Paris, C. (2025). Collaborative human-AI trust (CHAI-T): A process framework for active management of trust in human-AI collaboration. *Computers in Human Behavior: Artificial Humans*, 100200.

Mengliyev, I., Meylikulov, S., Fayzullayeva, Z., & Kobulova, M. (2024, November). Education artificial intelligence systems and their use in teaching. In AIP Conference Proceedings (Vol. 3244, No. 1, p. 030079). AIP Publishing LLC. https://doi.org/ DOI: 10.1063/5.0241443

Mishra, S. (2023). Exploring the impact of AI-based cyber security financial sector management. *Applied Sciences (Basel, Switzerland)*, *13*(10), 5875. DOI: 10.3390/app13105875

Mohamed, N., Taherdoost, H., & Madanchian, M. (2025). Comprehensive Review of Advanced Machine Learning Techniques for Detecting and Mitigating Zero-Day Exploits. *EAI Endorsed Transactions on Scalable Information Systems, 12*(1).

Mosqueira-Rey, E., Hernández-Pereira, E., Alonso-Ríos, D., Bobes-Bascarán, J., & Fernández-Leal, Á. (2023). Human-in-the-loop machine learning: A state of the art. *Artificial Intelligence Review*, *56*(4), 3005–3054. DOI: 10.1007/s10462-022-10246-w

Mtukushe, N., Onaolapo, A. K., Aluko, A., & Dorrell, D. G. (2023). Review of cyberattack implementation, detection, and mitigation methods in cyber-physical systems. *Energies*, *16*(13), 5206. DOI: 10.3390/en16135206

Mubarakali, A., Sharavanan, S., Elshafie, H., & Changalasetty, S. B. (2026). A secure and scalable home security system using IoT, 6G networks, AI-based hybrid deep learning models, blockchain, and smart contracts. *International Journal of Information Security*, *25*(1), 15. DOI: 10.1007/s10207-025-01178-x

Mughaid, A., AlZu'bi, S., Hnaif, A., Taamneh, S., Alnajjar, A., & Elsoud, E. A. (2022). An intelligent cyber security phishing detection system using deep learning techniques. *Cluster Computing*, *25*(6), 3819–3828. DOI: 10.1007/s10586-022-03604-4 PMID: 35602317

Murti, Y. S. & Naveen, P. (2023). Machine learning algorithms for phishing email detec- tion. *Journal of Logistics Informatics.*

Muthuswamy, V. V., & Absamatov, A. (2025). *Determinants of students engagement and their role in boosting students' academic performance among higher education institutions (HEIs).* Revista Electrónica de LEEME., DOI: 10.58262/LEEME.56.13

Muthuswamy, V. V., & Absamatov, A. (2025). Examining Mediating Role of Self Efficacy among Mobile Learning, Curriculum and Preventive Health Behavior. *Journal of Mind and Behavior*, *46*(2), 373–394. https://jmb-online.com/article-view.php?id=137

Naeem, S., Ali, A., Anam, S., & Ahmed, M. M. (2023). An Unsupervised Machine Learning Algorithms: Comprehensive Review. *International Journal of Computing and Digital Systems*, *13*(1), 911–921. DOI: 10.12785/ijcds/130172

Nasteski, V. (2017). An overview of the supervised machine learning methods. *HORIZONS B*, *4*, 51–62. DOI: 10.20544/HORIZONS.B.04.1.17.P05

Nawaz M, Javed A, Saudagar AKJ. (2026). PotatoGuardNet: a refined deep learning framework for potato leaf disease detection. Front Plant Sci. Jan 30;17:1720276. . PMID: 41696171; PMCID: PMC12901372.DOI: 10.3389/fpls.2026.1720276

Nazir, T., Iqbal, M. M., Jabbar, S., Hussain, A., & Albathan, M. (2023). EfficientPNet—An Optimized and Efficient Deep Learning Approach for Classifying Disease of Potato Plant Leaves. *Agriculture*, *13*(4), 841. DOI: 10.3390/agriculture13040841

Nettleton, D. F., Orriols-Puig, A., & Fornells, A. (2010). A study of the effect of different types of noise on the precision of supervised learning techniques. *Artificial Intelligence Review*, *33*(4), 275–306. DOI: 10.1007/s10462-010-9156-z

Niazkar, H. R., & Niazkar, M. (2020). Application of artificial neural networks to predict the COVID-19 outbreak. *Global Health Research and Policy*, *5*(1), 50. DOI: 10.1186/s41256-020-00175-y PMID: 33292780

Nithya, T., Chandrasekaran, V., Mahendrakumar, S., Keerthana, N., & Keerthana, A. P. (2026). Digital Innovation as the Backbone of Developing Economies: A Study. In *Digital Technologies and Transformations in Public Administration, Engineering, and Sustainable Business* (pp. 263-294): IGI Global Scientific Publishing.

Nouis, S. C., Uren, V., & Jariwala, S. (2025). Evaluating accountability, transparency, and bias in AI-assisted healthcare decision-making: A qualitative study of healthcare professionals' perspectives in the UK. *BMC Medical Ethics, 26*(1), 89. DOI: 10.1186/s12910-025-01243-z PMID: 40629303

Nuruddin, N. (2024). Hybrid Learning (HL) in Higher Education: The Design and Challenges. *International Journal of Instruction, 17*(1), 97–114. Advance online publication. DOI: 10.29333/iji.2024.1716a

Ochieng, T., Cogburn, D., & Wong, H. (2025). Introduction to the Minitrack on AI Safety, Cybersecurity, and Inclusion through Advanced Text Analytics.

Odufisan, O. I., Abhulimen, O. V., & Ogunti, E. O. (2025). Harnessing Artificial Intelligence and Machine Learning for Fraud Detection and Prevention in Nigeria. *Journal of Economic Criminology*, 100127.

Organization, W. H. (2021). *Ethics and governance of artificial intelligence for health: WHO guidance.* World Health Organization.

Osisanwo, F.Y., Akinsola, J.E.T., Awodele, O.,, Hinmikaiye, J. O., Olakanmi, O., & Akinjobi, J. (2017). Supervised Machine Learning Algorithms: Classification and comparison. *International Journal of Computer Trends and Technology, 48*(3), 128–138. DOI: 10.14445/22312803/IJCTT-V48P126

Panda, T., Nayak, S., & Mohanty, S. N. (2026). Temporal Analysis in Deep Learning-Based Recommender Systems for Predicting Plant Disease Outbreaks. In: Koganti, K.K., E., S.R., Gupta, N. (eds) Advanced Technologies in Electronics, Communications and Signal Processing. ICATECS 2024. Lecture Notes of the Institute for Computer Sciences, Social Informatics and Telecommunications Engineering, vol 620. Springer, Cham. DOI: 10.1007/978-3-031-94283-9_13

Pandey, D., Niwaria, K., Chourasia, B., (2019). Machine Learning Algorithms: A Review. *International Research Journal of Engineering and Technology (IRJET), 06*, 916. https://www.irjet.net

Pandey, S., Gupta, M., Mishra, A., Mishra, A., & Gangrade, J. (2025). Automated Potato Disease Classification Using Deep Learning - A Comparative Analysis of Convolutional Neural Networks. In Bairwa, A. K., Tiwari, V., Vishwakarma, S. K., Tuba, M., & Ganokratanaa, T. (Eds.), *Computation of Artificial Intelligence and Machine Learning. ICCAIML 2024.Communications in Computer and Information Science* (Vol. 2184). Springer., DOI: 10.1007/978-3-031-71481-8_26

Pandiri, D. N. K., Murugan, R., & Goel, T. (2025). ARM-UNet: Attention residual path modified UNet model to segment the fungal pathogen diseases in potato leaves. *Signal, Image and Video Processing*, *19*(1), 80. DOI: 10.1007/s11760-024-03566-7

Panjaitan, M. B. Hamdanah, Sirait, J., Sutikno, & Fatmawati, E. (2025). The role of emotional regulation in shaping students' perception of physics problem-solving tasks. TPM – Testing, Psychometrics, Methodology in Applied Psychology. https://tpmap.org/submission/index.php/tpm/article/view/139

Pattanaik, H., Patnaik, G., Gouda, A., Sahoo, M., & Das, M. (2024). A Comparative Study of Disease Detection in Potato Plants Using Machine Learning and Deep Learning Methods. In Tavares, J. M. R. S., Rodrigues, J. J. P. C., Misra, D., & Bhattacherjee, D. (Eds.), *Data Science and Communication. ICTDsC 2023.Studies in Autonomic, Data-driven and Industrial Computing*. Springer., DOI: 10.1007/978-981-99-5435-3_11

Paul, H., Ghatak, S., Chakraborty, S., Pandey, S. K., Dey, L., Show, D., & Maity, S. (2024). A study and comparison of deep learning based potato leaf disease detection and classification techniques using explainable AI. *Multimedia Tools and Applications*, *83*(14), 42485–42518. DOI: 10.1007/s11042-023-17235-3

Peri, S. S. S. R. G., Asokan, D., Goel, D., Anjali, A., & Keerthana, N. (2025). *Strategic Leadership and Digital Disruption: A Roadmap for Organizational Expansion using Adaptive Boosting (AdaBoost).* Paper presented at the 2025 3rd International Conference on Self Sustainable Artificial Intelligence Systems (ICSSAS).

Prabu, M., & Chelliah, B. J. (2022). Mango leaf disease identification and classification using a CNN architecture optimized by crossover-based levy flight distribution algorithm. *Neural Computing & Applications*, *34*(9), 7311–7324. DOI: 10.1007/s00521-021-06726-9

Purnamadewi, Y. R., & Zahra, A. (2025). Enhancing detection of zero-day phishing email attacks in the Indonesian language using deep learning algorithms. *Bulletin of Electrical Engineering and Informatics*, *14*(1), 505–512. DOI: 10.11591/eei.v14i1.8759

Qiu, H., Wang, X., Shen, J., Yang, S., & Zhao, W. (2026). A Survey on Crop Disease Prediction Detection: AI Models Trained on Multispectral and Hyperspectral Images for Early Disease Detection. In Chen, J., Luo, X., & Yu, Y. (Eds.), *Blockchain and Trustworthy Systems. BlockSys 2025. Communications in Computer and Information Science* (Vol. 2638). Springer., DOI: 10.1007/978-981-95-3483-8_14

Qu, J., Liu, A., & Liu, R. (2021). Research on Evaluation and Confirmation of College Students' Learning Behavior Based on Comprehensive Weighted Fusion Algorithm. 2021 IEEE 6th International Conference on Cloud Computing and Big Data Analytics (ICCCBDA), 121-125. DOI: 10.1109/ICCCBDA51879.2021.9442584

Radwan, M., Alhussan, A. A., Ibrahim, A., & Tawfeek, S. M. (2025). Potato Leaf Disease Classification Using Optimized Machine Learning Models and Feature Selection Techniques. *Potato Research*, *68*(2), 897–921. DOI: 10.1007/s11540-024-09763-8

Ragab, M., Basheri, M., Albogami, N. N., Subahi, A., Abdulkader, O. A., Alaidaros, H., Mousa, H., & AL-Ghamdi, A. A. L.-M. (2025). Artificial intelligence driven cyberattack detection system using integration of deep belief network with convolution neural network on industrial IoT. *Alexandria Engineering Journal*, *110*, 438–450. DOI: 10.1016/j.aej.2024.10.009

Raghu, N. V. N., T., L. N., D., Kumar B. M., H., & Shankaregowda, S. A. (2025). Enhancing Critical Thinking Through Problem-Based Learning: A Comprehensive Approach to Modern Education. In M. Lytras, P. Ordóñez de Pablos, & T. Aldosemani (Eds.), *Fostering Teacher Skills and Critical Thinking in Modern Education* (pp. 259-282). IGI Global Scientific Publishing. DOI: 10.4018/979-8-3373-1692-5.ch011

Rahman, Z., Yi, X., & Khalil, I. (2022). Blockchain-based AI-enabled industry 4.0 CPS protection against advanced persistent threat. *IEEE Internet of Things Journal*, *10*(8), 6769–6778. DOI: 10.1109/JIOT.2022.3147186

Raju, R., & Thasleema, T. M. (2026). Ensemble-based Deep Feature Extraction using Pre-trained CNNs for Black Pepper Leaf Disease and Nutrient Deficiency Detection and Classification: BPLDNDNet. *Evolutionary Intelligence*, *19*(1), 28. DOI: 10.1007/s12065-026-01149-8

Ramezanpour, K., & Jagannath, J. (2022). Intelligent zero trust architecture for 5G/6G networks: Principles, challenges, and the role of machine learning in the context of O-RAN. *Computer Networks*, *217*, 109358. DOI: 10.1016/j.comnet.2022.109358

Ravikumar, R. N., Aarthi, S., Rai, P. K., & Mamadiyarov, Z. (2026). Intelligent Code Analysis and Feedback Generation: A New Paradigm in Programming Education. In AI Applications in Instructional Education Strategies (pp. 137-170). IGI Global Scientific Publishing. DOI: 10.4018/979-8-3373-0598-1.ch006

Ravikumar, R. N., Aarthi, S., Ruzimova, F., & Mamadiyarov, Z. (2025). Training and development in AI-Driven Education scaling solutions. In Advances in computational intelligence and robotics book series (pp. 267–298). DOI: 10.4018/979-8-3373-2185-1.ch010

Raza, K. (2020). Artificial intelligence against COVID-19: A meta-analysis of current research. In *Big data analytics and artificial intelligence against COVID-19: Innovation vision and approach* (pp. 165–176). Springer. DOI: 10.1007/978-3-030-55258-9_10

Reddy, A. (2022). The Future of Cloud Security: Ai-Powered Threat Intelligence and Response. *International Neurology journal.*

Reddy, A. R. P. (2021). The role of artificial intelligence in proactive cyber threat detection in cloud environments. *NeuroQuantology : An Interdisciplinary Journal of Neuroscience and Quantum Physics, 19*(12), 764–773.

Reich, J. (2015). Rebooting MOOC Research. *Science, 347*(6217), 34–35. DOI: 10.1126/science.1261627 PMID: 25554779

Renugadevi, R. A., Viswanath, V., Reddy, B., Prakash, K. (2026). Intelligent Plant Disease Diagnosis: Harnessing Machine Learning and Deep Learning for Precision Agriculture. In: Sharma, H., Bhatt, A., Modi, C., Engelbrecht, A. (eds) Computer Vision and Robotics. CVR 2025. Lecture Notes in Networks and Systems, vol 1771. Springer, Cham. DOI: 10.1007/978-3-032-14041-8_27

Rezwana, J., & Maher, M. L. (2023). Designing creative AI partners with COFI: A framework for modeling interaction in human-AI co-creative systems. *ACM Transactions on Computer-Human Interaction, 30*(5), 1–28. DOI: 10.1145/3519026

Riza, A. Z. B. M., Jennsen, L., Anggani, P., Rafeen, A. I., Ruth, P. N. J., Sookun, D., . . . Luximon, L. (2025). Leveraging Machine Learning and AI to Combat Modern Cyber Threats.

Roshanaei, M., Khan, M. R., & Sylvester, N. N. (2024). Enhancing cybersecurity through AI and ML: Strategies, challenges, and future directions. *Journal of Information Security, 15*(3), 320–339. DOI: 10.4236/jis.2024.153019

Roy, R., Sabatini, A., Blasch, E., Kramer, K., Fasano, G., Majid, I., Crespillo, O. G., Brown, D. A., & Major, R. O. (2020). Avionics Systems Panel Research and Innovation Perspectives. *IEEE Aerospace and Electronic Systems Magazine, 35*(12), 58–72. Advance online publication. DOI: 10.1109/MAES.2020.3033475

Sadiq, S., Malik, K. R., Ali, W., & Iqbal, M. M. (2023). Deep Learning-Based Disease Identification and Classification in Potato Leaves. *Journal of Computing & Biomedical Informatics, 5*(01), 13–25. https://www.jcbi.org/index.php/Main/article/view/155

Sahami, M. (1998). A bayesian approach to filtering junk e-mail. *AAAI Workshop.*

Saha, S.. (2024). Deep Learning-Based Approach for Plant Disease Classification. In Nanda, S. J., Yadav, R. P., Gandomi, A. H., & Saraswat, M. (Eds.), *Data Science and Applications. ICDSA 2023. Lecture Notes in Networks and Systems* (Vol. 820). Springer., DOI: 10.1007/978-981-99-7817-5_18

Sah, S.. (2026). Cucurbita Pepo Disease Classification Through Attention-Enhanced Deep Learning Models. In Dutta, P. K., Singh, R., Haghi, A. K., & Hamad, A. A. (Eds.), *Harnessing AI to Reshape the Future of Agriculture*. Springer., DOI: 10.1007/978-3-032-12118-9_22

Sai Reddy, B., & Neeraja, S. (2022). Plant leaf disease classification and damage detection system using deep learning models. *Multimedia Tools and Applications, 81*(17), 24021–24040. DOI: 10.1007/s11042-022-12147-0

Salih, A. M., Raisi-Estabragh, Z., Galazzo, I. B., Radeva, P., Petersen, S. E., Lekadir, K., & Menegaz, G. (2025). A perspective on explainable artificial intelligence methods: SHAP and LIME. *Advanced Intelligent Systems, 7*(1), 2400304. DOI: 10.1002/aisy.202400304

Sandhia, G., Ranjani, M., Nithiyanandam, N., Prakash, U., Srinivasan, R., Girirajan, S., . . . Ramaprabha, J. (2025). Cybersecurity: The Part Played by Artificial Intelligence. In *Analyzing Privacy and Security Difficulties in Social Media: New Challenges and Solutions* (pp. 213-246): IGI Global Scientific Publishing.

Sangar, G., & Rajasekar, V. (2025). Optimized classification of potato leaf disease using EfficientNet-LITE and KE-SVM in diverse environments. *Frontiers in Plant Science, 16*, 1499909. DOI: 10.3389/fpls.2025.1499909 PMID: 40385236

Sarker, I. H. (2021). Deep cybersecurity: A comprehensive overview from neural network and deep learning perspective. *SN Computer Science, 2*(3), 154. DOI: 10.1007/s42979-021-00535-6 PMID: 33778771

Sarker, I. H. (2021). Deep Learning: A comprehensive overview on techniques, taxonomy, applications and research directions. *SN Computer Science, 2*(6), 420–420. DOI: 10.1007/s42979-021-00815-1

Sathya, R., & Abraham, A. (2013). Comparison of supervised and unsupervised learning algorithms for pattern classification. *International Journal of Advanced Research in Artificial Intelligence* 2(2), pp. 34–38. https://thesai.org/Downloads/IJARAI/Volume2No2/Paper_6-Comparison_of_Supervised_and_Unsupervised_Learning_Algorithms_for_Pattern_Classification.pdf

Sayeed, M., & Gupta, D. (2022). Automate Descriptive Answer Grading using Reference based Models. *2022 OITS International Conference on Information Technology (OCIT)*, 262-267. https://doi.org/DOI: 10.1109/OCIT56763.2022.00057

Shafik, W., Tufail, A., De Silva, L. C., & Apong, R. A. A. H. M. (2026). Lightweight vision transformer and ResNet-9 models for real-time plant disease detection and pest classification with SHAP explainability. *BMC Plant Biology*, *26*(1), 838. Advance online publication. DOI: 10.1186/s12870-026-08667-8 PMID: 41922963

Sharma, T., & Sethi, G. K. (2024). Improving Wheat Leaf Disease Image Classification with Point Rend Segmentation Technique. *SN Computer Science*, *5*(2), 244. DOI: 10.1007/s42979-023-02571-w

Shawon, S. M., Niha, F. L., Sinan, O. H., Abed, M. J., Al Qwaid, M., Sarker, M. T., & Zubair, H. T. (2026). Integrating Federated Learning and Explainable AI for Plant Disease Detection: A Systematic Review of Recent Advances in Precision Agriculture. *Int J Comput Intell Syst*, *19*(1), 138. DOI: 10.1007/s44196-026-01219-w

Shen, Y., Huang, Z., Li, J., Fey, M., & Brecher, C. (2025). A Survey on AI-Driven Digital Twins in Industry 4.0: Smart Manufacturing and Advanced Robotics. *Sensors (Basel)*. Advance online publication. DOI: 10.3390/s21196340

Silvestri, S., Islam, S., Papastergiou, S., Tzagkarakis, C., & Ciampi, M. (2023). A machine learning approach for the NLP-based analysis of cyber threats and vulnerabilities of the healthcare ecosystem. *Sensors (Basel)*, *23*(2), 651. DOI: 10.3390/s23020651 PMID: 36679446

Sinamenye, J. H., Chatterjee, A., & Shrestha, R. (2025). Potato plant disease detection: Leveraging hybrid deep learning models. *BMC Plant Biology*, *25*(1), 647. DOI: 10.1186/s12870-025-06679-4 PMID: 40380088

Singh, G., Kasana, G., & Singh, K. (2025). Improved Potato Crop Disease Classification Using Ensembled Convolutional Neural Network. *Potato Research*, *68*(2), 1501–1527. DOI: 10.1007/s11540-024-09787-0

Singh, G., & Yogi, K. K. (2025). Deep Learning-Based Detection of Early Blight in Potato Leaves Using CNN Architectures. *Potato Research*, *68*(4), 4139–4161. DOI: 10.1007/s11540-025-09921-6

Singh, M., Fuenmayor, E., Hinchy, E. P., Qiao, Y., Murray, N., & Devine, D. M. (2021). Digital Twin: Origin to Future. *Applied System Innovation*, *4*(2), 36. Advance online publication. DOI: 10.3390/asi4020036

Singh, R., Krishnan, P., Bharadwaj, C., Sah, S., & Das, B. (2025). Optimizing chickpea yield prediction under wilt disease through synergistic integration of biophysical and image parameters using machine learning models. *Scientific Reports*, *15*(1), 4417. DOI: 10.1038/s41598-025-87134-0 PMID: 39910102

Sinha, A. R., Singla, K., & Victor, T. M. M. (2023). Artificial intelligence and machine learning for cybersecurity applications and challenges. *Risk Detection and Cyber Security for the Success of Contemporary Computing*, 109-146.

Sipayung, M. S. Digital ESG Analytics: A Bibliometric Review of AI-Driven Sustainability Research (2010–2025).

Sireesha, C., Shanam, G. M., & Attaluri, K. (2026). MobileNet-Based Deep Learning for Accurate Potato Leaf Disease Detection. In: Mondal, A., Peng, S.L., Ahmed, T., Sarkar, J.L. (eds) Proceedings of International Conference on Advanced Communications and Machine Intelligence. MICA 2024. Smart Innovation, Systems and Technologies, vol 115. Springer, Singapore. DOI: 10.1007/978-981-96-5589-2_8

Smith, H. K. (2025). *Sustainable Intelligence at Scale: Algorithmic Innovations for Green AI Across Manufacturing*. Smart Cities, and Financial Cloud Platforms.

Stanton, I., Munir, K., Ikram, A., & El-Bakry, M. (2022). Predictive Maintenance Analytics and Implementation for Aircraft: Challenges and Opportunities. *Systems Engineering*. Advance online publication. DOI: 10.1002/sys.21651

Stonier, A. A., Gorantla, R. K., & Manoj, K. (2023). Cardiac disease risk prediction using machine learning algorithms. *Healthcare Technology Letters*, *11*(4), 213–217. DOI: 10.1049/htl2.12053

Suarjana, I. W. G., Sudirham, , Salam, I., & Aditama, M. H. R. (2023). Artificial intelligence in public health: The potential and ethical considerations of artificial intelligence in public health. *Journal of Public Health (Oxford, England)*, *45*(4), e834–e835. DOI: 10.1093/pubmed/fdad116 PMID: 37477239

Subramanian, D., Subramaniam, S., Natarajan, K., & Thangavel, K. (2024). Flamingo Jelly Fish search optimization-based routing with deep-learning enabled energy prediction in WSN data communication. *Network (Bristol, England)*, *35*(1), 73–100. DOI: 10.1080/0954898X.2023.2279971 PMID: 38044853

Sultonkhodjayeva, S., Rakhimberganova, M., Otakhonova, M., Batirovna, M., & Umarova, D. (2025). Multilingual sentiment analysis for emotion-aware feedback in language learning platforms. In *Proceedings of the 2025 International Conference on Next Generation Computing Systems: Intelligent Systems for Sustainable Development (ICNGCS 2025)*. IEEE. https://doi.org/DOI: 10.1109/ICNGCS64900.2025.11183447

Sun, H., Song, B., Sun, X., Cui, X. P., Liu, Z., Cong, M., Sun, M., Zhu, Z., Tian, Y., Liu, S., Xu, P., Dai, B., & Wang, L. (2025). Recent Representative Progress of Surface Coating Technology. *Chemical Record (New York, N.Y.)*, *25*(8), e202500054. Advance online publication. DOI: 10.1002/tcr.202500054 PMID: 40342263

Talab, H. K., Mohammadzamani, D., & Parashkoohi, M. G. (2024). Investigating the accuracy of classification in unbalanced data in order to diagnose two common potato leaf diseases (early blight and late blight) using image processing and machine learning. *Discover Applied Sciences*, *6*(6), 286. DOI: 10.1007/s42452-024-05959-2

Tauseef, A. (2022). Technology Under Siege: Reinforcing Device and Cloud Security Against Cyber Threats.

Tayfor, N. B., Majidpour, J., Ahmed, M. H., Hajianfar, G., & Arabi, H. (2026). Metaheuristic-driven feature selection in radiomics: Improving time-to-event survival prediction in glioblastoma. *Neural Computing & Applications*, *38*(8), 281. DOI: 10.1007/s00521-026-11991-7

Tiwari, N. K., Bajpai, A., Kumar, A., & Patro, B. (2026). Advancing Potato Crop Health and Disease Detection with Deep Learning. In: Shanker, U., Tiwari, R.K., Verma, A., Hassan, M.M. (eds) Proceedings of International Conference on Data Science and Artificial Intelligence. DSAI 2025. Studies in Autonomic, Data-driven and Industrial Computing.Springer, Singapore. DOI: 10.1007/978-981-96-9083-1_12

Trigwell, K., Ashwin, P., & Millan, E. S. (2012). Evoked prior learning experience and approach to learning as predictors of academic achievement. *The British Journal of Educational Psychology*, *83*(3), 363–378. DOI: 10.1111/j.2044-8279.2012.02066.x PMID: 23822526

Tukhtaeva, N., Ismanova, A., Allamuratova, Z., & Khayitboev, N. (2024, November). Using mind mapping in teaching computer science. In AIP Conference Proceedings (Vol. 3244, No. 1, p. 030028). AIP Publishing LLC. AIP Conference Proceedings. DOI: 10.1063/5.0241454

Tyagi, K., Rane, C., Sriram, R., & Manry, M. (2022). Unsupervised learning. In R. Pandey, S. K. Khatri, N. k. Singh, & P. Verma (Ed.) *Artificial Intelligence and Machine Learning for EDGE Computing*, pp. 33-52. Academic Press. DOI: 10.1016/B978-0-12-824054-0.00012-5

Usama, M., Qadir, J., Raza, A., Arif, H., & Yau, K.-L. A. (2017). Unsupervised machine learning for networking: techniques, applications and research challenges. *ArXiv*. https://arxiv.org/abs/1709.06599v1

Varal, A. S., & Sayyad, S. F. (2026). Enhancing agricultural sorting systems through image-based classification and machine learning. *Multimedia Tools and Applications*, *85*(2), 55. DOI: 10.1007/s11042-026-21155-3

Verma, K. K., Singh, B. M., & Dixit, A. (2019). A review of supervised and unsupervised machine learning techniques for suspicious behavior recognition in intelligent surveillance system. *International Journal of Information Technology*, *14*(1), 397–410. DOI: 10.1007/s41870-019-00364-0

Verma, P. R., Pantola, D., & Singh, N. P. (2026). *Architectural and Performance Analysis of Static and Dynamic Neural Networks in Plant Disease Detection*. Arch Computat Methods Eng., DOI: 10.1007/s11831-026-10498-7

Völker, B., Scholl, P. M., & Becker, B. (2022). A Feature and Classifier Study for Appliance Event Classification. In Afonso, J. L., Monteiro, V., & Pinto, J. G. (Eds.), *Sustainable Energy for Smart Cities. SESC 2021. Lecture Notes of the Institute for Computer Sciences, Social Informatics and Telecommunications Engineering* (Vol. 425). Springer., DOI: 10.1007/978-3-030-97027-7_7

Wang, W. Y., Zhang, S., Li, G., Lu, J., Ren, Y., Wang, X., Gao, X., Su, Y., Song, H., & Li, J. (2024). *Artificial Intelligence Enabled Smart Design and Manufacturing of Advanced Materials: The Endless Frontier in AI⁺ Era*. Materials Genome Engineering Advances., DOI: 10.1002/mgea.56

Wang, Z. (2024). Evaluation method for the comprehensive quality of students based on multi-source data fusion. *Asia Pacific Education Review*, 1–8.

Wang, Z., Liu, X., Chen, H., Yang, T., & He, Y. (2023). Exploring Multi-Fidelity Data in Materials Science: Challenges, Applications, and Optimized Learning Strategies. *Applied Sciences (Basel, Switzerland)*, *13*(24), 13176. Advance online publication. DOI: 10.3390/app132413176

Waseem, Q., Wan Din, W. I. S., & Aamir, M. (2025). A generalized three-tier hybrid model for classifying unseen (IoT devices) in smart home environments. *Scientific Reports*, *15*(1), 35388. DOI: 10.1038/s41598-025-19303-0 PMID: 41068230

Wazan, A. S., & Cuppens, F. (2023). Cybersecurity in networking: Adaptations, investigation, attacks, and countermeasures. *Annales des Télécommunications*, *78*(3), 133–134. DOI: 10.1007/s12243-023-00956-9 PMID: 36950453

Wazid, M., Das, A. K., Chamola, V., & Park, Y. (2022). Uniting cyber security and machine learning: Advantages, challenges and future research. *ICT Express*, *8*(3), 313–321. DOI: 10.1016/j.icte.2022.04.007

Wen, Z., Pizarro, O., & Williams, S. (2024). Active self-semi-supervised learning for few labeled samples. *Neurocomputing, 614,* 128772. DOI: 10.1016/j.neucom.2024.128772

Wild, G., Nanyonga, A., Iqbal, A., Bano, S., Somerville, A., & Pollock, L. (2025). Lightweight and Mobile Artificial Intelligence and Immersive Technologies in Aviation. *Visual Computing for Industry, Biomedicine, and Art, 8*(1), 21. Advance online publication. DOI: 10.1186/s42492-025-00203-z PMID: 40900374

Williams, F., Oke, A., & Zachary, I. (2019). Public health delivery in the information age: The role of informatics and technology. *Perspectives in Public Health, 139*(5), 236–254. DOI: 10.1177/1757913918802308 PMID: 30758258

Williamson, S. M., & Prybutok, V. (2024). Balancing privacy and progress: A review of privacy challenges, systemic oversight, and patient perceptions in AI-driven healthcare. *Applied Sciences (Basel, Switzerland), 14*(2), 675. DOI: 10.3390/app14020675

Wu, Y. (2025, November). Strategies for Integrated Learning Approaches in Multi-Source Data Fusion. In *2024 International Conference on Integrated Intelligence and Communication Systems (ICIICS)* (pp. 1-5). IEEE. DOI: 10.1109/ICIICS63763.2024.10859731

Wuyuan, C., & Wenjun, J. (2020). Research on Contributing factors of university students' online learning experience. Huadong Shifan Daxue Xuebao. *Jiaoyu Kexue Ban, 38*(7), 42. DOI: 10.16382/j.cnki.1000-5560.2020.07.003

Xu, L., Chen, X., Xu, P., Zhang, Y., & Zhao, J. (2026). Spectral image classification of asymptomatic peanut leaf diseases based on deep learning algorithms. *Plant Methods, 22*(1), 6. DOI: 10.1186/s13007-025-01485-3 PMID: 41423650

Xu, Y., Zhou, X., Qi, W., & Wu, J. (2022). Early Warning Method of Postgraduate Education Quality in Colleges and Universities Based on Multisource Information Fusion. *Wireless Communications and Mobile Computing, 2022*(1), 1888731. Advance online publication. DOI: 10.1155/2022/1888731

Yan, L., Xiao, J., Wu, X., & Li, X. (2022). Student Engagement Recognition Using Multimodal Fusion Analytical Technology. 2022 4th International Conference on Computer Science and Technologies in Education (CSTE), 231-235. https://doi.org/ DOI: 10.1109/CSTE55932.2022.00049

Yin, R., & Xu, H. Y. (2017). Construction of online learning engagement structural model: An empirical study based on Structural Equation Model. *Open Education Research, 23*(4), 101–111.

Zandi, D., Reis, A., Vayena, E., & Goodman, K. (2019). New ethical challenges of digital technologies, machine learning and artificial intelligence in public health: A call for papers. *Bulletin of the World Health Organization*, *97*(1), 2. DOI: 10.2471/BLT.18.227686

Zanzotto, F. M. (2019). Human-in-the-loop artificial intelligence. *Journal of Artificial Intelligence Research*, *64*, 243–252. DOI: 10.1613/jair.1.11345

Zhang, X., Zeng, Z., Peng, W., Chen, H., Chu, J., Wei, M. S., & Xu, R. (2024). Research and Implementation of Key Intelligent Detection Technologies Based on Deep Learning. https://doi.org/DOI: 10.1117/12.3055351

Zhang, A., Wu, C., Li, G., & Chen, S. (2026). Frequency-Aware and Residual-Attention CGAN with Two-Stage Training for Imbalanced Potato Leaf Disease Detection in Crop Management. *Potato Research*, *69*(2), 39. DOI: 10.1007/s11540-025-09979-2

Zhang, B., & Zhang, L. (2025). Development and Promotion of Multi-source Data Fusion Technology in Smart Classroom Construction. International Journal for Housing Science & Its Applications, 47(1). Li, X. (2025). Research on Intelligent Analysis Algorithm for Student Learning Behavior Based on Multi-source Sensor Data Fusion. *International Journal of High Speed Electronics and Systems*, 2540198.

Zhang, Y., Wang, Y., Xu, Y., & Yang, W. (2026). Effective automatic classification methods via deep learning for multi-type infectious keratitis diagnosis. *Graefe's Archive for Clinical and Experimental Ophthalmology*, *264*(1), 171–183. DOI: 10.1007/s00417-025-06996-2 PMID: 41134356

Zhang, Y.-y. (2021). The enlightenment of general education reform in harvard university on the construction of general education in Chinese universities. *Heilongjiang Researches on Higher Education*, *2*, 59–63.

Zhang, Z., Wei, Z., Court, S., Yang, L., Wang, S., Thirunavukarasu, A., & Zhao, Y. (2024). A Review of Digital Twin Technologies for Enhanced Sustainability in the Construction Industry. *Buildings (Basel, Switzerland)*, *14*(4), 1113. Advance online publication. DOI: 10.3390/buildings14041113

Zhao, Z., Baumann, A., & Ryan, E. (2024). Using Machine-Learning-Aided Computational Fluid Dynamics to Facilitate Design of Experiments. *Industrial & Engineering Chemistry Research*, *63*(49), 21444–21454. Advance online publication. DOI: 10.1021/acs.iecr.4c03042

Zhou, Y., Zou, S., Liwang, M., Sun, Y., & Ni, W. (2025). A teaching quality evaluation framework for blended classroom modes with multi-domain heterogeneous data integration. *Expert Systems with Applications*, *289*, 127884. DOI: 10.1016/j.eswa.2025.127884

About the Contributors

Mashael Asiri is an Associate Professor of Artificial Intelligence at King Khalid University (KKU), Abha, Saudi Arabia. She earned her Ph.D. in Computer Science from the University of Southampton, UK (2020), following an M.Sc. in Web Technology with Distinction from the University of Southampton (2015) and a B.Sc. in Computer Science from King Abdulaziz University, Saudi Arabia (2011). With over 13 years of academic and research experience, Dr. Asiri's work spans artificial intelligence, machine learning, deep learning, data science, and natural language processing, with applied contributions in healthcare, smart cities, cybersecurity, and education—advancing Saudi Vision 2030 priorities. She has published 30+ peer-reviewed papers in reputable journals and conferences, serves as a peer reviewer for international journals, and has supervised undergraduate and postgraduate research projects. Her leadership record includes serving as Head of the Computer Science Department at KKU (2021–2024) and leading multiple competitively funded projects from King Khalid University and the King Salman Center for Disability Research. Dr. Asiri holds a UK patent for a compact mini-computer for robotic machine-learning operations (IPO UK, 2024) and has developed several impactful AI systems, including multilingual RAG-based chatbots and models for medical imaging, traffic safety analytics, smart energy forecasting, and cyber-attack detection. She is a certified NVIDIA instructor in Generative AI (LLMs and Multimodal) and holds multiple professional certifications in AI and online teaching. Beyond academia, she contributes to national innovation activities as a judge and evaluator in major hackathons and mentors research teams across disciplines. Her current work focuses on trustworthy, efficient foundation-model customization, Retrieval-Augmented Generation pipelines, and scalable AI solutions for societal benefit.

***

N. Aparna is a Professor in the Department of Electrical and Electronics Engineering at J.J. College of Engineering and Technology, Tiruchirappalli. She holds a Ph.D. in Electrical and Electronics Engineering with specialization in Biomedical Image Processing. She has nearly two decades of teaching and research experience in engineering education. Her research interests include Image Processing, Biomedical Instrumentation, Artificial Intelligence, and Machine Learning. She focuses on developing robust and application-oriented computational methods for real-world problems. Dr. Aparna has published several research papers in national and international journals, including SCI and Scopus-indexed publications. She also holds multiple patents showcasing her research innovations. In addition, she actively contributes to curriculum development, Project guidance, and interdisciplinary collaborations.

Anorgul Ashirova is working as an Associate Professor at the Department of General Professional Sciences, Mamun University, Khiva, Uzbekistan

Arti Bhatt is an accomplished academician and media professional with over 8 years of experience in the media industry and 5 years of teaching experience in Mass Communication. She is currently serving as an Assistant Professor in the Department of Mass Communication at Shri Guru Ram Rai (SGRR) University, Dehradun, Uttarakhand, India. Dr. Bhatt holds a Ph.D. in Mass Communication. Her academic and research interests include media studies, digital communication, development communication and contemporary communication practices. She has made significant scholarly contributions, including 17 research papers published in reputed national and international journals, 7 research paper presentations at national and international conferences, and the editing of 5 academic books. In addition, she has contributed 8 chapters to edited volumes published by recognized academic publishers. Dr. Bhatt is also the holder of 1 utility patent, reflecting her engagement with innovation and applied research. As a research mentor, she is actively involved in guiding scholars and is currently serving as a Ph.D. supervisor to 2 doctoral candidates, thereby contributing to advanced research and academic leadership in the field of Mass Communication. Dr. Bhatt has also undertaken several capacity-building initiatives, including 3 Short-Term Professional Development Programmes, 2 Refresher Courses, 1 Faculty Induction Programme (FIP), and 1 MOOC course. Her commitment to continuous professional development is further reflected in her active participation in 30 workshops, 16 Faculty Development Programmes (FDPs), 64 seminars and webinars, 3 online intensive training programmes, 6 e-conferences, and 1 panel discussion, underscoring her dedication to academic excellence, lifelong learning, and collaborative knowledge exchange.

Susanta Das is a seasoned educator with a proven record of teaching and mentoring diverse student populations, working at multiple institutions, and contributing to various organizational initiatives. He received his Ph.D. and M.A. degrees in Physics from Western Michigan University (WMU), USA, and his M.Sc. degree in Physics from Banaras Hindu University (BHU), India. He continued his research as a Marie Curie Postdoctoral Fellow at Stockholm University, Sweden, working on beam diagnostics for DESIREE (Double ElectroStatic Ion Ring ExpEriment) under the DITANET project (Diagnostic Techniques for Particle Accelerators – a Marie Curie Initial Training Network). He also conducted research at the Indian Institute of Science Education and Research (IISER), Kolkata, India, on high-pressure physics as a Project Scientist-B, and at the University of Electro-Communications, Tokyo, Japan, on ion–surface interactions as a Postdoctoral Fellow. Throughout his career, Dr. Das has worked and collaborated with numerous researchers, Ph.D. scholars, master's students, and visiting scholars from different countries. He has visited several countries to present and discuss his research and has participated in international conferences in the UK, Italy, Germany, Greece, Belgium, Bulgaria, Romania, Brazil, and other countries. He worked at several institutions before assuming his current role at Ajeenkya D Y Patil University. He has received several prestigious awards and fellowships, including the Marie Curie Postdoctoral Fellowship (Sweden), the Science Academies' Summer Research Fellowship (India), the Gowen Frostic Doctoral Fellowship, the Department Graduate Research and Creative Scholar Award from WMU, and the Leo R. Parpart Doctoral Fellowship from the Department of Physics, WMU, among many others. Dr. Das has co-authored several research articles in WoS- and Scopus-indexed international journals, conference proceedings, and scholarly book chapters. He has also co-edited multiple books published by renowned international publishing houses, including IGI Global, Springer Nature, Wiley, Scrivener-Wiley, and Notion Press. Currently, Dr. Das is actively engaged in cutting-edge research with a keen interest in nanotechnology, the United Nations Sustainable Development Goals (UN SDGs), and data science. His multifaceted contributions in teaching, research, and academic leadership reflect a dedicated professional who significantly advances the vision and mission of the institutions he serves.

Chandra Bose Gurusamy got his undergraduate degree in Mechanical engineering from Bharathidasan University, his Master's degree in Aeronautical Engineering from Madras Institute of Technology, Anna University. Currently, pursuing his Doctorate from the Department of Aeronautical Engineering in Vel Tech Rangarajan Dr. Sagunthala R&D Institute of Science and Technology, Chennai. He has guided 5 PG & 60 UG scholars on their projects, he has published 8 publications in Journals and international conferences. He is a Life Member of the Institution of Engineers India, the Aeronautical Society of India, Indian Society for Technical Education.

Kritikka Kunte is a third-year undergraduate student pursuing a Bachelor of Technology in Artificial Intelligence and Data Science at the School of Engineering, Ajeenkya DY Patil University, Pune, Maharashtra, India. With a strong academic orientation toward data-driven problem solving, she has developed a focused interest in the domains of data analytics and data science, supported by both theoretical foundations and applied project experience. Throughout her academic journey, Kritikka has cultivated proficiency in core programming and analytical competencies, including Python, SQL, and Java, along with essential data science methodologies such as data preprocessing, exploratory data analysis (EDA), and machine learning techniques. She is proficient in industry-relevant tools and platforms, including Advanced Microsoft Excel, Matplotlib, Tableau, and Power BI, to derive insights from complex datasets and present them in a structured and interpretable manner. Her practical exposure includes the successful completion of projects such as Ocean Salinity Analysis, which involved analyzing environmental datasets to identify patterns and trends, and Speech Recognition and Translation, where she explored applied machine learning concepts in natural language processing. These projects reflect her ability to translate conceptual knowledge into functional, real-world solutions. Kritikka has further strengthened her technical profile through professional certifications, including the AWS re/Start Graduate credential from Amazon Web Services, a certification in Software Development, and Python training certified by Google. Her engagement in competitive and collaborative academic environments is demonstrated by her participation in the Smart India Hackathon (SIH) and by securing Second Runner-Up in an inter-collegiate Tableau competition, highlighting her analytical aptitude and visualization skills. With a growing interest in advanced transportation systems and data-centric engineering solutions, Kritikka brings a multidisciplinary perspective to the GHC Hyperloop Project Competition hosted at IIT Madras. She aspires to contribute meaningfully to innovative, technology-driven initiatives that integrate artificial intelligence, data science, and sustainable engineering to address complex global challenges.

Raghu N has Ten years of experience in Academic and Research. He received the Ph.D. (2020) in Electronics Engineering from Jain University, and B.E. in Electronics and Telecommunications Engineering from VTU University, Karnataka. His research interests were in RF Communication and Image Processing. He has published his research findings in various Scopus indexed Journals and International conferences. He is a member of various professional bodies.

Keerthana N V is an Assistant Professor with 8 Years of experience in teaching and 1-year experience in research (IUCAA LIGO Data Centre, Pune). Her area of interest is Network Security, Blockchain Security, and Machine Learning Algorithms. She is pursuing PhD at Anna University in Security in Blockchain. She has a working experience in High-Performance Computing (HTCondor) in LIGO INDIA Project. She has written many research articles in Network Security and assisted Scientists in analyzing Datasets in HTCondor.

Krutika Patre is an aspiring programmer and technology enthusiast, currently pursuing Engineering in Artificial Intelligence and Data Science. With a passion for learning, she is building experience in a variety of programming languages and technologies, including C, C++, Python, Data Structures (DS), HTML, CSS, and JavaScript, DBMS (My SQL). After learning this programming language, she has created interest in Full Stack Development. She had also attended an Arduino-Based Automation course at Dolphin Labs to improve my software knowledge. There, she learned how to work with sensors, microcontrollers, and circuit design. She has written review paper on Sustainable engineering on build environment. She is doing researching and learning many topics related to AI, Policy and governance and related to my interest. She has taken part in hackathons, workshops, and tech events to explore many fields. She is also working with a group on Hyperloop. Being part of this project has really helped her grow, especially in areas like teamwork, innovation, and systems thinking.

S Prabhu received the Bachelor's degree in Computer Science and Engineering from Anna University, in 2008, Master degree in Computer Science and Engineering from Anna University, in 2010 and Ph.D in Computer Science and Engineering from Anna University, Chennai (India), in 2020. He has 17 years experience in the teaching field. Currently, he is working as an Associate Professor, Department of Computer Science and Engineering (Cyber Security), in Nandha Engineering College (Autonomous), Erode, Tamilnadu, India. His field of interest includes Cloud Computing, Cyber Security &Web Programming. He has 14 Journal publication and published 03 books, 09 book chapters.

Sabyasachi Pramanik is a professional IEEE member. He obtained a PhD in Computer Science and Engineering from Sri Satya Sai University of Technology and Medical Sciences, Bhopal, India. Presently, he is an Associate Professor, Department of Computer Science and Engineering, Haldia Institute of Technology, India. He has many publications in various reputed international conferences, journals, and book chapters (Indexed by SCIE, Scopus, ESCI, etc). He is doing research in the fields of Artificial Intelligence, Data Privacy, Cybersecurity, Network Security, and Machine

Learning. He also serves on the editorial boards of several international journals. He is a reviewer of journal articles from IEEE, Springer, Elsevier, Inderscience, IET and IGI Global. He has reviewed many conference papers, has been a keynote speaker, session chair, and technical program committee member at many international conferences. He has authored a book on Wireless Sensor Network. He has edited 8 books from IGI Global, CRC Press, Springer and Wiley Publications.

Sundharesan R is a Doctorate holder in Aeronautical Engineering from Vel Tech Rangarajan Dr. Sagunthala R&D Institute of Science and Technology. His research specializes in the characterization and evaluation of protective coatings on aerospace materials, with a focus on improving corrosion resistance and wear performance.He has collaborated with ISRO-Vikram Sarabhai Space Centre on advanced rhenium and iridium coatings for carbon–carbon composites used in high-temperature aerospace applications.With over a decade of combined teaching and research experience, Dr. Sundharesan previously served as a Teaching Fellow at the University College of Engineering, Thirukkuvalai. He has published extensively in SCIE, Web of Science, and Scopus-indexed journals, authored several book chapters, and holds patents in coating technologies.He is currently working as an Assistant Professor at J.J. College of Engineering and Technology, where he continues his research in advanced coatings and aerospace materials.

Venkateswaran R is currently a senior faculty member in the Cyber and Information Security section of the Information Technology Department at the University of Technology and Applied Sciences, Salalah, Oman. He also serves as the counselor for the IEEE student branch at the university. With over 25 years of teaching and administrative experience in India and abroad, Dr. Venkateswaran is an active member of professional bodies like IEEE, ISACA, and other IT forums and reviewer of the IEEE conferences. He has published 40+ papers in international journals and conferences, including IEEE Xplore and Scopus. He has conducted numerous technical workshops and seminars for students and staff in his area of Expertise. He holds industry certifications such as Cisco Certified Academic Instructor, Certified Ethical Hacker (CEH) from EC Council, Microsoft Technology Associate (MTA) certifications, and Huawei Academic Certified Instructor. In recognition of his dedication and contributions, he received the best performing award multiple times, and his article was featured in the Oman Observer. He secured around USD 70000, funded by the MoHERI, Oman, for research.

Pranati Rakshit is the Principal of Tarakeswar Degree College, Tarakeswar, Hooghly, West Bengal, India. She belongs to Department of Computer Science. She previously served as Professor and Head of the Department of Computer Science and Engineering at JIS College of Engineering, Kalyani, West Bengal, India. She has 25+ years of teaching experience. She has completed her Ph.D. degree from Jadavpur University, Kolkata, West Bengal, India, in the field of Pattern Recognition, Machine Learning, Medical image analysis. She has completed her Master degree and B.E. Degree in Computer Science & Engineering. She has worked in the field of Pattern Recognition, Machine Learning, Deep Learning, Medical image analysis, Sentiment Analysis etc. She has supervised more than 22 M.Tech. Projects and presently supervising 1 Ph.D. student. She has 70 numbers of research publications in International journals and conferences including SCI and Scopus indexing. She has 43 patents (Granted-6, Published-37), 2 copyrights and 1 design IPR in her account. She is a life member of Indian Society of Technical Education.

Saravanakumar Ramachandran is a professor with over 20 years of experience in higher education, including more than 10 years of post-Ph.D. experience. His expertise lies in Artificial Intelligence, Data Analytics, and Healthcare Informatics, with a focus on developing intelligent and data-driven solutions for real-world challenges. He has published 47 research papers in reputed national and international journals, including SCI and Scopus-indexed publications, and has presented his work at various conferences. He is also a recognized Ph.D. supervisor under reputed university, currently guiding multiple research scholars in emerging areas of AI and analytics. Dr. Saravanakumar has filed seven Indian patents, with several granted, and has authored three academic books. He actively contributes to the academic community as a reviewer and editorial board member for international journals and has organized several conferences and seminars. His interests include AI-driven healthcare systems, predictive analytics, and interdisciplinary research, with a strong emphasis on innovation, outcome-based education, and academic excellence.

Gokulraj S holds a Bachelor's degree in Computer Science and Engineering from Paavai Engineering College, affiliated with Anna University, Chennai. He earned his Master's degree in Computer Science and Engineering from the same institution. He was awarded a Ph.D. in Computer Science and Engineering by Anna University, Chennai, with a research focus on Cloud Computing, Security and Optimization. With over seventeen years of academic experience, he has guided more than 100 undergraduate and postgraduate students in their academic and research projects. He has published over 20 research papers in reputed international journals and presented his work in various national and international conferences. In addition, he holds five patents published in the Indian Patent Journal and one registered copyright. Also he has actively participated in numerous conferences, workshops, and seminars across India. He also serves as a reviewer for various Scopus-indexed and peer-reviewed journals, including Springer and the International Journal of

Recent Scientific Research. As an active member of several prestigious professional organizations, he holds memberships in the Computer Science Teachers Association (CSTA), International Computer Science and Engineering Society (ICSES), and the International Association of Engineers (IAENG), which facilitate collaboration and knowledge sharing in his domain. At present, he is serving as Associate Professor in the Department of Computer Science and Engineering (Cyber Security) at Dr. N.G.P. Institute of Technology, Coimbatore, Tamilnadu, India.

Sunil Sankathala is pursuing B. Tech. in Computer Science and Engineering at Ajeenkya D Y Patil University, with a diverse range of interests that bridge technology, sustainability, and innovation. His academic focus lies in computer science fundamentals like programming, data structures, algorithms, and software development. He actively supplements this with hands-on experience in web development and robotics. Beyond the core curriculum, He has a strong research inclination in emerging and impactful fields. His current research interests include Artificial Intelligence in Healthcare, bioplastics, nano bioplastics, e-waste management, and solid waste management—areas where he believes technology can make a meaningful difference in solving real-world problems. He has been publishing research articles and book chapters in reputed national and international journals and books. He is also part of an ambitious Hyperloop project, which involves interdisciplinary collaboration and cutting-edge engineering aimed at revolutionizing transportation. Working on this project has enhanced his skills in teamwork, innovation, and systems thinking. In the tech domain, he has developed proficiency in web development using technologies such as HTML, CSS, JavaScript, and React. His interests in robotics further reflect building smart, responsive systems that interact with the physical world. Throughout his course, he has helped strengthen problem-solving and collaborative skills. He is proficient in languages such as Python, C, C++, MySQL, Ubuntu, Machine Learning and familiar with frameworks and tools like React, Git. He actively participates in hackathons, coding competitions, and tech events to challenge himself and learn from peers. He is also a quick learner and highly adaptable, with an eagerness to stay updated with the latest trends in the tech world. He aspires to become a skilled software engineer and contribute to building innovative solutions that have a positive impact on society. The long-term goal is to work in a dynamic environment where knowledge, grow professionally, and make meaningful contributions to the field of technology. Driven by a spirit of exploration and sustainability, he aims to contribute to technological solutions that address both human and environmental needs. The long-term goal is to become a versatile engineer and researcher, working at the intersection of computer science, environmental innovation, and human well-being.

Nithya Subramani is an Assistant Professor at Vel Tech Rangarajan Dr. Sagunthala R&D Institute of Science and Technology with 13 years of teaching and research experience in the field of engineering. Her research interests include aerodynamics, propulsion systems, advanced engineering technologies, and aerospace-related research. She has actively contributed to academic activities, student project guidance, and research publications.

Nurullayeva Gulnora Uktamovna is an accomplished academic affiliated with the Department of History at Karshi Turon University. With a strong commitment to advancing historical scholarship, her work focuses on regional history, cultural heritage, and interdisciplinary perspectives that connect the past with contemporary societal developments. She has actively contributed to teaching, research, and academic mentorship, guiding students in developing critical thinking and historical analysis skills. Her research interests include socio-political transformations, historical narratives, and the preservation of cultural identity. Dr. Nurullayeva has participated in various academic conferences and scholarly activities, reflecting her dedication to knowledge dissemination and collaboration. Through her academic efforts, she continues to support the growth of historical studies and contribute to the intellectual development of the academic community at both national and international levels.

Index

A

C

D

E

F

I

L

M

N

O

P

R

S

T

U

Z

www.ingramcontent.com/pod-product-compliance
Lightning Source LLC
LaVergne TN
LVHW080903300926
849162LV00003B/532

9798260032800